The Ayurvedic Cookbook

A Personalized Guide to
Good Nutrition and Health

DISCLAIMER

This book is not intended to treat,
diagnose or prescribe. The information contained herein
is in no way to be considered as a substitute for your own
inner guidance or consultation with a duly licensed
health-care professional.

Illustrations copyright by Robin Noren (R. Amadea Morningstar)
Digestive Organs Illustration and *Vata, Pitta, Kapha* signs, copyright Angela Werneke

Cover photo: Gordon King

Design & Typesetting: Casa Sin Nombre

First Edition, 1990   Second Printing, 1991

Printed in the United States of America

Library of Congress Cataloging-in-Publication Data
Morningstar, Amadea, 1952-
    The Ayurvedic Cookbook : a personalized guide to good nutrition and health / by Amadea
    Morningstar with Urmila Desai.
        p.   cm.
    includes bibliographical references.
    ISBN 0-914955-06-3
        1. Macrobiotic diet—Recipes. 2. Cookery, Indic. 3 Medicine, Ayurvedic.   I. Desai,
    Urmila, 1937- . II. Title.
    RM235.M67   1990   90-35806
    641.5'63—dc20   CIP

Published in 1991 by Lotus Light, PO Box 2, Wilmot, WI 53192

THE AYURVEDIC COOKBOOK

*A Personalized Guide to
Good Nutrition and Health*

Amadea Morningstar with Urmila Desai

Illustrations by Amadea Morningstar

LOTUS
PRESS

PO Box 2AC
Wilmot, WI 53192

DEDICATION

To Gord with much love.
May your Pitta be calm and bright

ACKNOWLEDGEMENTS

The authors wish to thank in alphabetical order:
All the friends who ate
LaVon Alt
Ivy Blank
Lenny Blank
Gordon Bruen
Chandrakant
Yogi Amrit Desai
Connie Durand
Dr. David Frawley
Gerald Hausman
Margie Hughes
Baba Neem Karoli
Alma King
Gordon King
Swami Kripalvanandaji
Dr. Vasant Lad
Lyn Lemon
Steven Lowe
Bob Noren
Margie Noren
Wes Pittman
Pranashakti
Staff of Kripalu Center, Lenox, Massachusetts
David Stafford
Students & Staff of The Ayurvedic Wellness Center,
Albuquerque, New Mexico
Dr. Robert Svoboda
Laura Ware
Angela Werneke

TABLE OF CONTENTS

Foreword: Yogi Amrit Desai
Introduction: Dr. David Frawley

PART THREE
Appendices

FOREWORD

The science of Ayurveda, like the science of Yoga, was inspired and developed by the great masters and seers of ancient India. The origins of Ayurveda and Yoga have common roots and play a highly complimentary role in spiritual evolution and the maintenance of physical well-being and vitality. Ayurveda is, perhaps, the oldest science of life, a system of diet, healing, and health maintenance that is deeply spiritual in origin. Unlike traditional Western medicine, Ayurveda is not confined to the healing of disease in a superficial treatment of symptoms. Instead, it evaluates the complete body mind of the individual.

Ayurveda sees medicine and diet as complementary rather than separate. No one can expect to retain vitality, recover from disease, or succeed in the practice of Yoga without the appropriate knowledge of the powerful effect diet has on physical health, mental clarity, and spiritual progress.

Indeed, yogis place great emphasis on diet as an integral part of the successful practice of any spiritual discipline. Ayurveda addresses not only healing but also prevention and maintenance of the vitality so crucial in the practice of Yoga. Ancient seers described the human body and the body of the universe as composed of *prana*—the primal energy, the vital life force which manifests in the form of earth, water, fire, air, and ether. Any imbalance of these elements in our body is experienced as illness, discomfort, or pain. These elements are kept in harmony by a healthy body that consumes them through breath, food, water, sunshine, exercise and sleep. Yogis perceived foods such as grains, fruits, vegetables, seeds, beans, herbs, and roots, as vital carriers and balancers for the energy of *prana* in the body. The power of these foods manifests only when they are used in the proper combinations and in complete coordination with the unique conditions of each individual. This is where the profound effects of Ayurvedic food reveal themselves.

The Ayurvedic preparation of recipes is most exquisite in its exotic taste, aroma, textures, and colors. When people raised on a traditional meat-oriented diet shift to a vegetarian style of eating as practiced in the West, they often experience positive changes in their health. But when they try Ayurvedic recipes, they discover a deep sense of fulfillment and satisfaction. Their whole system responds to the nourishment that comes from the subtle tastes and aromas of the special blend of spices. These subtle spices and aromas play a vital role in bringing us to a deeper level of health and well-being.

But Ayurvedic food should not be confused with the hot and spicy food of India. The blend and proportion of spices must be regulated to meet the physical constitutions and temperaments that are unique to a Western upbringing. Such an approach to Ayurveda—a practical Ayurveda for the West—is excellently co-created in the recipes by Urmila and Amadea—Urmila with her highly refined and intuitive traditional Indian cooking skills, and Amadea with her Western nutritional background and work with Ayurveda. Together, they represent the perfect blend necessary for a practical and contemporary presentation of this ancient science. I am particularly touched by the sensitivity with which Amadea has treated this complex subject, skillfully adapting Ayurveda to the Western way of cooking. Recipes are personalized to the different physical con-stitutions, and Ayurvedic principles are applied to many familiar Western dishes.

In my personal experience of Urmila's cooking, I have a profound respect for her and her art. As subtle as it may seem, the attitude with which she prepares food becomes a very integral and invisible part of the recipe. Without fail, such an attitude creates a dif-ferent vibratory constitution of the food that affects the consciousness of the person who eats it.

This is not just another recipe book, but a unique health manual that, if applied with proper understanding, can lead to a whole new dimension in the enhancement of health and the joy of eating. Amadea's and Urmila's fresh and lively perspective is a timely addi-tion to the interest in Ayurveda now flowering in the West.

Yogi Amrit Desai
Founder, Kripalu Center*
and Spiritual Director

*Kripalu Center is one of the leading yoga centers in the United States. It attracts thou-sands of people each year to its main center in Lenox, Massachusetts. Yogi Amrit Desai and Urmila Desai, together, serve to guide individuals in their yogic practices.

INTRODUCTION

In the past few years, Ayurveda, the traditional natural healing system of India, has become better known in the West. Ayurvedic books tell us what food items are good for different constitutions, but without the knowledge of how to cook Ayurvedically, and without specific recipes, such information remains limited. *THE AYURVEDIC COOKBOOK* fills this need very well.

According to the Upanishads, the ancient scriptures of India, food is Brahman, the Divine reality. The unity of all life is demonstrated by the process of eating in which we participate in the movement of creation in the material world. The physical body itself is born of and lives by food. Most disease is traceable ultimately to incorrect diet. The cure for such wrong eating is not in better drugs, nor necessarily in better restaurants, but in reclaiming our oldest right and duty, to cook for ourselves, and those we love. Though right diet may not always be enough to correct diseases, few diseases can really be alleviated without it. Moreover, right diet is the essence of disease prevention and the foundation of a healthy and happy life.

Indian cooking is based upon the therapeutic principles of the ancient Ayurvedic science of life. It is a rich tradition that makes American diet and cooking methods appear impoverished. While Indian cooking uses dozens of spices from cardamom to cayenne, American cooking uses only a few. It has been said that the art of cooking is diminishing in American culture and that addictions to sugar, coffee and artificial stimulants may occur because of a lack of freshly cooked food and spices that offer real nourishment.

While "fast food" meets the need for convenience, much is lost in the process. The life-force, which cannot be measured in terms of vitamins, minerals or calories, is destroyed or reduced by artificial preparations. Nothing can substitute for Nature, either in living or in cooking. The more we depart from Nature in our living habits, the more we must suffer in the long run. Ayurveda teaches that the more removed we are from the preparation of the food we take in, (and the more removed that food is from its natural state) the less likely it is to satisfy us.

It is a considerable task to write a cookbook that can be used for healing purposes. This requires, not only knowledge of the properties of different foods, but also tasty recipes. Amadea Morningstar has worked diligently, as the scope of this book indicates, and Urmila Desai adds her recipes and specific knowledge of Indian cooking, the touch of the Divine Mother. The recipes have a spiritual aspect, which reflect the authors' backgrounds and Mataji's Yogic tradition with her husband, Yogi Amrit Desai. The recipes are free of the excess use of spices, sugars and oils that characterize the commercial line of modern Indian cooking. Even those who have already cooked Indian dishes will find these recipes to be more subtle, and to afford a deeper level of nutrition.

Amadea offers macrobiotic and Western nutritional wisdom, as well as Ayurvedic recipes and lore. We should note that Ayurvedic cooking is not limited to Indian cooking anymore than Ayurvedic herbs are limited to Indian herbs. The principles of Ayurveda are universal and can be adapted on a global level.

According to Ayurveda, foods have therapeutic properties which are defined largely by the energetics of taste or (*rasa*). These are clearly outlined in the cookbook. Ways of preparing food to alter certain properties, or to antidote possible side-effects, are also covered. The art of using spices—cooking not only to make the food taste better, but to enhance therapeutic value—is fully discussed. Certain foods can be made useful for different individual constitutions by the use of the right spices, oils or cooking methods. *THE AYURVEDIC COOKBOOK* shows how such adaptation can be done and often points out how to adjust the same recipe for different constitutional needs. As this book indicates, an Ayurvedic diet can be rich and diverse whatever our constitution may be.

Most foods are neutral in energy and have mild properties. Condiments and spices have more pronounced effects, like the heating nature of garlic or ginger. For this reason it is only when consumed regularly that the capacity of most foods to aggravate the biological humors comes out. We do not have to avoid all the foods that may aggravate our constitution, but we do have to be careful of taking many of them on a regular basis.

Ayurveda, as part of the science of Yoga, teaches us to eat primarily *sattvic* food. In fact, it tells us that a *sattvic* diet is generally safe for everyone. *Sattvic* food is defined as food that is vegetarian, fresh, cooked in the appropriate manner, and not overly spiced or oily. The recipes in this book are of a *sattvic* nature. While Ayurveda explains the properties of different meats, for example, it tells us that meat is not necessarily for health.

THE AYURVEDIC COOKBOOK shows us a rich and tasty vegetarian diet. Much of vegetarianism in this country has been identified with raw foods and salads or macrobiotic cooking, and hence many people consider vegetarian cooking to be tasteless. Such raw food diets may also be found to be light and not nourishing enough for long term consumption, though they are very useful for short term detoxification. However, Indian and Ayurvedic cooking, with its wealth of spices, oils and cooking methods, offers a greater variety of food than would be possible through a heavy meat diet. It also shows us how to prepare vegetarian food that is nourishing and invigorating, that can impart the strength we usually associate with eating meat along with the sense of clarity that a vegetarian diet gives.

One of the most useful parts of the book is the outline of menus; different Ayurvedic constitutions are considered as well as a specific menu that is safe for all constitutions (*Tridoshic*). The menus give seasonal variations and suggestions for travelling. Different beverages are indicated in the book, including many herbal teas, for what we drink facilitates or hampers what we eat.

In Hindu eating the food taken in is given as an offering to the Divine Fire in the stomach, by whose grace we digest the food. It is said: *Annam Brahma, Rasa Vishnur, Bhokta Deva Maheshwarah!* "He who thereby remembers the Divine trinity in the process of eating cannot be harmed by the food he eats. The Ayurvedic preparation of food is part of this recognition.

David Frawley O.M.D., *Vedacharya*
Author: *Ayurvedic Healing, A Comprehensive Guide*
Co-Author of *The Yoga of Herbs* (with Dr. Vasant Lad)

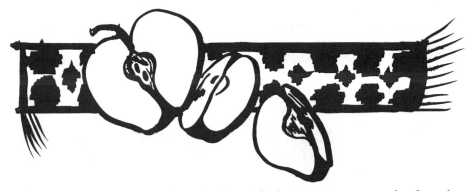

I (Amadea) first became interested in Ayurveda about seven years ago, when I saw that it offered a fresh perspective on my work as a nutritionist. Intrigued with its view of the world, so different from that received in my Western training, I looked further and began to apply its concepts practically. Like most health care professionals, I wanted to be of service to my clients and family. What I experienced was: the principles of Ayurveda work. I was delighted. I was also somewhat abashed at how little I really knew about this ancient Indian system of healing, and how useful my small scraps of knowledge were. These past seven years I have been learning about the basics of this system of healing and how to apply them.

Urmila's inspiration for Ayurvedic recipes grew from her practice of spiritual lifestyle. Her cooking reflects her personal experience with various dietary systems and the cultivation of her intuitive abilities. She began her life-long interest in nutrition and food in the small Indian village of Halol, in the Indian province of Gujarat. The middle of nine children, Urmila was trained as a young girl by her mother to prepare the indigenous diet based on Ayurvedic principles.

Mataji (Urmila) and I share a deep interest in food as a healing force. This, I think, is our strongest link in writing this book. We have each been cooking and eating and experimenting with nutrition for many years. Ayurveda has been friendly to us. It has given us the keys we need as we need them. And it offers a framework that can incorporate and utilize other systems of healing as well. It has coherence and structure. As practical and fairly eclectic people, we have appreciated this.

So what is Ayurveda? It is a system of healing which evolved in India some three to five thousand years ago in response to the needs of the time. It has both a philosophical and a practical basis, the practical perspective springing from its spiritual basis. The earth is perceived as being made up of five elements: ether, air, fire, water, and earth, manifestations of the Divine. These five elements form the basis for all things found in material creation, from the individual's constitution to the tastes of a food. Balancing the elements is key to maintaining health and successfully healing illness, whether physical or mental.

The India from which Ayurveda sprang is largely a mystery to us. And yet we know that the Indus River valley provided the richness and nourishment for a whole series of city-states to arise between 3,000 B.C. and 1,500 B.C. This great urban civilization was one of what are now considered the five cradles of civilization: Egypt, Sumer, Peru, China, and the Indus itself. Of these civilizations, there is surprisingly little known of the Indus culture, perhaps because the small amount of writing which did survive has as yet been indecipherable.

It is easy to imagine the *rishis,** the enlightened sages of ancient India, meditating among the pine trees in obscure spots in the Himalayas, bringing forth the knowledge which was to become Ayurveda, as tradition tells it. And yet it is vital to remember that the culture of their time was a tremendously supportive and sophisticated one. Sir Mortimer Wheeler, a specialist in Indus lore, characterized it as perhaps "the vastest political experiment before the advent of the Roman Empire." (This at a time when the old kingdom of Egypt flourished!) The Indian city-states of four thousand years ago encompassed an area of close to 500,000 square miles. These cities shared an elegant system of pictographic writing, a remarkably accurate standardized system of weights and measures and a strong inclination for well-organized city plans. The two greatest cities, Mohenjo-daro and Harappa, could each accommodate 20-50,000 people at their height, in city centers which covered the equivalent of six to seven miles. These urban centers were laid out in rectangular city blocks larger than those of Los Angeles or New York today, and were serviced by an intricate system of drainage and sewers. There was an extraordinarily high standard of public and private sanitation, which is reflected in the teachings of Ayurveda, with its emphasis on hygiene. Residential homes of brick stood wall to wall in solid rows, like the Victorians of San Francisco or the brownstones of New York, each resident intimately connected with the energetic flow of the city.

It was an affluent culture which worshipped the Mother Goddess. Like other nature-oriented civilizations of its time, it devoted large central areas to storage for grains. Major acreage was allotted for the cultivation of wheat and cotton. There was trade with Sumer via the Persian Gulf and the Arabian Sea. The port of Lothal existed as a center for agriculture and overseas trade. It had a huge dockyard for its time and giant brick kilns for the production of a wide variety of clay items. Among these earthen products were many toys for children, attesting to the prosperity of this culture and the apparent focus of its priorities. Toys were surprisingly sophisticated, often including functioning wheels and holes for pull-strings.

Out of this sophisticated and stable culture came the healing system of Ayurveda. Ironically, the traditional stories of Ayurveda describe how the *rishis* needed to remove themselves from this culture in order to be clear enough to receive the transmission of knowledge they sought. Sometime in the distant past, a large group of sages congregated in the foothills of the Himalayas to face the problem of disease and its effect on life and religious practice. Their concern was to eradicate the illness of all creatures, and they meditated together for this purpose. According to tradition, Lord Atreya came to them, delivering the information and perspective they needed most particularly to six of the disciples: Agnivesa, Bhela, Jatukarna, Parashara, Harita, and Ksharapani. It is said that when the disciples returned to the cities to propagate this knowledge, they fell into problems. Their understanding and memory faltered in the distractions of the cities. They needed to return to the Himalayas and Lord Atreya for the understanding once more. It is out of this second meeting that the system of healing known today as Ayurveda came.

*NOTE: The definitions of all italicized words are found in the text or glossary.

Ayurveda is Sanskrit for "the knowledge of life or daily living." The wisdom, depth and enduring utility of Ayurveda are a testimony to the civilization from which it came. This medical system emphasizes that humans come from nature, that we are an integral part of the universe, and that we have a responsibility to it. The balance of the universe lives within us. It is a system which focuses on physical health, believing that it is much easier to pursue spiritual studies or contribute to the life of the community if you are whole and healthy. It relies on the senses as primary tools of healing and diagnosis, utilizing them both as recipients of information and actors in restoring the balance. This process is described in more detail in the following chapters.

The city states of the Indus flourished for more than one thousand years, between 2,600 B.C. and 1,500 B.C. The body of information known as Ayurveda was transmitted for centuries orally, through songs and verses known as the *Vedas.* Because they were transmitted verbally for so many centuries before they were ever written down, their dates of origin can only be estimated. The *Rig Veda* (Sanskrit for "in praise of knowledge") is approximately four thousand five hundred years old, making it the oldest known song in the world. In 128 hymns it describes sixty-seven herbs and the practices of the medicine of ancient India. The *Atharva Veda* provides further information about the roots of this medicine. It was created some thirty-two hundred years ago.

The practice of Ayurveda continued. The first Ayurvedic medical text which is still accessible to us was the *Charaka Samhita,* written by the Ayurvedic teacher *Charaka* around 700 B.C. or earlier in the Punjab. About a century later, Susruta living near what is now present day Benares wrote the *Susruta Samhita. Charaka Samhita* contains extensive amounts of information about the practice of general medicine and the use of foods and herbs for healing. *Susruta Samhita* focuses on the practice of surgery in the Ayurvedic medicine of its time. Both are still available to Ayurvedic students today.

Ayurveda thrived particularly under Ashoka, who established one of the great empires of the ancient world. Ashoka was a powerful Hindu warrior living in India several centuries before Christ. At the peak of his power he renounced violence for the practice of Buddhism. Ayurveda was revitalized with the spread of Buddhism, and became the foundation for a number of highly respected systems of healing still existent today, including Tibetan Buddhist medicine and parts of Chinese medicine. It also influenced the practice of medicine in Japan and Indonesia. In the early centuries after Christ's birth, the third great work on Ayurveda was written by *Vagbhata* the elder and the younger. This two-volume set reviewed the work of *Charaka* and *Susruta* in *Astanga Samgraha* and *Astanga Hridaya.*

When the Moslems invaded India in 1100 and 1200 A.D., Ayurveda foundered, being forcibly replaced by the Islamic system of healing known as *Unani.* This system of healing is still in existence. For several hundred years it was the Moslems who held the best reputations as doctors on the international circuit, being consulted by Europeans and Indians alike. But it was in 1833 that Ayurveda received a particularly lethal blow. The British closed all the Ayurvedic colleges still surviving in India. Henceforth, only Western medicine was to be practiced, in the view of India's latest conquerors. It is a remarkable tribute to Ayurveda and its culture that it has survived so many assaults.

The turn of this century brought in India a tremendous sense of independence, the independence which was to be later articulated and symbolized so eloquently by Mahatma Gandhi. It was at this time of upheaval during the Swadeshi movement that Dr.

K.M. Nadkarni compiled his classic *Indian Materia Medica,* a superb collection of over two thousand Indian foods and herbs. Dr. Nadkarni was spurred by the desire to re-awaken his fellow Indians to the rich resources of their native healing methods. He emphasized a spirit of self-sufficiency and decried the growing reliance on Western medicine. After Indian independence, Ayurvedic schools and pharmacies arose again, with the active support of the Indian government.

The practice of Ayurvedic medicine traditionally included eight branches: pediatrics, obstetrics and gynecology, toxicology, ear-nose-and-throat (otolaryngology), general or internal medicine, ophthalmology, and surgery, which included plastic surgery. Training for *vaidyas* (Ayurvedic physicians) included the study of astrology, color and gem therapy, psychology, climatology, herbology, and nutrition. It provides an obvious and dynamic model for those of us today seeking a practical and integrated system of healing.

The ancient Ayurvedic texts cannot be used verbatim. The Indians of antiquity used what was available to them, and we need to use what is available to us. For example, Native American Indians of Canada used pine needles (a rich source of Vitamin C) to speed their healing from winter flus in centuries past. A native New Yorker of the 20th century is more likely to take a couple of Vitamin C tablets. In India, the equivalent high-dose Vitamin C would be the fruit *amla,* with over 700 mg of C per fruit. We use what we have. Most of us are unlikely to want to use crocodile semen or cow dung, even if we have access to them. Our cultural conditioning does not predispose us to them. But Ayurveda offers something beyond peculiar and exotic treatments (of which it has plenty!). It gives a clear system of concepts and principles, an understanding of natural laws which is invaluable to us at this time, as we struggle to birth a planetary culture and face the consequences of our years of mis-practice and neglect of the planet and natural laws.

This cookbook is a bit different from many, in that our primary interest is healing. Our aim was to discover the strengths of the foods and herbs we have here on this continent, using a structure (Ayurveda) which supports their effective use. While we have utilized many traditional Ayurvedic and Indian recipes, especially of the Gujarati region, we wanted to offer them with ingredients and directions readily available and understandable here in the West. We also wanted to create dishes that were quick and easy to prepare, and familiar to Americans. Our intent was to design recipes that would cause the least harm for all constitutions, so that families and other groups could eat them together. We also worked to develop dishes healing for particular constitutions. Some recipes are especially beneficial for only one type of person. It has been a delight to play in this way. We hope this same blessing of creative play is with you as you cook for yourself, your family, or friends.

The recipes included in this book have been developed to meet individual needs and conditions, and as you, the reader, sense and feel your response to the food, we welcome you to adopt the recipes to your own body and mind. Ayurveda has many levels of practice, and this is a simple beginning.

We live in times which cry out for a new kind of balance. The age of the simple soul, the old days when what we could not see would not hurt us, is no more. We live surrounded with intangibles on a planet which seeks our advocacy. How we make our contribution will differ from person to person. That we do participate in the healing is essential. This cookbook is one offering toward an inner balance. *Mataji* and I offer it up to you, and the healer within you, as *prasad.*

May your journey be fruitful.

NUTRITION FROM AN AYURVEDIC PERSPECTIVE

The ancients offered ten principles about a healthy diet and how it is to be eaten. They are:

1) Food needs to be hot (usually cooked).
2) Food needs to be tasty and easy to digest.
3) Food needs to be eaten in the proper amounts, not too much or too little.
4) Food needs to be eaten on an empty stomach, after your last meal has been digested, and not before.
5) Foods need to work together and not contradict one another in their actions.
6) Foods need to be eaten in pleasant surroundings with the proper equipment for their enjoyment.
7) Eating should not be rushed.
8) Eating should not be a horrendously drawn out affair, either.
9) It is best to focus on your food while eating.
10) Only eat food which is nourishing to your particular constitution and which suits your mental and emotional temperament.

(*Charaka*, p.XXXV)

These concepts may seem obvious, and yet if you think back over your last few days of eating, you are likely to find at least a few—perhaps many—examples of eating different from these. Of all the elements essential for the maintenance of positive health, food taken in the proper quantity is regarded as most important. In Ayurveda, food **is** medicine as well as nourishment, and what one eats matters vitally.

Why does food need to be "hot?" Hot can have a dual meaning here. The whole focus of Ayurvedic nutrition is to enhance digestion. In Ayurveda, foods which are considered heating in quality—whether or not they are hot or cold in temperature—usually stimulate digestion. And cooking food often enhances its digestibility; obvious examples are legumes and grains. A raw bean or dry grain of rice are unlikely to be received very well by the hardy body, let alone the sick one. Cooking tends to moisten and lighten many foods; these are qualities valued again in Ayurveda for the ability to stimulate or support digestion. Cooking is a valuable deterrent to bacterial growth and spoilage of food, probably a major issue in 700 B.C. or 2000 B.C.— and in parts of the world today. Raw foods **are** used, especially by those of *Pitta* and *Kapha* constitution. And in some cases today an Ayurvedic physician might recommend an all-raw fruit or juice fast for a particular constitution and circumstance. But much of the focus in Ayurvedic medicine is the proper and appropriate preparation of food. Usually this involves cooking.

In this view of healing, the body is made of up seven types of vital tissue or *dhatus.* These *dhatus* work together to ensure the smooth functioning of the body. They include *rasa* (plasma), *rakta* (blood), *mamsa* (muscle), *meda* (fat), *asthi* (bone), *majja* (marrow and nerves), and *shukra* and *artav* (reproductive tissue). Each *dhatu* nourishes the next. These are listed here in order from superficial to deep. A condition in which the blood (*rakta*) is malnourished is less serious and easier to rebalance than one in which the marrow (*majja*) has become involved. A poignant example of this from Western medicine is that of cancer. Usually if a malignant condition has spread to the bone marrow, it has advanced far indeed, and is much more difficult to treat with success than one restricted to the blood.

In Ayurvedic physiology, the *srotas* are also described. *Srotas* are the vital body channels through which energy moves. If a channel becomes blocked by wastes or by any other means, it will not function as effectively. Energy can accumulate at the points of blockage, or the flow of energy can be inhibited in other areas. This concept is probably familiar to most body workers, professionals who work with massage, acupuncture, acupressure, yoga or Rolfing, among others. It may seem less clear to those unfamiliar with energy work. While the *srotas* operate like blood vessels or nerves in their transmission of energy, they are the energetic equivalents of these, not the physical forms themselves. In Tibetan medicine one talks about the energy body or energy field in relation to the *srotas*. The *srotas* are the energetic condition out of which the physical condition arises.

In addition to the *dhatus* and *srotas,* a third basic concept in Ayurvedic physiology is that of *ama*. *Ama* is the waste that accumulates in the body, primarily through poor digestion and absorption. While polychlorinated biphenyls, DDT and sodium trichloroacetate were not around when the *rishis* developed Ayurveda, it is likely that their accumulation in body tissues today would be considered a form of toxic *ama*. Like food and drink, we absorb them from our environment, and if we do not effectively metabolize them and send them back out (a major task in industrial and urban environments especially), they gather in our tissues, to be dealt with.

In Ayurveda, good health can be maintained two ways: 1) by supporting and replenishing the vital tissues (*dhatus*) as they need it, through proper diet and regimen, and 2) by cleansing and removing any obstacles to the clear functioning of the system. This means clearing out *ama* and cleansing the blocked *srotas*. Traditionally the example of an oil lamp was used. The lamp must have adequate oil to burn to give off light. And it must be clean and protected from dust, insects, and wind in order to burn brightly. It is obvious by this definition of good health that few people in the world are maintaining it. Approximately three-quarters of the world's population do not receive enough nourishing food, while most of the remaining one-quarter are drowning in the wastes created through excessive consumption and pollution. In urban areas throughout the globe underprivileged children, especially, are struggling to maintain themselves on both levels. Many are malnourished, and so are less able to defend themselves against the high levels of pollution around them. This is as true of New York City as Brasilia.

A common example is lead. If a child has inadequate stores of calcium, she or he is more likely to absorb lead. Where does this lead come from? Primarily automobile, bus and truck exhaust in the big cities, though old paint in buildings is also a source. Ironically, lead, a heavy metal, tends to settle near ground level, so that children and pets breathe in more than the adults accompanying them. Taking in foods rich in calcium (dairy and greens) will directly strengthen the bones and nerves. At the same time the calcium will begin to displace the toxic lead, literally bumping it out of the body. One does not have to be poor to experience this condition. It has been estimated that 40% of children in American cities labor under a toxic load of lead (10ppm or more).

It is said that Spirit (*Purusha*) and Matter (*Pakruti*) come together to create cosmic intelligence (*Mahad*). Out of *Mahad* arises ego (*Ahamkar*). *Ahamkar* might also be translated as native body intelligence. *Ahamkar* then manifests as the five elements (*mahabhutas*) to create the inorganic and organic worlds. These five elements are earth (*prithi*), water (*Jala*), fire (*tejas*), air (*vayu*), and ether (*akash*).

The five elements come together in each creature in a different combination. And so each person is slightly different from every other person in their mixture of elements, and in the way they balance themselves. These differences need to be honored and worked with. What helps one person will not necessarily help another; each is unique. Essential to the healing in this system is the idea that our health and constitution are affected by what we eat. *In Ayurveda, food and actions are keys to healing.* If we eat and behave in ways which support our constitution and our environment, we and it are likely to stay clean, clear and healthy. If we eat and behave in ways which harm our bodies and the planet, knowingly or unknowingly, we are likely to suffer the consequences. This is becoming blatantly clear on a planetary as well as a personal level as we enter the 1990s. We are not separate from our environment. We are a part of it and it manifests in us.

The senses are considered the primary tools for gathering information about the body and its needs in Ayurveda. This might seem obvious, but it is not how Western medicine is generally practiced. An Ayurvedic physician will feel the client's pulse, smell the client's aroma, look at the overall appearance, listen to the quality of the voice and what the client is saying. The physician will recommend foods and herbs based on their tastes to balance the client's condition. Chinese and other traditional systems of healing operate in similar ways. In Western medicine, a blood test may be your primary entry into the realm of health assessment. The Western doctor looks at abstract numbers as a key to diagnosis. The good Western physician is also likely to use her/his senses, if they are wise. But in Ayurveda, it is at the basis of learning and treatment. The best *vaidyas* are those who can both feel and intuit the most subtle nuances of their client's pulses. They use their senses, and not some outside machine.

Herbs are used extensively in Ayurveda as a vital support to foods. By using particular herbs, one can profoundly alter the balance of the constitution. Herbs are used to stimulate digestion and enhance absorption. They are used to balance a wide variety of conditions.

With food, actions, and herbs, there is a fourth essential key to healing in Ayurveda. These are the thoughts and feelings of the person seeking healing. "A given diet or drug will not be effective if it is taken unwillingly by the individual . . . it will be more effective only when the individual has a feeling that by taking it she or he will be able to maintain his (sic) normal health or will be free from the malady from which he (sic) is suffering." (*Susruta* quoting *Charaka*). From our perspective here, that means a dish has to taste good to you, or you are unlikely to want to finish it, let alone eat it again. It is helpful to know why a specific food is recommended for your healing and balance. Knowing the "whys" can support your efforts. Ayurveda actively involves the individual. To utilize this system, you need to be willing to eat special foods, take specific herbs or herbal medicine and follow certain basic lifestyle routines. It demands more of one than the passive acceptance of treatment (often drugs or other pills) operative in Western medicine. Not everyone is willing to take such an active role in their own healing.

The nature of Ayurveda is commonsensical. For example, if you have a hot burning skin rash, you take cooling substances, internally as well as externally, to heal yourself. A dry rash would indicate the need for internal moisture. In Ayurveda what goes on inside the body affects the outside. Ayurveda operates in this way, cooling what needs to be cooled, warming what needs warming, moistening, or drying as required. The practice of Ayurveda addresses the individual body and constitution and what it needs for balance. It is specific for the individual. If you have heart disease, you will be treated with a program specific for your body, not for the general condition of heart disease.

Another appealing aspect of Ayurveda is that it offers a structure which makes sense. In these times there are dozens of recommendations available as to how best to deal with a given condition. This often leaves people bewildered and confused as to what to choose. My clients share this frustration frequently with me about nutrition. "I have read a lot about this problem," one said to me. "And I sense that the solution lies in nutrition. But how do I know which expert is offering the right advice for me?" By understanding your basic constitution and condition, you can utilize nutrition as a deep source of healing. This resource is largely under your control: it is you who eats for you, and no one else. This can be profoundly empowering. It is not as easy as taking a pill or defrosting a TV dinner. And yet its positive effects extend in directions far beyond what you might imagine.

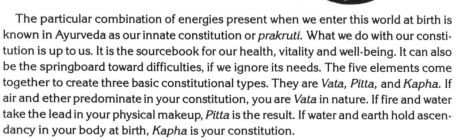

DISCOVERING YOUR CONSTITUTION

The particular combination of energies present when we enter this world at birth is known in Ayurveda as our innate constitution or *prakruti*. What we do with our constitution is up to us. It is the sourcebook for our health, vitality and well-being. It can also be the springboard toward difficulties, if we ignore its needs. The five elements come together to create three basic constitutional types. They are *Vata, Pitta,* and *Kapha*. If air and ether predominate in your constitution, you are *Vata* in nature. If fire and water take the lead in your physical makeup, *Pitta* is the result. If water and earth hold ascendancy in your body at birth, *Kapha* is your constitution.

How do you know this isn't simply some cultural stereotyping? This certainly was an issue for me in encountering Ayurveda. I have a real resistance to convenient systems of categorization, especially the categorization of people. Perhaps that is one reason it has taken me as long to investigate Ayurveda as it has. Humans are far more complex and remarkable than any standard description could convey, whether it be Ayurvedic, astrological, biochemical, or psychological. Also, people often use classifications as a way of getting safe. "Ah, I'm a *Kapha,* so that's why I have a weight problem." Or "Oh, I'm *Vata,* no wonder I rarely make commitments." Or "Ah, ha! being a *Pitta* of course I'm going to have a temper, let me share it with you!" Using limits to stay limited or to become more limited is not what we are after here. Yet understanding more about our natures and resources can be useful; it can give us support for healing and change. My answer to this question is, try it out for yourself. If it is useful, you will discover this.

What does understanding your constitution mean practically? Each constitution has different needs. Meeting these needs assures balance and better chances for good health and peace of mind. It also offers you more informed choices in what health care methods are most appropriate for you.

How can you discover your constitution? Ideally, a skilled Ayurvedic physician can assess your pulse and give you information about your *prakruti* (constitution). From pulse examination he or she can ascertain what elements are in balance, what is out, and what needs to be done. The pulse is utilized in Ayurveda in a way similar to Tibetan or Chinese medicine. Working with a talented Ayurvedic practitioner is an invaluable resource. But what if you live in Boise, Idaho, where there is no *vaidya?* Each constitution has certain characteristic physical, emotional, and mental attributes, which let us know what elements are present. The following questionnaire can assist you in getting a clearer idea about your constitutional type, so that you can use these recipes to maximum advantage.

Place a check next to the choice which best describes you. Occasionally there will be more than one choice.

Discovering Your Constitution

Place a check next to the choice which best describes you. Occasionally more than one choice may need to be made.

Vata	Pitta	Kapha
___ Thin, and usually have been; can be unusually tall or short	___ Medium, well-proportioned frame	___ Tend to be ample in build
___ Thin as child	___ Medium build as child	___ Plump or a little chunky as a child
___ Light bones &/or prominent joints	___ Medium bone structure	___ Heavy bone structure
___ Have a hard time gaining weight	___ Can gain or lose weight relatively easily, if you put your mind to it	___ Gain weight easily, have a hard time losing it
___ Small, active, dark eyes	___ Penetrating light green, grey or amber eyes	___ Large, attractive eyes with thick eyelashes
___ Dry skin, chaps easily	___ Oily skin and hair	___ Thick skin, cool, well-lubricated
___ Dark complexion relative to the rest of your family, tan easily	___ Fair skin, sunburn easily relative to the rest of your family	___ Tan slowly but usually evenly, skin stays cool longer than most
___ Dark, rough, wiry or kinky hair	___ Fine, light, oily hair, blond, red or early grey	___ Thick wavy hair, a little oily, dark or light
___ Prefer warm climate, sunshine, moisture	___ Prefer cool well-ventilated places	___ Any climate is fine, as long as it is not too humid
___ Variable appetite, can get very hungry, but may find your "eyes were bigger than your stomach"	___ Irritable if you miss a meal or can't eat when you are hungry; good appetite	___ Like to eat, fine appetite, but you can skip meals without physical problems if you have to (not that you like to)
___ Bowel movements can be irregular, hard, dry, or constipated	___ Easy and regular bowel movements, if anything, soft, oily, loose stools at least once to twice a day	___ Regular daily bowel movements steady, thick, heavy
___ Digestion sometimes good, sometimes not	___ Usually good digestion	___ Digestion fine, sometimes a little slow
___ Dislike routine	___ Enjoy planning and like routine, especially if you create it	___ Work well with routine
___ Creative thinker	___ Good initiator and leader	___ Good at keeping an organization or project running smoothly
___ Like to stay physically active	___ Enjoy physical activities, especially competitive ones	___ Love leisurely activities most

Discovering Your Constitution *continued*

Vata	Pitta	Kapha
You feel more mentally relaxed when you're exercising	Exercise helps keep emotions from going out of control for you	Exercise keeps your weight down in a way diet alone won't
Change your mind easily	Have opinions and like to share them	Change opinions and ideas slowly
Tend toward fear or anxiety under stress	Tend toward anger, frustration or irritability under stress	Tend to avoid difficult situations
Often dream, but rarely remember your dreams	Relatively easy to remember your dreams, often dream in color	Generally only remember dreams if they are especially intense or significant
Changeable moods and ideas	Forceful about expressing your ideas and feelings	Steady, reliable, slow to change
Like to snack, nibble	Like high protein foods, like chicken, fish, eggs, beans	Love fatty foods, bread, starch
If ill, nervous disorders or sharp pain more likely	If ill, fevers, rashes, inflammation more likely	If ill, excess fluid retention or mucus more likely
Light sleeper	Usually sleep well	Sound, heavy sleeper
You think that money is there to be spent	You think that money is best spent on special items or on purchases which will advance you	Money is easy to save for you
Sexual interest variable, fantasy life active	Ready sexual interest and drive	Steady sexual interest and drive
Brittle nails	Flexible nails, but pretty strong	Strong thick nails
Cold hands and feet, little perspiration	Good circulation, perspire frequently	Moderate perspiration
Thin, fast, variable pulse, hands cold	Strong full pulse, hands warm	Steady slow rhythmic pulse, hands cool
Variable thirst	Usually thirsty	Rarely thirsty

Add up all your checks. The constitution with the most checks generally indicates your primary constitution. If you have marked two constitutions nearly as often, you may be a dual dosha: Vata-Pitta, Pitta-Kapha, etc. Rarely, all three will be relatively equal, in which a Tridoshic or Vata-Pitta-Kapha type results.

If you checked aspects in a dosha different from your constitution as a whole, this may indicate an imbalance in that Dosha. For example, if you checked primarily Pitta aspects, but also marked off "brittle nails" and "light sleeper," this could indicate that while you are Pitta, you have an imbalance in Vata (see text for more information).

So what did you come up with? Did one description sound more like you than another? *Vatas* tend to be light, fast, wiry, creative people. *Pittas* have sharp minds, passionate feelings (sometimes submerged) and are likely to want to lead. *Kaphas* are solid, reliable, easy-going people, who shouldn't be pushed too far. Traditionally, the infuriated *Kapha* is compared to an enraged bull elephant about to charge.

Are you still uncertain as to your constitution? (*Vatas* often are.) Seriously, what kind of climate attracts you most? Temperature and humidity are keys here, as Dr. Robert Svoboda points out in his book, *Prakruti, Your Ayurvedic Constitution. Vatas* go for warm climes, *Pittas* for cooler ones and *Kaphas* for anything but humidity. Your body build as a child is another key. Use these aspects as tie-breakers if you are still in question.

Does more than one of these descriptions still fit you? It is possible. Many people are born with dual constitutions, or two *doshas* predominating. For example, a *Pitta-Kapha* would incorporate attributes of both these types. These individuals generally feel comfortable in leadership roles and have the momentum to achieve the goals they create. A *Vata-Pitta* is apt to react quickly, with plenty of mental energy and imagination. They are able to express themselves with feeling. While sweet taste calms this type, if they overdo it they are likely to find themselves coping with hypoglycemia. *Vata-Kaphas* face challenges. While mental agility and persistence are definite resources for them, fear and inertia can collaborate to do them in just as they are about to embark on that new plan. They need warmth to stay healthy and comfortable. A native *Vata-Kapha* of Arizona may experience difficulty moving to Philadelphia and its cold winters.

Did you check mainly one category with a few key aspects in another? If these aspects have developed only in the last few years, i.e.," weight change," "dry skin," "used to be quick to anger but now more often respond with fear," they could be describing your *vikruti.* If we abuse our constitution and natural needs, we can become imbalanced. This imbalance or disease state is known as our *vikruti.* This imbalance can show up in our constitutional *dosha* or in a *dosha* other than our innate constitution. For an example of the latter condition: say you were a little on the chubby side as a child. You were a kind person and tolerant of others' needs. As a teen you became interested in wrestling and became obsessed about making weight goals for meets. Over the next few years, high-protein diets, intense exercise, and out-and-out starvation became the norm as you managed to get yourself down to a svelte shape. However, problems arose. You found yourself experiencing panic attacks and insomnia. You began to have irrational fears about your body, performance, and self-image. You got off balance.

Here we are talking about someone whose original constitution (*prakruti*) is *Kapha*, but who has developed an imbalance in *Vata dosha* due to his lifestyle choices. This *Vata* imbalance would be known as his *vikruti.* From an Ayurvedic nutritional perspective, he would need to balance both *Kapha* and *Vata*, with an emphasis on the immediate imbalance, *Vata*. Calming, warming, cooked foods would be recommended. Clearly it could be useful to look at the psychological conditions underlying this person's choices. Here we would first offer enough nutritional guidance so that this person could begin to experience enough calm inside to be able to face the deeper issues in front of him. And this (dietary change) is something he can do for himself.

ATTRIBUTES AND NUTRITIONAL NEEDS OF EACH CONSTITUTION

Vata

The person with *Vata* predominant in their constitution is blessed with a quick mind, ready flexibility and creative resources. *Vata* is associated with the attribute of motion. You are likely to be on the go a lot, mentally, physically or both. *Vata* provides the essential motion for all bodily processes, and so is extremely vital for health. One purpose of dietary therapy for *Vata* is to ground or stabilize this motion. *Vata's* primary residence is the colon. This *dosha* can also be found in abundance in the brain, ears, bones, joints, skin, and thighs. *Vata* tends to increase with age, as witnessed by increased dryness and wrinkling of skin (dryness is another of the attributes of *Vata*.) On a seasonal basis, *Vata* is most prominent in the fall, and this is the most important time to attend to diet. Routine is also very useful in assisting you to ground all this moving energy effectively. You will find yourself getting rewarding results with greater use of regular patterns of healing and routine. On a daily basis *Vata* is most active in the late afternoon and early evening (2-6 p.m.) and before dawn (2-6 a.m.).

The other attributes of *Vata*, besides dryness and mobility, are light, cold, rough, subtle, clear, and dispersing. Any of these qualities in excess can imbalance *Vata*, while their opposites calm this *dosha*. For example, a lot of travel can derange *Vata*, especially if it is by plane. Rest, warmth and meditation can calm it. Loud noises, continual stimulation, drugs, sugar, and alcohol can all disequilibrate *Vata*. Soothing music, breaks, deep breathing, and massage balances it. Exposure to cold or cold foods really aggravate *Vata*, as do frozen and dried foods. Warm moist foods calm *Vata*.

Vata disorders are more likely to be noticed in the fall and winter. Some examples of common *Vata* imbalances include flatulence, bloating, tics or twitches, aching joints, dry skin and hair, brittle nails, nerve disturbances, constipation and mental confusion or chaos. These mental disturbances often relate to fear, anxiety or memory loss (or all of the above). Years ago I noticed an odd thing. Three clients in the space of a month gave me a medical history of memory loss, which in each case was immediately preceded by abdominal surgery. I thought this was strange, and wondered about the long-term implications of anesthesia in surgery. It wasn't until I got interested in Ayurveda that I saw a possible correlation. The seat of *Vata* is in the lower abdomen. Surgery in this area imbalances *Vata*. One symptom of *Vata* imbalance is memory loss. It is particularly important to tend to *Vata* after surgery in the lower torso, regardless of your constitution.

What you can do to balance *Vata*:
1. Keep warm.
2. Choose warming foods and spices (see the rest of this cookbook!)
3. Avoid extreme cold, and cold or frozen foods and drinks.
4. Minimize your intake of raw foods, especially raw apples and members of the cabbage family.
5. Take it easy on most beans, with a few key exceptions (see below).

6. Make sure your food is warm, moist, and well-lubricated. Soup, hot drinks and rice with a little oil or butter in it are some examples.
7. Emphasize sweet, sour, and salty tastes in your food choices.
8. Keep to a regular routine.
9. Create as safe, calm and secure an environment for yourself as you can.

Vatas need warmth, on all levels, from their environment to their friendships to their food. Cold causes *Vata* to constrict and tighten up and restricts the free flow of movement so vital to their well-being.

Raw foods, being cold, take more energy to digest. And *Vatas* do not usually have a great excess of digestive fire to waste. Members of the cabbage family, when eaten raw, can easily create gas. These include broccoli (which is the easiest of these to break down), cabbage, cauliflower, kale, kohlrabi, and Brussels sprouts. Gas, being airy, throws off *Vata*. Or more accurately, *Vata* gets thrown off and gas is the result. Most times when you have flatulence, *Vata* is at least temporarily out of balance. A light salad of lettuce and sprouts can be grounded with an oil and vinegar dressing; or marinated steamed vegetables can be eaten (see SALADS, pg. 201). If you do choose to eat raw foods, summertime or a warm climate are the best time and place to do it.

Beans tend to be cold, heavy and dry, not conducive to *Vata*'s best interests. And yet a few legumes can be helpful for *Vata*. Black lentils (*urud dal*) are warming and can be eaten in modest quantities. Split mung bean (*mung* or *yellow dal*) is quite good for *Vata*. Many *Vatas* handle certain well-spiced soy products well, like tofu or liquid soy milk. Some do not. Let your gut be the guide. Dairy is very calming to *Vata*, especially when it is warm.

Warm cooked whole grains ground *Vata*. Especially healing are basmati rice, brown rice, wild rice, oatmeal, and wheat products (as long as you are not sensitive to one or more of these!) Yeasted breads, sugar, and nutritional yeast can cause gas in *Vatas*. Chappatis, tortillas, papadums, unyeasted crackers, matzo, and quick breads (made with baking powder or soda) frequently are better tolerated. Pasta of all kinds is fine for *Vata*.

Fruit serves *Vata* well, so long as it is sweet, moist, well-ripened and not an apple, pear, cranberry, watermelon or dried fruit. All fruits are best taken alone or at the beginning of a meal, not mixed in with other foods. If *Vata* does choose to have dried fruit, it should be well-soaked or stewed.

Fermented products have a variable effect on *Vata*. Many *Vatas* find the sourness of pickles, umeboshi plums and vinegary foods stimulating to their digestion. A few find these upset their stomachs.

Eggs are best eaten in dishes or in a soft or well-spiced form. For example most *Vatas* enjoy scrambled eggs, omelettes or custards. Not all can handle hard-boiled or fried eggs. If you can, enjoy. If you can't, don't.

Most sweets are tolerated well by *Vata*, if you haven't developed excess yeast in your gut or elsewhere. Sugar is overstimulating to *Vata* and is best avoided. If you are cooking for yourself or other *Vatas*, sesame oil (or ghee) is your best choice. Its warmth and groundedness are beneficial for you. When cooking for other constitutions as well as yourself, sunflower oil is a good neutral choice.

Routine is remarkably grounding (though possibly distasteful!) for *Vata*. If you do nothing else, eating your usual foods at regular times can ground this *dosha* noticeably.

ABOUT EATING OUT.   Of all the *doshas*, you have the easiest time finding appropriate restaurants; you can do well almost anywhere with a few well-chosen limitations. Take it easy on the salad and mountains of raw food. Tomatoes and tomato-based dishes are best avoided; starch-acid combos like tomato sauce and pasta often do not sit well on the *Vata* gut. Icy treats are not great for you. You can find food suitable for your *dosha* at Thai, Indian, Chinese, American, Moroccan, Ethiopian, Japanese, Mexican, Spanish, and some Italian restaurants. Bon appetite!

 *Pitta*

The person with *Pitta* dominant in their constitution is blessed with determination, a strong will and probably good digestive fire. *Pitta* is associated with the elements of fire and water, and often it is the fiery quality about *Pittas* which is first noticed. It makes available to you large amounts of initiative and energy, as well as a good baseline of *agni* (digestive fire). The primary seat of *Pitta* is in the stomach and small intestine. Other seats of *Pitta* include the eyes, skin, blood, sweat glands, and fat. *Pitta* (and *Pitta* ambition) predominate in the middle of the life cycle, when we are young and middle-aged adults. It is important to channel this creative fire toward specific purposes, and to learn to express passionate feelings outwardly in a constructive way. Translation: Create! Express! *Pittas* are apt to have excellent abilities in taking charge of themselves, their lives and their healing processes.

The attributes of *Pitta* are oily, hot, light, mobile, and liquid. The idea is that any of these qualities in excess can imbalance *Pitta*. Their opposites will calm it. For example, summer and high noon are times of *Pitta* predomination. These are the times *Pitta* is most likely to encounter disturbances. In summer the weather is hot and light. We often get more mobile, going on vacations and side trips. During this time *Pitta* imbalances such as sunburn, poison ivy, prickly heat or short tempers often arise. Such *Pitta* disorders tend to calm naturally as the weather gets cooler, which gives some clues as to how best manage this constitution. For *Pitta* it is especially important to choose cooling foods in the summer, with a wide variety of raw foods. Warmer foods are best taken in winter, depending on the locale. On a daily basis *Pitta* is most active between 10 a.m. and 2 p.m. and from 10 p.m. to 2 a.m.

If the fire element is aggravated, you could notice any of the following: skin rashes, burning sensations, ulceration, fever, inflammations or irritations such as conjunctivitis, colitis, or sore throats, rapidly changing moods, irritation, anger, frustration, or jealousy. The water element in your constitution can sometimes show up as a tendency to produce large amounts of urine. In the extreme, with improper diet and lifestyle, the kidneys can become worn down and *Pitta's* normal vitality can lose its luster. These are all signals that your balance needs restoration.

What you can do to balance *Pitta*:
   1. Keep cool.
   2. Avoid excess heat, steam, and humidity.
   3. Avoid excess oils, fried foods, caffeine, salt, alcohol, red meat, and hot spices.

4. Emphasize fresh fruits and vegetables.

5. Enjoy ample amounts of milk, cottage cheese, and whole grains.

6. Emphasize sweet, bitter and astringent tastes in your food choices.

7. Get plenty of fresh air.

8. Trust your feelings and express them in ways that support you and those around you.

Lest you think that all joy is about to go out of your life, take heart. It is not so—you will just be losing excess aggravation! It is much easier to keep calm and focused eating a *Pitta*-supporting diet.

Keeping cool is vital. Take the time to find a shady spot in the middle of a hot summer day of work. Wear a hat to shade that active brain. Add a cool rinse after your shower. All these calm *Pitta*. Hot tubs, chilis, too much sun, all aggravate *Pitta*. Most oils, salt, alcohol, red meat, and hot spices are considered heating in quality by Ayurveda and so can be relied upon to irritate *Pitta*. While a few fruits and vegetables are heating, such as tomato and papaya, most calm *Pitta* down, as long as they are sweet and ripe.

Most dairy products are cooling in nature including all types of milk, cottage cheese, most soft cheeses, and ice cream. Hard cheeses, sour cream, buttermilk, and yogurt are best avoided, as their excess fat, salt or sour taste aggravate fire. Yogurt can be taken if prepared properly (see p. 82). Cooling whole grains relax and ground *Pitta*. These include barley, wheat, and basmati rice. Rice cakes and crackers are generally well-tolerated. Oats, while mildly warming in quality, ground *Pitta*, and so are helpful. *Pittas* can choose from a wide variety of wheat products, including breads, muffins, crackers, and pasta. Wheat-sensitive *Pittas* can benefit from the wheat-free recipes included here.

Pittas are often attracted to high-protein foods, and do seem to need a little more protein than other constitutions. Goat milk, cow milk, soy milk, egg white souffles, tofu, tempeh, and the aforementioned cottage cheese are all effective in balancing *Pitta*. Most beans—with the exception of heating lentils—are excellent. Their cool heavy sweet astringent tastes and attributes make them naturals for *Pitta*. Even the *Pitta* digestive tract can overdo them, though. Three to five times a week is a realistic amount without hazarding excess explosions from the direction of the gut. Check your own responses and eat accordingly.

Greens such as collards, turnip greens, dandelion greens, parsley, and watercress provide the bitter taste *Pitta* needs, as well as generous helpings of vitamin A, B complex, calcium, magnesium, and iron. Many *Pittas* seem to need more vitamin A-rich vegetables and fruits than other types, perhaps to replenish and vitalize their active livers.

Cooling spices are an important part of a *Pitta* diet. The best for you are cumin, coriander, saffron, dill, fennel, mint of all kinds, and parsley. You can also use cinnamon, cardamom, turmeric, and small amounts of black pepper, salt, and/or well-sauteed sweet onions. Garlic, sadly, is most aggravating for this *dosha* and should be avoided.

With your characteristically good digestive fire, you may be able to dare food combinations that would spell disaster for the other constitutions. Let your awareness be a guide. Notice what combinations you can digest well and which challenge you.

Maple syrup, brown rice syrup, barley malt, sugar, and raw young honey (6 months or less) are fine sweeteners for you. Sunflower oil, ghee, or unsalted butter are your best choices of fats, again in moderation. (Moderation is to *Pitta* what routine is to *Vata*: unfamiliar.)

ABOUT EATING OUT. It takes some planning. Vegetarian, continental-style restaurants, American, mild Indian, Japanese and Chinese spots (skip the eggroll) offer you a decent variety of choices on this program, as do salad bars. You are the one that can luxuriate at the ice cream parlor, if you like. Middle Eastern food can be an option, if you go for the dishes with mint (like tabouli), or cumin or fennel (such as Lebanese dishes) and pass up the fried and garlic-laden choices. Mexican, Italian, and fast-food places are likely to feel frustrating if you are sticking strictly to a *Pitta* diet. Your best bet is to avoid meat, fried food, caffeine, alcohol, and fast foods. Bon Voyage!

 *Kapha*

The person with *Kapha* preeminent in their constitution is blessed with strength, endurance, and stamina. *Kapha* is associated with the elements earth and water, and the qualities of faith, groundedness, calm, fluidity, and lubrication. While patterns and routines can seem easy to establish and follow for *Kapha*, frequent shifts in routine will actually help you create greater healing. It will also reduce your chances of getting stuck in a rut, physically or emotionally. Children tend to have a good deal of *Kapha* in them, as evidenced by their soft, fluid muscles and well-lubricated skin. *Kapha* decreases with age.

Your challenges as a *Kapha* are potential inertia and a tendency to want to possess things or people: what was called in the old days lust, greed, and attachment. Our infant daughter, a *Kapha*, provided a beautiful example of this when she was about nine months old. Her dad showed up to bring her home while she was in the middle of eating cornbread at the home of one of her godmothers. Iza, being practical, clutched her goodies in both fists as she was lifted into her carseat. She soon fell asleep in the darkness of the vehicle. However as they reached home and the car light came on, Iza stirred. She opened her eyes and without a blink directed the cornbread, still tightly held in both hands, straight for her mouth. Food and security are important to *Kaphas*. You wouldn't want to let them go. Clearly, everyone shares this quality with *Kapha* to varying degrees!

Lightening up on the holding on and letting go can be healing here. Often old attitudes and beliefs are held so strongly, they can become the source of waste in the physical body. Such wastes may even feel safe and familiar—again, hard to let go of. Two examples come to mind. One *Kapha* client had a tendency to retain excess fluid in his body. As he began to take diuretic herbs, he started to lose the excess water. He experienced sharp sensations of dehydration and thirst—although he still had more water in his tissues than the norm. The change was disorienting for him and he had a hard time continuing with the program. In another case, a client sensitive to wheat and dairy did a series of colon-cleansing techniques. Large amounts of excess mucus were cleared from her bowels by this treatment. The mucus, in part, was a reaction to past years of consumption of the offending substances. Rather than feeling good about this clearing, she was disturbed. She found herself eating a giant bowl of pasta with cheese late the same night, foods she hadn't eaten in months. She explained she felt like she needed grounding. She knew the food was likely to only create more *ama*, but that at least felt familiar.

The attributes associated with *Kapha* are oily, cold, soft, dense, heavy, slimy, static, and slow. Lest this list of qualities sound less than glamorous, comfort yourself in the knowledge that *Kapha* constitution was much valued by the ancients. Biologists substantiate this, acknowledging the primary importance of these attributes in sustaining life. *Kaphas* endure, unless they abuse their bodies greatly.

Kapha resides in the chest. Other sites of potential *Kapha* accumulation include the sinuses, head, throat, nose, lungs, joints, mouth, stomach, lymph, and plasma. *Kapha* is often correlated with the body's production of mucus. Mucus is both a useful lubricator in the appropriate amounts and a source of congestion, in excess. An imbalance of *Kapha* is likely to manifest as colds, congestion, sinusitis, depression, sluggishness, excess weight, diabetes, edema (water retention) or headache. *Kapha* can also accumulate as the moon gets full, and biologists have discovered a distinct tendency for organisms to retain more fluid at this time. The daily times of *Kapha* predominance are 6 a.m. to 10 a.m. and 6 p.m. to 10 p.m.

Kaphas can sustain a lot of exercise, and need to. As a *Kapha* you can tolerate more intense exercise of longer duration than any other constitutional type. You are also able to fast in a way that other constitutions cannot. Your natural body stores are able to carry you through a day of fasting with few repercussions. The temptation to be avoided is that of slipping into a horizontal lifestyle in front of the TV with your favorite edible goodies— else you may find the forces of gravity pulling most of your mass down toward your belly and hips.

What you can do to balance *Kapha*:
1. Get plenty of physical activity everyday.
2. Keep your consumption of fat to a minimum, including fried foods.
3. Avoid iced foods and drinks, sweets, and excessive amounts of bread.
4. Choose foods which are warm, light, and dry (see below).
5. Drink no more than four cups of fluid per day.
6. Emphasize pungent, bitter and astringent tastes in your food and herb choices.
7. Luxuriate in fresh vegetables, herbs and spices.
8. Get enough complex carbohydrates to sustain you and maintain an adequate energy intake.
9. Allow excitement, challenge and change into your life as much as possible.

Kaphas need variety and stimulation in their foods, friends and activities. It provides the perspective to shake up old ways of experiencing the world and support for the new. It also helps them move out of stagnation and into healing.

You will notice that many of the recipes here suited for *Kapha* contain little or no oil per serving. Oil or fat can increase *Kapha* like nothing else, except perhaps sweets or sour food. If you choose to adapt a *Vata* or *Pitta* recipe for your needs, cut the oil to one teaspoon or less, substituting water instead. A low-fat diet is one of your greatest therapeutic needs.

Most dairy is cool, moist and heavy, just like *Kapha*. It is best avoided. I use goat milk or small amounts of ghee to liven up my *Kapha* dishes at home.

When you do use oil, mustard oil, available at Indian groceries, is a good choice, as it is warming and pungent. Sesame oil, while warming, tends to be too heavy for *Kapha*.

Sunflower is a good oil when entertaining other *doshas*, as it is mild-mannered and non-assertive in nature, and a good source of polyunsaturated fats.

A program similar to the *Fit for Life* diet popular a number of years ago is useful for you. A light breakfast of fresh fruit and/or tea treats this *dosha* gently in the Kaphic time of dawn. Complex carbohydrates for lunch and/or dinner are important to provide fiber, minerals and B vitamins. The most light, warming and drying include millet, barley, rye, kasha, soba noodles, amaranth, quinoa, corn, oat bran, and toasted oats. These grains also keep your insulin pump primed, so you can continue to be able to handle starches effectively. An all-protein reducing diet seems to do a disservice for a *Kapha* body in the long run. Among other effects, it seems to imbalance the insulin mechanisms, making it less able to metabolize starch.

Light low-fat proteins serve you best, especially high-fiber beans. Anything which stimulates elimination tends to relieve *Kapha* (barley and beans being classic examples). Aduki beans are especially good, as are black turtle beans, though the latter are more difficult to digest. Soy beans and soy products are recommended less frequently. Over half of tofu's calories come from fat, surprisingly, while only 4% of black beans do. Still, soy products like soy milk tend to be less *Kapha*-enhancing than dairy.

Iced foods and drinks, being cold and heavy like *Kapha* itself, are not recommended. Fluids and salt increase *Kapha's* moisture and so should be kept to a minimum.

Hot, light spicy foods are great for you; you were born for Asian and Latin American cuisine (without the cheese). I had one *Kapha* client who reported losing thirty pounds travelling in Asia with no conscious intention whatsoever, and no gastrointestinal disasters either. She was served a diet ideal for her *dosha:* lots of vegetables, hot peppers, ginger, soy and soba noodles and well-spiced tea. No dairy or wheat, the ubiquitous bane of *Kapha* here in the States.

You can lighten up more in summer and in warm climates, eating more raw foods at these times, and save the warmer heavier foods for winter and cold climates. In general, light crispy foods will serve you best. Popcorn is a great example, as are rye crackers, corn tortillas, and steamed vegetables.

ABOUT EATING OUT.   Pleasurable choices include salad bars, Mexican restaurants (hold the cheese and sour cream and skip the fried dishes), vegetarian, Indian, Chinese, Thai, and Japanese restaurants (avoid the tempura and eggrolls). Italian and continental establishments could feel limited in their options for you, unless they specialize in great salads and vegetable dishes. Best bets are to stay away from fast food, meat, sweets and heavy fried foods. Bon appetite!

Often it is asked how important it is to stick with your constitution's food choices. This is a healing therapy. How strictly you choose to stay with the choices depends on how serious your condition is and how fast you want to get in balance. The closer you adhere to these guidelines, the sooner you will see results.

HOW TO IMBALANCE YOUR CONSTITUTION

Vata
Worry.
Fast.
Don't get enough sleep.
Eat on the run.
Keep no routine whatsoever.
Eat dry, frozen or leftover foods.
Run around a lot—in cars, planes, trains, or jogging shoes.
Never lubricate your skin.
Work the graveyard shift.
Avoid tranquil, warm, moist places.
Use drugs, especially cocaine and speed.
Have major abdominal surgery.
Repress your feelings.

Pitta
Drink plenty of alcohol.
Eat spicy food.
Engage in frustrating activities.
Emphasize tomatoes, chilis, raw onions, sour foods, and yogurt in your diet.
Exercise at the hottest time of day.
Wear tight hot clothes.
Use drugs, especially cocaine, speed, or marijuana.
Avoid cool fresh peaceful places.
Snack on highly salted foods.
Repress your feelings.
Eat as much red meat and salted fish as possible.

Kapha
Take nice long naps after meals.
Eat lots of fatty foods and oils.
Overeat as often and as much as possible.
Deny your creative self.
Luxuriate in inertia.
Become a couch potato.
Assume someone else will do it.
Avoid invigorating, warm, dry areas.
Don't exercise.
Live on potato chips and beer.
Use drugs, especially sedatives and tranquilizers.
Repress your feelings.
Make sure you get at least one dessert every day, preferably cheesecake or ice cream.

UNDERSTANDING AYURVEDIC NUTRITION: TASTE

Taste, or *rasa*, is the key to understanding Ayurvedic nutrition and being able to apply it practically to any constitution for healing and balance. From an Ayurvedic perspective, taste is made up of a number of different components.

There is the taste we experience when we put a food or herb in our mouths. That immediate experience of taste, and how it affects the body, is known as *rasa*. Then there is the effect that each taste has on digestion, its *virya*. A food with a hot *virya* will usually enhance your digestive function, while one with a cool *virya* can slow it down.

Taste also has a more long-term and subtle effect on the body and its metabolism. This long-term or post-digestive effect is known as the food's *vipak*. Some tastes will tend to lighten the body and promote weight loss over the long run, while others will have the opposite effect.

Each of the six tastes identified in Ayurveda has its own qualities or *gunas*. A taste can be light or heavy, moist or dry. These specific characteristics unique to each taste influence how it will affect us, both immediately and over the long term. Tastes which are light are generally easier to digest and assimilate, while those that are considered heavy from an Ayurvedic standpoint take more energy to digest. Moist tastes will have a lubricating effect on the body, as you might guess. A dry taste, eaten to excess, can be dehydrating.

It is not necessary to eat Indian foods in order to get the proper balance of tastes, though Indian cuisine offers many great examples of balanced taste. Each culture has developed its own way to prepare foods, many of them inherently balancing. Ayurveda offers a way to balance foods regardless of your particular cooking style and can be used in a wide variety of diets. Taste can be balanced in a Western dish as easily as in an Eastern one. The important thing is to become familiar with the tastes and their effects, so you can use them to support and assist you in creating good health.

Let's look at the six tastes to see how this works.

SWEET

Sweet taste is made up of the elements earth and water; it has a cooling *virya*. This means its immediate effect on digestion is to cool it down a bit, be mildly inhibiting. Its *vipak* is sweet. Sweet tends to be heavy and moist, and will create heaviness and moisture in the long as well as the short run. What this means practically is that sweet foods like sugar, sweets, candies, pastries, and ice cream will increase our bulk, moisture and weight when eaten in excess. No surprise? No, not particularly. As Americans, we have been experimenting with sweet taste in excess for more than a century, as our 35% rate of obesity testifies. And yet sweet taste in moderation can be most satisfying. It is also an excellent taste for stimulating growth and grounding, again, in moderation.

In Ayurveda, *rasa* can mean feeling or emotion as well as taste. And each of the tastes can have a subtle emotional or mental effect on our awareness, as well as a physical one. In balance, sweet can promote a feeling of love and well-being, a profound sense of satisfaction. In excess, it can induce complacency and inertia. (An experiment to test this effect can be easily done on one's own!) Sweet taste has a similar effect on digestion. It tends to be mildly satisfying, especially after a meal. At the same time, because it is cooling, it will not stimulate digestion; it will simply provide a sense of satisfaction.

There is a relieved feeling of "aah" that comes from sweet. For this reason, sweet taste can be most calming to the nervous mental energy of *Vata*. Sweet grounds *Vata* by offering it extra earth and water. These same elements in the cooling form of sweet are balancing and soothing to *Pitta*. *Kapha*, on the other hand, can become overloaded by sweet taste. Sweet offers *Kapha* what it already has in abundance: cool, moist earth and water, which can rapidly lead to inertia.

Here in the United States, sweets are readily available to calm us—or put us to sleep—whenever life might be getting too uncomfortable. Many of us have probably had the experience of finding ourselves heading toward the refrigerator with this agenda in mind: "Sweet..hm..sweet . . .what have I got in here?" The problem, of course, is that we can pay for this sedative relief in the long run, albeit with simple inertia, weight gain, depression or diabetes. Sweet deserves a place in each person's palate—the appropriate amount and kind for that individual.

SOUR

Sour taste is comprised of the elements earth and fire. The warming quality of fire shows up in the *virya* of sour, which is heating. Sour taste promotes digestion and has a mildly warming effect on the body as a whole. Its *vipak* is sour, which means that it continues to warm the body over time, as well as in its first impact. Anyone who has had an ulcer may have experienced this warming effect as something less than pleasant.

Other qualities associated with sour are a mild sort of heaviness and moisture. *Vata* benefits from the warmth, humidity and groundedness of sour taste. It can be quite helpful in stimulating digestion in *Vata* systems. *Pitta* can find it counterproductive because the heat of sour is more than *Pitta* needs. The gentle heaviness and moisture of this taste can be oppressive to *Kapha*, causing it to retain even more fluid and weight within itself. For *Pitta* and *Kapha*, sour taste is best balanced with other tastes. For *Vata*, sour foods like umeboshi plums or pickles or a bit of lemon can be excellent for stimulating an often delicate digestive tract.

On the emotional and mental levels, a small amount of sour taste conveys a refreshing sense of realism. There is a "wake-up" quality to sour which can bring us back to reality. An excessive amount of sour taste, on the other hand, can promote envy, jealousy, or what has been called "sour grapes" pessimism. Again, balance is important. A bit of sour can awaken consciousness and stimulate digestion on all levels. Large amounts might push us into unexpected envy and irritation.

Common examples of foods with sour taste are lemons, sour fruit and citrus, sour grapes, vinegar and pickled foods.

SALTY

Fire and water are the elements which constitute salty taste. Fire gives salt its heating digestive effect or *virya*. Like sour and sweet, salty taste tends to be somewhat moist and somewhat heavy. While sweet is the heaviest and most moist of the tastes, and sour less heavy and moist, salty taste is somewhere between the two. It will stimulate water retention faster than sour taste, yet will not promote weight gain quite as fast as sweet. Its *vipak* is sweet. This means that while salty is initially warming, its long-term action is not very warming, but more moistening and grounding. This long term effect can be seen in its ability to promote water retention in people eating many salty foods.

Because salty taste is mildly warming it slightly enhances digestive ability and *agni*. It is helpful for *Vata* because it warms and holds in moisture. *Pitta* can find its heat aggravating. While the warmth of salty tastes might stimulate *Kapha*, its tendency to promote weight and moisture is counterproductive for *Kapha*.

The effect of salty taste on the mind and feelings covers a range. A small amount of salty taste can lend an outspoken, grounded quality to an individual. Excessive use of salty taste seems to create several results. In some people it can produce a mind which is rigid, overly structured and contractive. In others it can result in an urgent and repeated desire for gratification of the senses. These two tendencies can unite in the person who takes tremendous pleasure in being "right" at all times. The addictive quality of potato or corn chips is a good physical example of this effect. Once you begin eating them, it is often difficult to stop.

Salt is used a good amount in our culture to stimulate and gratify our adrenals. It can be used as a way of pushing the adrenal glands to excessive performance by some in the same way that other people would use caffeine. Small amounts of salty taste are excellent for providing structure and enhancing digestion. Large quantities can create a system which is waterlogged and immobile (as in some kinds of heart conditions) or irritated and exhausted. The Japanese offer an example of this. While as a nation they have had a strikingly low rate of cancer in most areas when eating their traditional diet, their rate of stomach cancer is quite high. Medical researchers attribute this to the irritating effect that the high-salt Japanese diet has on the stomach (i.e. stimulating too much fire in one place, the gastric mucosa.).

Common salty foods include salt, seaweed, foods such as salted nuts, chips, and similar snacks. Fast foods and canned foods tend to be remarkably high in salt.

PUNGENT

Pungent taste is made up of the elements air and fire. It is the hottest of all the tastes and most stimulating to digestion. It is light and very dry in quality. Its *vipak* is pungent, that is, it stays hot, light and dry in its effect on the body from beginning to end. For this reason, it is a marvelous balancer for *Kapha*, drying out and warming up *Kapha's* excess dampness and mass. Small amounts of pungent taste can be useful for *Vata*, especially in conjunction with other less drying tastes. In these quantities it will warm and stimulate *Vata* digestion. Larger amounts of pungent foods can be most aggravating to *Vata* because the lightness and dryness create extra movement and dehydration in the system (examples: diarrhea and/or dry mouth; skin). A little bit of pungent taste balanced with sweet, sour and/or salty tastes can be quite good for *Vata*. This combination is often seen in Indian curries. The heat and lightness of pungent taste can be counted on to aggravate *Pitta* and is best taken with other tastes or avoided entirely.

Pungent taste's effect on awareness and emotion tends to be one of enlivening passionate movement. In moderation pungency can get a body moving, warm it up, get it motivated. It can be most clearing. A physical example of this is the effect of hot mustard sauce with Chinese egg rolls. While the egg roll is dense, heavy and fried, the hot mustard cuts through all this and has an immediate (and sometimes intense) clearing effect on the sinuses of the head. Pungent taste can act in a similar way on the mind. A bit of anger can bring some issues to a clarifying head. In excess, pungent taste can create unreasoning anger, aggressiveness and resentment. Again, it is the balance within the individual system which dictates what is too much or too little.

Examples of pungent taste include chili peppers, garlic, onions, and hot spices.

BITTER

Bitter taste is made up of the elements air and ether. It is the coldest and lightest of all the tastes. It also tends to be fairly dry. Bitter cold is a good way to begin to imagine the effect of bitter on the body. While its *virya* is cold, its *vipak* is pungent. This means that bitter continues to have a lightening and drying effect over time, yet its coolness is somewhat moderated or warmed by its pungent *vipak*. Short-term effects of bitter are definitely cooling.

Bitter taste provides an excellent balance for the heavy, moistening qualities of salty, sour and sweet tastes. It is also in relatively short supply in our national cuisine—unless you happen to journey down South. Dark leafy greens are one excellent example of a bitter food. They can lighten and enliven a meal, as well as providing generous amounts of vitamin A, iron, calcium, magnesium, and other nutrients. Many herbs also have a bitter effect on the body. Swedish bitters are a classic example. Burning food can create an excess of bitter taste, a method not recommended here.

Bitter taste being cold, light and dry is especially useful for *Pitta*. It is one of the best tastes for righting a *Pitta* digestive system which has gone out of balance (for example: with Swedish bitters, or other herbal stomach bitters). Its light, dry qualities and pungent *vipak* make it quite balancing for *Kapha* as well. It is contra- indicated for *Vata*, as one might suspect.

Bitter taste's effect on consciousness, in small quantities, is one of assisting a person to see clearly. Interestingly, bitter herbs have been used in many cultures during vision quests, or spiritual journeys. Bitter can stimulate a sense of slight dissatisfaction which helps us to push on and see things as they really are. In large quantities bitter taste can promote a chilling sense of disillusionment or grief. It is a taste which can be difficult to first enjoy, yet which balances the other tastes well.

ASTRINGENT

Air and earth compose the sixth taste, astringent. It has a cooling *virya*, not so cold as bitter, yet cooler than sweet in its effect on digestion, which it inhibits. It has a slight lightening and drying quality. Its *vipak*, or post-digestive effect, is one of pungency. In the short term it is cool, light and dry. Over time it continues to be light and dry, yet exerts less and less of a cooling effect on the body.

Its gentle coolness moderates *Pitta's* heat. Its light dry qualities help balance *Kapha*. Astringent taste is not at all useful for *Vata*, because, like bitter, it simply makes *Vata* more chilly and dry.

Astringent taste has a contracting effect on digestion and can slow it down. Astringency stimulates a constriction of the blood vessels flowing to the digestive organs, inhibiting the free flow of blood, enzymes and energy to this area. In herbology astringent herbs are valued precisely for this contractive quality, which can stop hemorrhage in a given area rapidly by constricting circulation (examples: wild geranium, shepherd's purse).

Mentally and emotionally, astringent taste in moderation promotes an ascetic, bare bones approach to life, a no-nonsense "let's see what's here" kind of perspective. In large quantities (which are hard to come by) astringent taste can promote a nihilistic philosophy or a loss of interest in life. Smaller amounts are useful in drying up the extreme emotionalism of some experiences and getting "back down to business."

There are very few foods that have a predominantly astringent effect on the body besides certain unripe foods like unripened bananas. Pomegranates and cranberries have some astringency, as do crabapples and quinces. Each of these also has a sour component as well, though. Many foods have a secondary taste of astringency. That is to say, most foods are made up of a combination of tastes, and often astringent taste is one of the underlying tastes. Many grains, beans and vegetables will have both a primary sweet and a secondary astringent effect on the body. For this reason, beans in particular can be helpful for *Pitta*. They offer the coolness of both sweet and astringent tastes, and have a balance of moisture (from sweet) and dryness (from astringent). And in fact, *Pitta* people do very well with most beans as long as their digestive fire is good. This same quality of coldness can make beans nigh impossible for the *Vata* gut to digest.

SUMMING IT UP

As you learn about the tastes you can see that sweet, sour and salty are most supportive to *Vata*, whereas pungent, bitter and astringent are those most enhancing to *Kapha*. Sweet, bitter and astringent tastes will be most helpful in balancing *Pitta*. In working with digestion, pungent, sour and salty tastes will most enhance digestion and assimilation, while sweet, bitter and astringent will mildly inhibit them. There are exceptions to these guidelines, at times, and yet, in general, this is exactly the way taste can be used to heal an imbalance in the constitution Ayurvedically. You can choose foods with tastes which balance both your constitution and your needs. In many ways, tastes are used in Ayurveda the way colors are utilized in painting. They can be used alone, for one effect, or mixed together to create another result.

GOING FURTHER

We are moving into the realm at this time in our culture, of being able to use energy in much more subtle ways than we have in the past. While we use the tastes physically to balance us, we can also create experiences which balance us much as the tastes do. That is to say, experiences can warm or soothe or moisten us that are not oral but experiential on another level. We can work with sweet aromas, sweet sensations, a sweet touch.

You can imagine this for yourself. What would a sweet experience be for you right now? Let yourself relax a moment, close your eyes, and experience whatever scene or sensation comes up in your mind. If you want, you can notice where in your body you feel this imagined experience most. Notice how this feels for you.

Each of the tastes can be experienced in this way. Some may be easier to imagine or more comfortable than others. And yet each of the tastes can be used in this way. For many people in our country, oral gratification has become so habitual or so painful that it is difficult to get a fresh perspective on foods and tastes. If you've experienced this challenge, you may want to introduce yourself to the tastes through the process above, imagining what a taste is like as an experience before you work with it as a food.

In my practice, I work with many people who struggle to overcome sweet cravings and yet who deny themselves sweet experiences in their lives. Often as we begin to allow in sweetness on other levels (loving, warmth, whatever sweet means for us) we find our bodies becoming more satisfied, relaxing. The craving for sweets begins to calm.

Ayurveda invites us to look more deeply. It invites us to use the tastes in a way that will enhance our consciousness as well as our health.

TASTES	ELEMENTS	QUALITIES	BALANCES	IN EXCESS AGGRAVATES
Sweet	earth & water	heavy, moist, cool	*Vata & Pitta*	*Kapha*
Sour	earth & fire	warm, moist, heavy	*Vata*	*Pitta & Kapha*
Salty	water & fire	heavy, moist, warm	*Vata*	*Pitta & Kapha*
Pungent	fire & air	hot, light, dry	*Kapha*	*Pitta & Vata*
Bitter	air & ether	cold, light, dry	*Kapha & Pitta*	*Vata*
Astringent	air & earth	cool, light, dry	*Pitta & Kapha*	*Vata*

DIGESTION

Digestion is the process by which we break down what is coming in from our outer environment in order to make it an integrated part of our inner environment. Absorption is the process by which we integrate these digested elements into our cells. Elimination is the means by which we let go of any unneeded elements, digested and not. How well the balance between these three processes is working dictates to a great extent how well-nourished we are, and how good we feel.

In Ayurveda the keys to fine digestion are good health, strength, and *agni* or digestive fire. *Agni* translates in Western terms into that ability of all the digestive organs to be lively, effective and coordinated in function when given an appropriate amount of food. This "appropriate amount of food" is an important part of the effective digestive process. Too much food can act like sand on a fire, dousing *agni*, and demanding more work of it than it can realistically deliver. Too little food can starve *agni*, like expecting a fire to burn brightly with but a few twigs to fuel it. [*Note:* It should be pointed out that fasting **is** one time-honored Ayurvedic method for cleansing. It can enkindle *agni* when properly carried out under the supervision of an Ayurvedic practitioner.] In these days of intense focus on dieting, obesity and anorexia, determining what is too much or too little can be a loaded question. Yet the reality is that your body, when balanced, can tell you how much you need through the simple messages of hunger and satiation. You can trust these messages. The rub is, it can sometimes take a long while—weeks, months or years—to create this inner balance, depending on your particular circumstances (see chapter about *The Chakras and Dietary Change* p. 33). The important thing to know is that it can be done.

The power of digestion always depends upon bodily strength. And the maintenance of strength is dependent upon good digestion. When one breaks down, the other is likely to be faltering as well. If you are having troubles with either your health or digestion, do not be discouraged. Know that each needs tending, and that the balance you create in one area will benefit the other. How can you know if your digestion is good? The well-greased operation moves smoothly with little sound or commotion. If you are experiencing gas, bloating, irritation, burping, belching, or whatnot, your digestion is likely to need some assistance.

In working with digestion, one looks at both the inner circumstances (how are the organs feeling and doing?) and the outer ones (what are you feeding yourself?). In a moment we will be looking at the organs in some depth. For now, let us look at the outer factors over which you have a great deal of impact.

In Ayurveda, one takes into account both the food and how it is prepared and combined. In general, foods considered light (*laghu*) by Ayurvedic standards are easiest to digest, while heavier foods are more difficult to digest. There is a wide variety of foods which are light, including lettuce, basmati rice, ghee, and egg white. There are also many heavy foods (*guru*), including avocado, cheese, banana, and black or tan lentils. These heavier foods, while they are useful for grounding, strengthening and nourishment, take more energy to digest, and so are best eaten in small quantities. Light foods can be taken in greater quantities and tend to stimulate the appetite and digestion. Heavy foods by nature suppress the appetite. An excess of heavy foods is viewed as a great way to create disease, unless you have tremendous digestive power and a superb metabolism tonified through exercise.

Foods are also classified as hot (*ushna*) or cold (*shita*) in Ayurveda. Foods considered hot by Ayurvedic standards stimulate digestive fire. These include most spices, chili, garlic, yogurt, red lentils, and honey, among others. Cold foods will tend to calm and/or slow digestion; these include milk, coconut, dill, and coriander, to name a few. A balance of heating and cooling foods and spices is optimal for best digestion.

The idea that a food can be heating or cooling may seem foreign at first, as in fact it is. It is relatively easy to see the burning effect of a "hot" food like chili or a "cold" food like milk. But the subtle fire of honey or red lentils may stretch your credibility or comprehension, as it did mine. I would recommend experimenting with foods. Let yourself notice whatever effects they have on you, if any. Do you perspire or heat up after certain foods? Do you digest particular foods with more ease or difficulty? How does adding spices to your food affect them? The recipes here will help give you guidance as to the focussed use of food and spices. In these ways you can build a repertory of experience which permits you to work with foods more adeptly for yourself.

The concept of heating and cooling foods is widespread in many cultures. And yet there is much disagreement between cultures (and practices of healing) as to what constitutes the relative attributes of a given food. For example, Indian Ayurveda considers yogurt heating. In neighboring Tibet, yogurt is regarded as cool. And this from two cultures which practice relatively similar forms of natural medicine, both with good results! Climate and lifestyle also have an influence on the effect of a food. Experiment for yourself, while allowing the experience of the centuries to guide you.

In these days of extensive usage of pesticides and other chemicals, it is possible that a given food may have unexpected effects based on contamination. For example, overexposure to some pesticides stimulates fever, diarrhea and other burning symptoms in people. These exposures can be and are mistaken for common flus and viruses, when in fact they are responses by the body to chemical overdose. For example, a grape treated with heavy doses of insecticides may cause such a feverish reaction. It is no longer cooling at all. Or it could be more cooling than normal, depending on the contaminating agent and response. How modern toxicology integrates with ancient Ayurveda is yet to be explored.

The attributes of oiliness and moistness (*snigdha*) and dryness (*ruksha*) also affect digestion. Oily foods in general will promote lubrication of the digestive tract and secretion of digestive elements, when used in moderation. In excess, they can be inhibiting by overworking the liver and gallbladder. Dry foods are usually less enhancing to digestion, though small amounts can effectively stimulate *agni*. Large quantities inhibit digestion. Examples of oily foods include ghee, vegetable oils, animal fats, soybeans, many vegetables and citrus. Dry foods include corn, buckwheat, rye, millet, most beans and dark leafy greens, to list a few. These latter listed foods will need moistening of some sort to be more easily digested by most people.

Foods which are slimy (*slakshna*) like okra or slippery elm bark tend to support lubrication and hence digestion (if you can enjoy them!). Soft (*mrudu*) foods will soothe digestion yet mildly inhibit *agni*. Tapioca is an example of this. Rough (*khara*) foods tend to move digestion and elimination along, as demonstrated by oat and wheat bran. And yet rough foods can be too harsh for some people, *Vata* in particular. Sharp (*tikshna*) foods like chilis stimulate digestion, on occasion too abruptly. Hard (*kathina*) and dense (*sandra*) foods behave much like heavy foods, putting more of a demand on *agni* while building the body. Nuts are an example of these. Foods which are liquid (*drava*) enhance lubrication and salivation, especially aiding the digestion of carbohydrates in the mouth. Static (*sthira*), gross (*sthula*) and cloudy (*avila*) attributes inhibit *agni* and digestion; a fast-food meal with a milkshake would be a good example. Whereas mobile (*chala*), subtle (*sukshma*) and clear (*vishada*) attributes stimulate the digestive processes of mind and body; the herb gotu kola would embody all of these.

What is important is the beginning of awareness: being aware in a relaxed fashion of what you are eating and how it feels to be eating it. Realize that the morrow will bring new data in the form of experience and observations for you to integrate, and that today's experiences are not the last word in your learning.

FOOD COMBINING AND PREPARATION

Skillfully combining attributes and tastes enhances and eases digestion. Proper food combining is a key to reducing potential *ama* and enhancing absorption. Lightening a heavy food like oatmeal with a pinch of ginger and/or cardamom (see SPICY OATMEAL, p. 282) will aid its digestion, absorption and assimilation. Moistening a dry food such as beans through soaking and thorough cooking will give the digestive tract a better chance of absorbing its vital nutrients without excessive elimination of gas. Warming a cold food such as milk promotes nourishment and minimizes the creation of *ama*, toxic wastes. The recipes which follow are specifically designed to enhance digestion and promote absorption using these principles.

Most vegetables are light and can be readily combined with most other foods in meals. Whether they are cooked (most light) or raw (a bit heavier from an Ayurvedic digestive perspective) will depend on the cook and her/his recipients. Most fruits are slightly oily, and so will promote digestion if eaten early in the meal, or before it. Fruits are best eaten alone. Again cooked fruit will tend to be most easy to digest for those with delicate systems, as the heat lightens the food.

The combination of concentrated proteins is generally avoided in Ayurveda. Mixing meats or fish with dairy, or beans with nuts, is generally not recommended for optimal digestion. An exception to this rule is yogurt, which is often added in small amounts to a meal to enhance its flavor and absorption.

Grains are considered a starch rather than a protein here. Whole grains can be added profitably to most meals and are an excellent source of calories, B vitamins and trace minerals.

BALANCING *AGNI*

Signs of insufficient *agni* are much more common than those of excess. Gas, burping, belching, sluggish digestion, difficulty in waking in the morning, scanty or no perspiration, and constipation can all be indicators of deficient *agni*. Overeating is one of the most common ways to inhibit *agni* and progressively repress its creation. Certain constitutions are most prone to insufficient *agni*, with *Vata* taking the lead.

Excessive *agni* can also result in burping or belching, although a burning sensation in the digestive tract is a more noticeable sign, especially in the stomach or duodenum. Diarrhea, irritability, hyperexcitability, and excessive talking can also occur. Excessive perspiration and thirst may result. Eating overly heating foods and going prolonged periods without eating are ways to over arouse *agni*, as is indiscriminate expression or repression of anger.

Eating smaller simpler meals is a good way to begin to rekindle balanced *agni*. Fresh lemon or lime in water is a gentle and cleansing stimulant to *agni*. Mild ginger tea is a stimulant for sluggish *agni* and reduces gas. Attending to appropriate combinations and using supportive herbs can make a large difference in digestion. The combination of ground cumin, coriander and fennel is a time-honored way to stimulate and tonify *agni*. Listening to your body and its needs is another.

For more radical balancing of the digestive tract, the consultation of a skilled Ayurvedic physician or nutritionist is most useful. Ayurvedic preparations such as *triphala, amalaki, bibhitaki, haritaki,* and *pippali* can be excellent tools when used with knowledgeable supervision.

THE DIGESTIVE ORGANS

The digestive organs themselves enact different functions. Digestion begins in our mouths where chewing and enzymes in the form of ptyalin in the saliva begin to break down food. How much we chew and the pH—acidity or alkalinity—of our food are the first effectors of digestion. The enzyme ptyalin needs a slightly alkaline environment to carry out its task of breaking down starch. If an acid food like orange juice is taken at the same time as a starch such as toast or cereal, the digestion of the starch is inhibited. This can result in gas, an upset stomach, or effects so subtle or negligible as to be unnoticed. A small amount of acid cooked in a food generally will not have this effect and can even be stimulating to digestion, for example, a bit of lemon in beans or vinegar in a green bean recipe. Large amounts of acid foods used to wash down starches can be difficult though for some digestive tracts. Besides orange juice and toast, salsa and chips, and tomato sauce on pasta are common challenging examples of these. One pregnant client of mine was amazed to find her midterm indigestion ceased when she stopped eating the tomato sandwiches of which she had been so fond.

Chewing provides important signals which initiate peristalsis. If you have a penchant for eating on the run, chewing may be something that has gotten lost in the rush. You may wish to welcome it back into your life. On the other hand, such a hullabaloo has been made about proper and adequate chewing, e.g. fifty times per bite and such, that some people work themselves into indigestion simply through the tension of the effort to chew properly. This is not necessary. Relaxing stimulates the smooth muscles of the gut, which enhances blood flow to the digestive organs. This increased circulation stimulates digestive juices and *agni*. Taking a moment before meals to focus and be aware of what you are about to do—eat—can be a relaxing stimulus to digestion.

The stomach is a major site of protein digestion, as well as the general sterilizer of incoming food. Hydrochloric acid, one manifestation of *agni*, begins both processes. This strong acid breaks down protein bonds (much the way a meat tenderizer would) and also kills bacteria and other microbes. Interestingly, people who attempt to block the natural workings of *agni* by taking antacids have been found to have more digestive difficulties in the long run—especially when travelling. Travelers using antacids have more gastrointestinal upsets than those who do not, because the inhibited hydrochloric acid of the stomach is not able to kill the bacteria it usually would. A bitter or sour taste is more useful than antacids as a preventive in this case. The herb *quassia* is excellent, or lemon or umeboshi plum is helpful. They stimulate *agni* and hydrochloric acid, thereby eliminating uncopacetic microbes.

The stomach also has a remarkably accurate secretion of acid in response to different proteins. It will secrete more acid at different rates and times, depending on the protein food eaten. Ayurvedic sages recommended centuries ago not to combine fish and dairy. Pavlov unknowingly substantiated this recommendation when he observed in his experiments on conditioned reflexes in the last century that milk, fish and meat each require a different rate of acid secretion in the stomach and a different concentration of acid. They are best digested when taken alone.

The balance of the *doshas* is demonstrated strikingly in the functioning of the stomach. Too much *Kapha* and excess mucus will slow digestion here, making the overall digestion sluggish and incomplete. Too little *Kapha* and/or too much *Pitta* can cause the lubricated mucus lining which protects the stomach from its own acid to break down. This acid is quite burning when activated, reaching a pH as low as 1 to 2. If the lubricated membrane is inadequately moistened with mucus, it can be burnt by the acid, causing an ulcer. Old-fashioned Western approaches in the 1940s and 50s to this condition fed a *Kaphic* cream and high-fat milk diet, inadvertently applying Ayurvedic principles. They often worked well. Another effective therapy here, besides the obvious avoidance of highly spiced and salted foods and alcohol, is increasing one's consumption of whole cooked grains. They can effectively soothe the stomach while provoking little secretion of gastric acid.

Contrary to popular opinion, the stomach does not break down everything. Little digestion of carbohydrates and only a very modest beginning of fat digestion occurs

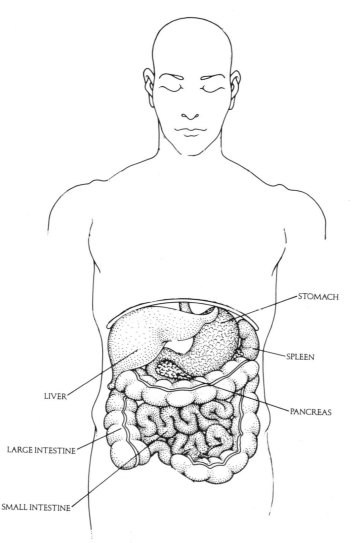

here. It is the small intestine which carries out these processes on a major scale, with the help of the liver and pancreas.

The small intestine in many ways functions like the cloverleaf intersection of a major freeway. The main route is stomach to small intestine to large intestine (see illustration). Yet several other thoroughfares enter on to the small intestine in the form of the pancreatic duct and the bile duct (from the liver and gallbladder). The small intestine is responsible for both producing enzymes to digest carbohydrates, fats, and proteins, and integrating the enzymes and bile introduced into it by the pancreas and liver. In Ayurveda, it is said that the small intestine is the organ most affected by overeating. Like the *Pitta* energy which activates it, the small intestine takes a leading role in digestion and excess food can impair this initiation markedly, causing sluggish, backed-up digestion.

The pancreas and liver take on essential supporting roles in this process. The pancreas produces copious amounts of bicarbonate to alkalize the acidic secretions dripping into the small intestine from the stomach. This enables the pH-sensitive enzymes of the upper small intestine (the duodenum) to do their catabolic work. The pancreas also creates enzymes like those made by the small intestine to digest fats, proteins, and carbohydrates. Its third function is an entirely separate one from digestion, that of regulating blood sugar. Frequently a craving for sweets will indicate a need to balance the pancreas through additional chromium, zinc, or protein snacks.

Protein is a primary fuel by which digestive enzymes in both the small intestine and pancreas are made. People will sometimes remark to me after they have been off heavy proteins such as beans or nuts for a while that they are having a hard time digesting protein, harder in fact than when they first chose to eliminate them. (Protein is not something I would usually recommend eliminating, or severely restricting, without a strong therapeutic reason.) It is often assumed that this difficulty in digestion is a sign that the food itself is too heavy, and should be avoided further. This is not necessarily true. It can be that the protein intake itself has gotten so low that digestive enzymes are not being made as abundantly, a classic example of too few twigs to stimulate the fire of *agni*. In this case, gradually increasing protein intake in the form of easily assimilated foods such as *kichadi*, miso broth, clear chicken broth or a bit of blue-green algae will usually strengthen digestion.

The liver carries out many roles. In digestion it specifically produces bile, which gives our feces their yellow to brown color. In hepatitis, the liver's energy becomes very low and digestion is disturbed. Unprocessed bile, usually excreted through the feces, backs up into the bloodstream. This creates the yellow skin, brown urine and light stools familiar to those who have had hepatitis. The bile pigments show up in the skin and urine and are minimal in the feces, accounting for their dramatic changes in color. Liver ailments like hepatitis can actually be good opportunities to strengthen this organ, as they let us know that it needs additional support. In Ayurveda, the analogy is made of a faucet watering the earth. If seeds of weeds (ill health) are present, excesses of diet or lifestyle can help them "sprout." A way to avoid developing illness is not to feed it, in this case not to eat high-fat, high-sugar, low-fiber foods.

Such diets stimulate problems not only in the liver but the colon as well. It has been well-documented that high-fiber low-fat diets promote the healthiest and most cancer-free colons. Such regimes allow the colon to keep itself clean and not excessively burdened with extra mucus or unfriendly bacteria (each of which supports the other). The colon is primarily responsible for reabsorbing fluids and electrolytes and for eliminating wastes. Interestingly enough, potassium has been found in Western nutrition to be essential for calcium metabolism. Potassium must be effectively absorbed through the colon, the seat of *Vata*, before it can support calcium in the bones, another *Vata* realm. This is modern substantiation for an archaic Ayurvedic observation: the colon must be clear and strong for the bones to be durable. Excess mucus and bacteria impair these functions, imbalancing *Vata* and inhibiting absorption. When *Vata* is balanced, elimination moves smoothly. When it is not, diarrhea, constipation, gas, and/or dry stools can result.

One can see from this discussion the importance of a healthy digestive tract, and how much of its happiness lies in our own hands.

THE CHAKRAS AND DIETARY CHANGE

For centuries the chakras have been acknowledged as the seven (or more) vital energy centers of the body. In this chapter we diverge from the traditional approach and present a modern transformationally-oriented view of the chakras. As my training has been in this modern system, I cannot say how different it is from the traditional Indian teachings. Southwestern College of Life Sciences in Santa Fe, in particular its president Robert Waterman, D.Ed., was originally instrumental in catalyzing my learning about this system. The summary of the chakras presented on p. 36 of this chapter is based directly on Dr. Waterman's transformational model as it relates to education. I would like to acknowledge this transmission and take responsibility for how it is applied to nutrition here. In my practice I have found it most helpful to work with the chakras in healing.

The body springs from a web of energy which dances through every cell; what occurs in one portion of our physical, emotional, mental, and spiritual beings is likely to have an impact on every other portion, to some degree. An understanding of this energy is useful in being able to affect the changes we want to make in our lives, including dietary transitions.

All of us come in with the potential equipment of seven chakras, or seven non-physical energy centers located within our auric fields. Their energy is expressed in our behavior, thoughts, words, and actions. While the endocrine glands have often been called the physical counterparts of the chakras, they are in fact distinct and separate entities, the former physical, the latter non-physical. If we look at the chakras and their realms of experience, we can get a sense of how we nourish ourselves and why—and where we may be starving ourselves, consciously or unconsciously. We begin to get a sense of where our priorities lie at the moment, and how changes can be made more creatively and effectively to meet our nourishment needs now.

For example: the first chakra is an energy center which is oriented toward keeping us alive and functioning on the physical plane. If one's mind decides that a fast would be a superb thing to do, but it fails to communicate that to the body, there is a strong chance that one will run into physical resistance to the project. An understandable response from the unknowing body might be the nonverbal equivalent of "Hey, wait a minute— are you starving us to death here?", fatigue, lethargy, even fear or panic. Whereas a creative awareness of the needs of the first chakra can assist us in designing a fasting program which is both security-enhancing and cleansing. It can also take into account the needs of our particular *dosha*. For example, you can let your body know what's going on before you plunge into whatever dietary change you are considering. How? You can make contact with your body in whatever way feels most comfortable for you: perhaps putting your hand on your belly, or giving yourself a comfortable place to sit, a warm bath, whatever. Then explain what you have in mind: that you think this fast or diet change is important for your health, long-term survival, mental clarity, whatever reasons you have. Make sure that at least one of these reasons is beneficial to the body and staying alive. If none of them are, the body is much less likely to go for the plan. Ideas about glamor and social acceptance make no impression on the first chakra whatsoever. Try the third chakra if you want to enlist support for a plan on that level. Once you've proposed your plan simply, sit and wait for a response. If you've trained in hypnosis or meditation techniques, you may already have a way of communicating with your body on a

"yes - no" level. These work well here. Occasionally you may come up with a nourishment plan that gets a strong "no" from the body. In that case I would recommend some
negotiation or further exploration of what may be causing a gap between the body's
desires and the mind's perceptions. Too often this gap is neglected or ignored. You will
get a better body-mind relationship with requests rather than demands.

First chakra energy is often much enhanced during pregnancy, as we are responsible
for creating and maintaining life for two at this time. And often eating habits will shift radically in response to this altered focus.

Second chakra energy is oriented toward learning more about our world through
experience and sensation. You see babies exploring a lot with their second chakras,
crawling around, sticking whatever they can in their mouths: what does it feel like, let's
check it out. At the adult level, if we have a deep yearning for a particular kind of sensation that we do not allow ourselves, second chakra energies can pop up in another area.
A very common way to express these energies is through food, using food for satisfaction. This works well if you are hungry and you need food. It doesn't work so well if what
you are really interested in is a sense of physical intimacy and you're trying to head yourself off at the pass by eating instead. Food is a great mirror for showing us where our
deepest healing can happen. One practical way to begin to get familiar with this area is
to simply notice what kind of textures your body likes. Does it want crunchy foods?
creamy ones? liquid ones? Consider incorporating these preferences into what you
choose to eat.

At the level of the third chakra, issues of relationship, power, nurturing, and belonging arise. Food choices can be strongly influenced by the habits of our families, friends
and teachers. There was a great column in a past *Ayurvedic Wellness Journal* by a
dancer who expressed this experience well. As a professional dancer in New York, she
had lived on what most of her fellow athletes had: diet foods, chocolate, stimulants, and
as few calories as possible. The pressure to choose such a diet was intense. And even-
tually her Kaphic constitution was badly imbalanced, with too much air (*Vata*). She was
tense, anxious, with unexplained panic attacks and sweats. When she consulted an
Ayurvedic practitioner in her area, she was astounded to hear him recommend the foods
she had avoided for years. This was a critical turning point for her, in that she had to rely
on her own power to make a choice for change. In breaking away from her old habits, she
created a major healing in her life. Yet only by trusting her own authority and power inside
could she do this. A useful way to allow third chakra energies to support you is by finding friends and family members who will accept you regardless of your dietary and
lifestyle choices. If you have this, you are fortunate indeed. Barring this, the first area of
work is trusting your own authority.

This sounds rather "highfalutin." What do we really mean by this? Power and food are
much entangled in this country. Eating for power, or to avoid power, is a common occur-
rence. It may feel more powerful to feel big than little, and so we overeat to achieve that
state. We may be afraid to express directly how powerful we really are, and so hide it by
directing our energies toward overeating or starving ourselves. It may feel safer and simpler to diet or eat than to take on Rockwell International, or a challenging meditation
practice, or that new job you want. It takes a lot of will to maintain a body at a weight that
is not naturally at its norm. Working with third chakra energies brings up the power of

choice. What are we choosing for ourselves now, and how are we going to let ourselves get it? If we deny our power, or give it away to another, this area will cry out for attention—often in the non verbal ways the body has for expressing itself with eating struggles, indigestion, or blood sugar imbalances. When we start to trust that what we really want to do in our lives **is** valid, this healing process has begun.

At the level of the fourth chakra, paradoxes begin to come up. This is appropriate, since it is here that we begin to learn how to balance opposite energies: female-male, light-heavy, dark-bright, warm-cold. We learn to co-exist with our yearnings, and give ourselves a more safe and healthy space for their expression. We open our heart to ourselves, and others. There is a joy in being able to share ourselves, our food, our gifts. If we try to repress one end of a polarity, imbalance can occur. I have known a fair number of people who eat instead of expressing their loving. Their love is so powerful it scares them. They want to share it, but don't know how. They haven't discovered how to do it yet. This tremendous desire to share can feel especially frustrated by eating or drug use, as it's not what the body and being are really yearning for. As the energy begins to open and relax in our hearts, a true blossoming can be experienced in all parts of our lives, especially in how we nourish ourselves and others. A practical way to start to work with this area is to begin to notice when you say one thing, and do another. You have two different things going on here. Interesting. Don't try to analyze this, simply be aware of the paradox. And if you can, keep looking at yourself with loving and compassion.

The fifth chakra frequently has a close relationship to the second chakra, as it is here that we express the truth of our experience. People working with bulimia are often seeking to discover a balance in their second and fifth chakras. There is frequently something important they need to communicate in the world, which is being denied or ignored. It is here, too, that we are more interested in food's symbolic messages rather than in its literal nourishment. When I was about eight, taking ballet lessons in the town next to ours, my mother and I had a ritual. After she would pick me up from dance class, we would stop at the corner drugstore down the block from the dance studio and buy an Almond Joy candy bar. Sitting in the car, we would carefully split it, eat it, and talk. Coming from a large family, these were rare moments for me alone with my mother. And periodically, I still find myself craving an Almond Joy, often when moments of quiet and intimacy have been short in my life.

Marion Woodman has written some excellent books about this realm particularly for women, *Addiction to Perfection* and *The Pregnant Virgin* among them. The fifth center involves the practical activity of receiving nurturance, being able to open to receive what Spirit, often in the form of others, has to offer us. As an opening to this area, you might notice what foods are important to you on a symbolic level. Or, if you frequently resist receiving help on some level, you might experiment with accepting it, being aware of how you feel as you do.

The issue of transformation is paramount at the level of the sixth chakra. Intuition is a resource which can aid us in making the nourishing choices which contribute most freely to our own transformation and that of others. Intuition can manifest in dreams, through meditative insight, through intuitive flashes, or in a sense of "knowing" in a deep and indisputable way. Again, here there is a correspondence energetically between the sixth and third chakras, for we must be able to trust our own power to trust our insight.

The sixth chakra can operate in rather Uranian ways, with sudden flashes of insight at unexpected times. It may communicate ideas and concepts about nourishing ourselves which are radically different than whatever is our accepted norm. Or it can provide a calming and peace-enhancing substantiation that we are on the appropriate path for us.

Acknowledging, accepting and acting upon our life purpose has a practical impact on how we nourish ourselves in the world from a seventh chakra level. The guiding force of our life purpose can be a powerful motivator in getting us to "get our act together," allowing our bodies to be fully strong enough to achieve our highest goals. Often when I ask clients what their life purpose is, they reply they don't know. That's a good thing to be aware of. It is useful to know what you are doing here: you are more likely to do it. It is also useful to be aware of ignorance in this matter: you may begin to consider how it is you are using your valuable energies on the planet at this time. Here we come full circle back to the first chakra, for without that vital life force which the first chakra offers us, our life purpose is more difficult to achieve.

DIETARY CHANGES

In truth, while the chakras have often been described in a linear way, from lower to upper, they can be perceived in another way as well: as a great symphony of energies. Each energy supports and nourishes the others, a glorious poem of sound which flows through each moment of our lives. If we imagine the chakras' interplay in this way, as one glowing dance, then how we relate to food is one blessing, one indicator of how these energies are flowing for us in the present moment.

To summarize:

Chakra

7. Transcendence—soul realization, life purpose, cosmic consciousness
6. Transformation—intuition, self-realization
5. Awareness—symbolic communication, receiving nurturance
4. Wholeness—unconditional loving, mediation of opposites, giving nurturance, service
3. Relationship—power, emotional, nurturing, sense of belonging (to a group), seat of "body brain"
2. Experience—sensation, security, safety
1. Energy—life, survival

Self-assessment on the current status of your own chakras as they relate to nourishment:

1. Have I got all the energy I need to do what I want to do? Is my diet meeting my basic physical needs? Am I getting enough calories, protein, nutrients?
2. Is my diet satisfying to me? Does it taste good? Are the textures and flavors and smells appealing to me?
3. Does it feel nurturing? How am I empowering myself by choosing this food?
4. Is this a food I would share with others, given the right circumstances and people? Can it encompass my extremes? What do I have to offer this food?

5. How do I receive this food? What is its symbolic value for me?
6. Intuitively, how does the way I am nourishing myself now contribute to my highest good and the good of others?
7. How does this food support my overall life purpose?

As you answer each of these questions for yourself, you may notice that some go smoothly and easily and with others you seem to run into snags. I often present this information on the chakras to groups. When asked to consider where much of their current eating behavior originates, many individuals groan, "It's all first chakra! I simply eat to survive!" Well, first off, surviving via eating is not such a dreadful activity. Most of the world engages in it or would like to! It is a practical way to get energy. And yet when we look at our behavior more deeply, often it isn't a survival issue at all. Frequently eating simply "anything" because one has let oneself go to the point of hunger with no thought for one's body, is a relationship issue. It is a matter of your relationship with your body: have you given it the same consideration you would give a friend, or even your dog? Often times we are far ruder to our bodies than we let ourselves notice. Treating ourselves with consideration is one practice which can make it easier for us to treat others naturally with consideration. Often this loving care for oneself is forgotten, especially by those who have a lot of responsibility in caring for others.

Then there is our relationship with time. Are we really grabbing a bite to eat "to survive?" Or are we doing this survival-style maneuver because we have not yet worked out a harmonious relationship with Old Man Time, or Cosmic Woman Time, as you would have it? Having enough consideration for ourselves and a healthy appreciation for the demands of time often shifts one's eating habits from touch and go to truly nourishing. We are talking about priorities here. Culturally little value is put these days on warm home-cooked meals, especially on their preparation. If you are a real fast food junkie, or restaurant frequenter, or live alone and abhor cooking for yourself, or all of the above, you might try a modest experiment to begin with: One warm home-cooked meal per week. If you are a less hardened "addict" than this, yet often find yourself staring into the recesses of your refrigerator with nary a scrap of nourishment in sight, here is another experiment: schedule two to three hours once a week to cook up goodies for yourself, a gallon of homemade soup, a pot of curry, a bowl of grain, whatever you choose. You might even want to ask a friend over to share it with you. Cooking this way, you still have the quick options, the cottage cheese or yogurt or eggs or whatever, and yet you also have some homemade fiber and nutrient-rich dishes as well. And your body begins to know that you really do care for it and are willing to share some time with it. If you've mastered these courses, try to buy and make enough food for dinner so that you have good leftovers for lunch the next day. Or browsing through the cookbook before you head for the store, so that you actually have the ingredients you need to make the dishes you want.

Often, when we simply allow ourselves to accept the information that our bodies offer us, something valuable happens. *Sushruta*, the ancient Ayurvedic physician, wrote about how craving can let us know what we need. Consider chocolate. Sometimes we will crave something like chocolate out of the blue. What many people don't realize is, chocolate is an exceptionally rich source of magnesium. It is a nutrient that has a powerfully relaxing effect on the body. I see this craving arise frequently in women immediately before their periods. This is a time when magnesium needs are high, to assist in smooth, rather than cramped muscle contractions. Chocolate also has both a strong sweet and bitter taste—tastes calming to *Pitta*. (Though due to its caffeine content, chocolate is not over-all a balancing food for *Pitta*.) A craving for chocolate could indicate a need for magnesium, more bitter tastes or more sweet tastes. Here sensation offers information. How we use this information is up to us. Other good sources of magnesium include broccoli, dark leafy greens, nuts, and chlorophyll-rich foods.

The Ayurvedic sages recommended a simple process for making dietary change. I think of it as "¼, ¼, ¼ . . ." They advised that when you are clear about an area of your diet or lifestyle that needs change, but are doubtful of your ability to change it, you begin to shift the habit one-quarter at a time. An example would be caffeine. Say you drink four cups of coffee per day. You enjoy it, but it is beginning to affect how well you sleep at night. You cut it by ¼, or one cup, for the first week or more. When you are comforta-ble with drinking three cups per day, cut your consumption again by ¼. Continue in this way until you are at the amount of coffee you want to be drinking, i.e., perhaps a cup per day instead of four. The same process can be used to increase certain foods or to reduce sweets or other addictive substances.

Making changes is a matter of beginning. Is there somewhere you would like to start?

EATING WITH THE SEASONS

From an Ayurvedic perspective, the constitutions balance and imbalance with the nat-ural changes of the seasons. These changes can be relieved or mitigated by astute shifts in diet and lifestyle. As we move, for example, from the scorching heat of summer to the cool crisp nights and mornings of early fall, we move from a *Pitta*-dominated season to one of *Vata* pre-eminence. *Vata*, encompassing the air and ether elements, is that within each of us which is cool, light, dry, and mobile, as you know. Each season has one or more elements and *doshas* which predominate, and in autumn it is *Vata* which is rising. *Vata* is an essential part of all of us. For the person with *Vata* predominant in their con-stitution, the qualities and attributes of this *dosha* can be more noticeable in the fall and winter than in any other season. *Vata* imbalances such as dry skin, creaky or achy joints, digestive gas, or nervous disorders are more likely to be noticed as the weather grows cooler. Fewer mosquito bites, skin rashes and *Pitta*-like sunburn will be showing up, and we may find ourselves coping with more subtle disruptions: a bit of nerves or anxiety about new fall starts or a struggle with spaciness as we orient ourselves after a high-flying summer.

The seat of *Vata* is within the pelvis. On an energetic level this area encompasses the first and second chakras, related to survival and security, some of our most basic needs. Autumn is a good time to re-evaluate how we are meeting these essential needs, both personally and planetarily. Those of *Vata* constitution can be particularly aware of what helps them to feel safe inside in a deep and effective way, and how they must act to achieve this. The time of the autumnal equinox is considered especially critical for health, present and future, and often some sort of physical or mental crisis will arise dur-ing this transition period.

Pitta and *Kapha* individuals may breathe a sigh of relief that the worst of the heat and humidity are over; however, *Vatas* may look with some regret at the passing of the summer's warmth and moisture. It is time to draw nourishment from the seeds of all that we have planted during the year, and move on.

Dietarily it is a good time to assess whether what we have been doing to nourish ourselves is really working. Regardless of one's constitution, more warm, moist, well-lubricated foods are required at this time, with a bit more emphasis on sweet, sour and salty tastes. Fortunately fall brings a renewed inclination in many of us to cook again, after a summer spent on the run. And this natural inclination to cook is vital in grounding *Vata*, reliant as it is on the earthy qualities of cooked grains, vegetables and light proteins for its nourishment. Cardamom is a nice spice for this season, being sweet and warm yet activating.

As we move into winter, a season in which *Kapha* predominates strongly, all the *doshas* must work together to preserve health. *Kapha* is the endurance which enables us to move through this season, but it needs the qualities of light and movement (*Vata*) and initiative (*Pitta*) to do so, else we are likely to simply crawl into our dens and sleep away until spring! *Kapha* promotes growth. It also strengthens and enhances natural immunity and resistance. It lubricates joints, is the essence of connective tissue, promotes healing, provides moisture to the skin and digestive tract, strengthens the memory and gives vitality to the lungs and heart. The thymus gland, which rests close to the seat of *Kapha*, is responsible for initiating many immune functions through its T-cells. It is also the gland responsible for creating growth hormones. Like *Kapha*, it is most active in its growth—promoting activities in youth. While *Vata* encourages breakdown of tissues and *Pitta* supports their maintenance, *Kapha* is the builder.

In winter, the digestive power is enhanced, so long as one is healthy. The contracting quality of cold actually concentrates *agni*, making it stronger. Now is the time when we can handle heavier foods, and more of them. And often we find ourselves yearning for more at this time. (This is not an unhealthy inclination, since *Vata* can be aggravated if one does not get enough food in winter.) Cold weather is not the time to embark on a fast. Contraindicated are cold drinks and frosty or frozen foods. Foods canned at home in the summer and fall provide one option to frozen foods in winter, and without the chemicals of commercial preparations. It is a time for warm cooked grains, especially rice and oats, soups, heavier protein foods, more beans, hot teas, honey, and warm milk. Many people, regardless of their constitutions, will find themselves putting on an extra five pounds as insulation against the drop in temperature which occurs in most temperate climates. This tendency must be balanced with an awareness so as to not build **too much**, especially over the holidays!

This season often brings an abundance of mucus, in the form of colds, coughs and flus, especially for children. While it may seem troublesome, even the thick mucus secreted by the lungs during a cold or cough serves its vital function. Surrounding bacteria and viruses, mucus encapsulates them and keeps them away from healthy lung tissue, thus protecting the lungs themselves. Echinacea is a friendly herb to use in this season, as it strengthens white blood cell function, improves chemotaxis (the ability of a white blood cell to discover newly arrived germs) and strengthens connective tissue's ability to repair and maintain itself. A bitter, pungent, and astringent herb, it is very appropriate for *Kapha*.

Children understand the ways in which to work with this *dosha* naturally. Rather than wall themselves off from its qualities, they jump in and play with them, having snowball fights, making snow forts and snow people. We are also offered the option to wade in and play: making gentle fun of our inertia, stuckness or greed at this time.

Spring is a time of new beginnings, and the release of the stored energy of the heart accumulated in winter. It is a time of planting the seeds of health for the coming year. In spring the accumulated *Kapha* in the system is melted by the heat of the sun, and the recently acquired bulk of winter goes with it (hopefully!). This release of excess *Kapha* into the body can disturb the power of digestion and generate various imbalances, like hay fever, spring flus and colds. Now is the time to work to reduce *Kapha*, choosing light bitter fresh foods. The classic "spring tonic" of dark leafy greens that many cultures have used is ideal. Dark leafy greens like nettles or dandelion (respectively good for the kidneys and liver) give light bitter dry pungent action to this otherwise rather soggy time, physiologically. Such a tonic moves out the accumulated debris of the cold wet months like a household undertaking spring cleaning. This is also a great time to exercise, cleanse in all ways, and to not oversleep. In preparing for this renewal, avoid heavy, oily, sweet, and sour foods. Ginger tea provides an excellent beverage for both spring and fall, warming the body and enhancing *agni* as it is imbibed.

In the summer the full strength of the sun's rays pour down upon the earth, evaporating the dampness of spring and creating an abundance of heat and dryness. Now *Pitta* predominates, and issues of fire and digestion come to the fore. Interestingly, while *Pitta* is often associated with digestive power, the increased heat of summer actually impairs *agni*. As Charak says, "Even as hot water extinguishes fire, so does *Pitta* suppress the digestive power (in hot weather)." For this reason it is best to eat and drink lightly, choosing sweet, moist, cool, and liquid items to placate *Pitta*, such as milk, rice, fruit, and tofu. Aloe vera juice is an excellent herbal therapeutic for summer, tonifying the liver and cooling the entire system. Ayurvedic texts also highlight the need to be judicious with alcohol in summer. If you do choose to consume it, it is best diluted generously with water. It can badly aggravate *Pitta* in the heat. Spicy, hot, pungent, sour, oily, or salty foods can have a similar action, adversely irritating *Pitta*.

The sages observed that in the rainy season, or times of heavy rain, all *doshas* can be thrown off. The chill of rain aggravates *Vata* and *Kapha*, while the acidity of the water from the rains was known to disequilibrate *Pitta* and *Kapha*. This environmental overview of acid rain was offered centuries before the advent of "acid rain" from industrial sources! One wonders how much more severe this effect is today in regions impacted by acidic industrial pollution. Even without contaminating influences, the rains of late summer and early fall can take skill to handle. One must attend to *Vata*, yet also take *Pitta* into consideration. Honey is a good sweetener for this time. Its warm drying qualities overcome the dampness without seriously irritating *Pitta*. The classic cup of tea with honey on a cold rainy day makes sense. Grains are also highly recommended at this time to strengthen the digestion. Barley, wheat and rice are particularly appropriate, as well as nourishing vegetable soups.

And then the autumn approaches once more, with its crisp coolness. Generally it is wise to follow the guidelines for the coming season starting about a week before the season actually arrives, to give the body a chance to align itself with the new changes as they come.

The ways of the seasons support our healing and engender an inner alignment with the cycles of the earth. What is recommended here is very similar to the way traditional peoples have eaten for centuries. Yet in our rush and sophistication, the common sense ways of the seasons have been forgotten by many. While initially attending to both constitution and season can seem bewildering, it is well worth the effort in terms of health. And in time it becomes second nature to have that hot pumpkin dish in fall, the cool mint tea in summer. And it is a pleasurable way to share with the earth and awaken to the wisdom of the seasons anew.

GETTING READY TO COOK

Cooking is a sacred and healing act. As a cook, you participate in the nourishment and vitality of yourself and all those around you. It is worth paying attention to this creative function. You may want to ground your intention by lighting a candle to *Agni*, the Hindu divinity of fire, or to whatever spirit of creativity and awareness you honor within. The more awareness you bring to this process the more genuinely healing results you will have.

On a more mundane level, you will need a clean space and adequate equipment. To cook Ayurvedically does not take a lot of complicated gear. The following list is likely to give you just about everything you need:

- One or two heavy skillets with lids. Iron works well.
- One small heavy skillet with lid. Ditto.
- Two or three medium-sized saucepans with lids. Stainless steel, enamel or copper can be used, depending on your needs.
- One large saucepan (about 8 quarts) with lid.
- One 4-or 6-quart stainless steel pressure cooker. If you have the 6-quart size, you can use it to can soups and other foods as well.
- One stainless steel steamer.
- One or two mixing bowls.
- One or two large (8 cup) measuring bowls. These usually come in glass or plastic in discount or department stores. They come in handy for measuring and storing veggies as you chop them for a curry or soup.
- Two sets of stainless steel measuring spoons.
- Two or three mixing and serving spoons, wooden or stainless steel.
- A soup ladle.
- One non-stick pan. This is essential for *Kaphas*, and helpful for those interested in making *masala dosas.*
- A blender.

And if all you have is one saucepan and a hotplate, persevere. You can make many dishes with those two items. You don't need an abundance of elaborate equipment to cook in this way. What is more important is cooking with awareness and using pure ingredients with understanding.

To cook any given recipe, you simply need to have each ingredient on hand plus the time it takes to make the dish. The preparation time is given at the top of each recipe.

Many of the recipes take a half hour or less to prepare. A few take hours. The bean recipes generally benefit from an overnight soak of the beans, especially if you are going to be serving them to a *Vata* crew. While you do not have to have every item on the following grocery list to get started, if you are so inspired, it will give you greater flexibility in making what you like from the cookbook whenever you feel like it.

- One pound black mustard seeds, or 1 ounce if you are cooking strictly for *Pitta* (cheapest from an herb store, Indian grocery, or other bulk store)
- One pound whole cumin seeds (herb store or Indian grocery)
- ½ pound fresh ginger root (found in the produce section of most supermarkets)
- 1 bunch fresh coriander leaves (cilantro) (produce section of most supermarkets)
- 1 cup plain yogurt, low-fat or regular
- ¼ pound ground coriander powder (1 ounce will do if that's all you can find— better fresh than a lot of it)
- 1 ounce ground cumin (ditto)
- 1 ounce fennel seeds
- 1 ounce fenugreek seeds
- 1 ounce ground cinnamon
- 1 ounce cardamon, in the pods, whole seeds, or ground. Green pods will be more fragrant if you can find them; the white are more available
- ½ pound shredded unsweetened coconut
- 1 ounce turmeric
- 1 ounce high quality Madras curry powder, mild to hot as you choose
- 1 pound dry mung beans, split if you can find them, whole if you can't
- 1 pound basmati rice or Texmati rice
- 1 ounce or small jar of *hing* or *asafoetida* (compounded asafoetida is fine) (Indian grocery item or imported food section of supermarket)
- 1 ounce cayenne or red chili powder
- 2 or 3 small hot chilis, fresh, green serranos or jalapenos (produce section. *Pitta* can omit)
- 1 quart cow, goat, or soy milk
- 1 pint sunflower oil, cold-pressed preferably
- 1 pound unsalted butter or ghee
- ¼ pound sea salt or rock salt (Kosher salt works well)
- For *Vatas*: 8 ounces sesame oil and 2 ounces sesame seeds—black are especially good.
- For *Kaphas*: 4 to 8 ounces mustard oil
- Fresh vegetables
- Grains
- Beans

Once you have what you need on hand, it's time to play, or to get to work, as your perspective inclines you. If you have never done any Indian cooking before, these long lists of spices can be horribly intimidating. Inside secret: they're not. Using all these spices takes about as long as it takes to measure them. Once you get the hang of the process, it's extremely easy and it provides you with many opportunities for lavish compliments from impressed friends and family. At the risk of sounding overly glowing, even kids like most of these recipes, which amazed me at first. They seem to appreciate the balance of tastes and the overall flavor of the food. Which is nice, since it is also very good for them.

Generally, the steps in three-fourths of these recipes are the same: you heat a little oil in a small or large skillet. You then put in some spices, very often black mustard seeds, sometimes other spices as well. Here is the only tricky part: you heat the mustard seeds in the oil, uncovered, until they pop. Literally, that's what they will do, start jumping out of the pan. So you want to be ready to throw the next ingredient in to calm them down as rapidly as possible. If they've moved faster than you have, you can always put a lid on the pan and take it off the heat. What you don't want to do is let them keep popping and cooking until they're thoroughly black and burnt, which can happen in two minutes or less if the oil is very hot. So be forewarned. You get through this step and it's smooth sailing from here. And if you don't, you can always toss out the blackened seeds and begin again. Learning.

1. Heat oil.

4. Immediately stir in next ingredients.

2. Add spices.

5. Add fluids, if recommended.

3. Seeds start to pop.

6. Cover and cook.

So, you then add the next ingredient or string of ingredients. Often this is turmeric or *hing.* This whole step of stirring spices into the oil is called making a *vagar.* Then you add the main vegetables, legumes, or grains you are using. Stir them around, coating them well with the flavor of the spices. This step is important for enhancing digestion. Then, add fluids if there are any, and mix again. From here on out the recipes diverge, sometimes adding a long list of flavors like ground coriander, sea salt, lemon and others. Here again, don't panic, just add the ingredients one by one. Usually there is no rush in this step, because whatever you are cooking is simmering away safely in its juices or water, and you can add the rest of the ingredients as leisurely as you like.

The last thing to know: the vast majority of these dishes keep well. If they don't we will say so in the recipe. This means you can make a dish in the morning, store it in the fridge or other cool place, and serve it for dinner, with an enhancement of flavors, if anything. They also make good leftovers for the next day for the same reason.

So! You're ready to go. Find a recipe you are interested in. We'll give you the rest of the orientation as you prepare to cook. On the upper right is listed how many the recipe will serve. Next, the seasons are listed. The following symbols represent the seasons: Spring = ✿; Summer = ✹; Fall = ☙; Winter = ❄. These let you know the **most** healing times to prepare this dish—summer, fall, what have you. You can serve anything in here any time you like, of course. However, this provides a seasonal guideline if you are interested in consciously preparing foods Ayurvedically. The "prep time" is listed on the upper left. This is how long it takes to fix the dish, from start to finish. Below this is how the dish affects the *doshas.* " – " means calms, helps this *dosha,* " + " means increases, aggravates this *dosha,* "0" means neutral effect. Then there is the list of ingredients, including those marked "(optional)." This means the dish tastes great without these foods, but if you like them, you can add them. Usually the optionals are items like onion, garlic, or pepper. These are best avoided by *Pitta.* And as we say, the recipes taste delicious without them. I know it's hard to believe, *Pitta,* that a food can have flavor without stimulating heat, but try it and see. Eliminating the onions, garlic and chilis also works well for those with tender tummies, children, and nursing mothers. There are also some fast separate dishes (see CONDIMENTS p. 216) for those who yearn for onions, and other hot spices and who find them healing.

Next you've got the directions. It is wise to read them through once so you know what you're getting yourself in for. After that, there's usually a "This goes well with . . . ." line, under **Comments**. Again, no need to slavishly follow our suggestions. This just lets you know some tasty combinations. Often healing garnishes are also given here.

So. There you have it. Enjoy!

PLANNING BALANCED MEALS EASILY

A balanced meal is not so imposing as you might think. A number of key anthropological and biological studies have found that a particular balance of nutrients best assures health and longevity. Unsurprisingly, this pattern is one that many human bodies have been choosing for centuries. In different cultures the specific foods used to create this balance have varied, but the overall pattern for health has not. This pattern includes: 40 to 60% whole grains, 10 to 20% high-quality protein, and 30 to 50% fresh fruits and vegetables. For the specific *doshas*, it works out best about like this for a day:

Vata	Pitta	Kapha
5-6 servings of whole grains	4-5 servings of whole grains	3-4 servings of whole grains
1-2 servings high quality protein	1½-2 servings high quality protein	2 servings high-quality low-fat protein
2-3 servings fresh cooked vegetables	3-4 servings fresh vegetables	4-5 servings fresh vegetable
1 serving fresh fruit or more	1-1½ servings fresh fruit or more	1 serving fresh fruit

What does this mean? An example:

Vata	Pitta	Kapha
Breakfast:		
⅔ cup oatmeal with *ghee* and sweetener	⅔ cup oatmeal with maple syrup	Fresh fruit (berries, apricots, etc.)
Chappati		Tea
Lunch:		
Dal, 1 cup	*Dal*, 1 cup	*Dal*, 1 cup
Basmati rice, ⅔ cup	*Basmati* rice, ⅔ cup	*Basmati* rice or barley, ⅔ cup
Steamed asparagus, ½ cup	Steamed asparagus, ½-1 cup	Steamed asparagus, 1 cup
Coriander chutney	Coriander chutney	Coriander chutney or dry ginger
Snack:		
Fresh fruit	Fresh fruit or sunflower seeds	
Dinner:		
Tridoshic vegetable curry, 1 cup (2 vegetables ½ protein)	*Tridoshic* vegetable curry, 1 cup	*Tridoshic* vegetable curry, ⅔ cup
Rice or bulgur, ⅔ cup	Rice or bulgur, ⅔ cup	Millet or barley, ⅔ cup
Papadums	1-2 *chappatis*	1 rye chappati
Lemon pickle or umeboshi plum	Medium salad	Large salad
Late night snack: (optional)		
Hot milk with ginger	Piece of fresh fruit	

A balanced meal includes a protein, one or more carbohydrates and one or more vegetables. *Kichadi* is a good example of a one-pot meal that includes all of these. Vegetable barley soup can be another, if you add some tofu or beans in the cooking. Vegetable curry over rice is an easy two-pot meal. Condiments add spice, literally and figuratively to a meal. For some ideas about their use as garnishes, see CONDIMENTS. They can take a meal from the mundane to the sublime, often in less than 15 minutes of preparation time.

For more ideas, see the menus which follow.

Just as each of the *doshas* has a predominant time in the year and in the life-cycle, each also has times of greatest strength during the day and night. At dawn, or 6 a.m., *Kapha* is just beginning to accumulate and continues to do so until about 10 a.m. This is a time to eat relatively lightly, especially for *Kapha*. You notice breakfasts are the lightest meals given in this example. *Vatas* may want to vary this by getting a somewhat more ample breakfast. *Kapha* really does best with little during this *Kapha* time. Around 10 in the morning, *Pitta* begins to rise. Many of my clients, especially *Pittas*, but not exclusively, tell me that this is when they first really begin to get hungry. In Ayurveda, 10 or 11 a.m. is when an early lunch would be served. This meal can be relatively substantial, as indicated in our example.

Some *Vatas* and *Pittas* find that a snack around 3 or 4 p.m. grounds them and helps their energy run smoothly until dinner. Such a snack would be superfluous for *Kapha*.

Vata predominates from 2 p.m. until about 6 p.m., when *Kapha* again begins to rise. *Kapha* is not an especially stimulating time for digestion. It is better to eat early if you can, around 6 p.m. Eating late encourages the accumulation of *Kapha*, especially for *Kapha*. *Vatas* may find themselves eating a smaller meal at dusk than at dawn. *Pittas* can eat supper with their usual hearty appetites. *Kaphas* do well to emphasize light foods, such as the large salad in our example. From 10 p.m. until 2 a.m., *Pitta* again predominates. Now is the time to let your digestive system assimilate what it has taken in during the day. With dawn the cycle begins again. You will notice from our example that there is usually a three-hour break or more between meals. This is to give the G.I. tract time to digest. For example, if you get into late afternoon snacking in a big way, your digestive fire is likely to be inhibited at dinner. Again, these are guidelines based on maximal functioning of the *doshas*. See how this works for you in your own life.

The following are sample menus for different constitutions:

TRIDOSHIC MENUS

SUMMER DAY

Breakfast

Fresh Fruit Salad
Juice or Tea
Breakfast Rice (if very hungry)

Lunch

Curried Parsnips & Carrots
Chappatis, Wholewheat or Rye, or Rice Cakes
Tossed Salad of Arugula, Lettuce, Sprouts
(with simple oil & vinegar dressing)

Snack

Fresh Sweet Berries or Choice of Fruit
Cool Mint Tea

Dinner

Asparagus Souffle
Saffron Rice
Summer Squash with Parsley and Dill
or
Mung Bean Sprouts Indian Style #1

Dessert

Carob Delights
(optional, for special occasions)

Choice of Beverage

Cool Mint Tea
Zingy Hibiscus Cooler
Lemongrass, Chrysanthemum, or Chamomile Tea
Fruit Shakes
Cool Bansha Tea
Soothing Chai
Mixed Vegetable Juice

FALL DAY

Breakfast

Hot Amaranth
Hot Spiced Milk

Lunch

Tridoshic Dal #1
Basmati Rice
Green Bean *Bhaji*
Coriander Chutney
Rye or Whole Wheat *Chappatis*

Snack

Toasted Sunflower Seeds

Dinner

Tridoshic Vegetable Curry #1
"Plain" Indian Rice
Hot Sicilian Salad

Dessert

Tridoshic Dal Payasam or *Kapha Shiro*

Choice of Beverage

Digestive Tea
Soothing Chai
Hot Spiced Milks
Hot Soy Milk
Hot Bansha Tea
Mixed Vegetable Juice
Miso Broth

WINTER DAY

Breakfast

Choice of Wheat, Rice, or Rye Toast with *Ghee*
Scrambled Tofu or French Toast
Hot Ginger Tea

Lunch

Vegetable Barley Soup
(with Split Mung Beans added)
Sage-Onion Quick Bread

Snack

Dry-Roasted Pumpkin Seeds or Hot Gingered Soy Milk

Dinner

Middle-Eastern Cabbage-Tofu Entree
"Plain" Barley or *Basmati* Rice
Leek-Daikon-Sunflower Salad

Dessert

Kapha Fruit Crumble

Choice of Beverage

Iron-Rich Breakfast Drink
Hot Apple Cider
Digestive Tea
Soothing Chai
Barley Tea or Barley Breakfast Brew
Osha Tea
Hot Ginger Tea #2
Hot Bansha Tea

SPRING DAY

Breakfast

Breakfast Rice
(with extra Ginger as desired)
Hot Herb Tea

Lunch

Tasty Chickpeas or Tofu and Mushrooms
Cream of Green Soup
Snow Pea Salad

Snack

Fresh Fruit or Simple Applesauce

Dinner

Potato-Green Pea Patties or Curried Potato Patties with Carrot
Carrot Raisin Salad

Dessert (optional)

Stewed Apricots

Choice of Beverage

Iron-Rich Breakfast Drink

Hot Apple Cider
Digestive Tea
Osha Tea
Ajwan Tea
Hot Ginger Tea #2
Hot Bansha Tea
Mixed Vegetable Juice

QUICK DAY

Breakfast

Choice of Favorite Ready-to-eat Cold Cereal (by constitution)
Cow, Goat, or Soy Milk

Lunch

Choice of Devilled Egg Salad or Curried Egg Salad
Sandwiches on Whole Wheat, Rice, or All- Rye Bread

Snack

Sunflower-Pumpkin Seed Mix or Soaked Raisins

Dinner

Tofu Pesto
over
Regular Wheat or Buckwheat Soba Noodles
Favorite Dark Leafy Greens

Dessert (optional)

Maple Tapioca (made with Goat's Milk ahead of time)

Choice of Beverage

Whatever is on the stove or in the refrigerator, made already!

WEEKEND DAY

Brunch

Masala Dosas with *Tridoshic Dal* or *Dosas* with Fruit Filling
Simple Applesauce or Blueberry Sauce

Snack

Sun Balls

Dinner

Mung Burgers
Tossed Salad
Gujarati-Style *Pulao*

Dessert

Indian Rice Pudding

Choice of Beverage

Soothing Chai
Digestive Tea
Whatever you choose of those already given

VATA MENUS

SUMMER DAY

Breakfast

Breakfast Rice
Hot Tea or Milk

Lunch

Zucchini and *Mung Dal*
Rice
Whole Wheat *Chappatis*
Yogurt (optional)

Snack

Fresh Figs, Apricots, Peaches, or Melon

Dinner

Buttermilk *Kadhi* over Noodles
Yam Salad

Dessert

Coconut Macaroons

Choice of Beverage

Cool Bansha Tea
Digestive Tea
Carrot Juice
Zingy Hibiscus Cooler
Cool Mint Tea
Caffix or Rana
Lemonade
Fruit Juice (diluted 1:1 with water)

FALL DAY

Breakfast

Cream of Wheat or Rice
Hot Gingered Milk or Hot Ginger Tea #1 or Hot Spiced Milk

Lunch

Simple Onion Soup
Whole Wheat Crackers or Bread
Asparagus Salad

Snack

Grapes or Sunflower or Pumpkin Seeds or Hot Tea

Dinner

Miso Tofu
Rice or Noodles
Curried Parsnips and Carrots

Dessert (optional)

Butterscotch Brownies

Choice of Beverage

Herbal Tea: Roastaroma, Almond Sunset, Mo's 24, Red Zinger, Orange Zinger,

Mandarin Orange, Emperor's Choice, Caffix, Pero, Roma
Hot Spiced Milks
Ginger Tea
Amasake
Grape Juice with Water

WINTER DAY

Breakfast

Spicy Oatmeal
Hot Tea or Milk

Lunch

Basic Warming *Kichadi*
Whole Wheat *Chappatis* with *Ghee*

Snack

Salted Cashews or An Orange or Hot Tea

Dinner

Tridoshic Vegetable Curry #1
Bulgur or Rice
Mother Ogg's Sweet Potatoes or Sweet Steamed Beets

Dessert (optional, special occasions)

Khir
Pumpkin Pie or Sesame Sweeties

Choice of Beverage

Herbal Teas: Cinnamon Rose, Mu, Caffix, Pero, Roma, Ginger, Amasake
Nut and Seed Milks
Warmed Juices
Hot Spiced Milks

SPRING DAY

Breakfast

Cream of Rice with *Ghee*
Ginger Tea or Warmed Milk

Lunch

Asparagus Cream Sauce over *Basmati* Rice or Noodles
Sweetened Carrots
Whole Wheat Muffins

Snack

Berries
Cherries
Mango or Papaya

Dinner

Cheese Sauce and Bulgur or Black Lentils with Yogurt and Rice
Artichoke with *Ghee*

Dessert (optional, special occasions)

Classic Oatmeal Cookies or *Shiro*

Choice of Beverage

Herbal Teas: Almond Sunset, Pelican Punch, Zingers, Blackberry Patch
Fruit Juices
Smoothies

QUICK DAY

Breakfast

Puffed Brown Rice or Wheat Cereal
Oatios
Milk or Soymilk
Rejuvenative Almond Drink

Lunch

Avocado Spread with Bread
Artichoke Heart Salad

Snack

Fruit in Season or Nuts or Seeds

Dinner

Fifteen-Minute Vegetable Curry
Whole Wheat Tortillas or *Chappatis*
"Plain" Indian Rice

Dessert (optional)

Papaya Salad

Choice of Beverage

Whatever is available:
Tea
Juice
Milk, Soy Choice of Beverage
Amasake

VARIATIONS

Breakfast

Whole Wheat Tortillas
or
Whole Wheat Toast and Shredded Wheat
or
Scrambled Eggs with Sauteed Onions
or
Buckwheat Pancakes
or
Corncakes
or
French Toast

Lunch

Hot Korean Vegetables and Noodles
or
Urud Dal and Rice
or
Gujarati Tridoshic Dal

Snack

Spiced-Up Yogurt

Dinner

Arugula Souffle
Spicy Rice and Potatoes
Radish and Cucumber Slices in Simple Oil and Vinegar Dressing

Dessert (optional)

Sweet Potato Halva

WEEKEND DAY

Brunch

Traditional *Masala Dosas*
or
Cottage Cakes
or
Crepes with Fruit Sauce
or
Eggs Chupadero

Snack

Four-Star Vegetable Soup or Hot and Spicy Soup

Dinner

Okra Curry
Brown or *Basmati* Rice (with a little Wild Rice)
Simple Acorn Squash

Dessert (optional)

Maple Tapioca

Choice of Beverage

As recommended in other *Vata* Menus

ON THE ROAD (WHEN TRAVELLING)

Breakfast

Oatmeal or Cream of Wheat or Shredded Wheat

Whole Wheat Toast, Tortillas, or Muffins
Scrambled or Poached Eggs or Cheese Omelette
French Toast, Pancakes, or Waffles

Lunch

Cottage Cheese, Macaroni Salad, Cooked Beets, Radishes at Salad Bar
Cheese Sandwich or Egg Salad Sandwich
Avocado and Cheese Sandwich and/or Vegetable Soups

Snacks (take your own)

Sunflower Seeds or Nuts
Fruit or Yogurt or Hot Soups or Choice of Beverage (in a thermos)

Choice of Beverage

Take Herbal Tea Bags, Caffix or Pero
Hot Teas
Hot Chocolate
Hot Milk
Fruit Juices

Dinner

Chinese Vegetables and Rice (with tofu, if well tolerated)
Egg Foo Young
Nori Rolls
Mild Indian Curries, Rice, and *Chappatis*
Quiche
Vegetarian Burritos or Cheese Enchiladas with Whole Grain Breads and Muffins

Dessert

Tapioca, Puddings, Rice Pudding or Pumpkin Pie

PITTA MENUS

SUMMER DAY

Breakfast

Puffed Rice or Crispy Granola with Wheat Flakes
Milk, Soy Milk, or Coconut Milk

Lunch

Avocado Spread
Whole Wheat or Rice Crackers or Whole Wheat *Chappatis* or Whole Wheat Tortillas
Large Tossed Salad

Snack

Unsprayed Grapes, Berries, or other Sweet Fruit in Season
or
Cool Mint Tea

Dinner

Mung Burger #2
or
Tempeh Burger on Whole Wheat Bun with Coriander Chutney
Fresh Cole Slaw
Fresh Dilled Zucchini

Dessert (optional)

Coconut Macaroons or Khir

Choice of Beverage

Herbal Teas: Chamomile, Chrysanthemum, Mint, Lemon grass and Nettle
Juices (dilute 1:1 with water)
Cantaloupe Smoothie
Milk
Soy Milk
Mint Julep

FALL DAY

Breakfast

Breakfast Rice or Cream of Wheat or Rice or Cooked Bulgur
with
Amasake, Cow, Goat, Soy, or Sunflower Milk

Lunch

Cream of Green Soup
Basmati Rice or "Plain" Barley
Snow Pea Salad

Snack

Pear, Apple, or other Fresh Fruit in Season

Dinner

Mushrooms in Yogurt over Pasta
Artichoke
Leek-Daikon-Sunflower Salad

Dessert (optional, special occasions)

Date Dream Balls or Sweet Potato Halva

Choice of Beverage

Hot Spiced Milks, Caffix, Pero, Roma
Coconut Milk
Herbal Teas: Comfrey, Mint, Almond Sunset, Roastaroma
Hot Apple Cider
Fruit Smoothies
Rejuvenative Almond Drink
Iron-Rich Breakfast Drink

WINTER DAY

Breakfast

Spicy Oatmeal or Cream of Barley
Hot Spiced Milk

Lunch

Vegetable Barley Soup with Beans or Split Pea Soup
Quick Wheat-Free Bread
or
Whole Wheat Muffin, *Chappati,* or Whole Wheat Tortilla

Snack

Sunflower-Pumpkin Seed Mix and/or Hot Tea

Dinner

Rajma or Cajun Red Beans

Mother Ogg's Sweet Potatoes
Favorite Dark Leafy Greens
Cornbread

Dessert (optional)

Shiro or Indian Rice Pudding

Choice of Beverage

Hot Spiced Milks
Hot Apple Cider
Hot Herbal Teas

SPRING DAY

Breakfast

Crispy Granola with Wheat Flakes or Breakfast Rice
Hot Herb or Bansha Tea or Barley Breakfast Brew

Lunch

Broccoli-Cauliflower Soup or East Indian Lima Beans
Chappatis or Whole Wheat Crackers
Indian-Style Bean Sprouts #1

Snack

Curried Garbanzos or Chevado

Dinner

Asparagus Souffle
Spicy Rice and Potato
Mushrooms and Peas

Dessert (optional, special occasions)

Baked Apples or Spiced Pears

Choice of Beverage

Dilute Juices
Herb Teas

Milks
Coconut Milk

QUICK DAY

Breakfast

Shredded Wheat and/or English Muffin
Milk
Digestive Tea

Lunch

Curried Egg Salad with Sprouts and Lettuce
or
Sunflower Butter and Jam on Rice Cakes or Whole Wheat Bread

Snack

Fresh Fruit
or
Dry-Roasted Pumpkin Seeds (made ahead of time)

Dinner

Fifteen-Minute Vegetable Curry
"Plain" Indian Rice
Mint Chutney
Whole Wheat *Chappatis*

Dessert

Classic Oatmeal Cookies (made ahead of time)
or
Khir

Choice of Beverage

What you have about
Fruit Juices
Teas
Milk

VARIATIONS

Breakfast

Scrambled Tofu and Herb Tea
or
Oat Bran Muffins and Mint Julep
or
French Toast and Tea or Milk

Lunch

Sweet Chickpeas and Pita Bread
or
Split Green Peas, Indian Style
or
Okra Curry and Rice
Asparagus Salad

Snack

Orange, Prunes, Raisins, Toasted Sunflower Seeds

Dinner

Santa Fe Pinto Beans with Whole Wheat Tortillas
Avocado Spread
Corn on the Cob or Cumin Zucchini

Dessert

Maple Tapioca

Choice of Beverage

As recommended in other *Pitta* Menus

WEEKEND DAY

Brunch

Cottage Cakes, *Pitta* Crepes, or *Dosas*
with
Blueberry or Simple Applesauce and Maple Syrup
Hot Tea

Snack

Date or Fig Shake

Dinner

Middle Eastern Cabbage-Tofu Entree with Rice or Barley
Rutabagas or Steamed Parsnips and/or Large Salad

Dessert

Khir

Choice of Beverage

As recommended in other *Pitta* Menus

ON THE ROAD (WHEN TRAVELLING)

Breakfast

Oatmeal, Shredded Wheat, Oatios/Cheerios, or Rice Cereals
Whole Wheat Toast or English Muffin or Pancakes or Waffles

Lunch

Salad Bar: Salad with Garbanzo Beans and Cottage Cheese
Baked Potato
Plenty of Vegetables or Bean Burrito and Salad

Snack (take them with you)

Fresh Fruit or Raw Cut-up Vegetables
Fruit Juices or Teas
Sunflower or Pumpkin Seeds or Applesauce

Dinner

Chinese Tofu Stir Fry with Rice and Chinese Vegetables
or
Red Beans and Rice with Vegetables
or
Salads and Soups
or
Broccoli-Stuffed Baked Potato

Desserts

Tapioca, Puddings, or Rice Pudding or Fresh Fruits

Choice of Beverage

Grape or Apple Juice
Water
Herb Teas
Milk
No Caffeine
Moderate alcohol (two drinks per week)

KAPHA MENUS

<u>SUMMER DAY</u>

Breakfast*

Fresh Fruit or Crispy Granola
Goat or Soy Milk with Cardamom

Lunch*

Cauliflower *Kahdi*
Cornbread
Snowpea Salad or Tossed Salad

Snack

Apricots, Berries, Peaches or other *Kapha* Fruits in Season

Dinner

Sauteed Tofu and Vegetables
Millet
Large Salad
Choice of *Kapha* Dressings

Snack or Dessert** (special occasion)

Unbuttered Popcorn or *Kapha* Fruit Crumble

Choice of Beverage

Apple, Pear, or Pomegranate Juice (dilute with water)
Cool Bansha Tea
Cool Herb Teas

Kaphas can often skip either breakfast or lunch with no ill effects
**It is highly recommended for *Kaphas* to not have dessert or eat dessert before
6:00 p.m. in place of a regular meal

FALL DAY

Breakfast

Fresh Fruit
Barley Breakfast Brew or Puffed Millet or Cream of Rye
Caffix or Hot Ginger Tea

Lunch

Simple Onion Soup
Rye Crackers
Spinach Salad

Snack

Apple or Pear

Dinner

Gingered Aduki Beans
Barley and Mushrooms
Simple Steamed Asparagus

Dessert

Stewed Apricots

Choice of Beverage

Hot Bansha Tea with Ginger
Hot Apple Cider
Hot Spiced Goat or Soy Milk
Hot Herb Teas: Caffix, Mint, Country Apple, Country Peach, Roastaroma, Blackberry

WINTER DAY

Breakfast

Herbed Millet or Hot Corn Cereal or Hot Amaranth Cereal
Hot Ginger Tea #2, Lotus Root Tea, Soothing Chai, Hot Soy Milk or Bansha

Lunch

Chana Dal Soup and Rye *Chappatis*
or
Black-Eyed Peas American Style and Cornbread
Spinach and Potato

Snack

Cranberries in Orange Sauce and/or Hot Tea

Dinner

Tasty Chickpeas or Sweet Chickpeas
Amaranth or Millet
Spicy Cumin Eggplant

Desserts

Baked Apple or Spiced Pear

Choice of Beverage

See above, breakfast
Hot Apple Cider
Hot Herb Teas

SPRING DAY

Breakfast

Fresh Fruit Salad or Cream of Rye, Millet, or Barley Cereal
Hot Ginger Tea #2 or Bansha Tea with Ginger

Lunch*

Daikon Radish Soup or Hot and Spicy Soup
Spicy Millet and Potato
Raw Vegetables: Celery, Sprouts, Lettuce or Asparagus Salad

Snack

Kapha Fruit in Season or Hot Tea

Dinner

Arugula Souffle
All-Rye Bread
Carrot-Raisin Salad

Dessert

Stewed Prunes or Figs or Delectable Prune Bars

Choice of Beverage

Fruit Juices (diluted)
Herb Teas
Bansha
Soy Milk
Water

QUICK DAY

Breakfast

Fresh Fruit
Oat Bran Muffin
Apple/Berry Smoothie

Lunch

Black Beans (made ahead of time or canned) on Corn Tortillas
as a Tostada or Burrito
with Sprouts, Chopped Lettuce, Raw Vegetables

Snack

Fresh Fruit
Tea

Dinner

Broccoli Sunflower Soup with *Basmati* Rice
or

Tofu Pesto over Buckwheat Soba Noodles and Carrot Sticks
or
Favorite Dark Leafy Greens

Dessert

Fresh Fruit or Simple Applesauce

Choice of Beverage

Whatever is available

VARIATIONS

Breakfast

Breakfast Rice or Puffed Oats or Scrambled Tofu

Lunch*

Broccoli Cauliflower Soup
Fresh Dilled Eggplant
Quick Wheat-Free Bread

Snack

Dry-Roasted Garbanzos
Toasted Corn Chips
Popcorn

Dinner

Tridoshic Vegetable Curry #2
"Plain" Indian Rice
Artichoke

Dessert

Kapha Shiro

WEEKEND DAY

Brunch

Buckwheat Pancakes with Blueberries, Honey and *Ghee*

or
Masala Dosas

Dinner

Hot Korean Vegetables and Noodles
Large Salad with Sprouts

Dessert

Fresh Fruit Salad

Choice of Beverage

See other *Kapha* Menus

ON THE ROAD

Breakfast

Granola or other *Kapha* Cold Cereal (bring it with you)
Goat or Soy Milk (bring it with you)
or
Fresh Fruit
Herb Teas (bring Tea Bags and dry Ginger Powder)
Poached or Soft Boiled Eggs
Rye Toast

Lunch

Chinese Stir Fry with Black Bean Sauce and Chinese Vegetables
or
Bean Nachos with Chili (hold the Cheese)
or
Soup and Salad
or
Bean Tostada and Salad

Snack

Any *Kapha* Fruit in Season

Dinner

Salad Bar with Garbanzo Beans, Beets, Plenty of Vegetables
Baked Potato or Indian Curry with Vegetables

Dessert

Fresh Fruit

Choice of Beverage

Spring Water
Herb Teas
Hot Ginger Tea

MAIN DISHES

ABOUT CURRIES

Curries are well-blended combinations of spices added to foods to aid digestion and tonify the body. They can be made up with as few as three or four spices, or as many as a dozen or more seasonings. Curries can also signify the dishes that are made up of these various spices. Curry powder came into existence as an easy way to approximate some of the flavors of an Indian curry. However, learning to make your own curries gives you a far wider range of tastes, dishes and medicinal actions. Homemade curry is also far fresher in flavor. Curry powder is occasionally used in our recipes to give a particular flavor.

One very basic way to begin a curry is to heat a small amount of black mustard seeds and whole cumin seeds together in warm oil. This is known as the vagar. *This activates the aromatic oils in the seeds, releasing their flavors and healing properties into the food which will be added to the oil. Cumin and mustard seeds are both warming herbs, ideal for* Vata *and* Kapha. *Black mustard seed in particular is pungent and mildly diuretic, making it quite useful for* Kapha. *Its warmth stimulates* agni *and overall digestion; it is beneficial in dispelling gas. Ayurveda values it for gout, arthritic and feverish conditions. It should be used in minimal amounts for* Pitta, *preferably balanced with cooling coriander powder or seeds. (Surprisingly, Americans eat more mustard every year than any other spice except black pepper. Usually it is mixed with turmeric in prepared mustard sauces. We do know something about enkindling* agni *with our hotdogs and hamburgers!)*

Whole cumin seeds as well as ground cumin are best used when they are fresh. Storing these spices for more than one year causes major losses in their medicinal and digestive properties, even when they have been well-sealed. Long-term storage can also make cumin more than slightly bitter. Cumin acts to dispel ama *and toxins; it is an excellent and gentle tonifier of the digestive tract. A few respected Ayurvedic writers have referred to cumin as cooling. In my experience it is not. Its pungency gives it a distinct warmth which is valuable in stimulating the functions mentioned above. In combination with coriander and fennel seeds, two very distinctly cooling herbs, it offers a cooling and relieving aid for excessive fire. But alone, its action is warming. Its slight bitterness will relieve* Pitta *as well as* Kapha. *It is also generally stimulating to* Vata *digestion.*

Turmeric is another fundamental spice in the curry armentarium. It is pungent, bitter and very slightly astringent. It is an excellent blood-purifier and anti-inflammatory. As Dr. Vasant Lad has pointed out in Ayurveda: The Science of Self-Healing, *it is an ideal addition to high-protein dishes. It stimulates complete digestion of the proteins and prevents the creation of toxins. It is good for dispelling flatulence and inflammation. Healing to the liver, its bright gold color gives curries their characteristic hue and adds an attractive tone, especially to vegetable combinations.*

Coriander is one of the most ancient spices in the classic curry. In use since 5000 B.C., it can be used as a powder or as seeds. It alleviates gas and tonifies the digestive tract. Pungent yet cooling, it is one of the best spices available for calming Pitta. *Its leaves are also often used as a cooling garnish in Indian dishes. Fresh coriander leaves can be found in Mexican or Chinese produce sections, under the names "cilantro" or "Chinese parsley." Regular parsley tastes and acts nothing like coriander and should not be used as a substitute in these recipes.*

Ginger is also frequently added to curries. It is hot, pungent and stimulating to both digestion and circulation. It is highly valued in Ayurvedic medicine for these purposes. The fresh root is best used for Vata, *while the dried powder is most beneficial for* Kapha. *Dry ginger specifically dispels gas, especially when used with hot peppers. Fresh ginger is diuretic and useful in alleviating colds and coughs, particularly as a juice. Both dry and fresh ginger stimulate appetite and calm indigestion. Dry ginger is considered less aggravating to* Pitta. *In a curry, either fresh or dried ginger can be used; the fresh grated root is most often utilized. Ginger relieves constipation and gas gently yet effectively, particularly in conjunction with other mild laxatives like fennel. Excessive use of ginger, particularly fresh ginger, can aggravate* Pitta. *It is also not recommended in excess for people with Bright's Disease or chronic heart conditions.*

Fennel cools and sweetens a curry, giving it body. It is especially serviceable in alleviating Vata *and* Pitta. *Its aromatic oils stimulate digestion. It must be used carefully, as its flavor can quickly dominate a dish. It stimulates perspiration, as well as milk production. It is often used as an after-dinner digestive aid.*

Black pepper offers pungency and warmth to a curry, enkindling agni. *It is also valuable for stimulating appetite and reducing gas. It is generally added in very small quantities, either as whole peppercorns or as ground pepper. It is rich in chromium, useful in preventing and alleviating adult-onset diabetes. Frequently these days diners shun pepper as well as salt, somehow assuming that if salt is bad for you, pepper must be too. In fact, black pepper is a real assistant to good health and digestion for most people. Black pepper is the native of India which set off the spice wars in Europe and stimulated the discovery of the New World.*

Other peppers are also used in Indian curries, in the form of cayenne, pip-pali (Indian long pepper), serranos, and chili powder. These peppers make the difference between a mild curry and a hot one, as they are quite pungent and fiery. They stimulate agni. *They are most useful for* Kapha *and in small amounts, for* Vata. *They aggravate* Pitta *indisputably. Indian long pepper, or pippali, is a great medicinal herb which promotes digestion and relieves gas and constipation. It can be obtained in some Indian food stores. Serranos is the Spanish name for the small hot green peppers used in this country in Indian cuisine. They are usually found in the Mexican section of produce stores. The hottest part of fresh peppers is around their seeds. You can remove the seeds if you want a milder dish, or leave them in for "killer" heat.*

Salt pulls the curry together and grounds it. As the Ayurvedic sutras say, "it brings out the deliciousness of the food." In times and areas where refrigeration is or was not available, it has also acted as a preservative, discouraging bacterial growth. Traditional Indian recipes often contain far more preserving salt than is needed today. Now we look to minimize its use, but not to eliminate it, as it is a valuable seasoning when used in moderation. It offers energy and strength as well as grounding.

Fenugreek is usually used in its seed form, and is found more often in Indian pickles than curries. It is bitter, pungent, sweet, and warming and a good rejuvenator. It has been used in many cultures as a female rejuvenative, perhaps because of its rich concentration of the B vitamin, folic acid. This herb stimulates blood and hair cell development, as well as weight loss. In Ayurveda, fenugreek is used for both women and men as a tonic. In small amounts it is excellent for fostering digestion and alleviating chronic cough. It has a strong bitter flavor which can take over a dish if you are too lavish in its use!

Hing, or asafoetida, is one of the best spices for balancing Vata. *It aids enormously in the digestion of a meal for this dosha, calming gas and bloating. It is pungent and should be heated before consumption.*

TRIDOSHIC VEGETABLE CURRY #1

Preparation time: 1 hour   Serves: 9-10
-Vata, -Pitta, -Kapha   ✿   ✳   🌿   ❄

   1 cup fresh green peas (frozen can be used if necessary)
   1 cup carrots, diced
   1 cup potatoes, diced
   2 cups green string beans or asparagus, cut in 1 inch pieces
   2 tablespoons sunflower oil or *ghee*
   2 teaspoons cumin seeds
   2 teaspoons black mustard seeds
   1 teaspoon sea salt
   1½ cups water
   2 teaspoons turmeric
   1 teaspoon coriander powder
   ½ cup yogurt

Heat oil or *ghee* in large heavy skillet. Add mustard and cumin seeds. When the
mustard seeds pop, add turmeric. Then add all the vegetables and the water. (If
using frozen peas, do not add until rest of vegetables are nearly done.) Cook covered
until the vegetables become tender, about 15-20 minutes. Then add yogurt and the
rest of the ingredients, stirring well. Simmer uncovered on low heat for another 15-
20 minutes.

Comments: Good with CUCUMBER *RAITA* (p. 224) and lime pickle for *Vata*. Serve
over rice or other grain. This easy-to-prepare curry is likely to garner you rave
reviews. The cooling qualities of the peas and potatoes are offset by the other vegetables and the curry spices. This small amount of yogurt, thinned with water, is
usually tolerated well by all *doshas* and aids digestion. Whenever you can, use tender fresh, rather than frozen peas, as they are more balancing for *Kapha* and *Vata*.

TRIDOSHIC VEGETABLE CURRY #2

Preparation time: 35 minutes   Serves: 8- 10
-Vata, -Pitta, -Kapha   ✿   🌿   ❄

   1 cup green string beans or asparagus, fresh, chopped
   $1/2$ cup ripe tomato, chopped in $1/2$ inch cubes (optional, omit for *Pitta.*)
   $1 1/2$ cups potatoes, cubed in $1/2$ inch pieces
   $1/4$ cup baby lima beans (optional)
   $1/2$ cup carrots, sliced
   $1/2$ bunch spinach (or other greens) well-washed, chopped
   1 to 3 tablespoons sunflower oil (the lesser amount for *Kapha*)
   1 teaspoon black mustard seeds
   1 teaspoon cumin seeds
   1 teaspoon turmeric
   1 teaspoon curry powder, mild
   3 cups water
   1 tablespoon coriander powder
   1 teaspoon sea salt
   1 hot green pepper, chopped (as garnish for *Kapha* only)

Wash, dry and chop vegetables. In large deep pan heat oil; add cumin and mustard seeds. When the mustard seeds pop, add tomatoes, curry powder and turmeric. Cook 3 to 4 minutes over medium heat. Add remaining ingredients, including water. Mix well. Cook for 20-25 minutes over medium heat or until soft. Garnish with fresh chopped coriander leaves if available.

Comment: This goes well with rice, barley, bulgur, or millet and a spinach-mushroom salad.

FIFTEEN MINUTE VEGETABLE CURRY

Preparation time: 15 minutes   Serves: 5-6
− *Vata,* − *Pitta,* 0 *Kapha*   ✿ ❋ ぇ ❄
   1 cup raw carrots (2 medium carrots)
   1 cup fresh or frozen green peas (1 lb.)
   2 tablespoons sunflower oil
   $1/8$ teaspoon *hing*
   $1/2$ teaspoon black mustard seeds
   1 teaspoon whole cumin seeds
   $1/2$ teaspoon sea salt
   $1/2$-1 pound tofu (optional, omit for *Kapha*)
   1 teaspoon curry powder
   1 teaspoon coriander powder
   $1/4$ cup water
   2 teaspoons brown rice syrup (use $1/2$ teaspoon for *Kapha*)
   $1/4$ hot green pepper, chopped (optional, omit for *Pitta*)
   $1/4$-1 cup plain yogurt (use the smaller amount for *Pitta* and *Kapha*)

Heat oil in heavy skillet. Add mustard and cumin seeds. When mustard seeds pop, add curry powder, salt, tofu, and vegetables. Cook uncovered for 5 minutes on medium heat, stirring occasionally. Add water and cover. Cook another 5 minutes (or until vegetables are tender) on low heat. Shake pan occasionally to prevent sticking. Add all remaining ingredients, mix well and serve.

Comment: Garnish with hot green pepper and dry ginger for *Kapha*.

This goes well with "PLAIN" INDIAN RICE (p. 129) or bread.

SPINACH AND POTATO CURRY

Preparation time: 30 minutes   Serves: 4·6
*mildly +Vata, 0 Pitta, −Kapha**   ✿ ✳ ⛄ ❄
*0 Vata, −Pitta, 0 Kapha***

> 3 medium potatoes or 6 medium parsnips
> 1 large bunch fresh spinach (1½ pounds)
> 1½ tablespoons sunflower oil
> ½ teaspoon mustard seeds
> ⅛ teaspoon *hing*
> ½ teaspoon turmeric
> 2 cups water
> 1 teaspoon sea salt
> 2 teaspoons coriander powder
> 2 tablespoons lemon juice
> ¼ green pepper, chopped (optional, omit for *Pitta*)
> 2 cloves fresh garlic, minced (optional, omit for *Pitta*)

Wash spinach and potatoes. Cut potatoes into ½ inch cubes; chop spinach. Heat oil in a heavy saucepan or skillet and add mustard seeds and *hing*. When seeds pop, add turmeric, potatoes and water. Stir. Cover and cook on medium heat for 5 to 7 minutes. Then add spinach and all other ingredients. Mix well. Cook covered for an additional 10 to 15 minutes. Serve.

Comments: This goes well with *rotalis* and CUCUMBER *RAITA* (p. 224) or yogurt. The bitter and astringent tastes of spinach balance *Pitta* and *Kapha* well; the cooling effect of the potato balances the pungent *vipak* of spinach for *Pitta,* making these two vegetables an excellent combinaton.

*With potato
**With parsnip

BUTTERMILK CURRY (*KADHI*)

Preparation time: 30 minutes   Serves: 6-8
— Vata, mildly +Pitta, +Kapha   🐌 ❄

2½ cups fresh buttermilk or yogurt
3½ cups water
¼ cup chickpea flour (available at Indian groceries and some health
food stores)
3 tablespoons melted butter or *ghee*
1 teaspoon cumin seeds
3 to 4 whole cloves
1 cinnamon stick, 1 inch long or ¼ teaspoon ground cinnamon
1 teaspoon sea salt
3 tablespoons barley malt or brown rice syrup
4 tablespoons lemon juice
¼ green pepper chopped (optional)

Mix buttermilk or yogurt, water and chickpea flour in large bowl with beater until completely smooth. In small skillet heat butter or *ghee;* add cumin, cloves and cinnamon. Heat until seeds turn dark brown but do not burn. Add this mixture to the buttermilk and chickpea flour mixture. Add remaining ingredients. Heat over medium heat just to boiling point, stirring constantly to avoid overflowing. Mixture will thicken slightly. Serve warm.

Comments: This goes well with tofu and vegetables or rice and vegetables. This warming dish can be served with cooler foods, such as tofu, cooling vegetables, or barley to be better balanced for *Pitta* and *Kapha*. It is an excellent dish for *Vata*.

CURRIED PARSNIPS AND CARROTS

Preparation time: 25 minutes   Serves: 4-5
— Vata, — Pitta, mildly +Kapha*   ✳ 🐌 ❄

6 medium parsnips (1½ pounds)
3 medium carrots (½ pound)
2 tablespoons sunflower oil or *ghee*
1 teaspoon black mustard seeds
⅛ teaspoon *hing*
½ teaspoon turmeric

¼ **cup water**
¼ - 1 **cup plain yogurt (the lesser amount for** *Pitta* **and** *Kapha***)**
¼ **cup additional water**
½ **teaspoon sea salt**
¼ **teaspoon cinnamon**
½ **teaspoon curry powder, mild**
1 **teaspoon coriander powder**
Shredded unsweetened coconut as garnish
Fresh coriander leaves, chopped, as garnish

Wash vegetables and dice into ½ to 1 inch pieces. Heat oil or *ghee* in large skillet; add mustard seeds and *hing*. When mustard seeds pop, add turmeric, ¼ cup water, parsnips and carrots. Stir well. Cover and cook on medium heat for 15 minutes. Add yogurt, rest of water, and rest of spices. Cook another 5 minutes, covered, over low heat. Garnish with coconut and fresh coriander leaves.

Comments: This goes well with rice, barley, or cracked wheat. This recipe also makes a good vegetable side dish, if you omit the yogurt and additional water.

*Kaphas can take a pinch of dry ginger with this to calm its effect for them.

OKRA CURRY

Preparation time: 25 to 30 minute   Serves: 5- 6
– *Vata,* – *Pitta,* + *Kapha*   ✿ ✳ 🐛 ❄

½ **pound fresh okra (2 cups chopped)**
1½ **tablespoons sunflower oil**
1 **teaspoon black mustard seeds**
½ **teaspoon cumin seeds**
½ **teaspoon turmeric**
2 **cups plain fresh yogurt or buttermilk**
3 **cups water**
4 **tablespoons chickpea (garbanzo) flour**
1 **teaspoon sea salt**
3 **tablespoons rice syrup or barley malt**
3 **tablespoons lime or lemon juice**
¼ **hot green pepper, chopped (optional)**

Wash and dry okra thoroughly. Cut into ½ inch pieces; throw the tops away. Heat oil in large (over 2 quarts) saucepan, add mustard and cumin seeds. When mustard seeds pop, add turmeric and okra. Cover and cook over low heat for 5 minutes. Combine yogurt, water and chickpea flour in a large bowl. Beat until smooth. Add this yogurt mixture to the okra, with remaining ingredients. Boil uncovered over medium heat for 15 to 20 minutes, stirring occasionally so that it will not stick.

Comment: This goes well with rice, *chappati,* and a vegetable side dish.

ABOUT DAIRY PRODUCTS

Eggs, milk, yogurt, and other dairy products are building in nature. They take a little more energy to digest than foods which have water as the basis for their broths. The following recipes are some of the lightest and easiest to digest of those using dairy products.

Hard cheeses, while delicious, are hard to digest at best. Too salty and oily for Pitta or Kapha, their blatant heaviness makes them a challenge for even the Vata digestive tract. "But they're so easy and tasty!" you exclaim. It's true. What can I say? Unless you are of a genetic heritage that has eaten cheese for centuries, it is best served at most occasionally, with a touch of warming spices like fresh basil leaves, black pepper or chili. Perhaps this is why raw onion is added to so many delicatessen-style sandwiches: you need to eat something quite hot to get the agni going enough to handle hard cheeses.

In Ayurveda, there is the concept of okasatmya. This term is used to describe diets and lifestyles which have become non-harmful to the body through regular and habitual use. Like the poison of a snake, they have become "part and parcel of the nature of the body" so that even though they would be harmful to another, to the snake they cause no harm. If you are of an ancestry that is used to eating large quantities of it, you may have a bit of an advantage in terms of being able to metabolize it. I once worked with a couple who were of Hispanic and Scandinavian descent, respectively. The Hispanic husband was struggling with a high cholesterol problem. The Swedish wife had eaten as much of their mutually adored Swiss cheese as her partner had, but with no elevation of blood fats whatsoever.

Hard cheese is not a regular part of Indian cuisine, so perhaps Ayurveda has not given it a fair shake. "The Healing Power of Cheese". . . well to be honest, I can't imagine it. Save it for your hungry kids, voracious and active teenagers and Vatas *in need of grounding.*

Sour cream is hot, sour and heavy. It is good to calm down an occasional Vata *baked potato, although yogurt or cottage cheese spread tastes scrumptious in that role as well.*

The regular use of evaporated milk is not recommended in Ayurveda.

Ice cream, the bane of Kapha, *is not bad for* Pitta *and chilly for* Vata. *One might want to try frozen yogurt. It has all the same cool moist sweet qualities as ice cream, but with a good deal less fat. Or try sherbet, or every now and then enjoy washing ice cream down with copious quantities of hot ginger tea and cardamom for balance. A dubious option.*

Buttermilk is light, sweet and sour. Regular use of fresh buttermilk tonifies the small intestine and can be serviceable in alleviating hemorrhoids. It is calming and grounding for Vata. Pittas *can best use it diluted and sweetened, not straight. Its lightness makes it an occasional option for* Kapha, *especially diluted with water. It should not be boiled, as its breakdown in this process makes it unhealthy. Buttermilk is used as an antidote to improper use of* ghee *in oleation therapy. Commercial buttermilk is more sour and heavy than the homemade variety.*

Homemade Indian buttermilk is the liquid left over after the churning of butter. Unless you happen to make your own butter from scratch, you are unlikely to have access to buttermilk as it was used in the ancient recipes. A reasonable equivalent is to dilute fresh yogurt one to one with water. It has many of the same tonifying effects on the digestive tract, and works well in the dishes here.

Ghee is highly valued in Ayurvedic healing as a rejuvenative and elixir. With milk or alone, it is particularly restorative to Vata *and* Pitta. *It is sweet, cool, light and oily.* Kaphas *can use it in small amounts to good benefit. It is easier to digest and aids absorption of other nutrients in a way that regular butter cannot. Whether it increases cholesterol levels or accumulates the chemicals found in butter currently on the market is not known. One can assume that it does contain cholesterol. It has been used for centuries as one of the most effective ways to absorb a wide variety of Ayurvedic medicinals. While it can be purchased in East Indian stores, it is simple and more inexpensive to make. The process takes about 15 minutes and uses 1 pound of unsalted sweet butter in a heavy saucepan (see p. 82).*

ABOUT YOGURT

Yogurt is a fascinating and useful food. It is particularly calming to the digestive tract, as people throughout the world have discovered. It can calm a

mild case of diarrhea or move along a constipated system. The addition of warming spices such as pepper or ginger will definitely assist in this latter action. Regular use of yogurt will frequently relieve long-standing bloating and restore a healthy bacterial balance to the colon. In action, it is initially cooling. Yet in the long run it is warming to the body. Its qualities and tastes are heavy, moist, sour, and astringent. It is especially calming for Vatas, and it can be used by them freely as a condiment and main dish. Pittas must take some care in preparing yogurt to ensure its balance for them. Taken plain and straight it is too hot and sour for regular Pitta use. Diluted one to one or more with water and sweetened with maple syrup, barley malt or fruit it is good for this fiery dosha, particularly if Pitta adds a bit of lemon juice and coriander powder or cinnamon to the mixture. A pinch of turmeric can also be added to enhance yogurt's digestibility, especially for Pitta. Kapha is best off consuming yogurt well-diluted in sauces, such as the curries offered here, or sweetened with honey as a drink (see KAPHA LASSI, p. 256). Honey, cinnamon, ginger, black pepper, and cardamom are especially appropriate for making yogurt assimilable for Kapha. Honey enhances the astringent qualities of yogurt, while the spices provide pungency. Yogurt and water can be added to many of the Indian vegetable side dishes for quick and easy main meals served over rice.

FRESH YOGURT

Preparation time: 1½ to 2 days
·*Vata, 0 Pitta, +Kapha**

Serves: 4-6

❁ ✴ 🐌 ❄

3 cups milk
½ cup yogurt

Heat milk in a large pan to boiling, take off heat and leave out at room temperature to cool. Then mix the yogurt in well with a spoon. Cover it with a suitable lid and leave it in a warm place (over the pilot light of the stove or near the radiator) for about 1½ to 2 days.

*Prepared as described above.

GHEE (CLARIFIED BUTTER)

Preparation time: 30 minutes
−*Vata, −Pitta −Kapha*

Makes: about 2 cups

❁ ✴ 🐌 ❄

1 pound sweet unsalted butter

In a heavy medium saucepan, heat butter over medium heat. Continue to cook at medium-low heat. The butter will bubble and make bubbling sounds. When it is almost done, milk solids will begin to collect on the bottom of the pan. When it is done, in about 15 to 20 minutes, it will be clear and become very quiet. Quickly take it off the heat before it burns, which it can do rapidly (if this happens it will begin to foam again rapidly and turn brown instead of golden). Cool slightly. *Ghee* is the clear golden liquid. Pour *ghee* through a metal strainer into glass or plastic container. Store at room temperature.

Comments: Superb aid for digestion and absorption. If you do not cook *ghee* long enough, it can mold. If you cook it too long, it will let you know immediately by burning. A touch of browning, though, can add a nice flavor. Some practitioners do not skim the foam off, valuing its medicinal elements; others do.

After making this once, you are likely to do it again and again, as it is simple and not nearly so difficult as the instructions make it out to be. Commercial *ghee* sold in markets is not infrequently adulterated with oil and often does not have the sweet light taste of true *ghee*. Plus, it is expensive.

ARUGULA SOUFFLE

Preparation time: 1 hour   Serves: 4-6.
*0 Vata, −Pitta, −Kapha**   ❀ ✳ ☙ ❅
*−Vata, −Pitta, +Kapha***

> 1 cup soy, goat or cow's milk
> 3 tablespoons *ghee*
> 3 tablespoons whole wheat flour or barley flour
> 1 bunch fresh raw arugula (or watercress) (equal to 1 cup cooked)
> 6 dried Shiitake mushrooms, soaked and chopped finely
> 1 egg yolk
> ½ teaspoon sea salt
> ¼ teaspoon nutmeg
> ¼ teaspoon paprika
> Black pepper to taste
> 4 egg whites
> ⅛ teaspoon cream of tartar

Wash, chop and steam arugula until tender (5 minutes or less.) Puree in the blender until smooth.

Melt *ghee* in medium saucepan; slowly stir in flour to make a paste. Gradually add milk, stirring constantly over medium heat. Continuing on medium heat, bring the mixture to a boil. Stir in the pureed greens and chopped mushrooms. Reduce heat to low and gently stir in the egg yolk. Cook for 1 to 2 minutes on low, adding the herbs and spices as you cook it. Remove from heat and let cool.

While vegetable mixture is cooling, beat egg whites with cream of tartar in clean bowl until stiff (peak). You will get best results if there is no egg yolk or fat in the whites at all and they are at room temperature. Gently fold egg whites into cooled vegetable mixture and place in an ungreased souffle or baking dish (one that is about half as deep as it is wide). Bake at 325 degrees for 30 to 45 minutes, or until the souffle is firm. Best eaten immediately, though it usually will hold its height for up to 10 minutes after removing from the oven.

Comment: Good with rice or bread and a salad.

*when made with goat milk and barley flour
**when made with soy or cow milk and whole wheat flour

ASPARAGUS SOUFFLE

Preparation time: 1 hour   Serves: 4-6
0 Vata, − Pitta, − Kapha*   ✿   ✳   ঽ
− Vata, − Pitta, + Kapha**

> 1 cup milk (soy, goat, or cow)
> 3 tablespoons *ghee*
> 3 tablespoons barley flour or whole wheat flour
> 1 pound fresh asparagus (about 1 cup cooked)
> 1 egg yolk
> ½ teaspoon sea salt
> ¼ teaspoon fresh ground black pepper
> 4 egg whites
> ⅛ teaspoon cream of tartar
> Paprika as garnish

Wash asparagus and chop into 1 inch pieces. Steam until tender, about 8 minutes.

Melt *ghee* in medium saucepan; slowly stir in the flour. Add the milk gradually, stirring constantly over medium heat. The sauce will thicken as it cooks. Bring the mixture to a boil and stir in the cooked asparagus. Reduce heat to low and stir in the egg yolk. The mixture will thicken a bit more as you continue to cook it for another 1 to 2 minutes. Stir in the salt and pepper; remove from heat and let the mixture cool.

Beat egg whites with cream of tartar in a clean pottery, enamel, or stainless steel bowl (plastic will slow down the process somewhat). When egg whites are stiff enough to peak, fold them gently into the cooled asparagus sauce. Place the whole mixture in an ungreased souffle or baking dish (one that is about half as deep as it is wide). Sprinkle top with paprika. Bake at 325 degrees for 30 to 45 minutes, or until souffle is firm. The souffle will keep for a few minutes after taking it out of the oven before it falls, but it is best eaten immediately.

Comment: This goes well with salad and bread or rice.

Variation: Sprinkle with ¼ cup parmesan cheese for *Vata.*

*when made with goat or soy milk and barley flour
**when made with cow's milk and whole wheat flour

ASPARAGUS CREAM SAUCE

Preparation time: 20 minutes   Serves: 4
−Vata, moderately +Pitta, +Kapha*

  ½ pound fresh asparagus
  3 tablespoons *ghee*
  2 tablespoons barley flour
  2½ cups buttermilk
  ½ teaspoon sea salt
  Paprika as garnish

Wash asparagus and chop into ½ to 1 inch pieces. Warm *ghee* in heavy saucepan or skillet; saute asparagus in *ghee* until tender. Stir barley flour into *ghee*, pushing the asparagus aside as you do. Add buttermilk slowly, stirring well into the flour-*ghee* mixture to avoid creating lumps. Cook over low heat until thick. Add salt. Sprinkle paprika over the sauce on serving.

Comments: Good over rice, toast, or eggs, used like a Hollandaise sauce. Barley flour and buttermilk were an ancient way to calm and tonify the digestion. Together they make a light tangy, lemon-flavored sauce.

*Fine for occasional use.

SPICY BUTTERMILK

Preparation time: 15 minutes   Serves 3-4
—Vata, moderately +Pitta, +Kapha*   🐌 ❄️

> **2 cups buttermilk (or 1 cup plain yogurt with 1 cup water)**
> **1 teaspoon sunflower oil**
> **1 teaspoon cumin seeds**
> **1 teaspoon sea salt**
> **¹/₂ teaspoon ground cumin**
> **¹/₂ teaspoon freshly ground black pepper**
> **1 teaspoon Sucanat**

Heat oil in a small skillet. Add cumin seeds and heat until they are brown. Mix in the buttermilk (or yogurt and water) and the rest of the ingredients. Mix well. Heat to warm over low heat, but DO NOT LET IT BOIL. (This would ruin its digestibility, as well as its looks.)

Comments: Traditionally, this dish is served over *dhokalas, pudas,* or *vatas.* It makes an excellent sauce over most of the Indian-style vegetables offered in the VEGETABLE section (p. 147), turning them into quick main dishes with rice. Cut out the salt in either the buttermilk sauce or the vegetables if you combine them in this way.

*Fine for occasional use.

ABOUT MUSHROOMS

    Mushrooms are light, dry and cool—unless they are placed in a heavy moist sauce. Then, warmed and spiced, they can be suitable for Vata. *Plain, they benefit* Pitta *and* Kapha. *Shiitake mushrooms are similar in their effects, but have more salt and pungency to their flavor. Thus they warm more than regular mushrooms. They enhance immune function significantly. Dried Shiitake mushrooms offer the most economy and flexibility, as they can be kept on hand and used whenever needed. Well-soaked, they are beneficial for all constitutions, especially* Kapha. Vatas *need to eat them in moderation as large amounts of the dried variety can be aggravating to them.*

MUSHROOMS IN YOGURT

Preparation time: 15 minutes

Serves: 3-4

—Vata, +Pitta, +Kapha

> **2 cups mushrooms, sliced (½ pound)**
> **1½ cups plain yogurt**
> **2 tablespoons *ghee* or melted butter**
> **½ teaspoon cumin seeds**
> **½ teaspoon ground cumin**
> **½ teaspoon sea salt**
> **¼ teaspoon black pepper, fresh ground if you have it**
> **¼ teaspoon nutmeg**

Wash, dry and slice mushrooms.

Heat *ghee* or butter in a medium sauce pan. Add cumin seeds. When they turn brown, add sliced mushrooms and cook over low heat for 5 to 7 minutes. Then cool. Add yogurt and remaining ingredients and mix well. Serve.

Comments: This rich dish goes well with bread or rice.

Variation: *Pitta-Vata** Version of MUSHROOMS IN YOGURT OVER PASTA:
Increase the mushrooms to 4 cups. While the mushrooms are cooking, stir in 2 tablespoons chickpea flour. Use ¾ cup plain yogurt and ¾ cup water in place of the 1½ cups yogurt; stir the yogurt and water together. Stir this into the mushroom mixture and heat over low heat for about 5 minutes or until sauce begins to thicken. Add the rest of the ingredients, plus 1 teaspoon brown rice syrup and 1 teaspoon ground coriander. Serve warm. Good over pasta.

* —Vata, —Pitta, moderately + Kapha.

ABOUT BEANS

Beans, served with grains, form the staple food for many main dishes around the world. They are used for both cleansing and building in Ayurveda. Not only are they low in fat and high in fiber, they also provide significant amounts of protein, iron, B vitamins and other trace minerals. As a food crop, they nourish the soil rather than rob it of vital nutrients, through their function of nitrogen fixation. Nitrogen-fixing bacteria in beans can pull in over one hundred pounds of nitrogen from the atmosphere per year per acre and offer it in usable form to the soil they grow in. This is a valuable alternative to the synthetic nitrogen fertilizers, which are generally made from oil or natural gas products. The latter have harsh effects on the earth and are becoming increasingly short in supply.

The trick, of course, is how to digest beans. If you are just beginning to add them to your diet, it is wise to try them no more than once or twice per week for the first few weeks. The average person can usually tolerate legumes three to four times per week with acculturation, balanced agni, and sound preparation. Expecting yourself to eat more than this, unless you grew up eating beans daily, is probably unrealistic and may only create the largest methane-producing digester in your area (you). The key is to discover which beans are most appropriate for you, and how to properly prepare them so as to minimize gas-producing qualities. The following recipes emphasize this.

Split mung beans are one of the most popular staples in India and are highly regarded in Ayurveda. They are lighter and easier to digest than most other beans and are used widely for healing, especially in the restorative and cleansing Indian dishes kichadi and dal. They tend to be slightly cool in their effect on the body; Vata and Kapha diners seeking to offset this effect can do so easily with warming spices such as ginger, black pepper, cumin, and mustard seeds. They are fine "as is" for Pitta, or can be served with the above spices balanced with a healthy amount of coriander powder or leaves. In the United States it can be difficult to find split mung or mung dal as it is called, unless you have an Indian grocery in your area. It is also sold as "yellow dal." Whole mung beans are more readily available, yet not quite so easy to digest. A good way to approximate split mung with whole mung is to soak the whole bean overnight, rinsing frequently. Even better, soak the whole bean until it sprouts, about three or four days, rinsing once to twice daily. The husk can then be removed and you have the split bean. They are an excellent legume for year-round use, especially in spring, summer and fall.

TRIDOSHIC DAL

Preparation time: 1 hour   Serves: 6
−Vata, −Pitta, 0 Kapha*   ✿   ✳   🍵   ❄

      1 cup split mung *dal*
      8 cups water
      2 cups summer squash, in ¼ to ½ inch slices
      1 cup carrots, in ¼ to ½ inch slices
      ⅛ teaspoon hing
      2 tablespoons sunflower oil or *ghee*
      1¼ teaspoons turmeric
      1 tablespoon lime or lemon juice or 1 tablespoon *amchoor* (dried mango powder)
      1 teaspoon sea salt
      ½ tablespoon fresh ginger root, minced
      1 small hot green pepper, chopped finely or ¼ cup prepared salsa (omit for *Pitta,* and easy on this for *Vata*)
      1¼ tablespoon cumin seeds
      ½ teaspoonto 1 tablespoon black mustard seeds (the smaller amount for *Pitta,* the greater amount for *Vata* and *Kapha*)

Garnish: Fresh coriander leaves, chopped and shredded unsweetened coconut

Wash *dal* until rinse water is clear. Wash and chop vegetables.

Warm 1 tablespoon oil or *ghee* in large heavy saucepan. Add *hing*, turmeric, and lemon juice and saute for 30 seconds over low heat (be careful, it is easy for turmeric to burn). Stir in the beans and saute for another 1 to 2 minutes. Add the chopped vegetables and stir another minute or two. Add water, salt, ginger, and pepper (if you are using it); bring to a boil on high heat. Then cover and reduce heat to medium-low. Let soup simmer for 45 minutes or until beans have dissolved. Warm remaining tablespoon of oil or *ghee* in a small skillet, add cumin and mustard seeds, heat until the mustard seeds begin to pop. Add to soup, which is now ready to serve. Garnish with fresh chopped coriander leaves and coconut.

Comments: *Dals* are an easy and popular way in India to get a nourishing protein-rich meal. They are good served with "PLAIN" INDIAN RICE (p. 129) and a vegetable side dish. This *dal* originally evolved from one served by the Hari Krishna people here in the States.

Dals are always prepared with something sour in the *vagar* (mixture of spices and *ghee*) to stimulate digestive fire. In Bombay, *tamarind* is often used, while in the Gujarati province, lemon, lime or *amchoor* add this stimulating sourness. It must be added in the early stages of cooking for best effect.

*Serve with warming condiments such as chopped scallion, fresh green chili or dry ginger to calm Kapha.

GUJARATI *TRIDOSHIC DAL*

Preparation time: 40 minutes plus 2 hour soak for split mung
1 hour 15 minutes plus 2 hour soak for whole mung   Serves: 6-8
−*Vata,* −*Pitta,* −*Kapha*

> 1³⁄₄ cups split mung *dal* or whole mung beans
> 6¹⁄₂ cups water
> 1 tablespoon sunflower oil or *ghee*
> ¹⁄₂ teaspoon mustard seeds
> ¹⁄₂ teaspoon turmeric
> ¹⁄₈ teaspoon *hing*
> 1 teaspoon sea salt
> 1¹⁄₂ teaspoons barley malt or brown rice syrup
> 1¹⁄₂ teaspoons lime or lemon juice
> 1 teaspoon coriander powder
> ¹⁄₂ teaspoon cinnamon
> ¹⁄₄ teaspoon curry powder, mild
> ¹⁄₄ green pepper, chopped (optional, omit for *Pitta*)
> 1 clove garlic, minced (optional, omit for *Pitta*)

Soak mung for 2 hours, then drain. In large heavy sauce pan heat oil or *ghee* and add
mustard seeds. When they pop, add turmeric, *hing,* mung, water, and remaining
ingredients. Mix well. Cover and cook for ¹⁄₂ hour if split mung, 1 hour if whole
mung, or until mung is quite soft.

Comments: This is good with *chappatis,* BUTTERMILK CURRY (p. 78), rice, and
vegetables. Good all-purpose *dal* from the Gujarati region. The soaking is important
to minimize gas. The beans can be soaked overnight if this is more convenient for
you. *Kapha* needs to garnish with peppers and dry ginger for this recipe to be
calming.

TUR DAL

Preparation time: 2 hours   Serves: 6
−Vata, + +Pitta, −Kapha   ✿ ⚘ ❄

Follow the recipe for *TRIDOSHIC DAL* (p. 89), and substitute 1 cup *tur dal* (available in Indian groceries) for the split mung *dal*. Prepare as directed, adding 2 to 3 cloves of garlic with the salt and ginger and the maximum amount of spices in all choices. You may need as much as 12 cups of water to cook this *dal* until soft. Add 1 teaspoon ground coriander before serving to calm and relax the flavor of the beans a bit and to aid digestion.

Comments: *Tur dal* is a hot, light, dry bean helpful for *Vata* and *Kapha* and definitely aggravating for *Pitta*. Not for those with inflamed gastrointestinal tracts. Easy to find in India, this legume is rarely found anywhere in this country besides Indian groceries. It is often oiled and packed in small plastic bags.

ZUCCHINI AND MUNG DAL

Preparation time: 1 to 1½ hours, plus 2 hours to soak   Serves: 4-5
−Vata, −Pitta, −Kapha   ✹

> 1 cup split mung *dal* or whole mung beans
> 1½ tablespoons sunflower oil
> ½ teaspoon mustard seeds
> ½ teaspoon turmeric
> ⅛ teaspoon *hing*
> 1 tablespoon lime juice
> 4 cups water
> 2 cups zucchini cut in ½ inch cubes
> 1 teaspoon fresh ginger root, finely minced
> 1 teaspoon sea salt
> ½-1 teaspoon coriander powder
> ¼ hot green chili pepper, chopped (optional, omit for *Pitta*)

Soak mung in 4 cups water for 2 hours. Heat oil in heavy skillet, add mustard seeds. When they pop, add turmeric, *hing,* lime juice, and drained mung beans. Add fresh ginger root and 4 cups of water. Cover and cook over medium heat for 20 minutes if split mung, 1 hour or more if whole mung beans. Add zucchini and remaining ingredients and cook 15 minutes or until beans are soft.

Comments: This goes well with rice and *rotali. Pitta* needs to garnish lavishly with chopped coriander leaves or coriander powder to offset the fresh ginger.

MUNG *DAL* WITH SPINACH

Preparation time: with pressure cooker, 45 minutes   Serves: 3-4
Without pressure cooker, 1 hour or more   ✿ 🐌 ❄
−*Vata, moderately* +*Pitta, 0 Kapha*

> 1 cup split mung *dal*
> 4½ cups water (1-2 cups more for high-altitude chefs)
> ⅛ teaspoon *hing*
> 1 tablespoon sunflower oil
> ½ teaspoon mustard seeds
> 1 teaspoon cumin seeds
> 3 cloves garlic, minced
> 1 teaspoon turmeric
> 1 teaspoon sea salt
> ¼ hot green chili pepper (optional, best for *Kapha*)
> 1½ teaspoons coriander powder
> 1 teaspoon brown rice syrup (optional, omit for *Kapha*)
> 1 tablespoon lime or lemon juice
> 2 cups fresh spinach, chopped

Garnish: fresh coriander leaves, chopped

Wash the *dal* well and put it in the pressure cooker with the water and *hing*. Bring to pressure and cook for 15 minutes. Or, use a regular pot, bring to a boil, cover and cook until tender, about 45 minutes.

In a small skillet, warm the oil and add the cumin, garlic and mustard seeds. When the mustard seeds pop, stir in the turmeric and combine the mixture with the cooked mung *dal*. Add the rest of the ingredients except the spinach and cook for 10 minutes. Then add the spinach and cover and cook until tender, 5- 10 minutes more over medium heat.

Comments: This goes well with *chappatis* and a vegetable side dish. If *Pitta* yearns for this dish, omit the mustard seeds and substitute 2 tablespoons chopped onion for the garlic, sauteing it until sweet, with the spices. Then, 0 *Pitta*.

AMA-REDUCING *DAL*

Preparation time: 3 days to sprout mung, 30 minutes to 1 hour to make the soup
−*Vata,* −*Pitta,* −*Kapha** 	 Serves: 5-6
−*Vata,* +*Pitta,* −*Kapha*** 	 ✿ ✳ 🐌 ❄

2 to 3 cups sprouted mung beans
2 to 3 cups vegetables, chopped (broccoli, carrots, greens, sprouts, green beans or asparagus work well)
1½ tablespoons *ghee* or olive oil
1 to 2 inches of garlic, or fresh ginger root, peeled and chopped finely
1 to 3 cloves crushed (omit if *Pitta* is high)
½ to 1 teaspoon cumin seeds
1 teaspoon coriander seeds
½ to 1 teaspoon turmeric
½ teaspoon fresh ground black pepper
2 to 3 bay leaves
⅛ teaspoon each of fennel seed, *hing*, cinnamon, and cardamom
½ cup fresh coriander leaves, chopped

Garnish: coconut and more chopped coriander leaves

In a pressure cooker, cook sprouted mung for about two minutes after reaching full pressure, or cook the beans in water in a covered saucepan until soft. Using the cooking water, puree mung in blender. Set aside.

In soup pot, warm *ghee* or oil. Add spices and toss until coated and their aromas emerge. Add chopped vegetables to spices and oil and toss until coated. Stir for two minutes, then add 4 to 6 cups of water. Mix well. Bring to boil, then reduce heat and simmer covered until veggies are cooked. Add pureed mung beans to soup pot. Stir. Bring to boil again. Reduce heat and let soup simmer for five minutes. Add more water if a thinner consistency is desired. Add salt to taste, about ½ teaspoon.

Comments: This recipe comes from Ivy Blank, Director of The Ayurveda Center of Santa Fe, based on a dish made by Drs. Smita and Pankaj Naram of Bombay. It is specifically designed to reduce *ama* and rest the digestive tract during illness, convalescence or rejuvenation therapy. The mung beans are cooling by nature, yet are warmed by the addition of the ginger and the other warming spices. Amounts of the spices and the type of vegetables used can be adjusted to suit the individual. One stick of kombu can also be added to reduce gas and add trace minerals. This is an excellent one-dish meal which can be served a few times each week to rest the system, if you like.

NOTE: If you are using this dish during *Pancha Karma* therapy, increase the oil or *ghee* to 5 to 6 tablespoons for best effects. Greater amounts of oleation are needed during this process.

*without garlic
**with garlic

ABOUT BLACK LENTILS

Black lentils (urud dal) *are especially useful as a restorative for* Vata. *They are used in small amounts in the later stages of convalescence from illness as well. Yet because they are heavy, digestive assistance is usually necessary. Cumin and* hing *(asafoetida) provide warmth and carminative action.* Asafoetida *also acts to enkindle* agni *and discourage the growth of parasitic worms in the large intestine. A pinch of* hing *can be added to almost any bean dish in the early stages of preparation to make it more assimilable and balancing for* Vata.

BLACK LENTILS WITH YOGURT

Preparation time: 1 hour   Serves 4-5
−*Vata,* +*Pitta, moderately* +*Kapha*

> ½ **cup dry black lentils** *(urud dal)*
> 3 **cups water**
> ½ **teaspoon sea salt**
> 1 **teaspoon ground cumin**
> ⅛ **teaspoon** *hing*
> 1 **clove garlic, finely minced**
> 1 **tablespoon barley malt or brown rice syrup**

Garnish: yogurt to taste

Wash lentils. Cook covered in water with *hing* until soft, 25 to 30 minutes over medium heat. Add salt, cumin, garlic, and barley malt. Cook 20 more minutes.

Comments: This goes well with bread and vegetables or rice. Excellent dish for *Vata* as it is very strengthening. It should be tried in very small quantities at first, as it is a concentrated food. Can be eaten occasionally by *Pitta* and *Kapha,* but it is imbalancing if eaten on a regular basis. Serve with yogurt for *Vata,* or CAULIFLOWER KAHDI (p. 190) for *Pitta* and *Kapha.*

URUD DAL (BLACK LENTIL DAL)

Preparation time: 1½-2 hours
—Vata, +Pitta, +Kapha

Serves: 5-6

¾ cup split urud dal (split black lentils, ivory in color, available in Indian groceries)
6-8 cups water
⅛ teaspoon *hing*
1 stick of kombu
3 cups fresh vegetables (carrots and zucchini are good)
2 tablespoons sunflower oil or *ghee*
1 teaspoon black mustard seeds
1 teaspoon cumin seeds
1 tablespoon lemon juice or *tamarind*
3 cloves of garlic, minced
½ medium onion, chopped
1 teaspoon turmeric
1 tablespoon sesame seeds (optional, enhances *Vata* calming effect)
1 teaspoon sea or rock salt
1 tablespoon fresh ginger root, minced
3 tablespoons fresh coriander leaves, chopped
Small green chili pepper (optional)

Garnish: chopped coriander leaves, ginger or yogurt

Wash *ukrud dal* well; drain.

Put *dal, hing,* kombu, and 6 cups of water in a large saucepan and bring to boil over high heat. Reduce to medium-low heat and cover. Cook until *dal* is soft, about 1 hour. In the meanwhile, wash and chop the vegetables and onion. Carrots are attactive slicd in half-moon shapes (cut the carrot in half lengthwise then slice crosswise) with zucchini in full-rounds. When the *dal* is close to being cooked, warm the oil or *ghee* in a medium-sized skillet and add the mustard and cumin seeds. When the mustard pops, add the lemon juice, onion, garlic, sesame, and turmeric. Stir well and saute until onion is tender.

When the *dal* is soft, stir the spices and onion into it. Add the salt and chopped vegetables. Cover and cook over medium heat another 20 minutes. While it is cooking, put the ginger, coriander, pepper, and 1 cup of water in the blender and blend. Ten minutes before serving, add this blended mixture and cook ten minutes more. Add more water if the soup needs to be thinned; it should be the consistency of a very thick pea soup.

SWEET CHICKPEAS

Preparation time: 20 minutes, if using pre-cooked chickpeas   Serves: 4
mildly +Vata, −Pitta, 0 Kapha   ❁   ✳   ❄

> 2 cups cooked chickpeas (garbanzos)
> 2 cups parsnips grated (about 2 medium parsnips)
> 1 large onion, grated
> 1 to 2 tablespoons sunflower oil (the lesser amount for
> **Kapha**)
> ½ teaspoon *ajwan*
> ⅛ teaspoon *hing*
> ½ teaspoon turmeric
> ½ teaspoon sea salt
> ½ cup water

Garnish: Fresh coriander leaves, chopped

Warm the oil in a large skillet and add the *ajwan* and *hing*. Brown them lightly. Stir in the chickpeas, parsnips, turmeric and onion and saute about 5 minutes. Add the rest of the ingredients and cook an additional 10 minutes or until the parsnip and onion are sweet and tender. Garnish with fresh chopped coriander leaves.

Comments: For some *Vatas*, this could moderately imbalance them. The more thoroughly the chickpeas are cooked, the less chance of this. Really scrumptious and easy dish. If you are making the chickpeas from scratch, and have a pressure cooker, allow an extra 40 minutes. Combine 1 cup of dried chickpeas, 4½ cups of water, 1 stick of kombu, and ⅛ teaspoon *hing* in a pressure cooker. Cover and bring to pressure; cook for 30 minutes.

MUNG BURGERS

Preparation time: 1½ hours with a pressure cooker
2 hours without
0 Vata, 0 Pitta, 0 Kapha*
−Vata, −Pitta, moderately +Kapha**

Serves: 5-6

✿ ✳ 🌰 ❄

> 1 cup whole mung beans
> 4-5 cups water
> 2 tablespoons brown or wild rice
> 1 stick kombu
> ¹⁄₁₆ teaspoon *hing*
> 1 teaspoon sunflower oil
> ½ medium onion, finely chopped
> ½ teaspoon cumin seeds
> ½ teaspoon dry oregano
> 2 medium red potatoes, unpeeled
> 1 egg white
> 1 teaspoon-2 tablespoons stoneground mustard (the lesser for *Pitta,*
> *Vata* and *Kapha* can use up to the maximum as they like)
> 1 teaspoon sea or rock salt
> ¼ teaspoon freshly ground black pepper
> 2 tablespoons barley or whole wheat flour

*VERSION 1: Combine the mung beans, water, rice, kombu and *hing* in a pressure cooker and bring to pressure and cook for 25 minutes (if you like your burgers chewy, make it 20 minutes). If you are not using a pressure cooker, bring the beans to a boil with the rest of these first ingredients and then cover and cook over medium heat for an hour, or until soft.

While the beans are cooking, wash the potatoes and cut them in quarters, then eighths. Chop the onion. Warm the oil in a large skillet and add the cumin, oregano and onion. Saute until the onion is tender and the herbs are lightly browned. Set aside and wait for the beans to be done.

When the beans are done, cool the pot in cool water to bring it down from pressure, open it, and add the potatoes. Cook uncovered until the potatoes are soft, about 20-30 minutes. Add the beans and potatoes to the herbs in the skillet and mash. Stir in the egg white, mustard and salt and pepper. Add the flour if the burgers need thickening. Form into patties and cook on a non-stick pan until brown, flipping to brown the other side. Or cook them on a cookie sheet in a 350 degree oven for 20-30 minutes. Makes 10 to 12 3" to 4" burgers.

Comment: This goes well with ARTICHOKE HEART SALAD (p. 205).

**VERSION 2: Substitute 1 large sweet potato for the 2 red potatoes. Wash and peel it and add it the same time the potatoes would have been added, after the beans have cooked. Omit the oregano and mustard and add 1 teaspoon fresh ginger root, finely chopped or minced, and 1 teaspoon mild curry powder.

Comments: These disappear rapidly when served at our house. A no-cholesterol option to good old beef burgers.

MATAJI'S POTATO & GREEN PEA PATTIES

Preparation time: 1 hour
moderately +Vata, −Pitta, −Kapha

Serves: 5-6

✿   ✳   ❄

> 5 medium red potatoes
> 1 tablespoon sunflower oil
> ½ teaspoon mustard seeds
> 1 teaspoon sea salt
> 1 tablespoon lemon juice
> ½ teaspoon freshly ground black pepper
> 1 tablespoon sesame seeds
> 2 teaspoons Sucanat
> 3 cups frozen green peas

Put water on to boil in a large pot for the potatoes. Boil potatoes with their skins on. Cool. While the potatoes are cooking, heat oil in a medium-sized skillet and add mustard seeds. Blend the peas in the blender. When the mustard seeds pop, add green peas and salt to the oil. Cook over low heat for about 10 to 15 minutes or until all the water is absorbed. Add remaining ingredients and mix well. Cool. Take pota-toes and mash them in a separate bowl, then make 10 to 12 balls. Flatten the potato balls into patties, then place pea mixture in their centers. Fold and seal, pressing together with hands and reforming into round patties. Heat iron pan, and add enough oil to keep from sticking. If making for *Kapha,* use a non-stick pan and no oil. Cook patties over low heat until brown on both sides. Serve hot.

Comments: If you add extra *ghee* as a garnish for *Vata,* these are OK for occasional use.

One of Mataji's favorites, these are scrumptious on toast for lunch, or served with *raita* and a vegetable side dish for dinner.

CURRIED POTATO PATTIES WITH CARROTS

Preparation time: 1 hour
Serves: 8
− *Vata,* + *Pitta,* − *Kapha*
✿ 🐚 ❄

>   6 large or 8 small red potatoes
>   2 large carrots (2 cups grated)
>   1½ tablespoons sunflower oil
>   1 tablespoon black mustard seeds
>   1 tablespoon curry powder
>   1 to 1½ teaspoons sea salt (to taste, the lesser amount for *Kapha*)
>   ⅔ cup green onions, finely chopped
>   ½ cup fresh coriander leaves, finely chopped (optional)

Put water in a large pot to boil for the potatoes. Wash the potatoes well and leave on their skins. Put them in the water to boil until tender, about ½ hour. While they are cooking, wash and finely grate the carrots. Wash and finely chop the green onions. Put the oil in a large skillet and add the mustard seeds. When they pop, add the grated carrot and cook just long enough to wilt them slightly. Stir in the curry powder and salt. When the potatoes are done, drain them and let them cool enough to handle them. Mash them well, with a fork or your hands, and stir or mash in the rest of the ingredients, including the uncooked green onion and coriander leaves. Form the mixture into patties and cook on a skillet, browning them 1 to 2 minutes on each side. Serve hot. If you are working with *Kapha* or *ama,* use a non-stick pan and no oil. Makes 16 4 inch patties.

Comments: This goes well with CUCUMBER *RAITA* (p. 224), and a vegetable side dish. Garnish with extra *ghee* for *Vata.* These delicious patties come from Martha Callanan, cook and caterer extraordinaire in Santa Fe. She provides many of the dishes for the Marketplace Deli, and is about to offer a catering service for people looking for balanced dinners at home. Her interest in Ayurveda and her creative skill are reflected in this recipe.

When making this recipe for a mixed group of *Vatas* and *Kaphas,* you can make up the original recipe with a minimum of oil and make the *Kapha* patties first. I then add an extra tablespoon or two of oil or *ghee* to the remaining mixture before making patties for the *Vatas.*

Cucumbers and potatoes are a good way to understand more about how Ayurveda views foods. Both are cold and sweet, and yet cucumber is considered relieving to *Vata* and aggravating to *Kapha,* while potato is considered the opposite. It aggravates *Vata* and calms *Kapha.* Why so? How is it that starchy potato calms *Kapha* while burpy cucumber balances *Vata?* It is due to the effect of their *gunas.* Cucumber is moist, which *Vata* needs. And potato is dry, which *Kapha* needs. So *Vata* needs additional moisture with potatoes. The best bet is to try these and see for yourself what works.

TASTY CHICKPEAS

Preparation time: with pressure cooker, 40 minutes, without pressure cooker,
5 hours (can also be made in crock pot)   Serves: 6-7
+ *Vata,* − *Pitta,* − *Kapha*   ❀ ❄

> 1½ cups dry chickpeas (garbanzos)
> 2½ cups water (up to 4 cups for high- altitude cooking)
> 2 tablespoons sunflower oil
> ½ teaspoon mustard seeds
> 1 ripe tomato, cut in ½ inch pieces (optional, but delicious)
> 1 teaspoon curry powder, mild
> 2 tablespoons sesame seeds
> 1 teaspoon sea salt
> 1 teaspoon coriander powder
> ½ teaspoon turmeric

Soak the beans overnight, if possible. Discard water, use fresh water and pressure cook chickpeas at 15 pounds pressure over medium heat for 25 to 30 minutes.

Or boil in 4 cups of water for 2 minutes, then let soak in same water for 3 to 4 hours. Drain, discarding this water and add 2½ cups fresh water. Bring chickpeas and water to a boil, then cook at medium heat for 50 minutes or until quite soft.

When peas are cooked, heat oil in a heavy skillet, adding mustard seeds when oil is warm. When seeds pop, add chopped tomato and curry powder. Cook for 2 to 3 minutes. Add sesame seeds, chickpeas, salt, coriander, and turmeric. Mix well. Heat for 2 to 3 minutes.

Comment: This goes well with *chappatis* and is excellent with rice. Garbanzos are the most drying of all legumes, and so are especially excellent for damp *Kapha*. Being cool and dry, they need the help of garlic or mustard seeds to warm them, as well as a good long time to cook. A small amount of sesame seeds are often added to garbanzo (chickpea) dishes to make them more unctuous—warm and lubricated.

If this dish is made with Indian chickpeas (*kala chana*), which are dark brown, it makes a very pretty meal with cornbread and a colorful vegetable like sauteed broc-coli or sweetened carrot.

HOT KOREAN VEGETABLES AND NOODLES

Preparation time: 45 minutes   Serves: 3-4
– Vata, O Pitta, O Kapha   🐌 ❄

> 2 ounces cellophane noodles (mung bean noodles, Harasame or Saifun
> work well, available in Asian stores or import section of groceries)
> 4-8 dried Shiitake mushrooms
> 1 tablespoon sunflower oil
> 2 inches of fresh leek, finely sliced, or
> ½ small onion, finely sliced
> 1 unpeeled clove of garlic
> 1 cup carrots, thinly sliced or ½ cup snowpeas
> 1 cup spinach, finely chopped or broccoli, finely chopped
> 1 cup yellow crookneck summer squash, finely sliced
> 1 cup bean sprouts
> 2 teaspoons coriander powder
> 1 tablespoon tamari
> 1 teaspoon Sucanat
> 1 teaspoon oil
> 3 small cloves of garlic, minced (omit for *Pitta*)
> ½ teaspoon red chili powder or 1 hot red Chinese pepper, dried (omit for
> *Pitta*)

Soak the cellophane noodles and mushrooms in a medium-sized bowl, with enough water to cover them, for ½ hour. Wash and chop the vegetables. Drain the noodles and mushrooms well and thin-slice the Shiitake mushrooms.

Warm the oil in a large skillet and add the leek or onion with the unpeeled clove of garlic. Saute until sweet. Take out the clove of garlic. Add mushrooms, carrots, spinach, broccoli, and summer squash and saute until tender and bright in color, 3-5 minutes. Add the snowpeas and saute another minute. Stir in the bean sprouts and cook over medium head about 30 seconds. Add the noodles, coriander, tamari, and Sucanat and toss well.

Stop here and serve if you are working with any *Pitta* at all. If not, cover and set the dish aside for a moment, and in a small skillet warm 1 teaspoon oil (1 tablespoon if you are working with *Vata* alone) and saute the minced garlic until tender. Stir in the red pepper, crumbled if it is whole. Serve as a garnish on the side for *Vata* and *Kapha,* or mix into the noodles if there is not an ounce of *Pitta* in the company.

Comment: This goes well with MISO TOFU (p. 102).

ABOUT TOFU

Tofu and liquid soy milk tend to be cool and heavy, yet oilier than most other bean products. This oily lubricating quality helps their digestion, as does the pre-processing they have undergone as legumes. Like split mung, they can be used relatively easily by all types with just a bit of modification. Eaten in excess, they will increase Kapha. Warming preparation, in the form of heat or warming spices such as ginger, tamari, cumin, turmeric, cinnamon or mustard seeds, aid their healthy breakdown in the system. Beans can be idiosyncratic in effect though; if your experience doesn't match the descriptions given here, trust your direct experience first. Some people have a hard time digesting tofu in almost any form; an allergy to soy may be present. It was popular in the sixties and seventies to serve tofu cold, cubed and plain at health food-type salad bars. This is about the most difficult way to try to consume an already chilling food. Try tofu marinated, spiced and cooked, then make up your mind about its digestibility for you.

MISO TOFU

Preparation time: 15 to 20 minutes

−*Vata,* −*Pitta,* −*Kapha*

Serves 2-3

✿ 🌰 ❄

        1 carton (1 pound) tofu
        1 tablespoon sunflower oil
        ½ medium onion, finely sliced (optional)
        ⅛ teaspoon black pepper
        1 tablespoon barley miso or mellow white miso
        1 tablespoon tamari
        ¾ cup water
        3 dried Shiitake mushrooms (optional, tasty)

Put mushrooms in water to soak. Warm oil in heavy skillet and saute onion until tender, about 5 minutes. Drain tofu and cut into 1 inch cubes. Add it to the onion and stir-saute 5 minutes, sprinkling black pepper over it. Drain mushrooms, reserving water to be used in next step. Add mushrooms to sauteing tofu. Mix miso and tamari with water, pour over tofu in skillet. Heat another 3 minutes, then serve.

Comments: *Vata* needs to garnish with fresh grated ginger root to be balanced, *Kapha* should garnish with a pinch of dry ginger. The cooking, miso, and tamari warm the otherwise "cool" tofu. Salt is kept to a minimum by adding minimal amounts of miso and tamari, yet enough to enhance *agni* and make the tofu more easy for *Vata* to digest. Shiitake mushrooms add flavor and strengthen the immune system.

MIDDLE EASTERN CABBAGE-TOFU ENTREE

Preparation time: 45 minutes, plus overnight freeze and thaw   Serves: 4
mildly +Vata, −Pitta, mildly −Kapha

1 pound frozen tofu (or 2 cups cooked garbanzos)
1 large onion, chopped
2 tablespoons *ghee* or sunflower oil
1/4 teaspoon allspice
1/8 teaspoon fennel seeds
1/2 teaspoon turmeric
1 parsnip, chopped
1 small cabbage (3 cups chopped, raw)
1 large tomato or 1 cup tomato puree (optional, good, omit if *Pitta* is high)
3/4 teaspoon sea salt
2 tablespoons sunflower seeds
1 tablespoon pinon nuts (optional)
1/2 teaspoon spearmint, dry

Take tofu out of the freezer to thaw. (If you haven't frozen tofu before, all you need to do is put the package of tofu in the freezer overnight or longer. It creates a different chewier texture which is quite appealing in this dish.)

Wash parsnip and chop it into 1/2 inch pieces.

Put *ghee* in large skillet and add chopped onion. Add allspice and saute for 1 minute. Add turmeric and fennel, then chopped parsnip. Stir. Continue to saute until onion is tender and sweet. Add tomato. Tear tofu roughly into pieces, 1/2 to 3 inches in size. Stir into the sauce. Cover and simmer 20 minutes. While the dish is cooking, wash and chop the cabbage into 1 inch wide pieces. After dish has finished simmering, add the cabbage. Cover and cook for another 10 minutes. Stir in rest of ingredients, simmer 2 to 3 minutes.

Comments: Very good over "PLAIN" INDIAN RICE (p. 129). A really tasty dish. If you want to strongly calm *Kapha,* cut the *ghee* or oil to 1 teaspoon and add cup water instead. Skip the pinon nuts and garnish lavishly with black pepper.

With the frozen tofu, *Vata* should add a bit of extra *ghee* and black pepper or dry ginger for best balance.

TOFU AND MUSHROOMS

Preparation time: 50 minutes   Serves: 3-4
—Vata, —Pitta, —Kapha*   ✿   ✳   🐚   ❄

> 1 (1 pound) package of tofu
> 6 dried Shiitake mushrooms (available in Asian food stores, interna-
> tional section of groceries and in many health food stores.)
> 2 cups water
> ¼ teaspoon black pepper
> 1 tablespoon or more tamari (natural soy sauce)

Soak mushrooms in water for 20 minutes. While they are soaking, cut tofu into 1 inch cubes. Put tofu, mushrooms and soaking water into large heavy skillet. Cook covered on medium-low heat for 25 minutes. Add black pepper and tamari, serve.

Comments: Good with rice, barley or millet and vegetable side dish. Strengthening for the immune system, gently focussing for the mind.

*When served with ginger for Vata and Kapha. Vatas need to keep their dried Shiitake mushroom consumption moderate.

TOFU PESTO

Preparation time: 15-20 minutes   Serves: 4-6
—Vata, +Pitta, —Kapha*   ✳   🐚
—Vata, —Pitta, —Kapha**

> 1 carton (1 pound) tofu, drained and steamed for 5 minutes over high
> heat
> 1 bunch fresh basil (1 ounce or 1 cup lightly packed), chopped
> 2 tablespoons olive oil
> 1-2 cloves fresh garlic, minced (optional, omit for *Pitta*)
> 1 tablespoon barley miso or mellow white miso
> 2 tablespoons sesame tahini
> 3 tablespoons water

Steam tofu and cut in about 4 pieces. Puree basil and oil in blender on low for ½ minute. Add rest of ingredients and blend until smooth. Do not over blend as this can spoil the flavor of the delicate basil.

Or grind the basil into the oil in a *suribachi* (an Oriental mortar and pestle), then grind in rest of ingredients until smooth.

Comments: This is the best way we have found to serve pesto without heating up *Pitta* or greasing up *Kapha*. It is also lower in fat and higher in protein than most pestos, while retaining the rich flavor of the dish. It makes an elegant and very simple party dish, or a fast supper after a long day out.

As prepared, it is relatively thick and can be used as a spread with crackers or raw vegetables. To serve over pasta, a little water can be added in the blending preparation to thin it to the consistency desired. Or *Vata* can add extra oil, if desired. It is healing for the nerves and digestion.

*with garlic
**without garlic

SAUTEED TOFU AND VEGETABLES

Preparation time: 30-40 minutes
−*Vata,* −*Pitta,* −*Kapha**
mildly +*Vata,* −*Pitta,* +*Kapha***

Serves: 2-4

Use any favorite vegetable side dish recipe in this cookbook, such as mushrooms and peas, sauteed okra, spinach and potato, or cauliflower and potato. Add one carton (1 pound) of fresh or frozen tofu, drained and cubed, to the vegetables as they are cooking. Cook until the tofu has taken on the flavor of the spices in the dish (15 to 20 minutes). This can be served over rice or millet as a main dish by itself, or with SPICY BUTTERMILK (p. 86), or BUTTERMILK CURRY (p. 78), as a sauce.

Comments: Frozen tofu offers more texture than regular fresh tofu and picks up more of the flavors of a sauce. However, it is best used only occasionally by *Vata* and *Kapha,* i.e., once or twice a month at most, as more regular use can be overly cooling. Well-spiced fresh tofu can be used frequently without harm, as long as it is well-tolerated.

*With fresh tofu (depending on the vegetables)
**With frozen tofu. Garnish with dry ginger for Kapha and fresh grated ginger root for Vata to balance this effect.

ABOUT ADUKI BEANS

Aduki *beans look like tiny red kidney beans, and are well-known for their ability to rebuild adrenal function and kidney energy. They are somewhat easier for* Vata *to handle than many larger beans. They are a delicious staple for* Pitta *and* Kapha. *Still, being cold, dry and heavy in nature, they require soaking, plenty of cooking and warm spicing for best digestion. Ginger and tamari are good for this, and onions and garlic can be added for a flavorsome dish.*

GINGERED ADUKI BEANS

Preparation time: with pressure cooker, 45 minutes plus overnight soak. Serves: 5-6
Without pressure cooker, 3 hours plus overnight soak.   ✿   ✷   ❊
mildly +Vata −Kapha, −Pitta

> **1 cup dry aduki beans**
> **6 cups water**
> **1 stick kombu**
> **⅛ teaspoon** *hing*
> **1 teaspoon grated fresh ginger root**
> **1 tablespoon tamari**
> **½ medium onion, chopped fine (optional, can be omitted for** *Pitta*)
> **1-2 cloves fresh garlic, minced (optional, needs to be omitted for** *Pitta*)
> **1 tablespoon sunflower or sesame oil (optional, can be omitted for** *Kapha*)
> **½ teaspoon crushed** *neem* **(curry) leaves, if available**

Sort the beans and soak them overnight. After soaking, drain and put beans in pressure cooker with fresh water, kombu and *hing* and cook at 15 pounds pressure on medium heat for 25 minutes or until quite soft.

Without a pressure cooker, again, soak the beans overnight, rinsing them periodically to reduce gas potential. Put drained beans in large saucepan with fresh water, *hing* and kombu. Bring to a boil, then reduce to medium heat. Cook for 2 to 3 hours or until quite soft.

In large heavy skillet, heat oil, garlic, onion and ginger. Add cooked beans and *neem*, stir-sauteing for 10 to 15 minutes. Add tamari in last few minutes of cooking before serving. (If omitting oil, onion and garlic, heat 3 tablespoons of water in the skillet, add ginger and cook for 3 minutes, then stir in beans and simmer the mixture for 10 to 15 minutes, again adding tamari in the last few minutes of cooking.)

Comments: This goes well with "PLAIN " INDIAN RICE (p. 129) and FAVORITE DARK LEAFY GREENS (p. 154). The *neem*, being bitter, is good for calming *Pitta* and beneficial for *Kapha* as well. *Vata* can eat this only in small amounts.

SANTA FE PINTO BEANS

Preparation time: with pressure cooker, 45 minutes. Serves: 6-8
Without pressure cooker, 9-10 hours; can be made in crockpot. ✿ ✸ ❄
+*Vata*, −*Pitta*, −*Kapha**

> 1½ cup dried pinto beans
> 6 cups water
> ¼-½ medium onion, finely chopped (use the smaller amount for *Pitta*)
> 1-2 cloves garlic, minced (omit for *Pitta*)
> ½-2 teaspoons chili powder (use the smaller amount for *Pitta*)
> 1 bay leaf
> ½ teaspoon dried oregano (2 teaspoons fresh if available)
> ½ teaspoon dried basil (2 teaspoons fresh if available)
> ½ teaspoon whole cumin seeds
> ⅛ teaspoon *hing*
> 1 teaspoon coriander powder
> 1 teaspoon spearmint, fresh if available
> Salt to taste, about 1 teaspoon

Sort and wash beans, soaking overnight if possible. Place all ingredients except coriander, mint, and salt in pressure cooker, bring to 15 pounds pressure, cook at medium heat for 30 minutes. Take off heat, stir in coriander, mint and salt, cook 10 minutes on medium.

Or soak at least 4 hours, rinsing half a dozen times to reduce the gas-producing raffinose in the outer coating of the bean. Place beans in large pot with fresh water and bring to a boil, cook two minutes. Drain beans, discarding the cooking water and add a fresh 6 cups water. Let sit 2 hours in this water. Add all ingredients except coriander, mint and salt, bring to a boil in pot or crockpot uncovered, cover and reduce heat to medium-low. Cook covered for 3 to 4 hours or until beans are quite soft. Add rest of ingredients, cook 10 minutes on medium. Stir, serve.

Comments: This dish goes well with corn or wheat tortillas or cornbread and a fresh vegetable or salad. The salt should not be added until the end as it makes the beans tough. The *hing,* kombu and cumin substantially aid digestion of this dish for *Vata*. Spearmint assists digestion and cools the other herbs and spices for *Pitta*. Excellent for *Kapha*.

If well-soaked and served with ghee or oil, this is well-tolerated by Vata in small amounts.

Santa Fe Pinto Beans can be used in a wide variety of dishes, including:

BEAN BURRITOS

moderately +Vata, −Pitta, −Kapha

Warm a whole wheat tortilla (for *Vata* and *Pitta*) with ½ teaspoon butter or oil in a heavy skillet. Turn once so both sides are heated. *Kaphas*, heat a corn tortilla in a non-stick pan without oil. Place on a serving plate and spoon enough hot beans into the tortilla to make a substantial yet manageable serving (½ cup for flour tortillas, ¼ cup for corn tortillas). Put any of the garnishes you desire on top of the beans, and roll the tortilla around the hot mixture like a crepe, securing with a toothpick if you like. Good fast lunch or supper, popular with kids and adults.

Garnishes: Grated cheese (*Vata*) Yogurt or sour cream (*Vata*)
Green chile salsa (*Vata & Kapha*) Cottage cheese (*Pitta & Vata*)
Red chile salsa (*Vata & Kapha*) Sauteed onions (*Vata & Kapha*)
Lettuce & grated vegetables (*Pitta & Kapha*)
Steamed mushrooms (*Pitta & Kapha*) Chopped avocado (*Vata & Pitta*)
Chopped raw onion (*Kapha*)

TACOS

moderately +Vata, −Pitta, −Kapha*

Buy prepared taco shells (simply pre-folded, pre-toasted corn tortillas). Or make your own tacos using yellow or blue corn tortillas, warm them on both sides on an oiled skillet for *Vata* and *Pitta*, fold in half as you take them off, let cool slightly on a paper towel, and fill. Keep them soft for *Vata* and *Pitta* by warming them rapidly. Cook more slowly at lower heat on an unoiled, non-stick pan to get them crispy for *Kapha*. Filling should include beans and shredded raw vegetables for certain, and then any of the garnishes listed above.

*Unless heavily garnished with cheese, yogurt, sour cream or salsa, in which case it is mildly +Vata..

QUESADILLAS

—Vata, +Pitta, +Kapha

Warm one side of a flour tortilla (whole wheat preferably) on an oiled skillet. Turn it over and add 2 to 2 tablespoons grated cheese. Reduce heat to low, cover and cook until cheese has melted. Tasty fast snack.

Split peas, like adukis, are sometimes easier for Vata to digest, though not every Vata will find this to be true. Split peas tend to be lower in protein than many of the beans and higher in starches. Both Pitta and Kapha can benefit from their use, and can substitute them in recipes calling for black (urud) or (regular) common lentils.

SPLIT GREEN PEAS, INDIAN- STYLE

Preparation time: 1 hour 20 minutes, plus overnight soak Serves: 8-10
mildly + Vata, −Pitta, −Kapha

> 2 cups dry green split peas
> 8 to 11 cups water
> 1 to 2 tablespoons sunflower oil (the lesser amount for *Kapha*)
> ½ teaspoon mustard seeds
> 1 medium size fresh tomato, cubed (optional, tasty—but do not include if you want to calm *Pitta*)
> ½ teaspoon curry powder, mild
> 2 tablespoons lemon juice
> 2 tablespoons grated coconut
> 1 teaspoon sea salt
> ½ teaspoon turmeric
> 1½ teaspoons coriander powder
> 1 teaspoon fresh ginger root, chopped or ¼-½ teaspoon dry ginger powder
> Green pepper, chopped (optional)

Garnish: chopped fresh cilantro leaves

Soak peas overnight to reduce cooking time and propensity for gas-formation. Then wash and cook one hour with water.

In small frying pan heat oil and add mustard seeds. When they pop, add tomato, curry powder and turmeric. Mix well, add to pot of peas. Add rest of ingredients and cook over medium heat for 15 minutes.

Comment: This goes well with *basmati* rice, barley or *chappatis.*

BLACK-EYED PEAS, AMERICAN STYLE

Preparation time: with pressure cooker, 30 minutes.   Serves: 5-7
Without pressure cooker, 4-5 hours.   ✳ 🍵 ❄
+*Vata,* −*Pitta,* −*Kapha*

> **1½ cup dried black-eyed peas**
> **6 cups water**
> **1 large onion, chopped**
> **1 clove garlic, minced (needs to be omitted when cooking for *Pitta*)**
> **1 bay leaf**
> **Salt and fresh black pepper to taste**
> **1¼ tablespoon Bernard Jensen's Broth or seasoning powder**

Sort and wash the peas. Place them in the pressure cooker with water, onion, garlic, and bay leaf. Cook at 15 pounds pressure for 20 minutes at medium heat.

Or soak the beans overnight or for a minimum of 4 hours, rinsing six times. Then place in large pot with onion, garlic, and bay leaf and 6 cups fresh water. Bring to a boil, then lower heat to medium-low and cook covered for 45 minutes to 1 hour or until peas are quite soft.

When done, add salt (about 1 teaspoon), pepper (¼ teaspoon) and the vegetable broth. Stir and serve.

Comment: Adding a teaspoon of *ghee* or oil to *Vata's* portion or serving aids digestibility significantly (as good Southerners know).

SPICY WHOLE MUNG BEANS

Preparation time: with pressure cooker, 45 minutes, plus overnight soak. Serves: 8-9
Without pressure cooker, minimum of 3 hours.   ✿   ✳   🍃   ❄
0 Vata, −Pitta, −Kapha

> 1½ cups dry whole mung beans
> 9 cups water
> 1 teaspoon sea salt
> 1 medium onion, chopped
> 1 carrot, diced finely
> 2½ tablespoons lemon juice
> ½ teaspoon curry powder, mild
> 2 teaspoons coriander powder
> 1 tablespoon fresh ginger root, minced
> 1 to 2 tablespoons sunflower oil (the lesser amount for *Kapha*)
> ½ teaspoon mustard seeds
> ½ teaspoon cumin seeds
> 1 teaspoon turmeric
> ⅛ teaspoon black pepper
> ½ green pepper, chopped (optional, omit for *Pitta*)

Soak beans overnight. Drain them and cook with 6 cups of water in pressure cooker for 20 minutes or until quite soft. Without pressure cooker, soak beans at least 2-3 hours. Rinse, then place in large pot with 9 cups of water and cook for 40 to 50 minutes or until quite soft.

In small frying pan, heat oil. Add mustard and cumin seeds. When the mustard seeds pop, add turmeric, then add the warmed spices to the cooked mung beans. Add all remaining ingredients and mix well. Cook for 15 minutes over medium heat.

Comments: This goes well with barley and steamed vegetables, or *rotali* and rice. Can also be served as a soup. Garnishes: cayenne (*Vata* and *Kapha*), yogurt (*Vata*), generous amounts of coconut and chopped coriander leaves (*Pitta*).

Some *Vatas* may find the whole mung beans hard to digest; split mung is usually much easier for *Vata*.

ABOUT KIDNEY BEANS

Red kidney beans are specific for Pitta *(and no one else!).* Pittas *lost in the heart of Louisiana, home of red beans and white rice, do well. It's not the diet for* Vatas *or* Kaphas, *though the traditional hot Cajun spices help them.*

CAJUN RED BEANS

Preparation time: 1 hour with pressure cooker
4 to 5 hours without
+*Vata,* −*Pitta,* +*Kapha*

Serves: 4-6

✳ 🫘 ❄

2 cups dry kidney beans
8 cups water
¼ teaspoon *hing*
2 bay leaves
1 stick of kombu (seaweed)
2 tablespoons sunflower or walnut oil
2 *neem* leaves, if available
½ medium onion, finely chopped
½ teaspoon whole cumin seeds
1 teaspoon fresh thyme (½ teaspoon dry)
1 teaspoon sea salt
1 small jalapeno, chopped (optional)
1 tablespoons coriander powder

Put kidney beans, water, *hing*, bay leaf, and kombu in the pressure cooker. Bring to pressure and cook 30 minutes. Or place same ingredients in large saucepan and bring to a boil. Reduce heat and simmer on medium until tender, about 3 to 4 hours.

Warm oil in large skillet and add onion, cumin, thyme and crumbled *neem* and other bay leaf. Saute for 1 to 2 minutes. Add cooked kidney beans, salt, jalapeno, and coriander and simmer for an additional 20 to 30 minutes.

Comments: This goes well with "PLAIN" INDIAN RICE (p. 129). For best results, follow with fennel seeds, toasted and chewed after the meal. Even so, some *Pittas* will need to forego the jalapeno in this to keep their fire calm. The *hing*, kombu, cumin, bay and coriander aid digestion, making this dish an occasional option for *Vata* and *Kapha*. The thyme brings a bit of pungency plus the flavor of New Orleans to the beans.

RAJMA

Preparation time: 1½ hours with pressure cooker   Serves: 6
3 hours without.   ✿ ⁊⤍ ❄
+Vata, −Pitta, +Kapha

1 cup dry kidney beans
5 cups water
½ stick kombu
¹⁄₁₆ teaspoon *hing*
1 medium onion, chopped
1 teaspoon fresh ginger root, grated (omit if *Pitta* is high)
1 tablespoon *ghee*
1 tablespoon cumin seeds
¼ teaspoon fennel seeds
½ teaspoon turmeric
⅛ teaspoon dry ginger powder
½ teaspoon sea salt
1¼ tablespoon Sucanat (optional)
1 tablespoon grated organic orange peel
1 teaspoon coriander powder

Put the beans, water, kombu, and hing in the pressure cooker or large saucepan. If pressure cooking, bring to pressure and cook for 30 minutes at 15 pounds pressure. If cooking without pressure cooker, bring beans to boil, then lower heat to medium and cover and cook beans until tender: 1½ to 2 hours. (You may need to add extra water when cooking in this slower way.)

Spoon the *ghee* into a medium-sized skillet and add the cumin and fennel. Warm over medium heat until cumin is lightly browned, about 2 to 3 minutes. Add the turmeric and stir well. Add in the onion and ginger and saute over low heat until onion is sweet and tender, about 5 minutes. Stir in the cooked beans and cook uncovered over medium heat until most of excess water is gone. Add rest of ingredients, stir well. Cook over medium heat another 5 to 10 minutes.

Comments: I first fell in love with *rajma* traveling in northern India, where it is served hot with *chappatis* and sometimes stewed green chili. This somewhat unorthodox version is designed expressly for *Pittas*, since they are the primary (and only) folks this legume benefits. A concentrated dish, it is best eaten in small amounts with cumin, coriander and fennel on the side. Traditionally, a pinch of cloves would be added, which gives a nice zing. However, most *Pittas* have plenty of zing without adding this extra. (Translation: cloves are very heating.)

EAST INDIAN LIMA BEANS

Preparation time: with pressure cooker, 1 hour, plus 1 hour soak.   Serves: 8-10
without pressure cooker, 1 hour 15 minutes plus 3 hour soak.   ✿   ✳   ❄
+*Vata,* −*Pitta,* 0 *Kapha*

    1½ cups dry lima beans
    7½-10 cups water
    2 tablespoons sunflower oil (this can be reduced to 1 tablespoon for
    Pitta and *Kapha,* if desired)
    ½ teaspoon mustard seeds
    1 tablespoon sesame seeds
    ½ teaspoon turmeric
    2 tablespoons barley malt or brown rice syrup
    2 tablespoons lemon juice
    1 teaspoon sea salt
    3 tablespoons grated coconut
    1 tablespoon fresh ginger root, grated
    1 teaspoon curry powder
    ½ teaspoon cinnamon

Garnish: fresh chopped coriander leaves, if available

Soak lima beans in water in uncovered pressure cooker for 1 hour. Drain, add 7½ cups of fresh water, cover and bring to 15 pounds pressure. Cook over medium heat until beans are quite soft, about 25 minutes.

If pressure cooker is not available, soak beans for 3 hours. Drain, add a 10 cups of fresh water, bring to a boil, reduce to medium heat, cover and cook until soft, about 45 to 50 minutes.

When beans are cooked, heat oil in small frying pan. Add mustard seeds. When they pop, add sesame seeds and turmeric. Stir this mixture into cooked beans. Add remaining ingredients to the beans and mix well. Cook about 15 to 20 minutes over medium heat without covering. The beans will thicken. When ready to serve, garnish with chopped cilantro leaves.

Comments: This goes well with "PLAIN" INDIAN RICE (p. 129), and *TRIDOSHIC VEGETABLE CURRY #2* (p. 75). This delicious dish is likely to bring back memories for those who have travelled in southern India. If you wish to create a simple *tridoshic* meal from this recipe, simply add tofu in the last 15 to 20 minutes of cooking. A 1 pound cube of tofu can be cut into 8 large pieces and added with the remaining ingredients. *Vata* diners can eat the spicy tofu, while *Kaphas* eat the limas. *Pittas* can choose between the two (0 *Vata,* −*Pitta,* 0 *Kapha*).

KICHADIS

ABOUT *KICHADIS*

Kichadis *are at the core of Ayurvedic nutritional healing. They are a relatively simple stew of basmati rice and split mung dal, which are suitable for almost every dosha.* Kichadis *take on endless variations depending on the herbs, spices and vegetables used in them. They are the primary food in Pancha karma, Ayurvedic cleansing therapy, because of their ease of digestion and assimilation. The kichadis which follow are designed for specific purposes. They are best eaten fresh when used therapeutically. Let your own sense of the herbs and your constitution guide you as you create healing modifications.*

BASIC FORMAT:
Ghee: *for lubrication and assimilation*

Warmed with: *Spices, any of the following:*

*Asafoetida (*hing*): calms* Vata, *aids assimilation, potent carminative*
Bay leaf: warms, digestive
Black mustard seeds: digestive with pronounced warming effects
Black peppercorns: warms, digestive, carminative
Cardamom: calms and stimulates digestion
Cinnamon: warms and sweetens, a digestive
Cloves: quite heating, digestive
Coriander: cooling, soothing, carminative and digestive
Cumin: carminative, digestive, balances all doshas
Fennel: cools, sweetens, digestive, tonifying to the stomach
Fenugreek: warming, digestive, tonifier, reducer of mass
Garlic: warming, strengthening, reduces ama
Ginger: warms, potent digestive stimulant
Kombu: non-traditional (a seaweed); digestive, removes heavy metals
Neem (curry leaves): cooling, bitter, clears and removes wastes
Saffron: cooling, tonifying, digestive, balances all doshas
Turmeric: tridoshic, *specific for aiding protein digestion*

Combine these with: *Split mung dal, basmati rice, and vegetables. This is sometimes varied; other beans and grains can be used for specific healing purposes, if they are very well-cooked. For example here we use aduki beans in the kidney kichadi, as adukis are outstanding in their ability to support the kidneys. Similarly, we utilize non-traditional herbs or spices when they are especially useful, e.g., dandelion root to promote the excretion of fluids, or burdock root to cool and purify the blood. Again, allow your intuition and self-knowledge to guide you in these adventures.*

Cook: *Cook until both beans and grain are very soft, but not gummy.*

COOLING *KICHADI*

Preparation time: about 2 hours
0 Vata, − Pitta, − Kapha

Serves: 5-6

❀ ✳

> ½ cup *basmati* rice
> ¼ cup split mung *dal*
> ½ burdock root, (about 8 inches)
> 1½ cup green beans
> 2 tablespoons ghee
> ½ teaspoon fennel seeds
> 1 teaspoon cumin seeds
> 1 tablespoon amaranth (optional)
> 1 stick *kombu*
> 6 to 10 cups water
> ½ teaspoon sea salt
> 1 tablespoon coriander powder

Garnish: chopped coriander leaves

Wash rice and mung until the water is clear; drain. Wash burdock root and peel it; then slice in inch slices like a carrot. Wash green beans; chop into 1 inch pieces.

Warm *ghee* in medium saucepan. Add fennel and cumin seeds and saute for 1 to 2 minutes. Add rice and mung and saute for another couple of minutes. Put burdock and green beans in immediately after the rice and beans, stir saute for 1 minute. Add 6 cups of water and bring to a boil. Put kombu, amaranth and salt in once the *kichadi* has come to a boil, and reduce to medium-low heat. Cover and cook until tender, 1 to 1½ hours, adding water as needed to keep the mixture moist. Before serving, add the coriander powder, stir well. Garnish with fresh chopped coriander (cilantro) leaves.

Comments: This dish is a potent blood purifier. Burdock clears the kidneys and blood, while the green beans act as a diuretic. A good one for summer skin break-outs, or excess water retention. Useful in diabetes, as well as in increased *Pitta* states.

BASIC WARMING *KICHADI*

Preparation time: 2 hours   Serves: 2-3
−*Vata*, +*Pitta*, −*Kapha*   ✿ 🐌 ❄

> ½ cup *basmati* rice
> ¼ cup split mung beans
> 6 cups water
> 1 tablespoon *ghee*
> 1 teaspoon cumin seeds
> ⅛ teaspoon *hing*
> 1 teaspoon coriander seeds
> ¾ teaspoon cardamom seeds
> 1 teaspoon black peppercorns
> 1 bay leaf
> 2 more tablespoons *ghee*
> ¾ teaspoon cinnamon
> ¼ teaspoon ground cloves
> 1 teaspoon turmeric
> ¾ teaspoon salt, rock salt if you can get it
> 1 tablespoon fresh ginger root, grated
> ½ small onion, chopped
> 1-2 cloves of garlic (optional)
> ½ teaspoon ground cumin
> 2-4 cups fresh vegetables: carrots, greens, string beans or zucchini are
> possibilities, chopped
> 2 more cups water, as needed

While this is an imposing list of ingredients, it's actually as easy to make as all the other *kichadis.* Wash the rice and split mung until the rinse water is clear. Warm as tablespoon of *ghee* in a medium saucepan and add the whole cumin seeds and *hing.* Lightly brown them. Add the rice, mung and water and bring to a boil. Cook for about 45 minutes.

Warm the last 2 tablespoons of *ghee* in a small skillet. Add the coriander, cardamom, peppercorns, and bay leaf and saute for 2 to 3 minutes. Then stir in the rest of the spices and the onion (and garlic, if you use it). Put the sauteed spices in the blender with a little (½ cup or less) water and grind well. Pour this spice mixture into the rice and mung. Rinse out the blender with the last 2 cups of water and add it to the *kichadi* as well. Add the vegetables. Cook for 20 minutes or more.

Comments: This healing brew is also good for stimulating digestion and circulation. Easy to eat. Based roughly on the proportions of a Punjabi *garam masala* in its spicing.

SAFFRON-ASPARAGUS *KICHADI*

Preparation time: 1½ hours Serves: 4

–Vata, –Pitta, –Kapha ✿ ✷ ❧ ❄

⅛ teaspoon saffron
2 tablespoons *ghee*
½ teaspoon cumin seeds
¼ teaspoon fenugreek seeds
3 to 4 *neem* leaves (curry leaves, available in Indian groceries, fresh if you can get them)
1 tablespoon onion, finely chopped
⅛ teaspoon *hing*
½ cup split mung dal
¾ cup *basmati* rice
1 pound fresh asparagus (2-3 cups chopped)
1 teaspoon sea salt
6 cups water
¼ teaspoon ground cumin

Dry-roast the saffron in the bottom of a heavy pan. Add the *ghee*, cumin and fenugreek seeds and warm over low heat until cumin is brown. Add the *neem*, onion, and *hing* and stir. Slow saute until onion is tender, a minute or two. Wash the *dal* and rice until the rinse water is clear, drain and add to the spice mixture. Add the water and salt and cook until tender, about an hour. While the *kichadi* is cooking, wash and chop the asparagus into 1 inch slices. Fifteen minutes before serving, steam the asparagus (see p. 148) and stir it and the ground cumin into the *kichadi*. If working only with *Vata*, the asparagus can be sauteed in an additional tablespoon of *ghee* until tender, then added to the *kichadi*.

Comments: This subtle dish is designed specifically to tonify both the female and male reproductive systems. Useful for fertility and healing of potency and menstrual issues. It is especially good during the summer.

SPLEEN-PANCREAS *KICHADI* #1

Preparation time: 2 hours   Serves: 4-5
 −*Vata, 0 Pitta, mildly −Kapha*   ✿   ✳   🐚   ❄

> 1 teaspoon sunflower oil
> 1/4 teaspoon black mustard seeds
> 1/4 teaspoon cumin seeds
> 1/2 teaspoon turmeric
> 3/4 teaspoon sea salt
> 3 *neem* (curry) leaves (available in Indian groceries)
> 1 teaspoon fresh grated ginger root (or to taste)
> 1/4 cup split mung beans ("yellow *dal*")
> 1/2 cup Texmati rice, *basmati* rice or bulgur
> 1/2 onion, finely chopped
> 3 carrots, sliced
> 6 cups water

Garnish: fresh coriander leaves, chopped (optional)

Warm oil in a medium saucepan; add black mustard seeds and cumin. Warm until the mustard seeds pop, then add turmeric, onion, salt, *neem*, and ginger. Stir well and saute onion until tender. Wash beans and grain until the rinse water is clear. Add them to the sauteing mixture, stirring well. Add water, bring to boil and let cook covered over medium heat for an hour or more. Add carrots and cook another 15 minutes. Garnish with chopped coriander leaves to enhance digestion.

SPLEEN-PANCREAS *KICHADI* #2

Preparation time: 2 hours   Serves: 4-5
 0 Vata, −Pitta, 0 Kapha   ✿   ✳   🐚   ❄

> Same spices as above through ginger root
> 1/2 cup split mung *dal*
> 1 cup dry pearl barley
> 1 onion, chopped
> 2 parsnips, chopped
> 1 cup string beans, chopped
> 1/2 stick kombu
> 8 cups water

Garnish: green onion, chopped (optional)

Prepare spices as above. Saute onion with spices until tender. Again, wash beans and barley until rinse water is clear. Stir them into the sauteed onions and spices. Add water, bring to boil and add rest of ingredients except scallions. Cook covered for 1¼ hours. Garnish with scallion.

LUNG *KICHADI* #1

Preparation time: about 2 hours   Serves: 2-3
−*Vata*, +*Pitta*, −*Kapha*

Follow the recipe for BASIC WARMING *KICHADI* (p. 118) with the following changes:

Wash 2 medium sweet potatoes and dice into ½ to 1 inch pieces. Add ½ teaspoon *ajwan* and saute with the cumin and *hing*. Add the sweet potato plus 1 stick of kombu when you add the mung, rice and water. Again, cook for about 45 minutes.

Omit the bay leaf and fresh ginger and cut the cardamom to ¼ teaspoon (about 1 pod). Cut the *ghee* or oil in the second step to 1 tablespoon and add the coriander, cardamom, peppercorns, and ¼ teaspoon of dry ginger. Saute for 2 to 3 minutes. Then stir in the rest of the spices and the onion and 4 cloves of garlic. Follow the rest of the recipe as described. If you like, you can add 1 tablespoon flaxseed in the last 15 minutes of cooking to enhance clearing of the lungs. Simply mix it into the *kichadi* as it is cooking.

Comments: This is an excellent *kichadi* for fighting winter colds, flus and rampaging bronchitis. It is also tasty enough to be served as a company dinner. *Ajwan* and ginger work to decongest the lungs, while the onion and garlic warm and stimulate the immune system and circulation. Sweet potato is rich in vitamin A, which soothes the lung membranes and bronchioles, and supports the immune system. Kombu assists in removing heavy metals like lead, if you are living in a polluted or urban environment. The dish is relatively hot and spicy.

LUNG *KICHADI* #2

Preparation time: about 1½ hours   Serves: 4-5
0 Vata, 0 Pitta, −Kapha   ❁ ☙ ❋

>½ cup dry garbanzos
>6 cups water
>⅛ teaspoon *hing*
>1 to 2 tablespoons *ghee*
>½ teaspoon black mustard seeds
>1 teaspoon cumin seeds
>1 teaspoon turmeric
>1 large onion, chopped
>2 cloves garlic, minced (omit for *Pitta*)
>1 tablespoon dry sage, crumbled
>1 cup *basmati* rice
>2 to 4 more cups of water (as needed)
>½ stick *kombu*
>1 parsnip, chopped (optional)
>1 carrot, chopped
>1 cup cabbage or broccoli, chopped (omit for *Vata*)
>¾ teaspoon sea salt
>1 teaspoon ground coriander
>1 tablespoon sesame seeds

Wash the beans and rice. Put the garbanzos, water and *hing* in a pressure cooker and bring to pressure. Cook for 30 minutes on 15 pounds pressure or medium heat. While the beans are cooking, warm the *ghee* in a medium-sized skillet and add the mustard and cumin seeds. When the mustard seeds pop, add the turmeric, onion, garlic, and sage. Stir over low heat for 2 to 3 minutes. Add the rice and stir. Set aside until garbanzos are done.

When the garbanzos are cooked, open the pressure cooker and add the spiced rice mixture. Add the kombu, parsnip, and extra water. Cook for 45 minutes or until rice is tender. Add rest of vegetables and spices and simmer covered for another fifteen minutes.

Comments: The garbanzos cool and dry irritated inflamed lungs. Sage dries hyper-secreting lung mucosa, while warming a touch. The carrot, cabbage and broccoli add vitamins A and C respectively. Good for lungs exposed to irritating chemicals or pollution, or a body recuperating from a cold or cough. Nice for children.

DIGESTIVE *KICHADI*

Preparation time: 1½ hours
Serves: 3-4
−*Vata,* +*Pitta,* −*Kapha**

      ❀   🐌   ❄

> ½ teaspoon cumin seeds
> 2 tablespoons *ghee* or sunflower oil
> 3 bay leaves
> 1 teaspoon coriander seeds
> ½ teaspoon turmeric
> 1 teaspoon oregano, dry
> ½ teaspoon sea salt
> 1 stick kombu
> 1 teaspoon fresh ginger root, grated
> ½ cup *basmati* rice
> ¼ cup split mung *dal*
> 4 to 6 cups water
> 3 cups fresh vegetables, such as carrots, zucchini, or sum-
> mer squash, diced

Wash the rice and beans until rinse water is clear.

Warm the *ghee* in a medium saucepan. Add the cumin seeds, bay, coriander and oregano. Brown slightly, until aromatic (you can smell them). Stir in turmeric, rice and *dal.* Add water, salt, kombu, and ginger. Simmer covered over medium heat until beans and rice are soft, about 1 hour. Wash and dice vegetables. Add them and cook until tender, 15 to 20 minutes more.

**Pitta* can garnish generously with fresh chopped coriander leaves to neutralize this effect. If Kapha is making this kichadi for themselves alone, the ghee or oil can be cut to 1 teaspoonful. Additional ghee can be added after cooking if other doshas, especially Vata, are to be sharing in the eating.*

KIDNEY *KICHADI*

Preparation time: about 1½ hours, with pressure cooker   Serves: 5-6
— *Vata,* — *Pitta,* — *Kapha*

1 burdock root (12 inches) (available in the produce section of Asian or natural groceries)
½ cup dry aduki beans
½ stick kombu
6 cups water
2 tablespoons *ghee*
1 teaspoon cumin seeds
¼ teaspoon fennel seeds
1 large onion, chopped
1 teaspoon turmeric
2 bay leaves
⅛ teaspoon *hing*
3 curry leaves (also called *meetha neem,* available in Indian groceries) (optional, to be added if you can get it)
⅛ teaspoon cinnamon
2 carrots (or 1 acorn squash)
1 cup *basmati* rice
¾ teaspoon sea salt
2 more cups of water (as needed)

Wash and peel the burdock root. Slice it in inch slices. Wash aduki beans. Put adukis, 6 cups water, burdock, and kombu in pressure cooker. Bring to pressure and cook at 15 pounds pressure 25 to 30 minutes. (You can do this step without a pressure cooker; it takes an extra 2½ hours of cooking.) While the beans are cooking, heat the *ghee* in a medium skillet and add the cumin and fennel seeds. Then add the onion, turmeric, bay leaves, *hing,* curry leaves, and cinnamon. Saute until the onion is tender; set aside.

Wash the carrots (or squash) and slice or chop into small pieces (¼ inch for the carrots, 1 inch for the squash). Wash rice well. Saute the rice and vegetables in with the onion and spices for 1-2 minutes.

When the beans are done, pour the sauteed rice and vegetable mixture with spices into the opened pressure cooker (or pot). Add an extra 2 cups of water. Put the pressure cooker back on the heat, but use it as a pot, not a pressure cooker. Let it simmer covered, but not sealed for another 20 to 30 minutes. Add salt and serve.

Comments: Garnish with dry ginger and yogurt for *Vata* and coriander leaves and/or soy milk for *Pitta.* This sounds strange, but tastes quite good. If making strictly for *Kapha,* you can cut the *ghee* to 1 teaspoon and leave all else as is.

LIVER-GALLBLADDER *KICHADI*

Preparation time: 1½ hours
0 Vata, −Pitta, − Kapha

Serves: 5·6

✿   ✴   ☙

> 1 tablespoon sunflower oil or *ghee* (or less)
> 1 teaspoon cumin seeds
> ½ teaspoon black mustard seeds
> ½ teaspoon whole coriander seeds
> 1 teaspoon turmeric
> ⅓ cup dry split mung *dal* (yellow *dal*)
> 1 cup dry pearl barley
> 6 inch burdock root, peeled and chopped (available in produce sections and Asian stores)
> 1 parsnip, chopped (optional)
> 1 tablespoon dry dandelion root, chopped (available in herb sections of stores)
> 1 teaspoon fresh grated ginger root
> ½ stick kombu
> ½ pound fresh broccoli
> and/or
> 1 bunch fresh dark leafy greens (dandelion greens are especially good if you can get them)
> ¾ teaspoon sea salt
> 1 tablespoon coriander powder

Warm *ghee* in 4 quart saucepan. Add cumin, mustard and coriander seeds. Saute until mustard seeds pop. Add turmeric and split mung beans and stir-saute 30 seconds. Add 6 cups water and barley, then burdock, dandelion, ginger, and kombu. Bring to a boil, then cook covered over medium heat for 50 minutes or until barley is tender. Add additional water (about 4 cups) to keep the *kichadi* moist, stirring occasionally to prevent it from sticking on the bottom. Wash and chop the broccoli or greens. Fifteen minutes from serving, add the vegetables, salt and coriander powder. Stir, cover again and cook another 10 to 15 minutes more.

Comments: This *kichadi* is mildly laxative and diuretic, as well as being a cholagogue (liver-bile stimulator). If you are on a "zero fat" diet, the spices and mung can be dry roasted in the saucepan before the water and other ingredients are added. Shiitake mushrooms can be added if you are recovering from an infection. The parsnips are added primarily to sweeten and cool the dish.

ABOUT GRAINS

Grains are the primary food for much of the world. From a Western nutritional perspective, grains need to be complemented with at least a small amount of protein to be considered a main dish. Yet in much of the world, if one has access to enough grain to satisfy the appetite, it is considered a perfectly good and nourishing meal. If a little protein is added, it is usually in the form of beans or dairy. It can also be provided by nuts or seeds, appropriate vegetables like greens, or animal flesh. From an Ayurvedic point of view, what is most appropriate will depend on your constitution, needs and preferences.

In ancient times, grains provided the backbone for a wide variety of healing Ayurvedic gruels. Rice was prepared as a thin stew, with specific spices and foods added to treat the illness at hand. Dried grains were also used in healing. The Ayurvedic classic **Charak Samhita** recommends a thin dish of roasted corn flour, water, honey, and ghee with spices to counteract excessive eating, impaired digestion and foggy memory and intellect see MORNING AFTER CEREAL (p. 285 for modern-day replica). Another gruel of powdered barley mixed with buttermilk was used to "eradicate stomach pain."

In general grains have a sweet taste and a sweet vipak. This sweet attribute can be discovered for one's self by slowly chewing almost any unsweetened cooked grain. As you chew, the bonds which hold the simple sugars of the grain together dissolve, allowing you to taste its true sweetness. This sweetness makes whole grains useful for grounding. Frequently we are drawn to grains precisely for this grounding and calming quality. Western researchers have found that when a generous helping of grains is eaten, levels of the amino acid tryptophan rise in the brain, an hour or two later. The brain safely utilizes tryptophan to make the compound serotonin, among other things. This compound creates a feeling of well-being and calm in the body.

The following recipes are designed for use with whole grains, not refined grains, as whole grains are far more nutritious and balancing. Cooked whole and undiluted, grains tend to be starchy with just a bit of protein in them. They are also a rich source of B vitamins, trace minerals and fiber. Vatas and Pittas will benefit most from goodly servings of whole grains, while Kapha can take it a bit easier on them. All doshas balance from some warm, cooked whole grain each day, for grounding and smooth metabolic functioning.

Each grain has unique qualities which are helpful in healing. White basmati rice is the one grain which is tridoshic in effect; it can be eaten by all constitutions with benefit. It is slightly cooling, sweet, light, and moist. It is useful in calming an irritated or inflamed gut. Because it is lighter than many other grains, it can be eaten by Kapha, in small quantities. Its coolness, sweetness and moisture are valuable for Pitta. And its sweet moist attributes balance Vata. It is easy to digest. Texmati is a good substitute for Indian basmati rice in this country. It is a cross between Indian basmati and American long-grain white rice. Two cloves can be added to the rice pot when cooking basmati or Texmati rice. This gently warms the slight coolness of the grain. The parboiling which is a part of the preparation of basmati for market does reduce its B vitamin content compared to brown rice. Yet this same process makes this grain easier to digest and least likely to produce gas. Brown basmati rice is a variety of commercial rice which actually is closer to regular brown rice in its attributes. American Texmati and brown basmati have not been parboiled before marketing, to the best of our knowledge.

Brown rice does not have the same effects as basmati rice; it is a different species of rice and it has been prepared differently. Its husk has been left intact. This gives it a more warming, heavy, moist, and rough effect. It is sweet and astringent in nature. These qualities make it balancing for Vata; it grounds, warms and moistens. These same qualities are slightly imbalancing for Pitta and Kapha. Sometimes the roughness of brown rice can irritate the gut, compared to basmati. Some Ayurvedic practitioners use brown rice very little, preferring basmati. I use it fairly often. In my experience, its high fiber content and abundance of B vitamins alleviate constipation, especially in our culture, where fiber intake can be sporadic. It is also one of the most grounding of grains, without having the striking heaviness of wheat. Prepared half and half with barley, brown rice can be an appropriate grain for Pitta. Both rice and barley are reputed to dispel fatigue in Ayurvedic practice.

Wild rice is similar to brown rice in its qualities and effects. However, it is 50% higher in protein, which makes it slightly more warming in its action.

"PLAIN" INDIAN RICE

Preparation time: 20 minutes with *basmati* rice
45 minutes with brown rice
—*Vata, mildly +Pitta, mildly +Kapha**
—*Vata, —Pitta, 0 Kapha***

Serves: 3-4

✿ ✳ 🐌 ❆

>   1 cup brown or *basmati* rice, uncooked
>   1 teaspoon sunflower oil
>   ¹/₂ teaspoon mustard seeds
>   ¹/₂ teaspoon cumin seeds
>   3¹/₂ cups water
>   1 teaspoon sea salt
>   ¹/₄ teaspoon fresh ground black pepper

In medium-sized saucepan heat oil and add mustard and cumin seeds. When the mustard seeds pop, add water, rice and salt. Bring to a boil. Cover and reduce heat to low. Cook for 15 minutes for *basmati*, 35 to 40 minutes for brown rice. Add black pepper; mix well and serve.

Comment: Very good, very simple.

Variation: PEAS AND RICE: Add 1 cup fresh or frozen green peas when you add the *basmati* rice, water and salt.

mildly +Vata, —Pitta, —Kapha

*With brown rice
**with basmati rice

SAFFRON RICE

Preparation time: 30 minutes
—*Vata, —Pitta, 0 Kapha**

Serves: 4

✿ ✳ 🐌 ❆

>   ¹/₈ teaspoon saffron
>   1 teaspoon cumin seeds
>   1 cup *basmati* rice
>   3 cups water
>   ¹/₂ teaspoon sea salt

Wash the rice. Dry roast the saffron and cumin in the bottom of a heavy medium-sized saucepan for 2 to 3 minutes to bring out their flavor. Add the rice, water and salt, bring to a boil, cover, reduce heat to low. Cook until done, about 15 minutes.

Comments: This is the kind of dish that gets you to thinking about raising *Crocus sativa*, the plant from which this comes. It has a subtle light flavor which goes well with *dals* and with a simple vegetable on the side, like steamed broccoli. Not for those on an economy budget—a packet slightly smaller than a tablespoon costs $7.00 or more. The amount of saffron in this recipe gives a lovely flavor prepared as it is here. If you are after a more brilliant yellow color, double the amount recommended.

when eaten in modest quantities by Kapha

PULAO

Preparation time: 30 minutes with *basmati* rice,   Serves: 5-6
1 hour with brown rice   ✿ ✳ ⬤ ❄
−*Vata, −Pitta, 0 Kapha**
−*Vata, +Pitta, +Kapha***

    1 cup *basmati* or brown rice, uncooked
    ¼ cup *ghee* or butter
    3 cups water
    1 tablespoon sunflower oil
    ½ teaspoon mustard seeds
    1 teaspoon turmeric
    1 cup green peas
    ½ cup green bell pepper, chopped (optional)
    ⅛ cup cashews, chopped or ⅛ cup pumpkin seeds
    ¼ cup raisins
    ½ teaspoon sea salt
    1½ teaspoons curry powder, mild

In medium-sized saucepan heat the *ghee* or butter. Add the rice. Stir constantly over low heat for 3 minutes, watching carefully. When it is coated all over and glistens slightly, add water. Cook until soft: 15 minutes for *basmati*, 35 to 45 minutes for brown rice. Cool in the saucepan.

In a medium-sized skillet heat oil and add mustard seeds. When they pop, add turmeric and vegetables. Cook for 3 to 4 minutes. Add nuts or seeds and raisins and mix well. Add cooled rice, fluffing it with a fork as you take it from its pan. Add salt and curry powder. Mix well. Serve.

Comments: This goes well with yogurt and a side dish of eggplant and is an especially good dish for *Vata*.

*With *basmati* and pumpkin seeds*
**With brown rice and cashews*

SPICY RICE AND YOGURT

Preparation time: 10 minutes

Serves: 4-5

−*Vata*, +*Pitta*, +*Kapha**

−*Vata*, −*Pitta*, 0 *Kapha***

     ❋ 🌰 ❄

> 2 cups cooked brown or *basmati* rice
> 2 cups yogurt or ½ cup yogurt and ½ cup plain soy milk
> 1 to 2 tablespoons sunflower oil (the lesser amount for *Kapha*)
> ½ teaspoon mustard seeds
> ½ teaspoon cumin seeds
> ⅛ teaspoon *hing*
> 1 teaspoon sea salt
> ½ teaspoon black pepper
> ½ teaspoon cinnamon
> ¼ hot green pepper, chopped (optional)

Garnish: ⅛ cup raw almonds as a garnish (optional)

Heat oil in medium-sized deep saucepan. Add mustard seeds and cumin seeds. When mustard seeds pop, add the rice and yogurt. Then add all other ingredients (except almonds) and mix well. Heat to boiling point. Serve hot.

Comments: This is a delectable and easy lunch or dinner dish if you have some rice prepared on hand. Made with the full amount of yogurt, it is a superb meal for *Vata*. Made with soy milk, which is lighter and cooler than yogurt, it is suitable for *Pitta* and *Kapha* as well.

*With 2 cups yogurt
**With ½ cup yogurt and ½ cup soy milk, and basmati rice

RICE AND POTATOES

Preparation time: 30 minutes with pre-made rice   Serves: 4-5
45 - 75 minutes with fresh rice
− Vata, 0 Pitta, + Kapha

> 1 cup dry rice, *basmati* or brown (3 cups cooked)
> 3 medium potatoes
> 3 tablespoons sunflower oil
> 1 teaspoon mustard seeds
> 1 teaspoon turmeric
> ½ cup water
> 1 teaspoon sea salt
> 1 bunch fresh dark leafy greens, chopped (optional)
> 1½ teaspoon lemon juice
> ½ hot green pepper, chopped (optional, omit for *Pitta*)
> 1 teaspoon honey

Garnish: cup fresh coriander leaves, chopped

Cook the rice in two cups of water and cool. While rice is cooking, cut the potatoes into ¼ inch pieces. Wash twice with water, draining each time.

In a large saucepan, heat oil and mustard seeds. When the seeds pop, add turmeric, potatoes, greens, ½ cup water, and ½ teaspoon salt. Mix well. Cook over low heat for about 15 minutes or until the potatoes are soft. Combine the rice with the cooked potatoes. Add lemon juice, pepper and rest of salt and mix well. Cook for an additional 3 minutes, then add honey, drizzling it over the dish then stirring it in well. Garnish with fresh coriander leaves.

Comments: Serve it as a lunch or light supper. Extra lemon can be squeezed on top by *Vata* as a garnish. A way for *Vata* to have white potatoes happily. The preparation warms and moistens the potato.

SPICY RICE AND POTATO

Preparation time: 10 to 15 minutes   Serves: 2-4
— Vata, mildly + Pitta, mildly + Kapha*   ✿ ⁂ ❄
— Vata, 0 Pitta, 0 Kapha**

    1½ cup cooked brown or *basmati* rice
    1 medium potato, well scrubbed
    ¼ hot green pepper, chopped (optional, omit for *Pitta*)
    2 tablespoons sunflower oil
    ⅛ teaspoon *hing*
    ½ teaspoon mustard seeds
    3 tablespoons water
    ½ teaspoon sea salt
    ½ teaspoon curry powder
    1 teaspoon fresh ginger, chopped or grated

Garnish: Fresh coriander leaves, chopped, if available

Dice potato. Heat oil in frying pan and add mustard seeds and *hing*. When the mustard seeds pop, add potatoes and curry powder. Stir. Add water and cook over low heat for 5-7 minutes, stirring occasionally to keep potatoes from sticking. Add cooked rice and all other ingredients. Mix well and remove from heat.

Comments: This goes well with yogurt or vegetable curries. The moist quality of the rice and oil tends to balance the drying effect of the potato for *Vata*.

*With brown rice
**With basmati rice

OATS AND ASPARAGUS

Preparation time: 2 hours, or overnight soak plus 1 hour   Serves: 3-4
(Most of it unattended)
−Vata, −Pitta, mildly +Kapha

>   1 cup oat groats, dry
>   6-8 cups water
>   1 tablespoon *ghee* or sunflower oil
>   ¾ teaspoon cumin seeds
>   ⅛ teaspoon *ajwan*
>   1 tablespoon coriander seeds
>   ½ teaspoon sea salt
>   Black pepper to taste
>   ½ pound fresh asparagus

Wash the oat groats until the rinse water is clear. Put them on to boil with the water in a medium saucepan. While they are coming to a boil, warm the *ghee* or oil in a small skillet and add the cumin, *ajwan* and coriander seeds. Heat for 1 to 2 minutes or until cumin is lightly brown. Add the spices plus salt to the oats, cover and cook over medium heat until tender, 1 hour with overnight soak, 2 hours otherwise.

Ten minutes before you want to serve the dish, wash and chop the asparagus. Steam it until tender, 5 to 8 minutes. Stir into the cooked oats, serve.

Comments: This medicinal recipe is very soothing for an irritated bladder. Barley will also work well here, substituted for the oat groats. Try it with BLACK BEAN SOUP (p. 194) for a healing and tonifying supper for the bladder.

ABOUT BARLEY

Barley's attributes are coolness, lightness and dryness. I was initially confused by the Ayurvedic attributes of barley, since it seemed to be such a moist almost gooey grain when cooked up. Then I started investigating how it affects the body. It is diuretic and laxative in action. It pulls water into the body, but then it pulls an even greater amount out. Understanding its dynamic action, I could see why it would be so beneficial for Kapha—and not so useful for Vata. Its cool grounded qualities make it helpful for Pitta. It is serviceable for preventing constipation, especially in those of Pitta and Kapha persuasion. It also can heal chronic diarrhea with mucus. Barley can be used to alleviate Vata if it is well-spiced with medicinal herbs like fennel and calamus, and moistened with oil and vinegar. Delicious, eh? Diluted as a thin grain drink (see BARLEY TEA, p. 268) it can be drunk to bring down fevers and calm inflamed urinary tracts. It is also a nutritious food for infants.

SEASONED BARLEY

Preparation time: 1 hour
Serves: 4-5
mildly +Vata, −Pitta, −−Kapha*

❀ ❄

    1 cup dry barley
    6 cups water
    1 burdock root (12 to 15 inches)
    1/2 teaspoon sea salt
    1 onion, chopped (optional)
    1/2 stick kombu
    1 teaspoon dry sage
    Black pepper and *ghee* to taste

Wash and peel the burdock root; chop it finely. Place all ingredients except sage, black pepper and *ghee* in medium saucepan and bring to a boil. Cover and lower heat to medium-low. Cook until tender, about 50 minutes. Add sage, black pepper and *ghee* and simmer another 5 minutes.

Comments: This dish is specifically useful for ulcerative, mucus, or nervous colitis, or combinations thereof (the raw twingy gut).

* +Vata if used regularly (fine for occasional use)

Variation: Instead of sage, add 1/2 teaspoon thyme, 1/2 teaspoon oregano, 1/4 teaspoon savory, all dried, and 1/8 teaspoon black pepper. This formula works more on the upper digestive tract, enhancing digestion in the stomach. Good served with tamari.

"PLAIN" BARLEY

Preparation time: 1 hour   Serves: 4-5
*moderately +Vata, −Pitta, −Kapha**   ✿ ⁂ ❄

1 cup barley, uncooked
5 cups water
½ teaspoon sea salt
2 tablespoons fresh parsley, chopped
1 teaspoon ground cumin

Put barley, water and salt in medium saucepan and bring to boil. Then cover and reduce heat to medium-low and cook until barley is done (tender), about 50 minutes. Add parsley and cumin.

*Serve with ghee for Vata to calm this effect; it is then only mildly imbalancing; fine for occasional use. Year-round for Kapha and Pitta.

BARLEY AND MUSHROOMS

Preparation time: 1 hour 15 minutes   Serves: 4-5
mildly +Vata, −Pitta, −Kapha   ✿ ❄

1 cup dry barley
3 cups water
½ cup Shiitake mushrooms
3 tablespoons butter or *ghee* (reduce to 1 tablespoon for *Kapha*)
1 teaspoon mustard seeds
1 tablespoon sesame seeds
2 cloves
1 teaspoon sea salt
¼ teaspoon fresh ground black pepper
3 tablespoons fresh parsley, chopped fine

Garnish: with extra *ghee*, sesame seeds and clove to calm *Vata*.

Put barley with water in large pot. Bring to a boil uncovered; then cover, lower heat to simmer and cook until done, 50 minutes to 1 hour. While barley is cooking, soak Shiitake mushrooms in enough water to cover them, for at least 15 minutes. Drain mushrooms and slice.

When barley is done, heat butter or *ghee* in small frying pan. Add mustard seeds. When they pop, add sesame seeds, cloves and sliced mushrooms. Cook over low heat for 4-5 minutes. Then add remaining ingredients plus sauteed mushroom mixture to barley; mix well. Cook 2-3 minutes.

ABOUT RYE, MILLET, AND BUCKWHEAT

Rye, millet and buckwheat are all hot, light, dry grains. For this reason, they are ideal for Kapha. *Rye and millet are particularly balancing grains for* Kapha, *as is barley. Their light dry qualities make them inappropriate for* Vata *if eaten alone. The sweet* vipak *of millet, rye and buckwheat balance their heat to some extent for* Pitta, *making them less imbalancing when prepared with extra moisture. Interestingly, rye and buckwheat have usually been served with wheat down the generations. This gives cold heavy moist wheat a chance to balance the other grains' opposing light and dry qualities. This combination is helpful for* Pitta *and* Vata. *These two can usually handle a bread made from rye and wheat flours more easily than a 100% rye bread. Not so for* Kapha, *who is best off with the all rye product, preferably toasted. 100% rye crackers are especially valuable for* Kapha. *100% buckwheat noodles (soba) are also helpful for the* Kapha *who misses the joys of regular pasta. They can be found in Asian groceries and Western health food stores. Commercial buckwheat pancakes, while delicious, usually have more wheat than buckwheat in them. They are more useful for* Pitta *and* Vata *than* Kapha, *ironically enough. Check out the BUCKWHEAT PANCAKES (p. 277) under BREAKFASTS, to keep* Kapha *calmer.*

SPICY MILLET AND POTATO

Preparation time: with pre-cooked grain, 10-15 minutes   Serves: 2-4
with fresh grain, 40-55 minutes   ✿ ❄
+ *Vata, 0 Pitta, — Kapha*

> 1½ cup cooked millet
> 1 medium potato, well-scrubbed
> 2 tablespoons sunflower oil
> ⅛ teaspoon *hing*
> ½ teaspoon mustard seeds
> ½ teaspoon curry powder
> 1 teaspoon fresh ginger chopped or ⅛ teaspoon dry ginger powder
> ½ teaspoon sea salt

Garnish: fresh chopped coriander leaves, if available

Wash and dice potato. Heat oil in medium frying pan and add *hing* and mustard seeds. When the mustard seeds pop, add potatoes and curry powder. Stir and cook over low heat for 5 to 7 minutes. Add cooked millet and all other ingredients. Mix well and remove from heat.

Comment: This goes well with goat yogurt and vegetable curries.

HERBED MILLET

Preparation time: 35 minutes   Serves: 4
+ *Vata, + Pitta, — — Kapha*   ❄

> 1 cup dry millet
> 2½ to 3 cups water
> ¼ teaspoon sea salt
> ½ small onion, finely chopped
> 3 small cloves of garlic, unpeeled (or 1 peeled and minced)
> 1 teaspoon sage

Put all the ingredients in a medium saucepan and bring to a boil. Cover and reduce heat to low. Cook 30 minutes or until millet has absorbed all the moisture of the water. It's a good idea to check it at 20 minutes, as sometimes the millet cooks faster.

Comments: This goes well with AJWAN TEA (p. 271) or OSHA TEA (p. 267), especially on those bloggy mornings or evenings when a cold might be upon you.

A good breakfast or dinner dish. Add the greater amount of water if you like a creamy consistency or are working to calm *Vata*, the lesser if you prefer it like a dinner grain. Good in rainy weather.

Fine for occasional use for Vata and Pitta: use the larger amount of water for Vata, and skip the garlic for Pitta.

SOUTHWESTERN POSOLE

Preparation time: overnight, plus 3 hours   Serves: 4
(about 15 minutes of actual preparation)   ✿ ❄
+ *Vata*, + + *Pitta*, − *Kapha*

> 2 cups dry yellow or blue corn posole (about 12 ounces, available primarily in the Southwest, occasionally in Mexican sections of groceries elsewhere)
> 8 cups water
> 1 large onion, chopped
> 2 cloves garlic, minced
> 1 tablespoon sunflower oil (optional)
> 1 teaspoon or more red chili powder, or 3 red chili pods
> 1 teaspoon oregano
> 1 teaspoon sea salt
> 1 tablespoon coriander seeds
> ½ teaspoon cumin seeds

Soak the posole overnight in water, then rinse well and drain. Put the posole and water in a large pot and bring to a boil. Cover and lower heat to medium and cook for 2½ hours. Add the rest of the ingredients and cook for another ½ hour, or until posole is tender. Stir occasionally. This can be made in a crockpot.

Comments: This goes well with SANTA FE PINTO BEANS (p. 107) and a salad. This recipe is included because it tastes good and is balancing to *Kapha*. So often, *Kaphas* shun starch, having been taught from infancy onward that it is "bad" for chunky types. In reality, modest amounts of complex carbohydrates are quite useful for *Kapha* and keep insulin mechanisms running smoothly. Obviously, if you have not found this to be the case for you, don't take my word for it. Try a little and see how it affects you.

Other healthy starch options for *Kapha* include 100% buckwheat soba noodles, good with chopped parsley and *ghee* or steamed vegetables, corn tortillas, popcorn, and Jinenjo wild potato noodles. The latter usually have some wheat in them, so they should be used occasionally rather than regularly. However, they are quite a tasty and tender pasta for those looking for wheat-limited options.

GREEN CHILI POSOLE: add ½ cup stewed green chilis to the recipe above, when you add the other spices.

TURKEY OR CHICKEN POSOLE: traditionally posole has red meat in it. A lower fat but still non-vegetarian option is to add 1 pound of lean chicken or turkey, cubed, to the posole in the last hour of cooking. Popular here in the mountains of New Mexico.

ABOUT WHEAT

Wheat is the most widely used grain in the United States. And it is the heaviest and most moist of the grains as well. This is its strength and its drawback. It is excellent for balancing a dry bean like garbanzo. For example, it can be used to make pita bread with falafel or humus. It is very grounding when served with something cool and moist like cheese. It is the best grain to use if you are interested in gaining weight (as long as you don't have an allergy to it). You might guess from this discussion that wheat is great for Vata and highly imbalancing for Kapha. True! It is also balancing for Pitta in that it is cool as well as heavy.

Wheat sensitivities are widespread in this country at this time, perhaps partially due to the infant feeding practices of a generation ago. We introduced grains to infants as early as three weeks of life, in the well-meaning but mistaken belief that babies needed this extra nourishment. In truth, the intestinal lining is not ready to break down grains at such an early age. Instead, food can look like a foreign substance at this age, and be treated as such. Antibodies can be made to the undigested grains, with allergies resulting. Symptoms of grain sensitivity range from sluggishness after consuming them, to indigestion, headache, joint pain, and moodiness. If you are sensitive to wheat or any other grain, avoid it, regardless of what is recommended here in the Ayurvedic charts for your constitution. At times, these sensitivities can be healed and the food reintroduced. Supporting agni and avoiding the offending food for a time, plus skilled assistance in enhancing digestive and immune power, is most effective in healing allergies.

ROTALIS OR CHAPPATIS

Preparation time: 2 hours
–Vata, –Pitta, +Kapha

Makes: 20 to 25

✿ ✳ ଈ ❄

> 2 cups whole wheat flour
> 2 teaspoons sunflower oil
> 1 cup warm water
> ¾ cup whole wheat flour in separate bowl
> *Ghee*

In a deep bowl mix flour and oil with your hands, then add water and prepare a dough. (This dough is softer than other doughs.) Cover and let sit for one hour. Add 1 additional teaspoon of oil and mix it in so that it thoroughly penetrates the dough.

Prepare 20 to 25 small balls from the dough. Squeeze and knead between your palms. Cover balls with dry flour, and roll with a rolling pin on a wooden board to about 3 to 4 inch circles. Sprinkle with dry flour again, then roll each *rotali* to its full size of about 6 inches in diameter.

Transfer each *rotali* to a hot iron pan over medium heat. Turn it over after ½ minute or when you see small bubbles. Let it cook another ½ minute. Then transfer it to direct flame of stove until it puffs like a balloon. Take it out to a dish and spread *ghee* on it.

Comments: This goes well with rice and soup or any vegetable preparation. The classic Indian flat-bread. A good yeast-free alternative to regular bread. One teaspoon to 1 tablespoon each of cumin seeds and black peppercorns can also be pressed into the dough for a more pungent flavor which stimulates digestion (*–Vata, –Pitta, moderately +Kapha*).

For children, you can use rice syrup and nut butters and roll the *chappati* into a "log," a popular option (*–Vata, +Pitta, +Kapha*).

RYE CHAPPATIS

Preparation time: 30 minutes or less
moderately +Vata, moderately +Pitta, –Kapha

Makes: 5 *chappatis*

✿ ✳ ଈ ❄

> ½ cup rye flour
> ½ teaspoon *ghee*
> ⅛ cup cold water

Rub the *ghee* into the rye flour with your fingertips. Add the water. Mix and knead the dough until a smooth consistency has been achieved. Divide the dough into 5 equal-sized balls. Roll the balls in rye flour on a well-floured surface. With a floured rolling pin, roll the balls out to 5½ to 5¾ inches in diameter.

Cook on a hot dry pan for 15 seconds to 1 minute or until bubbles appear on the top side. A non-stick frying pan works well for this. Turn the *chappati* and cook another 15 seconds to 1 minute on the other side or until the *chappati* is lightly browned.

If you have a gas stove, finish cooking the *chappati* directly over the flame without a pan. The *chappati* will puff up. As soon as it puffs, flip once to complete cooking. After cooking, coat one side lightly with *ghee*.

If an electric stove is available, use a second pan lightly coated with oil. Cook the *chappati* lightly on both sides.

CORN BREAD

Preparation time: 45 minutes   Makes: 1 loaf or 9-12 squares
Vata, Pitta, Kapha (see below)   ✿ ❄

> 1 cup cornmeal
> 1 cup barley or rice flour
> 1 teaspoon sea salt
> 2 ½ teaspoons baking powder (2 teaspoons at high altitude)
> 2 egg whites or 1 egg
> 1½ to 4 tablespoons sunflower oil or ghee
> 1 tablespoon sweetener: apple concentrate, maple syrup, or brown rice syrup
> 1 cup milk (cow, goat, or soy)

Preheat the oven to 400 degrees. Lightly oil an 8 by 8 inch baking pan and put in the oven to heat for 5 minutes. Sift together the dry ingredients well. (This step is important, especially if you are making cornbread for *Kapha*, with the minimum of oil. It keeps the bread lighter.)

Lightly whisk the egg whites or egg and stir in the rest of the wet ingredients. Stir the two mixtures together with a few quick whisks of a spoon. Pour the batter into the hot pan and bake for 25 to 30 minutes or until done (a toothpick stuck into the center of the bread should come out clean).

Serve hot.

For *Vata:* use rice flour, egg whites or egg, 4 tablespoons of fat, maple syrup or rice syrup, and cow's milk (– *Vata,* – *Pitta, moderately* +*Kapha*)

For *Pitta:* use barley or rice flour, egg whites, 2 to 4 tablespoons fat, any of the sweeteners, and any of the milks (*0 Vata,* – *Pitta, moderately* + *Kapha*)

For *Kapha:* use barley flour, egg whites or egg, as little oil as you can still enjoy, apple concentrate, and goat or soy milk (+ *Vata,* – *Pitta,* – *Kapha*)

Tridosha: use either flour, egg whites, 3 tablespoons fat, maple or brown rice syrup and soy milk or ½ cup cow's milk diluted with ½ cup water (– *Pitta,* – *Vata, 0 Kapha*)

Comments: The trick here is adding enough fat to make the cornbread delicious, without adding so much fat that it no longer calms *Kapha.* In making cornbreads for this cookbook, I began to realize that most commercial cornbreads do not help *Kapha,* but aggravate it. Most use at least ¼ cup of fat, which calms and sweetens the bread in the long run, making it more suitable for *Vata or Pitta,* ironically enough. If you do make this recipe with the minimum of oil and need to warm the cornbread up to re-serve it, STEAM IT, DO NOT TOAST IT. The steam gives added moisture, while toasting makes an already border-line dry bread too dry. In all cases, *Vata* and *Pitta* can serve with extra butter or *ghee* and sweetener to calm this warm drying effect.

EGGLESS CORN BREAD

Preparation Time: 2 hours, most of it unattended   Makes: 1 loaf or 9-12 squares
moderately + *Vata, 0 Pitta,* – *Kapha*

> 1 cup cornmeal
> ½ cup barley flour
> ½ cup oat flour
> ½ teaspoon sea salt
> 1 teaspoon baking powder (¾ teaspoon if cooking at high altitude)
> 1½ cups buttermilk, or ½ cup plain low-fat yogurt and 1 cup water
> 1 tablespoon apple concentrate

Sift the dry ingredients together. Then mix all ingredients in a bowl. Let stand covered for one hour. Preheat oven to 350 degrees. Bake in well-greased bread pan or 8 by 8 inch baking pan for 40 to 45 minutes. Serve immediately.

Comments: This moist, slightly sour dough flavored bread is an easy one for those looking to avoid eggs. If you like, you can bring the cup of water to a boil and pour it over the cornmeal first before adding the rest of the ingredients. This calms the slight bitterness of the cornmeal and brings out a bit of sweetness. *Pitta* and *Vata* can balance this recipe with additional *ghee* and/or appropriate sweetener.

BANANA MUFFINS

Preparation time: 35 minutes   Makes: 6 large muffins
– Vata, 0 Pitta, + Kapha

> **2 large ripe bananas**
> **¼ cup sunflower oil**
> **¼ cup maple syrup**
> **½ teaspoon ground cardamom**
> **½ teaspoon cinnamon**
> **2 dates, chopped**
> **1¼ cups flour, barley and Indian rice flour, half and half, or 1¼ cups whole wheat flour**
> **1½ teaspoons baking powder (1 teaspoon at high altitude)**
> **½ teaspoon sea salt**

Preheat oven to 350 degrees. Mash the bananas in a medium mixing bowl and stir in the oil and syrup. Mix in the spices and the dry ingredients. Spoon into well-oiled muffin tin and bake 25 minutes or until done.

Comments: Really good and quite easy. We keep meaning to see if these muffins keep well, but we never have a chance, they get eaten too fast.

Variation: Substitute ¼ cup all fruit sweetened jam for the maple syrup. Apricot jam or orange marmalade work well. These jams have no sugar and are sweetened with fruit juice concentrate. They can be found at most whole-food or health food stores.

ABOUT OAT BRAN

Oat bran has become popular recently as a source of fiber and as one way to lower blood cholesterol levels. It is far lighter and dryer than regular oats. It is most balancing for Kapha, served as a cold breakfast cereal like oat bran flakes. It is relatively neutral for Pitta. Unless it is well-moistened, it can definitely imbalance Vata. Vata can get the benefit of the oat bran fiber naturally present in cooked rolled oats. Oat bran can also be added to muffin or bread recipes to lighten their effects and add fiber (see OAT BRAN MUFFINS which follows). Aptly enough, in Ayurveda, rough dry foods like oat bran are highly regarded as a way of counteracting the effects of consuming too many sweet heavy foods, such as meat, wine, cheese, and sweets.

OAT BRAN MUFFINS

Preparation time: 45 to 50 minutes
+ *Vata*, − *Pitta*, − *Kapha*

Makes: 12 3-inch muffins

❁ ✳ ☙ ❄

2 cups oat bran (or about 4 cups rolled oats)
1 teaspoon sea salt
2 teaspoons baking powder
¹/₂ teaspoon cinnamon
¹/₄ teaspoon ground cloves
¹/₈ teaspoon dry ginger powder
2 cups goat milk
¹/₂ cup dried figs, or ¹/₂ cup unsweetened applesauce
¹/₂ cup raisins
¹/₄ cup *ghee* or sunflower oil
1 egg (or 2 egg whites, if you're looking for zero cholesterol)
¹/₂ cup sunflower seeds (optional)

Preheat oven to 425 degrees and grease muffin tin. If using rolled oats, grind them dry in the blender to give them the crumbly powdered texture of oat bran. The volume of the rolled oats will reduce from about 4 cups to that of the oat bran, 2 cups when ground.

Mix the oat bran or ground oats with salt, baking powder, spices, and sunflower seeds in a large mixing bowl. In a small saucepan, bring the goat milk to a boil. Pour it and all the wet ingredients except raisins into the blender and blend until figs are finely chopped and egg is blended. Pour liquid into dry ingredients and stir quickly, using a minimum of strokes to avoid making the muffins tough. Stir in raisins. Fill greased muffin tins ²/₃ to ¾ full with the batter. Bake at 425 degrees for 20 to 25 minutes or until done (a knife stuck in the center of a muffin will come out clean when done).

Comments: Good with *ghee* and hot tea. *Pitta* can substitute soy or cow milk in this recipe if they like. However, the astringency of goat milk is beneficial for *Pitta* as well as *Kapha*.

Variation: Substitute 2 cups rolled oats and 1 cup whole wheat flour for the oat bran. Grind up the rolled oats as directed. Use cow's milk rather than goat's milk, and add ½ cup sweetener—maple syrup, rice syrup, or Sucanat in place of the figs or applesauce (− *Vata*, − *Pitta*, + *Kapha*).

QUICK WHEAT-FREE BREAD

Preparation time: 40 minutes   Serves: 6-8
mildly + Pitta, mildly +Vata, −Kapha *   ❀ ❄

> 1½ cups oat bran
> ¾ cup cornmeal
> 1 teaspoon sea salt
> 2 teaspoons baking powder (1½ teaspoons at high altitude)
> 2 cups soy milk or cow's milk (soy for *Kapha*)
> 1-2 tablespoons maple syrup (the greater amount for *Vata* and *Pitta*,
> the lesser for *Kapha*, or as your tastes dictate)
> 1 large egg, beaten
> 1 tablespoon sunflower oil or *ghee*
> ¼ cup sunflower seeds (optional)

Preheat oven to 425 degrees.

In a medium mixing bowl mix together the dry ingredients: oat bran, cornmeal, salt, and baking powder. In another bowl beat the egg and then beat in the soy milk, maple syrup and oil. Add wet ingredients to dry ones, with a minimum of strokes. The mixture will be soupy in consistency. Pour into a greased 8 inch square baking pan and bake for 20 to 25 minutes or until done (knife inserted in center will come out clean). Makes 16 2 inch squares, or one dozen muffins.

Comments: The advantages of this bread are that it is moist, holds together and tastes good, no rare thing in a wheat-free bread, as those of you who have tried them know. It also works well as a quick fruit bread, with mashed banana, apricots, or dates added in place of some of the liquid.

*Both Vata and Pitta can ameliorate this a great deal with the addition of butter and jam, or ghee *and sweetener.*

Variation: SAGE ONION BREAD: saute in the 1 tablespoon of oil, 1 small onion, chopped. Omit the sweetener and add 1 teaspoon dry sage. Stir these into liquid ingredients and proceed as above. Savory and light.

+Vata, mildly +Pitta, −Kapha

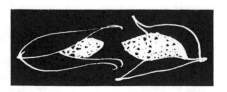

VEGETABLES

ABOUT VEGETABLES

Vegetables are a delightful way to lighten up a meal, and balance the taste of it for your constitution or family. Rich in vitamins and low in calories, they offer nourishment without ponderous mass. Being in general light and moist, they are some of the easiest foods to digest when properly prepared. They combine well with most foods, including proteins, grains and fats. Vegetables have a wide range of tastes, from sweet (winter squash), bitter (dark leafy greens), astringent (asparagus), and pungent (watercress) to salty (celery). This means they can be used in a wide variety of ways to heal. Like most foods, vegetables are classified as cool or warm, light or heavy in Ayurveda. The warming vegetables tend to be most advantageous for Vata and Kapha, the cooling ones for Pitta. Heavy roots are used to balance light Vata and leafy vegetables are more often advised for substantial Kapha.

Asparagus is one of the few vegetables that can be eaten by all doshas with no alteration. Sweet, astringent, and bitter, cool, light and moist, it is ideal for Pitta. It stabilizes Vata, being easy to digest, and lightens and stimulates Kapha. It can be steamed and eaten as it is here, or used in a wide variety of curries, kichadis, and main dishes. It is used medicinally in Ayurveda as a mild laxative, cardiac and nerve sedative, tonic, aphrodisiac, and demulcent. Calm your distraught partner (or yourself) after a long day at work with this vital veggie! A less potent relative of the rejuvenative Indian preparation Shatavari.

SIMPLE STEAMED ASPARAGUS

Preparation time: 15 minutes or less
– *Vata,* – *Pitta,* – *Kapha*

Serves: 3-4

❁ ✳ ৯৯

> **1 pound fresh asparagus**
> **1 cup water**
> **1 tablespoon *ghee* or butter**

Put water in medium-sized heavy skillet; heat on medium heat. Wash and trim asparagus, cutting any woody ends off (these can be saved for use in a soup stock if you like). Leave asparagus stalks whole. When water has come to a boil, put asparagus in skillet and cover. Steam until tender, 5-8 minutes. (A fork will go through them easily when they are tender.) Drain and serve with *ghee* or butter.

ASPARAGUS AND PARSNIPS

Preparation time: 30 minutes
Serves: 4-5

−Vata, −Pitta, 0 Kapha

✿ ✳ ❧ ❄

> ¾ pound fresh asparagus (2½ to 3 cups chopped)
> 3 medium parsnips (2 to 2½ cups chopped)
> 1 to 2 tablespoons sunflower oil or *ghee* (the greater amount for *Vata*
> and *Pitta,* the lesser amount for *Kapha*)
> ½ cup water
> ½ teaspoon fenugreek seeds
> ¼ teaspoon black mustard seeds (omit for *Pitta*)
> ⅛ teaspoon *hing*
> ½ teaspoon turmeric
> ½ teaspoon rock or sea salt
> ½ teaspoon ground cumin
> ¼ teaspoon freshly ground black pepper
> 1 tablespoon coriander powder

**Garnish: small green chili pepper, chopped (for *Kapha,* and a little for *Vata*),
and with chopped pepper and dry ginger (for *Kapha*)**

Wash the asparagus and parsnips well. Dry them and cut the asparagus into 1 inch
pieces, the parsnips into ½ inch cubes. Bring ½ of the oil to warm in a large skillet,
add the fenugreek and mustard seeds. When the mustard seeds pop, stir in the *hing*
and turmeric and the chopped parsnips. Mix well. Add the water and cover and cook
over medium heat for about 4 minutes. Warm the rest of the oil in a separate pan
and saute the asparagus until flavorful, about 5 to 8 minutes. Add the remaining
ingredients to the parsnips and stir well. Cook over low heat for another 5 to 10 minutes. Just before serving, mix the sauteed asparagus in with the parsnips.

Comments: This goes well with *KADHI* BUTTERMILK CURRY (p. 78) and rice. This
tasty dish is based on the old Gujarati favorite of okra and potatoes. If you want to
make it in the original, use ¾ pound fresh okra instead of asparagus and 2 small
potatoes instead of the parsnips. The dish is also good with green beans substituted
for the asparagus. As it stands, ASPARAGUS AND PARSNIPS is a good dish for
tonifying the reproductive tract in both men and women.

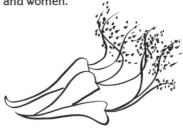

ABOUT ARTICHOKES AND OKRA

Globe artichokes are nearly as tridoshic as asparagus. Like asparagus, they are cool, light, moist, sweet, and astringent. They lack the slight bitterness of asparagus and so do not relieve Kapha and Pitta quite as much. Still, they are a food that can be eaten by all types without loss of balance. They need to be well-cooked, and preferably warmly herbed, to be assimilable by Vata.

Okra is used more frequently in India than in the United States, with the exception of the American South, as it grows best at tropical temperatures. This slippery tropical vegetable, the "edible hibiscus," relieves Pitta, has a neutral effect on Kapha, and very mildly increases Vata. It is cool, diuretic, soothing, and softening. Cooked to enhance its moistening qualities,it is well-tolerated by all doshas. It acts as an anti-inflammatory in cystitis, sore throat, fevers, bronchitis, and irritable bowel.

ARTICHOKES

Preparation time: 50 minutes   Serves: 2
with pressure cooker: 15 minutes (8 minutes if small artichokes)* ❀ ✳ 🐌 ❄
— Vata, — Pitta, — Kapha

> **2 large healthy artichokes**
> **3 cups water**
> **1 bay leaf**
> **¼ teaspoon sea salt (optional)**

Wash artichoke and trim off base. Put water in large saucepan; bring to boil; add salt and bay leaf. When the water is boiling, add the artichokes. Cover and cook on medium heat until artichokes are tender, about 45 minutes.

If using pressure cooker, put all ingredients in cooker, cover. Bring to pressure at 10 pounds and cook 12 minutes (8 minutes if using small artichokes), or until tender. Cool, open.

Comments: The bay leaf warms and eases digestion for *Vata* and *Kapha.* A nice dish for a beleaguered liver.

Good served with lemon, *ghee,* mayonnaise, or CUCUMBER RAITA (p. 224).

*For high-altitude cooking, cook artichokes 3-5 minutes.

SAUTEED OKRA

Preparation time: 30 minutes   Serves: 4-5
— *Vata*, — *Pitta*, + *Kapha*   ✳ 🍃

>   1 pound fresh okra
>   4 tablespoons sunflower oil or *ghee*
>   ½ teaspoon fenugreek seeds
>   ½ teaspoon turmeric
>   ⅛ teaspoon *hing*
>   ½ teaspoon sea salt
>   2 teaspoons coriander powder
>   ¼ teaspoon black pepper
>   ¼ teaspoon ground cumin

Wash okra and spread it on absorbent paper towel or cloth to dry thoroughly. Cut okra in ½ inch pieces, throwing away the tops.

In heavy skillet heat oil and add fenugreek seeds. When they turn brown, add turmeric, *hing,* salt, and okra. Mix well, cover and cook over low heat for 10 minutes. Cook uncovered another 10 minutes over very low heat, stirring occasionally to keep the okra from sticking. Add remaining ingredients and mix well. Serve.

Comment: This goes well with SPLIT GREEN PEAS, INDIAN STYLE (p. 109), and "PLAIN" INDIAN RICE (p. 129).

GREEN BEAN *BHAJI*

Preparation time: 45 minutes   Serves: 4-6
— *Vata*, — *Pitta*, — *Kapha*   ❀ ✳ 🍃 ❄

>   4 cups fresh green beans
>   1 tablespoon sunflower oil or *ghee*
>   ½ teaspoon black mustard seeds
>   ⅛ teaspoon *hing* (optional, helpful for *Vata*)
>   1 teaspoon turmeric
>   2 to 6 tablespoons water
>   ½ teaspoon sea salt
>   1 inch fresh chopped ginger root
>   1 small fresh green chili pepper (omit for *Pitta*)
>   ½ cup chopped fresh coriander leaves

Garnish: shredded unsweetened coconut, chopped coriander leaves

Wash the beans and chop into one inch pieces. The fresher they are, the less likely they are to agitate *Vata*, and *Pitta* and *Kapha* will not object either. Warm the oil or *ghee* in a large skillet with a lid. Add the mustard seeds and warm them until they pop. Add turmeric and *hing* and stir well. Put in the chopped green beans and 2 to 3 tablespoons water. Cover and cook on low until the beans are tender (about 15 to 30 minutes).

Put the rest of the water and the remaining ingredients (salt, ginger, chili, coriander, and coconut) in the blender and puree. Pour over the cooked beans and mix well. Simmer for 1 to 2 minutes or until well-mixed. Garnish with more coriander and coconut.

Comment: This goes well with *dal* and *basmati* rice.

Garnish liberally with coconut and coriander for *Pitta*, add extra *ghee* for *Vata*, and take it easy on the coconut for *Kapha*.

This makes a good company dish and an easy way to introduce people to Ayurvedic cooking. I owe the flavor of this dish to Usha Lad, Dr. Lad's spouse. When I (A.M.) was first trying to teach myself Indian cooking, a fair number of humbling flops occurred, and this was an early one. The beans were tender, but very bland in flavor. I hadn't a clue as to how to proceed. Usha said, "Here, look . . ." and pulled out the chili, ginger and coconut from the refrigerator, and popped them in the blender with a bit of water. Aah. Much better. And a delicious example of south Indian cooking.

PUNJABI-STYLE STRING BEANS

Preparation time: 1 hour   Serves: 5-6
−*Vata*, −*Pitta*, −*Kapha**   ✿   🐛   ❄

> 1 pound fresh string beans
> 2 tablespoons sunflower oil
> 1/2 teaspoon mustard seeds
> 1/2 teaspoon turmeric
> 1/8 teaspoon *hing*
> 3/4 teaspoon sea salt
> 1 cup water
> 1 tablespoon coriander seeds
> 1-2 cloves garlic (optional, omit for *Pitta*)
> 1 teaspoon cumin seeds
> 5-6 whole black peppercorns
> 1 teaspoon rice syrup
> 1/2 teaspoon curry powder (mild)
> 1/2 hot green pepper, chopped (optional, omit for *Pitta*)

Garnish: Fresh chopped coriander leaves

Wash and dry string beans. Cut lengthwise and then cut into 1 to 2 inch pieces, about 4 to 5 cuts per bean. Heat oil in a large saucepan and add mustard seeds. When they pop, add turmeric, *hing*, string beans, and salt. Stir, mixing well. Then add ½ cup water. Cover and cook over medium heat for 15 to 20 minutes.

While beans are cooking, heat 1 teaspoon of oil in a small frying pan and add cumin seeds, coriander seeds and black peppercorns. Saute for about 3 minutes. Cool, then blend in blender. Leave this mixture in blender and add hot green pepper and rest of water (½ cup). Blend again. Add this mixture plus remaining ingredients to cooked string beans and cook an additional 5 minutes uncovered. Garnish with fresh coriander leaves.

Comments: This goes well with *CHANA DAL* SOUP (p. 193) and *chappatis.* This dish takes a relatively long time to make, and it's worth it. Cutting the beans alone consumes about a quarter of an hour, but they take up the spices in a most wonderful way, when so cut. Good fancy dish for company, or when you're feeling like playing in the kitchen. The fresher and juicier the string beans, and the longer they cook, the more likely they are to calm rather than aggravate *Vata*. Dry or poorly cooked green beans indisputably increase *Vata*.

*Pitta needs to garnish with coriander and coconut in order to be balanced.

ABOUT GREENS

As Dr. Vasant Lad says, "Bitter is better!" and dark leafy greens are one of the best ways to get bitter taste pleasantly. We find ourselves recommending dark leafy greens very frequently, as an excellent way of counteracting the heaviness and lack of nourishment in much of the Western diet. Light, pungent and rich in both vitamins and minerals, dark leafies like kale, collards, arugula, dandelion, chicory, mustard and turnip greens are all specific healers for the liver and immune system. They also provide superb support for the skin, eyes, and mucus membranes. Properly prepared, they are easy to digest and will stimulate elimination. They can be eaten as much as three to four times per week or more for their healing properties. They make an especially excellent spring tonic. Most greens have a pungent vipak, which is why it is best to prepare them with generous amounts of cooling coriander powder.

Spinach, swiss chard and beet greens are a bit different. While fast to cook, they are a concentrated source of oxalic acid. This compound binds

*with calcium, preventing its absorption. An occasional meal of these veg-
etables does no harm, but they are best not eaten as regularly as the other
greens recommended above.*

*Spinach cools, nourishes and soothes, with light, dry attributes and a
pungent vipak. In large quantities it is aggravating to Pitta and Vata, and best
served to Kapha. Small amounts are well-tolerated by all, and are useful
medicinally in the treatment of lung and liver disorders.*

*Some greens are obviously more pungent than others: mustard greens
being hotter than collards or kale for example. Pittas especially need to take
taste into account when choosing their greens. The more pungent greens—
mustard, arugula, turnip greens, watercress—are easier for most Kaphas
and Vatas to catabolize, and are best minimized by Pitta. Vatas do well to
take their greens well-cooked, not raw. Pitta and Kapha can handle them
either way.*

FAVORITE DARK LEAFY GREENS

Preparation time: 10 to 20 minutes   Serves: 2-4
−Vata, −Pitta, −Kapha*   ✿   ✳   🐚   ❄

> 1 bunch dark leafy greens: kale, collards, mustard, turnip or dandelion
> greens
> 1/2-3/4 cup water
> 1 teaspoon sunflower oil or *ghee*
> 1/2 teaspoon whole cumin seeds
> 1 teaspoon coriander powder

Wash the greens and chop them, taking out the stem in the process. Bring water to a
boil in a heavy bottomed skillet. Put in chopped greens, cover, lower heat to simmer.
Cook on low heat for 7 to 15 minutes or until greens are tender. Drain, saving water,
if not too bitter, for use as soup broth.

Heat oil in small frying pan over low heat. Add cumin seeds. When they begin to
brown, stir in coriander. Brown, do not burn. Pour this mixture over the drained
greens, mixing well. Serve immediately.

Comments: This is a great dish to introduce yourself or others to greens. As one
person put it, "it's user-friendly!" Nutritious and easy to digest, the spices take the
edge off the usually bitter greens.

Traditionally, greens are cooked for long periods of time and the water is not saved for further use. This is still very appropriate when working with wild greens, such as lambs quarters or purslane (which taste delicious prepared in this way, by the way). Wild herbs tend to have more potent medicinal qualities. Cultivated greens' effect is much milder, though they offer goodly amounts of vitamin A, B complex, iron, magnesium, and calcium, some of which ends up in the cooking water. This dish is good for the liver, skin and colon.

Occasionally you may encounter a batch of greens so bitter these amounts of herbs won't calm them. In this case, increase the coriander powder to as much as 1 tablespoon. If still too bitter, stir in 2 tablespoons plain yogurt before serving.

* *Most calming for Pitta and Kapha, an occasional option for Vata.*

ABOUT POTATOES AND THE NIGHTSHADE FAMILY

The nightshades—tomato, white potato, eggplant, peppers, and tobacco—were used in the New World for centuries with little difficulty. But their reception by the Old World has been a bit problematic. The deadly nightshades get their name for a definite reason: they concentrate poisonous alkaloids in various parts of their anatomy, particularly their leaves. This is why chewing on a potato or tomato leaf is never recommended. When the potato was first discovered in North America and sent back to Queen Elizabeth the First for her consumption, her chef unfortunately erred and served her the potato leaf and stem, and threw out the root! Elizabeth was unimpressed. And potatoes did not make it as a staple food in Europe for another two hundred years. Nightshade leaves were used, ground up with poisonous mushrooms, as a deterrent to flies in the Old World. But their fruits were highly mistrusted. Are they all dangerous? We're not sure. The solanines in them certainly are. It is often recommended to avoid the nightshade family if you are seeking to eliminate a condition of rheumatoid arthritis.

White potatoes are cool, light and dry; therefore they imbalance Vata, assist Kapha, and essentially have a neutral effect on Pitta. They are one of the few nightshade fruits that can accumulate enough toxins in their edible portion to be overtly toxic. Fortunately, it is relatively easy to tell if they have done so. If a potato has a green shade to its peel, it is suspect. The toxic alkaloids solanine and chaconine accumulate close to the surface of the peel in these areas, especially if potatoes are allowed to sit in light, or are stored in very cold or fairly warm places. A cool dark storage spot serves potatoes best. Cooking will not remove these toxins. Cutting out the green portion, usually the surface ⅛ inch or less, will. Besides greening, a sharp, burning sensation on the tongue upon eating the potato is another sign of excessive alkaloid levels. Cutting the potato to eliminate these areas is usually sufficient.

The preparation of the humble potato has a great deal to do with whether it is calming or irritating to a given dosha. While potato is beneficial to Kapha, french fries, potato chips and baked potato with sour cream are not. Each of these contains a lot of oil; the inherently light potato has become heavy by preparation. Similarly, many Vatas can handle a baked potato on occasion if it has generous amounts of ghee, yogurt or sour cream on it. (Though much sour cream can get a Vata digestive tract rumbling ominously.) Pittas and Kaphas do best with their potatoes boiled or stewed in dishes, not fried. Baked potatoes are fine for Pitta if they do not overdo it on the fatty condiments. Vatas need their potatoes well-spiced and moistened, as they are in the following recipe. Potatoes, being rich in Vitamin C, have been used in Ayurveda as a cure for scurvy for centuries. They are also recommended as an easy to digest starch for those with nervous indigestion or indigestion related to liver weakness.

TRIDOSHIC MASHED POTATOES

Preparation time: 45 minutes   Serves: 4
0 Vata, − Pitta, − Kapha   ❀   ✳   ☙   ❄

  8 new potatoes with skins
  ¹/₂ cup goat milk, hot
  ¹/₄ cup (4 tablespoons) *ghee*
  1 teaspoon sea salt
  1 tablespoon fresh parsley, chopped (optional)
  1 teaspoon fresh marjoram, chopped (optional)

Garnish: liberally with *ghee* **for** *Vata*

Put 2 to 3 quarts of water in a medium saucepan and bring to a boil (should be enough water to cover the potatoes). While the water is heating, wash the potatoes, scrubbing well. When the water has come to a boil, put in the potatoes, whole. Boil until tender, about 20 minutes. Drain the water and put the potatoes in a large bowl. Mash with a fork or potato masher, stirring in the hot goat milk and *ghee* as you mash. Season with salt and herbs as desired. Very good.

Comment: The *ghee* and milk warm and moisten the dry potatoes.

ABOUT PEAS

Green peas behave much like the legume they are, being cool and heavy, sweet and astringent. They alleviate Pitta and Kapha well. Best to serve them well-spiced to Vata, else they could stimulate gas. The following dish is fast and particularly scrumptious with Shiitake mushrooms.

MUSHROOMS AND PEAS

Preparation time: 15 minutes
mildly +Vata, −Pitta, 0 Kapha*
+Vata, −Pitta, +Kapha**

Serves: 3-4

✿   ✱   ❄

> ½ **pound fresh mushrooms or 6 large dried Shiitake mushrooms**
> 3 **tablespoons** *ghee* **or butter**
> ½ **teaspoon cumin seeds**
> ½ **teaspoon ground cumin**
> ½ **teaspoon sea salt**
> ½ **teaspoon fresh ground black pepper**
> 2 **cups fresh peas (frozen can also be used)**

If using fresh mushrooms, wash and dry them well; slice. If using Shiitake mushrooms, immerse in ½ to 1 cup water in small bowl; soak for 10 minutes or more. Drain and slice.

Steam fresh peas if you are using them. Put aside.

Heat *ghee* or butter in medium-sized skillet. Add cumin seeds. When they turn brown, add sliced mushrooms and saute until tender. Then add salt, ground cumin and black pepper. Mix well. Add steamed peas; stir. If using frozen peas, add them directly to the mixture in the skillet and stir until they are cooked and fresh green in color, about 3 minutes. Serve.

Comment: This goes well with rice and *dal.*

*The fresher the pea, the milder the effect on Vata
**Frozen peas.

GARDEN MEDLEY

Preparation time: 30 minutes　　　　　　　　　　　　　　　　Serves: 6-8
−Vata, mildly +Pitta, −Kapha*　　　　　　　　　　　❁　✴　🌰　❆

> 1 teaspoon-2 tablespoons sunflower oil or olive oil (the lesser amount for *Kapha,* the greater amount for *Vata*)
> 1 medium onion
> ½ teaspoon cumin seeds
> 1 teaspoon fresh oregano leaves (½ teaspoon dried)
> 1 sprig fresh savory (½ teaspoon dried)
> 1 tablespoon parsley
> 1 fresh mint leaf
> 4 tomatoes (optional)
> 3 small zucchini
> 1 small eggplant
> 1 medium yellow crookneck squash
> 1 tablespoon Bernard Jensen's Broth or Seasoning (powder)
> ¼ teaspoon black pepper
> 1 teaspoon coriander powder

Cube onion. Heat oil in large saucepan; add onion, cumin, oregano, savory, and parsley; cook on low for 2 to 3 minutes. Add mint and tomatoes and cook for another 2 to 3 minutes. Wash and chop zucchini, eggplant and yellow squash into ½ inch slices. Add to pot and cook on medium heat for 15 minutes or until tender. Add remaining ingredients; mix well. Serve.

Comments: If you are an omnivore, this is an easy dish to which you can add poultry or fish. Add ½ pound already cooked chicken or turkey, cut up in 1 inch pieces, the same time that the squash is added. If using fish, cut it into 1 inch pieces while raw and add in the last 8 minutes of cooking. A good stew.

*With tomatoes, definitely +Vata and +Pitta
With chicken or turkey, −Vata, mildly +Pitta, 0 Kapha
With sea fish, −Vata, +Pitta, +Kapha
With freshwater fish, −Vata, mildly +Pitta, 0 Kapha

ABOUT SQUASH

Summer squashes—zucchini, scaloppine, yellow crookneck—are light, cool, and easy to digest. They are perfect for relieving Pitta, especially on a hot summer day. And with warming spices like garlic, mustard seed, onion, or cumin, they balance Kapha and Vata.

CUMIN ZUCCHINI

Preparation time: 15 minutes
−*Vata,* −*Pitta,* −*Kapha*

Serves: 4

❀ ✳ 🌿 ❄

2 medium zucchini
3 Shiitake mushrooms, dried (omit for *Vata*)
2 tablespoons *ghee* or butter
½ teaspoon whole cumin seed

Soak Shiitake mushrooms in cup of water for 10 minutes, or until tender.

Heat butter or *ghee* in medium-sized heavy skillet. Add cumin seeds, heat until they are brown. Wash and slice zucchini. Drain and slice mushrooms. Add zucchini and mushrooms to *ghee*-cumin mixture, stir. Cook for 5 minutes on medium heat.

Comments: If cooking for a mixed *doshic* group, the mushrooms can be included in the cooking of this dish, then avoided by *Vata* in the serving and eating of it. Nice flavor, but a little too drying for *Vata.*

FRESH DILLED ZUCCHINI

Preparation time: 20 minutes
− −*Vata,* − −*Pitta, mildly* +*Kapha*

Serves: 4-6

✳

2 medium zucchinis
1 bunch fresh dill
2 tablespoons sunflower oil
½ teaspoon turmeric
⅛ teaspoon *hing*
½ cup water
1 tablespoon barley malt or brown rice syrup
2 tablespoons lemon juice
1½ teaspoon coriander powder

Wash dill and chop finely. Wash zucchini and slice inch thin. Heat oil in medium sized skillet. Add turmeric, *hing*, zucchini and water. Cover and cook 5 minutes. Then add rest of ingredients and cook 5 minutes more.

Comment: Good served with a bit of yogurt.

SUMMER SQUASH WITH PARSLEY AND DILL

Preparation time: 20 to 30 minutes   Serves: 3-4
– Vata, – Pitta, 0 Kapha*   ✳ 🐚

    4 small yellow crookneck squash, or one large one
    ¹/₂ small onion
    1 clove garlic, unpeeled
    3 tablespoons *ghee* or butter
    ¹/₂ teaspoon sea salt
    ¹/₄ teaspoon fresh ground black pepper
    1 teaspoon fresh dill weed, or ¹/₂ teaspoon dried
    1 tablespoon fresh parsley

Wash and dry squash and slice thinly. Chop onion, dill and parsley, keeping separate. Warm *ghee* or butter in medium saucepan, add onion and unpeeled garlic. Saute 2 to 3 minutes. Add sliced squash and cook uncovered over medium heat for 5 to 10 minutes, or until tender. Add all other ingredients, cover, and cook on medium heat for another 10 minutes. Remove garlic.

*Reduce ghee to 1 tablespoon to calm Kapha

SPICY SQUASH AND *CHANA DAL*

Preparation time: 45 minutes or less, plus overnight soak   Serves: 4-6
moderately + Vata, – Pitta, – Kapha   🐚 ✳

    1 large white scaloppine squash or 2 small yellow crookneck squash
    ¹/₂ cup *chana dal* (soaked overnight)
    3 cups water
    1 to 2 tablespoons sunflower oil (the lesser amount for *Kapha*)
    1 teaspoon mustard seeds (¹/₂ teaspoon for *Pitta*)
    ¹/₈ teaspoon *hing*
    ¹/₂ teaspoon turmeric
    ³/₄ teaspoon curry powder
    1 tablespoon rice bran syrup
    ¹/₂ to 1 teaspoon sea salt
    1 tablespoon coriander powder
    1 tablespoon fresh ginger, grated
    ¹/₄ hot green pepper, chopped (optional, omit for *Pitta*)
    1 clove garlic, minced (optional, omit for *Pitta*)

Soak *chana dal* overnight in water. Drain and discard water. Put 3 cups fresh water plus *chana dal* in medium saucepan and bring to a boil. Reduce heat to medium and cook until soft, about 30 minutes. Set aside.

Wash and cut squash into 1 inch cubes. Heat oil in deep skillet, add mustard seeds. When the mustard seeds pop, add *hing*, turmeric and squash. Then add remaining ingredients. Cover and cook over medium heat for 5 minutes. Add cooked *chana dal* and cook 5 minutes more.

Comments: This goes well with rice and bread. This well-spiced and warming dish makes a good fast main dish as well.

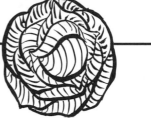

ABOUT CABBAGE

The cabbage family is one group of vegetables truly best avoided by Vata, as it is cold and heavy. Like beans, it takes energy and fire to digest. Its members include cabbage, broccoli, cauliflower, Brussels sprouts, kohlrabi, and kale. Rutabagas and turnips are distant cousins. Of these, simple steamed broccoli fares best in most digestive tracts, being the lightest and easiest to handle, as well as the richest in vitamins A and C. If Vata ventures into cabbage culinary experiments, it is wisest to take it cooked and well-spiced as it is here, rather than raw. A few Kaphas will find the cabbage family goitrogenic, that is, slowing to their thyroids. But most Kaphas and Pittas will find them beneficial, with the added advantage of a cancer preventive action.

SOUTH INDIAN STYLE BROCCOLI

Preparation time: 30 minutes or less
0 Vata, − Pitta, − Kapha

Serves: 4- 5
✿ ✸ ❄

> 1 bunch fresh broccoli (6 cups chopped)
> 1 tablespoon sunflower oil or *ghee*
> ½ teaspoon cumin seeds
> ½ teaspoon black mustard seeds
> 1 teaspoon dry *urud dal*
> ⅛ teaspoon *hing*
> 1 tablespoon onion, finely chopped
> 1 tablespoon sesame seeds

Wash and chop the broccoli into 1 inch pieces. Warm the oil or *ghee* in a large skillet and add the cumin and mustard seeds. When the mustard seeds pop, add the rest of the ingredients except the broccoli and cook over medium heat for 1 to 2 minutes. Add the broccoli and stir. Cook until bright green and tender. Serve with an extra tablespoon of *ghee* for *Vata* or *Pitta*.

SAUTEED BROCCOLI

Preparation time: 20 minutes   Serves: 5-6
mildly + Vata, − Pitta, − Kapha*   ✿ ✳ 🍵 ❄

> 2 large heads of broccoli (about 5 cups chopped)
> 1 teaspoon-3 tablespoons *ghee* (lesser amount for *Kapha*, greater for *Pitta* and *Vata*)
> ½ teaspoon mustard seeds
> ¼ teaspoon cumin seeds
> ⅛ teaspoon *hing*
> 1 clove garlic, minced (optional, omit for *Pitta*)
> 1 teaspoon turmeric
> 2 teaspoons coriander powder
> ¾ teaspoon sea salt
> 1 tablespoons lime or lemon juice

Wash and pat dry broccoli. Chop in ½ inch pieces. Heat *ghee* in medium-sized heavy skillet; add mustard and cumin seeds, the *hing* and garlic. When mustard seeds begin to pop, add turmeric, then broccoli. Stir well. Add remaining ingredients as broccoli is cooking, mix well. Cook uncovered until broccoli is tender but still bright green, stirring occasionally, about 10-15 minutes in all.

Comment: This goes well with rice and soup.

*Serve with extra ghee and/or lime pickle to mitigate this effect for Vata

---

"PLAIN" INDIAN CABBAGE

Preparation time: 15 minutes   Serves: 4-5
moderately + Vata, − Pitta, − Kapha   ✿ ❄

> 1 medium cabbage
> 1- 2 tablespoons sunflower oil (lesser amount for *Kapha*)

½ teaspoon mustard seeds
½ teaspoon whole cumin seeds
⅛ teaspoon *hing*
½ teaspoon turmeric
1 teaspoon sea salt
1½ teaspoon coriander powder
1 tablespoons lemon juice
1 teaspoon honey or maple syrup
¼ green pepper, chopped (optional)

Garnish: Chopped fresh cilantro leaves (optional)

Wash and chop cabbage into small (½ inch) shreds. Heat oil in large heavy skillet, add mustard seeds, cumin seeds and *hing*. When mustard seeds pop, add turmeric, cabbage and remaining ingredients, except honey if you are using it. Cook 5 to 10 minutes. Stir in honey, if you are using it, after taking cabbage off heat. Serve.

Comments: This goes well with any kind of soup, grain and *rotali*. This is the way to eat cabbage if you are a *Vata,* as the *hing* calms *Vata* and the mustard and cumin seeds aid digestibility. However, it is still not the vegetable to balance *Vata.* Great for other constitutions.

GUJARATI-STYLE CAULIFLOWER

Preparation time: 15 minutes   Serves: 4-5
+ *Vata,* – *Pitta,* – *Kapha*   ✿   ✳   ❄

1 medium cauliflower (5 cups chopped)
1 tablespoon sunflower oil
½ teaspoon mustard seeds
1 teaspoon turmeric
½ teaspoon sea salt
½ teaspoon curry powder, mild
¾ cup water
1 tablespoon coriander powder

Cut cauliflower into small pieces about ¼-½ inch; wash. In a medium-sized skillet heat oil and add mustard seeds. When they pop, add turmeric, salt and cauliflower. Mix well. Cover and cook for 5 minutes over medium heat. Then add rest of ingredients, including water. Cook another 5 minutes over low heat, covered.

Comment: This goes well with rice and *dal*.

CAULIFLOWER WITH POTATOES

Preparation time: 15 minutes
moderately +Vata, −Pitta, −Kapha

Serves: 4-6

❀ 🍃 ❄

> **1 small cauliflower**
> **2 medium potatoes**
> **3 tablespoons sunflower oil**
> **½ teaspoon mustard seeds**
> **⅛ teaspoon *hing***
> **1 teaspoon turmeric**
> **1 teaspoon sea salt**
> **1½ tablespoons coriander powder**
> **¼ teaspoon cinnamon**
> **½ teaspoon curry powder**
> **1 tablespoon brown rice syrup or barley malt syrup**

Wash the cauliflower and potatoes well; drain and cut into small (½ inch) pieces. Heat oil in a medium skillet. Add mustard seeds. When they pop, add turmeric and potatoes; stir well. Cover and cook 7 to 8 minutes over medium heat.

Then add cauliflower and salt. Cover and cook an additional 5 minutes. Add remaining ingredients; mix well and serve.

Comment: This goes well with LIMA BEAN AND RICE SOUP (p. 196).

ABOUT TOMATOES

Tomatoes are most aggravating to Pitta and least for Kapha, being light and warm. They have a sour vipak, which makes heavy consumption of them undesirable for either Kapha or Pitta in the long run. Vatas generally find their peel and seeds most aggravating, and so can usually handle tomato more easily as a paste, sauce or juice in very modest quantities. Tomato sauces are an excellent way to increase Pitta. A native of the South American Andes, tomato was brought into cultivation in Mexico and found its way to Europe in the early 1500s. Old World suspicion about this fruit-vegetable are reflected in its Latin name, Lycopersicon esculentum, "edible wolf's peach!" Its current English name comes from the Nahuatl Indian language of Mexico. Tomatoes are a rich source of vitamins A and C, and were much championed by Thomas Jefferson, who raised them in large quantities on his plantation in Virginia. His fellow Americans were not so sure about this practice—it took us a good 150 years before we were ready to embrace pizza, spaghetti sauce and catsup.

ZUCCHINI AND TOMATO

Preparation time: 15 minutes
−Vata, +Pitta, −Kapha*

Serves: 4-5

✳ 🐚

2 tablespoons sunflower oil
2 medium tomatoes, cubed
1 teaspoon oregano leaves
1 teaspoon coriander powder (up to 1 tablespoon for *Pitta*)
1 teaspoon sea salt
4 cups zucchini, chopped
2-4 tablespoons water
3-4 bay leaves

Heat oil in a saucepan or skillet. Add tomatoes, bay leaves, coriander powder, salt, and oregano. Cook over low heat 3-4 minutes. Add zucchini, stir in well, cook for 5 minutes on low heat. Add water and cover and cook over medium-low heat for 10 minutes more. Serve.

Comments: Delicious served with *dal* and rice or *PULAO* (p. 130). Excellent fast summer dish, using produce from the garden.

*Pitta can garnish with fresh coriander leaves, but dish is still warming—not recommended on a regular basis for Pitta.

ABOUT
BEETS

Beets sweeten, warm, moisten, and add mass. They are a lovely way to calm Vata in the autumn. In small amounts as a juice they are particularly therapeutic for Pitta liver conditions. In excess, they will aggravate fire. Beets are best for Vata and Kapha, with an occasional foray into them for Pitta. Medicinally, beets are utilized in Ayurveda for uterine disorders, constipation and hemorrhoids. Their rich content of folic acid may be part of their benefit to the female reproductive system.

SWEET STEAMED BEETS

Preparation time: 30 minutes   Serves: 4-6
–Vata, 0 Pitta, –Kapha*   ✿ ❦ ❄

> **4 cups raw beets (5-6 medium beets)**
> **2 tablespoons *ghee* or butter**
> **2 tablespoons lemon juice (or lime juice)**
> **1 tablespoon coriander powder**

Wash and slice the beets in ⅛ to ¼ inch slices. Pour one inch of water in the bottom of a heavy medium-sized pot, put in stainless steel steamer, and bring water to boil. Place sliced beets in steamer and steam until tender, 20 to 25 minutes. Drain.

Melt the *ghee* or butter in a small pan. Put steamed beets in a serving bowl and drizzle the *ghee* or butter and lemon juice over them. Add the coriander powder and stir well. Serve.

Comments: This is a pleasurable way for anyone to eat beets. Beets are usually considered best for *Vata* and *Kapha,* as they are heating. The coriander here cools the beet, making it appropriate for *Pitta.* And the steaming alleviates the somewhat heavy quality of the beet, making it more digestible.

*Occasional use only for Pitta

SPICY CUMIN EGGPLANT

Preparation time: 15 minutes   Serves: 4-5
moderately +Vata, moderately +Pitta, moderately +Kapha   ✿ ❄

> **1 medium eggplant, peeled**
> **1 bell pepper, chopped (optional)**
> **4 tablespoons sunflower oil**
> **¾ teaspoon cumin seeds**
> **½ teaspoon mustard seeds**
> **½ teaspoon turmeric**
> **⅛ teaspoon *hing***
> **1 teaspoon sea salt**
> **½ cup chickpea flour**
> **1 tablespoon onion, chopped (optional)**
> **½ teaspoon chili powder**
> **2 teaspoon coriander powder**

Wash and peel eggplant; cut into 1 inch cubes. In heavy skillet heat oil, add mustard and cumin seeds. When the mustard seeds pop, add turmeric, *hing*, onion, and pepper (if using). Then add eggplant and salt; mix well. Cover and cook 5 minutes over medium heat. Eggplant will get very soft. Remove lid and add chickpea flour and remaining ingredients. Mix well and cook uncovered 5 to 7 minutes over medium heat. Stir occasionally so flour will not stick or burn.

Comments: This goes well with spicy *bhakhari*, *dal* and rice, barley or millet. Delicious as this is, it is best eaten only occasionally. Despite the cooling chickpea flour, eggplant, and coriander, this dish is warming overall due to the chili powder and mustard; helpful for *Kapha*, but not for *Pitta*. The chickpea flour, while well-balanced with spices, can cause *Vata* to increase. *Pitta* can omit the mustard and chili for a balanced dish, while *Kapha* needs to keep the oil to a minimum.

ABOUT BELL PEPPERS
AND EGGPLANT

Bell peppers are sweet, light, oily, and warm. They are most calming to Kapha. *Cooked, they can often be tolerated by* Vata, *though this seems to be idiosyncratic in effect—some folks do fine with them, others do not. Bell peppers are mildly aggravating to* Pitta, *with their slight warmth and pungent* vipak.

Eggplant on the other hand, is sweet, light, oily, and cool. How it is prepared is critical in its effect on the doshas. Warmed and spiced with a little oil, it can be tolerated by Vata. *Served with a minimum of oil and a fair amount of warmth and spices, it benefits* Kapha. *Served again with a scarcity of oil, it balances* Pitta *(see the following FRESH DILLED EGGPLANT for more on this.) This is one of the few natives of the nightshade family which did not originate in the New World, being East Indian in origin.*

FRESH DILLED EGGPLANT

Preparation time: 25-30 minutes   Serves: 5-6
very mildly +Vata, −Pitta, 0 Kapha

1 bunch fresh dill
1 medium eggplant
3 tablespoons sunflower oil
½ teaspoon turmeric
⅛ teaspoon *hing*
1 cup water
¾ teaspoon sea salt
1 teaspoon curry powder
2 tablespoons honey or barley malt
2 tablespoons lemon juice
¼ green pepper, chopped (optional)
1 teaspoon coriander powder

Wash the dill and chop finely. Wash and peel the eggplant; cut it into 1 inch cubes. Heat oil in medium sized cooking pan. Add turmeric, *hing*, eggplant, dill, and water. Cover and cook 10 minutes over medium heat. Add rest of ingredients and cook 5 minutes more.

Comments: There is some disagreement in Ayurvedic circles over the effect of egg-plant on *Pitta*. Eggplants available in the United States are cool, yet slightly oily in effect. How they are prepared becomes pivotal. Served with cooling dill, our egg-plant is balancing. Fried or served in a tomato sauce such as eggplant parmesan, it warms and is aggravating to *Pitta*. In India the eggplants are distinctly different, being small, greenish, round, and heating in effect. Here is one source of the confu-sion. The lightness and slight astringency of eggplant, both Indian and American, makes it useful for *Kapha,* when cooked with a minimum of oil.

ABOUT CARROTS

Carrots are an easy and nutritious vegetable to eat, with 10,000 i.u. of vitamin A in each carrot. Indigenous to Kashmir, Afghanistan and the west-ern Himalayas, they are most often recommended for Vata *and* Kapha. *At first glance they look like an ideal food for* Pitta: *they are sweet, bitter and astringent in taste, with a cooling virya. However, their overall action or vipak is pungent, heating. So in the long run in large quantities carrots will aggravate* Pitta *while relieving* Kapha *and* Vata. *I have seen this occur with* Pittas *choosing to go on self- imposed carrot juice fasts. Eating the appar-ently cool sweet carrot juice day after day, their fire increases. A few carrots in fresh vegetable juices are fine for* Pitta *when balanced with generous amounts of cooling celery, cucumber or lettuce. And an occasional carrot in dishes is not going to aggravate* Pitta *significantly.* Vatas *and* Kaphas *can eat as many carrots as they like. Carrots purify the blood and tonify the kidneys.*

SWEETENED CARROTS

Preparation time: 15 minutes
— *Vata, moderately* + *Pitta*, — *Kapha*

Serves: 5-6

❀ 🍃 ❄

4 cups sliced carrots (4 medium carrots)
1 tablespoon sunflower oil
½ teaspoon mustard seeds
½ teaspoon turmeric
⅛ teaspoon *hing*
½ teaspoon sea salt (or less)
1 teaspoon coriander powder
¼ hot green pepper, chopped (optional, omit for *Pitta*)
3 tablespoons water
1 teaspoon maple syrup

Wash and slice carrots. In heavy skillet heat oil and add mustard seeds. When they pop, add turmeric, *hing*, carrots, salt, coriander, and pepper. Cook uncovered over medium heat, stirring frequently for 2 to 3 minutes. Add water and maple syrup; cover and cook for 5 minutes more over low heat.

Comments: Good side dish with GINGERED *ADUKI* BEANS (p. 106).

ABOUT PARSNIPS

The parsnip was a very popular staple in Europe and America before the introduction of the white potato. Now it makes far rarer appearances in markets, at least here in the West. A member of the carrot family, its qualities include coolness, sweetness, heaviness, and moisture. It is very calming to Vata *and beneficial for* Pitta. *It mildly increases* Kapha. *Parsnips can often be substituted for potatoes in recipes to good effect.*

STEAMED PARSNIPS

Preparation time: 20 minutes
—Vata, —Pitta, +Kapha

Serves: 3-4

3 large parsnips (about 1 pound)
4 tablespoons *ghee*
1 tablespoon maple syrup
Salt and pepper to taste

Wash parsnips, scrubbing well. Slice in ½ inch wide strips lengthwise. Put 1 to 2 inches water in large covered saucepan, put in steamer and bring to boil. Place sliced parsnips on steamer tray and reduce heat to medium. Continue to steam, covered, until tender, about 15 minutes. Remove from heat, place in serving bowl and drizzle with *ghee* and maple syrup. Parsnips can be served as is, or sliced or mashed.

Comment: This mildly sweet dish goes well with entrees like TASTY CHICKPEAS (p. 100).

ABOUT PUMPKIN

Pumpkin is considered sweet, hot and heavy in its attributes. For this reason, it is best used by Vata from an Ayurvedic perspective. Some say that because pumpkin has a hollow core and is so heavy in quality, it can even increase Vata. Warmed and spiced as it is here this is unlikely.

PUMPKIN AND GREEN BEANS

Preparation time: 40 minutes
—Vata, mildly +Pitta, moderately +Kapha

Serves: 6-8

2 cups string beans (½ pound)
3 cups pumpkin (1 pound)
½ cup water
3 tablespoons sunflower oil
½ teaspoon mustard seeds
½ teaspoon fenugreek seeds
⅛ teaspoon *hing*
1 clove garlic
¾ teaspoon sea salt
2 teaspoons coriander powder
1 tablespoon brown rice syrup
½ teaspoon curry powder

Wash and dry green beans; chop them in 1 inch pieces. Wash pumpkin, cut in 1 inch wedges, peel, then slice in ½ inch pieces.

Heat the oil in a large skillet and add mustard and fenugreek seeds. When mustard seeds pop, add *hing*, whole uncut garlic and green beans. Cook over medium heat for about 5 minutes. Then add chopped pumpkin, salt and water. Cover and cook for another 15 minutes over medium heat. Add remaining ingredients and mix well.

Comment: This goes well with any kind of soup and bread.

ABOUT SWEET POTATOES

Sweet potatoes and yams are often spurned as potential members of the nightshade family due to the "potato" in their name. They are not night-shades at all, but relatives of the morning glory clan. They can often be eaten by those who have difficulties with white potatoes. True yams, while short on certain nutrients, serve well as anthelmintics and antihemorrhoi-dals. Other varieties of true yams are used as poultices to reduce swelling.

MOTHER OGG'S SWEET POTATOES

Preparation time: 45 minutes
— Vata, — Pitta, + Kapha

Serves: 4-6

4 large sweet potatoes
3-4 tablespoons *ghee*
2 tablespoons barley or wheat flour
2 cinnamon sticks
½ teaspoon fresh ginger root, grated
2 cups goat milk
½ teaspoon sea salt
¼ teaspoon black pepper

Wash and scrub the sweet potatoes well, and chop in about 4 to 5 pieces each. Bring a medium-sized pot of water (about 2 quarts) to a boil, add the sweet potatoes and cook on medium heat until soft, about 20 to 30 minutes. Drain the potatoes. Melt the *ghee* in large saucepan or skillet, break up the cinnamon sticks into a few large pieces and add them and the ginger to the *ghee*. Stir-saute for 2 to 3 minutes. Add the potatoes, mashing them slightly into the *ghee* and spices with a fork or potato masher. Clear a space in the center of the pan and stir in the flour until it is mixed well with the *ghee*. Mash the flour and *ghee* into the potatoes. Slowly add the milk, stirring as you go. Heat until hot. Add salt and pepper. Remove the cinnamon sticks before serving.

Comments: This goes well with CAJUN RED BEANS (p. 112) and rice. Boiling the sweet potatoes before you spice them brings out their sweetness more strongly. Sweet potatoes are warm and heavy in nature. Sweet potatoes and the quasi-yams sold in this country (actually also sweet potatoes) have abundant quantities of beta carotene (vitamin A), unlike true yams, which are found in Africa, India and the Caribbean and lack vitamin A. The brighter in color the sweet potato is, the more nutrients it contains. Mildly laxative in nature, they can create gas. The cinnamon and ginger in this recipe forestall that possibility substantially.

SIMPLE ACORN SQUASH

Preparation time: 45 minutes   Serves: 6
 −Vata, −Pitta, +Kapha   ✴   🐚   ❄

> **3 acorn squash**
> **3 cups water**

Bring water to boil in large covered saucepan. Wash squash well and cut in half lengthwise. Put squash in boiling water. Cover, reduce heat to medium and cook until tender, 35 to 40 minutes. Serve with *ghee* and maple syrup, or plain with salt and black pepper.

Comments: Acorn squash is gently warming, sweet and heavy. Like sweet potato it is a rich source of beta carotene and is nutritive for the membranes and skin. Grounding, a good sweet vegetable for *Vata* and *Pitta*. Eaten in excess, i.e., daily, its heat could aggravate *Pitta*.

RUTABAGAS

Preparation time: 15-20 minutes   Serves: 4-6
 −Vata, −Pitta, moderately +Kapha   🐚   ❄

> **4 medium rutabagas (1 pound)**
> **1 cup water**

Wash the rutabagas and peel them (the skin tends to be bitter). Put water in a medium saucepan and place steamer on bottom; bring water to boil. Slice rutabagas about ¼ inch thin and put on steamer. Cover and reduce heat to medium-low and cook until tender, about 15 minutes. Serve with *ghee* (and lemon if you desire).

Comments: This sweet, bitter and astringent vegetable is ideal for *Pitta,* while being mildly warming to *Vata.* It is a bit too heavy and sweet for *Kapha* on a regular basis, but fine for occasional use. Its name is Old Nordic for "baggy root," aptly enough.

STEAMED MUSHROOMS

Preparation time: 15 minutes   Serves: 3-4
moderately +Vata, −Pitta, −Kapha   ✿ ✳ ❄

1 pound fresh mushrooms, in good shape

Wash mushrooms well and trim stems if needed. Heat large heavy skillet with tight fitting cover on low heat. When it is warm, put in mushrooms whole and let them steam covered on low heat in their own juices until done, about 10 minutes. Serve warm.

FRUITS

ABOUT FRUIT

When serving fruit, it is best to eat it alone or at the beginning of a meal. Fruit is so readily digested that it deserves to be first on the stomach's list. Otherwise, it ferments, caught in the layering effect which occurs in the stomach. Whatever goes into the stomach first is digested first, and sets the pace for the rest of the meal to come. Fats and proteins are digested much slower than most fruits and vegetables. If fruits are eaten after bread and butter and beans, for example, they are forced to wait in the stomach for as long as it takes these heavy foods to digest before they can be broken down. This delay in a hot wet acid environment causes fermentation, gas and belching, unnecessarily.

Fruits are one of the most cleansing and valuable of foods. Used in proper proportion and at the appropriate time, they are key to calming the doshas and clearing ama out of the system. They must be ripe and unpolluted to have this effect, otherwise they will create ama themselves. Unfortunately, most of the produce being sold in Western markets today is neither ripe nor chemical-free. Fruit is picked green, often with a heavy residue of pesticides and other synthetics. Such produce can not be used for cleansing; in fact it is best not eaten at all. Chemical ingestion can cause a wide variety of ills, including skin rashes, headaches, fever, and diarrhea.

Fruit grown without chemical interference is most desirable. This can be homegrown fruit or certified organic fruit purchased in stores. Or it can be produce culled from abandoned old trees and bushes in your area. Homegrown fruit is actually easier to produce than one might guess. Planting a fruit tree takes a sunny, well-augmented spot of soil, a few hours of hard work and once to twice weekly soaks of water. And patience: the tree is likely to take two years or more before it begins to bear fruit in any substantial quantity. When it does, you will have a superb source of food you can trust. At the same time your tree(s) will be contributing much needed oxygen to the biosphere, beginning to offset damage wreaked by automobiles and tree logging. One tree might seem like a very small contribution. And yet seven trees, planted over time, will feed a family of four and make significant contributions to the environment.

If you live in a warm wet area like Florida, a mango tree would be a great choice for planting. Ripe mangos are balancing to all three doshas *and are a rich source of vitamin A and C. Vitamin A, like mangos themselves, is soothing and regenerative for the gut and throat. This nutrient is also being explored by the National Cancer Institute as a effective preventive for cancer. It is useful in tonifying the skin and all tender tissues. Again, mango has been used Ayurvedically for centuries for these purposes. It has also been utilized for scurvy, roundworms, diarrhea, and chronic dysentery. Unripe mango is another business. Sour rather than sweet in taste, it strongly aggravates* Pitta *and* Kapha *and can irritate many a gut. Many prepared cooked mango chutneys are made from unripe mangos. You can make your own fresh mango chutney, if you like, with the recipes included here (p. 220). One way sour unripe mango is used to good advantage is in dals as amchoor. This dried mango powder provides stimulation for digestion when cooked in foods in small amounts, much the way lime, lemon or tamarind does.*

If you are a Kapha *or a* Pitta *living in a cooler, more temperate area, as most of the United States is, you would do well to consider planting an apple tree or two: sweet, light and cool, apples can live for 75 to 100 years, bearing for at least three to five decades of that time. A healthy dwarf apple can be especially appropriate for urban living and can produce 50 to 150 pounds of fruit per year.* Vatas *can join* Kaphas *and* Pittas *in their feasts if the fruit is well-cooked and spiced (see SIMPLE APPLESAUCE, p. 185). Apples are useful for cleansing, particularly in autumn fasts, to reduce* ama *related to aching joints, sinusitis and headaches.*

Apricot trees are another possibility. Apricots are sweet and astringent, but with a hot virya *and a sweet* vipak. *This unexpected heating quality makes a sweet apricot ideal for both* Vata *and* Kapha. *Sweet taste being cool and sour taste being hot, sweet apricots can be used well for* Pitta, *while sour apricots cannot. Sweet cherries are another light fruit handled well by all* doshas, *being sweet, cool, light, and moist, and therefore easy to digest—in moderation! Large quantities can get the gut moving in a way most diners would not desire. A sour apricot or cherry will aggravate* Pitta *and not help* Kapha *much either. Sweet apricots and cherries specifically calm* Pitta *and* Vata *and are light enough to be handled well by* Kapha.

Peaches and nectarines are in the "swing" category. That is, they are heavier than cherries or apricots, making them a bit more difficult to digest. And being heavy, they subtly increase Kapha. The ancient Ayurvedic sages recommended eating heavier fruits in smaller quantities than the light ones, thereby solving that dilemma. An occasional peach or nectarine will not harm Kapha at all. For a fast, though, Kapha would be best off choosing the lighter fruits: cranberries, blueberries, apricots, sweet cherries, apples and strawberries, unless specifically told to do otherwise by a trusted practitioner. Sweet peaches and nectarines are balancing for Vata and well-tolerated in moderation by Pitta.

Most berries are sweet, sour and light. Their lightness makes them well-suited for Kapha, while their taste equilibrates Vata. A few berries will not aggravate Pitta, but their sour lightness makes them not the fruit of excess for Pitta.

Sweet purple grapes are a food that can be eaten in moderation by all doshas. Best for Vata and Pitta, they are light enough to be eaten in small quantities by Kapha with benefit. Grapes are a fruit which has been sprayed heavily with chemicals by commercial growers. It is important to know your source and to consider the effects that such chemicals have on the people who work in the fields with them. They are deadly. For these reasons, organic grapes and raisins are an especially wise health choice, for everyone concerned. Dried grapes (raisins) are one of the oldest of foods. When well-soaked in water, they balance each dosha. Both grapes and raisins are highly regarded in Ayurvedic medicine for a wide variety of debilitated and toxic conditions.

Kiwis are a newly popular and frequently expensive addition to the North American fruit scene. Yet they need not be costly. Also known as the Asiatic (or Siberian) gooseberry, they can be prolific producers in the home garden when well-watered. They are a rich source of vitamin C and store well in cool places for months on end. Like many other berries, they are sweet, light and cool, with just a touch of sour and astringency in their taste. Best used by Vata and Pitta, they can be eaten in moderation by Kapha. Why only in moderation, the Kapha asks, if they are a berry? Because they are considerably more moist than most other berries.

Lemons and limes are often seen on the Ayurvedic "no" lists for Pitta and Kapha. However, I would not recommend a sour lemon or lime juice fast in most cases for either Pitta or Kapha, a small amount of lime or lemon added to a dish after cooking can stimulate agni, cleanse ama and clear the palate. While sour in taste, both lemon and lime have a cooling virya and a sweet vipak. Lime is especially useful, in that it tends to be lighter than lemon in its effects on the body. It is thus less aggravating to either Kapha or Pitta, and suitable for Vata.

Citrus is best enjoyed by Vata. Oranges in particular, with their moist sweetness, are quite relieving to Vata. They purify the blood, stimulate the appetite, and are recommended for those with liver weakness. Interestingly, citrus was first grown in India, as well as China and Japan. The word "orange" is a Hindi one. Other citrus is best avoided by Pitta, unless it is very sweet. Neither sweet nor sour tastes benefit Kapha, so despite the lightness of most citrus, including grapefruit and tangerine, it will aggravate Kapha in the long run. While oranges are thousands of years old, the popular Ruby Red grapefruit sold in supermarkets today was discovered as an unplanned mutation but a scant sixty years ago in south Texas. This highlights the wide difference in practical experience of these foods. In order for a food to have value in Ayurvedic healing, it need not have been used for centuries; its properties simply need to be clearly understood. Yet the continual addition of new foods to our diet challenges the assessment skills of a good Ayurvedic practitioner. (Ruby Red grapefruit are good for calming Vata.)

Bananas offer the most healing when they are allowed to ripen on the stem. Picked green as they are in most markets in the States, they are distinctly less healthy. Their qualities include sweetness and heaviness with a cool virya, as might be expected from this very sweet tasting fruit. However, their long term effect (vipak) is sour. This souring influence makes bananas poor for Kapha and in excess unhelpful to Pitta. The sweet and sour heaviness of banana is calming for Vata and specifically useful for putting on weight. Banana is used therapeutically in hangovers, intestinal malabsorption, inflamed gastrointestinal tract, heartburn, gas, and painful menstruation. Plantain, its starchy look-alike, is specific for calming inflammation of all kinds.

Outwardly sour and astringent pomegranate has an unexpectedly sweet vipak. This fruit is most useful to Pitta; it counters the ill effects of consuming too many sour foods, sugar or salt. It also balances Kapha well. It is mildly aggravating to Vata. Medicinally it is beneficial in chronic diarrhea, tapeworm and gastrointestinal weakness.

Figs are a paradox. While dried stewed figs are frequently used in Ayurveda as specific for constipation, fresh ripe figs are not. While nourishing, fresh figs are heavy and thereby delay digestion. Fresh figs are best for Vata and Pitta, while Pitta and Kapha utilize dried figs most effectively. Fresh figs are an especially good tonic for people in a weakened condition who are experiencing cracked lips or splits in mouth or tongue. They are used both internally and as a poultice in healing these.

Pears, a member of the rose family, are considered heavy and dry and so, consequently difficult for Vata to digest. Their heaviness is usually handled well by the undaunted agni of Pitta, while their dryness suites Kapha. The rose family has contributed many a fruit to humankind, including apples, pears, apricots, cherries, strawberries, raspberries, blackberries, peaches, and plums.

Melons are actually kin to the squash family, as many gardeners might guess from the appearance of the plants. Watermelon is the largest and most widespread of the melons; it has been a part of Indian cuisine since prehistoric times. It was enjoyed on the tables of Egypt as early as 4000 B.C. It features prominently in several Ayurvedic teaching tales. Its cool heaviness can challenge the Vata gastrointestinal tract in particular. The Ayurvedic antidote for this is to serve watermelon with a bit of salt or salt and chili peppers, to enkindle agni. Most melons, being sweet, are well-suited to Pitta and Vata. Cantaloupe in particular is a superb source of vitamins A and C, which are strengthening to the immune system. Cantaloupe molds rapidly and needs to be used when it is fresh for best benefits. Melons, being cool, sweet, heavy, and moist, only add to Kapha's tendencies in these directions.

Papaya warms and sweetens, providing moisture and heaviness. It is used in Ayurveda to treat a wide variety of conditions including impaired agni, delayed or scanty menstruation, indigestion, hemorrhoids, chronic diarrhea, amoebic dysentery, and round worm. It is best for Vata, mildly imbalancing to Kapha, and definitely aggravating to Pitta. Ripe papaya eaten daily is excellent for clearing chronic constipation in Vata. The seeds and milky unripe juice of the papaya are one of the best ways to eliminate roundworms in children. Dried, salted papaya is used to reduce enlarged spleen and liver.

ABOUT TRIDOSHIC FRUIT

A number of fruits can be used by all constitutions, as has been mentioned. Preparation and proper combination are the doorway to healing tridoshic use. Well-ripened mangos are well-tolerated by all doshas. Stewed or soaked raisins are appropriate for all constitutions. Sweet purple grapes, sweet cherries, sweet apricots, and fresh sweet berries can be enjoyed in moderation by all. Raw sweet pineapple is best for Vata and Pitta, but can be eaten in moderation by Kapha. It calms gastritis and overactive liver and acts as an anthelmintic. Apples and pears can be stewed or baked with liquids to suit all doshas. Ripe banana is fine served plain for Vata. It can be prepared with a pinch of dried ginger for Kapha and a bit of turmeric for Pitta. Dried figs can be stewed and served as they are for Pitta and Vata; Kaphas can eat them with a pinch of ginger or nutmeg as a balancing garnish. Cranberries can be sweetened with sweet orange and cinnamon to make them workable for all doshas in small amounts.

PAPAYA SALAD

Preparation time: 5-10 minutes — Serves: 2
$--Vata, +Pitta, +Kapha$ — ✿ ✳ ᴥ

    1 ripe papaya
    1 tablespoon lime juice
    Sea salt to taste

Wash the papaya and slice it in half, removing the seeds. (In India the seeds are used to expel roundworm in children, eaten with the fresh milky juice. They are bitter and pungent and a touch hot in flavor.) Cut the papaya in wedges, cutting off the peel as you go. Cut the wedges in 1 inch pieces or whatever size you like. Salt the papaya lightly but thoroughly and pour the lime juice over it all.

Comments: Eat on an empty stomach. Very good for stimulating the digestion of protein, and for clearing excess mucus out of the GI tract. Though . . . this is such a good salad you don't really need a reason for enjoying it!

FRESH PINEAPPLE SALAD

Preparation time: 15 minutes — Serves: 4-5
$-Vata, 0 Pitta, +Kapha$ — ✿

    1 fresh pineapple, ripe and sweet
    1/2-1 cup dates, pitted
    1/4 cup shredded unsweetened coconut
    1 tablespoon fresh mint leaves

Peel, core and cut pineapple into 1 inch cubes. Chop dates and mix all ingredients in medium serving bowl. Can be eaten immediately or stored in the refrigerator for 6 to 8 hours.

Comment: The pineapple *must* be sweet for this recipe to work and calm *Pitta* as well as *Vata*.

CRANBERRIES IN ORANGE SAUCE

Preparation time: 25 minutes   Serves: 4-6

mildly + Vata, mildly + Pitta, − Kapha   ✿ ❄

> **12 ounces cranberries, raw**
> **3 fresh oranges or 1 cup orange juice concentrate**
> **¹/₂ cup water**
> **2 teaspoons cinnamon**
> **2 cloves**
> **¹/₄ teaspoon dry ginger**

Mix all ingredients together in a medium saucepan and cook uncovered on low heat for 15 to 20 minutes. Serve. This can be blended if you want a sauce.

FRESH FRUIT SALAD

Preparation time: 10 minutes   Serves: 3-4

− Vata, mildly + Pitta, − Kapha   ✿

> **¹/₂ cup fresh sweet blueberries**
> **¹/₂ cup sweet apricots**
> **¹/₂ cup peaches**
> **¹/₂ cup fresh strawberries**
> **1 tablespoon lemon or lime juice**
> **1 tablespoon honey (optional)**
> **Mint leaves for garnish (optional, excellent for *Pitta*)**

Chop larger fruit into ½ to 1 inch pieces. Halve strawberries; leave blueberries as they are. Put all fruit into serving bowl. Drizzle juice and honey over fruit. Mix well and serve, garnish with mint leaves as desired.

Comment: Good opening dish for summer lunch or dinner. Generously garnish with mint and omit honey and use brown rice syrup or maple syrup instead (or sugar) and you have a dish which is *0 Pitta*.

BLUEBERRY SAUCE

Preparation time: 15 minutes   Serves: 3-4, or 2 very gluttonous people
–*Vata, 0 Pitta, –Kapha*   ✿   🐸   ❄

 2 cups sweet blueberries
 ¼ cup water (or juice)
 2 tablespoons honey

Put berries in water in a small saucepan and warm over medium heat for 10 minutes. Pour the hot berries and liquid into blender. Add honey. Blend until smooth.

Comments: This bright-flavored sauce is good with pancakes and waffles and over desserts. Use a *Pitta*-calming sweetener like maple syrup if *Pitta* wants to enjoy this.

STEWED FIGS OR PRUNES

Preparation time: 20 minutes   Serves: 2
–*Vata, –Pitta, –Kapha*   ✿   🐸   ❄

 ¼ cup dried figs or prunes
 1 cup boiling water

Place figs or prunes in heatproof cup or bowl. Pour boiling water over dried fruit. Let soak 15 minutes, covered if possible. Serve.

Comments: Can be used regularly by *Pitta* and *Kapha* on long-term basis. Excellent cleanser. Best used by *Vata* for short periods of time (10 days or less). Good breakfast opener.

SPICED PEARS

Preparation time: 20 minutes   Serves: 4
−Vata, −Pitta, −Kapha   🫖 ❄

> **5 ripe medium pears (about 4 cups chopped)**
> **½ cup apricot nectar**
> **¼ cup water**
> **⅛ teaspoon dry ginger powder (omit for *Pitta*)**
> **3 cloves (omit for *Pitta*)**
> **3 cardamom seeds (about 1 pod)**
> **⅟₁₆ teaspoon sea salt**

Wash, quarter, and core pears. Chop in ½ inch pieces. Put all ingredients in medium saucepan and cook uncovered over medium heat for 15 minutes or until soft. Serve hot or warm.

STEWED APRICOTS

Preparation time: 15 to 30 minutes   Serves: 2
0 Vata, −Pitta, −Kapha   🫖 ❄

> **1½ cups dried apricots, without preservatives**
> **2 cups water**
> **1 cup apple or apricot juice**
> **1 teaspoon lemon juice (optional)**
> **1 tablespoon apple concentrate (optional, add if needed to sweeten a tart batch of apricots)**
> **2 cloves (omit for *Pitta*)**

Simmer all ingredients in a small saucepan until apricots are tender. Serve hot or cold.

SIMPLE APPLESAUCE

Preparation time: 30 minutes   Serves: 4
0 Vata, − Pitta, − Kapha   ✿   ✳   🍵   ❄

> **6 raw apples (organic Golden Delicious work well)**
> **1 cup apple juice**
> **¼ teaspoon cinnamon (*Kapha* and *Vata* can add more as desired)**

Wash and chop apples into 1 inch cubes, cutting out the core. Bring apple juice to a boil in a medium-sized saucepan. Put in apples and cinnamon immediately. Reduce heat to medium-low and simmer for 20 minutes or more. Serve hot or cooled.

Comments: This dish works well as a snack, a dessert, or an opener for breakfast. The cinnamon warms the recipe and can be used generously by *Kapha.* Golden Delicious apples are especially rich in pectin, a soft fiber excellent for stimulating elimination; however, many varieties of apples taste good in this recipe. The juice sweetens the dish without adding the heavy quality of most sweeteners.

ABOUT FRUIT JUICES

Fruit juices are a concentrated sweet and are best used therapeutically. In general they will have similar medicinal effects to the fruits themselves. Most calming to Vata *and* Pitta, *they can increase* Kapha *unless well-diluted.* Kapha *is better off with herbal teas or juices diluted 1 to 5 or more with herbal tea or mineral water with a pinch of ginger. In particular, blackberry juice is a good astringent antidote for diarrhea, while excessive consumption of apple juice can cause diarrhea, gas or constipation, as it throws* Vata *off balance in the system.*

Best bets with fruits are to relax, enjoy, eat them whole and usually alone. Bon appetite!

SOUPS

ABOUT SOUPS

Soups make an excellent, nourishing and usually easy meal. They can be made ahead of time and warmed up, for a hearty lunch, dinner, or breakfast if you so desire. Clear soups are easy to digest and least challenging to agni. Especially good in fall and winter, they serve as a support in convalescence and older age, and any age. They offer a good way to begin to tonify the gut and nervous system which have been traumatized or neglected with many fast meals on the run. Milk-based soups are considered a little more challenging to digest, and so are recommended for times when the digestive fire is good.

FOUR STAR VEGETABLE SOUP

Preparation time: 30-60 minutes
– Vata, mildly + Pitta, 0 Kapha

Serves: 2-3
✿ 🐌 ❄

> 1 teaspoon sunflower oil (can use up to 1 tablespoon if you like)
> ½ teaspoon cumin seeds
> ⅛ teaspoon *hing*
> 1½ teaspoons coriander seeds
> 2 tablespoons dry *urud dal*
> 2 cloves garlic, minced (omit for *Pitta*)
> 1 teaspoon fresh ginger root, grated
> 1 carrot, sliced
> 1 zucchini, sliced
> 1 cup other vegetable: asparagus, summer squash, string beans, onion, or greens
> 4 cups water
> 1 teaspoon salt, rock salt if you can get it

Warm the oil in medium-sized saucepan. Add the cumin, *hing* and coriander seeds and saute until brown, 3 to 5 minutes. Stir in the *urud dal*, garlic and ginger and saute for another 2 to 3 minutes. Add the vegetables and stir. Pour in the water and bring to a boil. Reduce to medium heat and cook for ½ hour or more. The longer you cook it, the more tender everything will be. Add salt and serve.

Comment: Good with *chappatis* and CUCUMBER *RAITA* (p. 224).

This soup fills your nostrils with the smells of South India's kitchens. It is a good way to introduce split black lentils to *Vata,* as there is a very small and tasty amount to meet! In the south of India this legume is used for flavor and aroma, as well as being valued as a potent nutritive. It is invariably paired with *hing* because of its gas-producing qualities; almost always it is also served with garlic. A good soup to tonify digestion and vital energy.

VEGETABLE BARLEY SOUP

Preparation time: 1 - 1½ hours   Serves: 12
0 Vata, − Pitta, − Kapha   ❀ 🍵 ❄

> ¾ cup barley, uncooked
> 1 tablespoon sunflower or olive oil
> 2 teaspoons whole cumin seed
> ½ medium onion, red or yellow, chopped
> 1 clove garlic, chopped (omit for *Pitta*)
> 3 stalks celery, chopped
> 7 cups water
> 1 cup peas, fresh or frozen
> 3 new potatoes, in ½ inch cubes
> 1 large carrot, halved lengthwise then sliced
> ¼ bunch fresh parsley, chopped
> 1 cup string beans, in ½ inch slices
> 3 large Shiitake mushrooms, dried
> ½ teaspoon ground cumin
> ¼ teaspoon fresh ground black peppercorns
> 1½ teaspoon sea salt

Warm oil in large saucepan. Add whole cumin, gently browning. Add onion, garlic and celery and saute 3 to 4 minutes, until tender. Add water, bring to a boil. Wash and chop vegetables. When water is boiling, put in barley and vegetables (if you are using frozen peas, do not add them until the soup is nearly done). Crumble dried mushrooms in small bits into the soup for flavor. Cover and reduce heat to low, simmer for 1 hour or until barley and vegetables are tender. Will make a thick soup; you can add more water if you prefer a thinner broth. When barley is tender, add frozen peas, ground cumin and salt. Simmer 5 more minutes. Serve with a teaspoon of *ghee* in each bowl of soup if you like.

Comments: A ½ cup of uncooked split mung *dal* or 1 pound cube of tofu can be added when you put in the barley, if you want to make a one-pot meal. Serve with extra broth and a garnish of *ghee* to calm *Vata.*

SIMPLE ONION SOUP

Preparation time: 1 hour   Serves: 6-8
−Vata, mildly +Pitta, −Kapha   ✿ 🍵 ❄

>   2 tablespoons *ghee*
>   3 large onions, cut in quarters then sliced finely
>   2 cloves garlic, chopped
>   1 tablespoon barley flour
>   7 cups water
>   ½ bunch fresh parsley, chopped
>   3 tablespoons barley miso
>   Slices of lemon for garnish

Put *ghee* in large saucepan and add onions and garlic. Slow saute the onions in the *ghee* over low heat until tender and sweet, about 45 minutes. Stir occasionally to prevent sticking. Add flour and stir into *ghee* (this will be easiest if you clear a space in the center of the onions so the flour and *ghee* can be mixed easily without trying to stir the flour into the onions, too). Gradually add water, stirring into the *ghee*-flour mixture over low heat. Increase the heat to high and bring the soup to a boil.

Put the miso and about 3 cups of the soup mixture into a blender. Add ½ the chopped parsley and puree. Stir the blended soup into the rest of the soup, add rest of parsley, heat for 2 minutes, serve.

BROCCOLI CAULIFLOWER SOUP

Preparation time: 20-30 minutes   Serves: 4-6
+Vata, −Pitta, − −Kapha   ✿ ✳ ❄

>   2 cups fresh broccoli, chopped
>   2 cups fresh cauliflower, chopped
>   3 cups water
>   ½ cup onion, chopped
>   1 cup asparagus (optional)
>   1 teaspoon *ghee* or sunflower oil
>   1 teaspoon cumin seeds
>   ½ teaspoon black mustard seeds
>   2 teaspoons fresh ginger, chopped
>   1 teaspoon sea salt

Steam the broccoli, cauliflower and onion over the water until tender; puree in the blender. Steam the asparagus, chopped in 1 inch slices, separately.

Make a *vagar* by heating the *ghee* in a small skillet and adding the cumin and mustard seeds. When the mustard begins to pop, add the ginger and stir for 30 seconds. Put these ingredients plus the salt in the blended vegetables and stir. Add the steamed asparagus. Garnish with chopped scallion (for *Kapha*) or fresh chopped coriander leaves (for *Pitta*).

CAULIFLOWER *KADHI*

Preparation time: 30 minutes   Serves: 3
moderately + Vata, 0 Pitta, – – Kapha   ✿   ❄

> 1 cup cauliflower, diced
> 3 tablespoons rolled oats, dry
> ¹/₄ - 1 cup onion, chopped (depending on your tastes, *Pitta* does better with less)
> 3 cups water
> ¹/₂ teaspoon fenugreek seeds
> 1 tablespoon *ghee* or sunflower oil
> ¹/₂ teaspoon black mustard seeds
> 2 whole cloves
> ¹/₂ teaspoon cumin seeds
> ¹/₂ teaspoon turmeric
> 4-5 curry leaves, fresh if you can get them
> ¹/₂ teaspoon fresh ginger root, grated
> 1 teaspoon sea salt
> 1 teaspoon lime or lemon juice

Garnish: Fresh chopped coriander leaves

Put the cauliflower, oats, onion, and water in a medium saucepan and cook over medium heat until soft, about 10 minutes. While they are cooking, prepare the *vagar* by heating the *ghee* or oil in a small skillet and add the fenugreek, mustard, cloves, and cumin. When the mustard seeds pop, add the turmeric and curry leaves, warm for an additional 30 seconds. Pour the blended vegetables back into their saucepan and add all the ingredients. Stir well. Boil uncovered for 10 to 15 minutes, stirring occasionally. Garnish with fresh chopped coriander leaves.

Comments: Good for *Kaphas*, *Pitta-Kaphas*, *Kapha-Vatas* and other *Kaphic* souls. The mustard, cloves, ginger, and fenugreek make this too warming to calm *Pitta,* but the rest of the ingredients soothe *Pitta* enough that the overall dish has a neutral rather than aggravating effect.

HOT AND SPICY SOUP

Preparation time: 25-30 minutes
0 Vata, +Pitta, −Kapha*

Serves: 6

❀ 🐚 ❄

> **5 cups water**
> **1 inch fresh ginger root**
> **⅓ cup *basmati* rice**
> **1 clove**
> **3 peppercorns**
> **1 medium carrot, sliced**
> **1 cup raw cabbage, chopped or 1 cup fresh greens**
> **1 umeboshi plum**
> **1 large Shiitake mushroom (optional, *Vata* can skip eating it, but good for flavor)**
> **1/16 teaspoon *pippali* or cayenne**
> **1 tablespoon tamari**
> **1 teaspoon raw honey (optional)**

Bring water to boil in medium saucepan. Peel and slice the ginger into 4 or 5 pieces. Add to the boiling water, cover and turn to low. Let simmer while you wash the rice and drain it. Add it to the soup and turn heat up to medium, cover again. Wash and slice the carrot and chop the cabbage. Add them to the brew. Simmer 10 minutes more. Add cayenne or *pippali*, tamari and honey just before serving.

Comments: This goes well with MISO TOFU (p. 102). A nice brew to sip during a cold, flu, cough, or hay fever. Warms the body and supports the immune system. The cabbage is a rich source of vitamin C, and carrot provides generous amounts of vitamin A (if you use greens as well, they give you an extra dose of both these vitamins). Ginger stimulates circulation and digestion.

*Vata can garnish with sesame seeds or gomasio if they like.

BROCCOLI SUNFLOWER SOUP

Preparation time: 15 minutes   Serves: 4
moderately +*Vata*, −*Pitta*, −*Kapha*

          ✿ ✳ ☙ ❄

> 4 cups broccoli, chopped (about 1 bunch)
> 2 cups water
> 1 tablespoon miso
> ¼ cup raw shelled sunflower seeds
> 2 to 3 cloves of garlic (omit for *Pitta*)
> 2 scallions, finely chopped (omit for *Pitta*)
> ½ teaspoon dry oregano
> Black pepper to taste

Wash and chop the broccoli and scallions. Put the broccoli in a steamer over the water. Cover and steam until tender and bright green, about 5 minutes. While it is steaming, grind the sunflower seeds in the blender into a fine powder. Leave them there. When the broccoli is done, put it and the cooking water plus the rest of the ingredients in the blender with the ground sunflower seeds and puree. Serve immediately.

Comment: A good quick lunch on a cold day.

CREAM OF GREEN SOUP

Preparation time: 30 minutes   Serves: 2-3
−*Vata*, −*Pitta*, +*Kapha**
0 *Vata*, −*Pitta*, −*Kapha***

          ✳ ☙ ❄

> 1 bunch tender greens, chopped
> 2 tablespoons *ghee*
> ¼ teaspoon black mustard seeds
> ½ small onion, chopped
> 1 cup fresh mushrooms, sliced
> 2 tablespoons barley or whole wheat flour
> 2 cups milk (soy, goat or cow)
> 1 teaspoon sea salt
> ¼ teaspoon black pepper

Wash the greens thoroughly and chop them in 1 inch pieces. Put them in a steamer in a saucepan over boiling water. Cover and steam until tender 5 to 8 minutes. While they are steaming, saute the mustard seeds in the *ghee* until they begin to pop. Add the chopped onion and sliced mushrooms and saute until the onion is sweet. Stir in the flour. Slowly pour in one cup of milk, stirring it as you go to create a smooth creamy sauce. When the greens are finished steaming, drain them and put them in the blender (no need to save the cooking water here). Add the last cup of milk to the blender and blend the greens and milk on "puree" speed. Stir into the cream sauce in the saucepan and simmer for a minute or two.

Comments: This goes well with *chappatis* or toast. Rich in minerals and beta-carotene and easy to digest.

* *With whole wheat flour and cow's milk*
* **With barley flour and soy or goat's milk*

CHANA DAL SOUP

Preparation time: 1-2 hours
+*Vata,* −*Pitta,* −*Kapha*

Serves: 8-10

1½ cup dry *chana dal*
7 cups water
1 tablespoon sunflower oil
½ teaspoon mustard seeds
1 teaspoon sea salt
1½ tablespoons rice syrup
1½ tablespoons lemon juice
2 teaspoons coriander powder
¼ hot green pepper, chopped (optional, omit for *Pitta*)

Wash *chana dal*; drain. Cook *chana dal* in water in medium-sized saucepan covered over medium heat until soft, about 45 minutes or 1½ hours, depending on the *dal!*

In a small frying pan heat sunflower oil and add mustard seeds. When mustard seeds pop, combine the oil-seed mixture with the cooked *dal*. Add remaining ingredients to the saucepan and mix well. Cook an additional 10 minutes. Serve.

Comments: This goes well with Indian bread or rice and a vegetable side dish. This warm spicy dish is a good one for *Pittas* and *Kaphas* in the autumn and winter.

BLACK BEAN SOUP

Preparation time: 1 hour 20 minutes with pressure cooker
4 hours without
moderately +Vata, −Pitta, −Kapha

Serve 6-8
❀   ❄

> 2½ cups dry black beans
> ⅛ teaspoon *hing*
> 9 cups water
> 3 tablespoons *ghee*
> ½ medium onion, chopped
> 1 clove garlic (optional, omit for *Pitta*)
> 3 bay leaves
> 1 stalk celery, finely chopped
> ¼ teaspoon coriander powder
> 2 teaspoons sea salt
> Black pepper to taste

Garnish: fresh lemon juice and *ghee*

Place the black beans, *hing*, water, and 1 bay leaf in a 6 quart pressure cooker (filled no more than ½ full) and bring to 15 pounds pressure. Cook for 30 minutes on medium heat or until beans are tender. While beans are cooking, saute the onion, garlic, celery, and remaining 2 bay leaves in the *ghee*. Add the sauteed ingredients to the beans. Add salt and coriander and simmer for another 40 minutes, or as long as you like to develop the flavor. Can be served with lemon slices.

Comments: Garnish with lemon and *ghee* for *Vata*, with a slice of fresh lemon peel for *Pitta* and *Kapha*.

CREAM OF GIRISOLE SOUP

Preparation time: 30 minutes
−Vata, −Pitta, +Kapha*
− −Pitta, 0 Kapha, 0 Vata* *

Serves: 4-6
❀   ✳   🦞   ❄

> 8-10 Jerusalem artichokes (3 cups cubed)
> 2 tablespoons *ghee*
> 1 teaspoon dry marjoram
> 1 bay leaf
> 3 tablespoons barley or whole wheat flour

> 3 cups cow or soy milk
> 1 teaspoon Sucanat (optional, skip for *Kapha*)
> ½ teaspoon sea salt
> Black pepper to taste

Garnish: 2 tablespoons fresh parsley, chopped

Wash the Jerusalem artichokes well and cube into ½ inch pieces. Heat *ghee* in medium saucepan over low heat; add marjoram and bay leaf and stir saute for 1 minute. Add barley flour, stirring in well. Then add the cubed Jerusalem artichokes, mixing them well with the *ghee*, herbs and flour. Saute for one minute. Slowly add the milk, stirring the soup as it thickens. When all the milk has been added, cook over medium heat until the soup is the thickness you desire. Add Sucanat, salt and pepper. Garnish with chopped parsley. Good with a light tossed salad of lettuce, sprouts, or arugula.

Comments: For a nourishing lunch or a soothing supper (with mild tonifying benefits for the reproductive tract) this soup is a good one. However, if you have plans to serve it at your next elegant dinner party, think again. It has all the appearance and flair of gravy!

*With cow's milk and whole wheat flour
**With soy milk and barley flour

"PLAIN" *KICHADI* SOUP

Preparation time: 45 minutes
–*Vata*, –*Pitta*, 0 *Kapha*

Serves: 4-5

✿ ❋ 🐌 ❄

> ½ cup *basmati* rice
> ¼ cup split mung (yellow *dal*)
> 1 tablespoon *ghee*
> ½ teaspoon cumin seeds
> ½ teaspoon sea salt
> ½ teaspoon ground cumin
> 6 cups water

Garnish: Fresh coriander leaves, chopped

Warm *ghee* in a medium saucepan. Add whole cumin seeds and saute for 1 to 2 minutes or until slightly browned. Wash rice and *dal* well (until water is clear), add to *ghee* and stir. Saute for another minute. Add water and bring to boil, then cover, cook over medium-high heat for 30 minutes. It will still be broth-like, rather than the thick stew that traditional *kichadi* is. Add salt and ground cumin, garnish with coriander, serve.

Comments: This is good garnished with lime pickle for *Vata.* Vegetables can be added as desired in the cooking. A pinch of dry ginger on serving enhances its utilization for *Kapha,* and *Pitta* can garnish with coconut as well as coriander for extra cooling.

LIMA BEAN AND RICE SOUP

Preparation time: 20-25 minutes   Serves: 5-6
moderately + *Vata,* −*Pitta,* −*Kapha*   ✿ ❄

> ¼ cup cooked *basmati* rice
> ½ cup cooked lima beans
> 1-2 tablespoons sunflower oil (the lesser amount for *Kapha*)
> ½ teaspoon mustard seeds
> ½ teaspoon turmeric
> 2 cups chopped carrots
> 4 cups water
> 1 green pepper, chopped (optional, omit for *Pitta*)
> 2 teaspoons coriander powder
> 1 teaspoon sea salt

In a saucepan heat oil and add mustard seeds. When they pop, add turmeric and carrots. Cook for 3 to 4 minutes. Then add rice, lima beans, water, and remaining ingredients. Boil for 15 minutes over medium heat. Serve hot.

Comments: Good recipe for using leftovers. Works well for a quick lunch or supper.

SPLIT PEA SOUP

Preparation time: 2 hours 10 minutes   Serves: 8-10
moderately +*Vata,* − −*Pitta,* − −*Kapha*   ✿ ❄

> 2 cups dry split peas
> 10 cups water
> 3 large carrots, sliced
> 2 stalks celery, finely chopped
> 1 large onion, chopped
> 1 teaspoon sea salt (or to taste)
> ½ teaspoon freshly ground black pepper
> 1 teaspoon barley (*mugi*) miso

Put peas and water in large pot, bring to boil. Add carrots, celery and onion; cover. Simmer for two hours or until peas dissolve into a thick soup. Add salt, black pepper and miso. Serve hot.

Comments: Good as lunch dish or hearty supper with unleavened bread. The carrots, onion, and spices warm the otherwise "cool" peas, enlivening them and enhancing their digestibility. Some *Vata* people will do well with this recipe. Try it and see.

CHICKPEA AND GREENS SOUP

Preparation time: with pressure cooker, 1 hour plus overnight soak   Serves: 8-10
without pressure cooker, 3 to 4 hours plus overnight soak   ✿ ✳ ❄
+ *Vata,* − *Pitta,* − *Kapha*

> 1½ cup dry chickpeas (garbanzo beans)
> 6-9 cups water
> 2 tablespoons sunflower oil
> 1 teaspoon mustard seeds
> 1 teaspoon turmeric
> 2 teaspoons sea salt
> 2 teaspoons sesame seeds
> 1½ tablespoons barley malt
> 3 tablespoons lemon juice
> 1 tablespoon coriander powder
> 1 bunch fresh greens, chopped (can use kale, collards, mustard or turnip greens. Dandelion or spinach are also good.)

Garnish: Chopped coriander leaves

If using a pressure cooker, soak the beans overnight. Then put them in the cooker with 6 cups of water and cook at 15 pounds of pressure for 35 minutes or until soft.

If not using a pressure cooker, soak the beans in 9 cups of water for 4 to 5 hours or overnight. Drain, add fresh 6 cups of water. Bring to a boil, cover, reduce heat to medium and cook for approximately 1 hour or until the beans are quite soft.

In small skillet, heat oil and add mustard seeds. When the seeds pop, add turmeric. Combine this mixture with beans in cooking pot. Add remaining ingredients. Stir well. Cook for 15 minutes on medium heat. Garnish with fresh coriander leaves.

Comment: This goes well with *chappatis* or rice.

DAIKON RADISH SOUP

Preparation time: 1 hour   Serves: 2
−Vata, mildly +Pitta, −Kapha   ❀ 🐌 ❄

    ½ large daikon radish (½ pound, 2 cups grated)
    2 teaspoons toasted sesame oil
    ½ teaspoon fresh ginger root, peeled and grated
    ¼ teaspoon cumin seeds
    2½ cups water
    ½ teaspoon sea salt or 1½ teaspoon tamari
    1 tablespoon fresh parsley, chopped
    2 tablespoons onion, finely chopped (optional)

Wash daikon and grate it. Set aside. Put sesame oil in medium saucepan to warm
over low heat. Add ginger and cumin seeds (and onion if you are using it) and saute
for 1 minute. Add the grated daikon and slow saute for 10 minutes, stirring occasionally. Add water and cover; cook on medium heat for 30 to 45 minutes or until
daikon is very tender. Add salt or tamari and parsley. Serve hot.

Comments: This soup is based on an ancient brew for curing hemorrhoids. It is
good for the liver as well.

RED LENTIL SOUP

Preparation time: with pressure cooker, 30 minutes   Serves: 5-6
without pressure cooker, 2 hours   ❀ ❄
0 Vata, +Pitta, −Kapha*

    1 cup dry red lentils
    6 cups water
    1 tablespoon sunflower oil
    ½ teaspoon mustard seeds
    ¼ green pepper, chopped (optional)
    1½ teaspoon sea salt
    2 teaspoons coriander powder
    3 tablespoons lemon juice
    2 tablespoons barley malt
    1 tablespoon fresh ginger root, chopped

Wash lentils. Cook in pressure cooker with 3 cups of water until soft (about 10 min-utes). If pressure cooker is not available, soak lentils for one hour, drain, and cook with 4 cups of water about 30 minutes.

In a small frying pan, heat oil and add mustard seeds. When they pop, add turmeric. Combine with cooked lentils in open pressure cooker or large pot. Add 3 cups of water and remaining ingredients. Cook for an additional 10 minutes over medium heat.

Comments: This goes well with a vegetable side dish and *rotalis.* This tasty thin soup makes an excellent opening dish for a dinner or the main course for a light lunch. One thing to know: lentils, being rich in uric acid as well as heating, can indirectly but effectively aggravate a case of gout.

*Pitta can garnish with chopped coriander leaves to offset this effect to some extent.

BASIC MISO BROTH

Preparation time: 5 minutes   Serves: 1
−Vata, +Pitta, +Kapha*

> **1 teaspoon miso paste—yellow, white or red**
> **1 cup water**
> **Scallions (optional garnish for *Kapha*)**

Bring the water to a boil. Put the miso in a cup or small bowl. Pour a little of the water into the miso, mash with a spoon into a smooth paste. Add the rest of the water and stir well.

*The miso can be cut to ½ teaspoon per cup of water for a broth which is neutral in effect for Pitta and Kapha. Excellent nerve and stomach calmer for Vata. Hot and soothing on a cold day. The basis for many simple vegetable soups, using steamed vegetables and a bit of cooked rice or soba noodles.

SALADS

ABOUT SALADS

Salads are a light and cool way to balance a meal, particularly for Pitta *and* Kapha. Vatas *do better to have their salads warm, or at least initially cooked. Marinades and salad dressings make salads accessible and grounded for* Vata.

Leafy lettuce, endive and escarole are most actively relieving for Kapha, *due to their lightness. Their cool moisture makes them an appropriate food for* Pitta *as well. While lettuce's demulcent, mildly sedative attributes can be appealing to* Vata, *it is modestly increasing to* Vata. *Oil and vinegar or dairy-based dressings will calm this effect for* Vata *substantially, but many people find that if their* Vata *is off balance, they tolerate salads poorly. Romaine lettuce is one of the more nutritious of the lettuces, being richer in folic acid and vitamin A than most. Arugula, watercress and nasturtium leaves are more warming than lettuce due to their greater pungency. Watercress in particular is stimulating and diuretic; it is valued as a spring tonic. Watercress seeds have a wide variety of uses in Ayurvedic medicine, including as a restorative.*

Fresh sprouts behave much the same as lettuce, but with some of the qualities of their original seeds. Therefore, mung sprouts are slightly cooling, like mung beans themselves. Steamed or cooked bean sprouts have a neutral effect on all doshas. *Raw, they are best tolerated by* Kapha *and* Pitta. *Alfalfa and soy sprouts are slightly aggravating to* Vata *as well and need to be grounded with an oil-based dressing. Radish sprouts have more pungency and so are more actively relieving to* Kapha *than* Vata. *They aggravate* Pitta.

Parsley's slightly warming diuretic action benefits Kapha. *It mildly imbalances* Pitta. *In small amounts it can be used by* Vata.

Cucumber is considered cool, soothing, nutritive, heavy, and moist. This is why, even though it is recommended as relieving to both Vata *and* Pitta, *some* Vatas *find it hard to digest (due to its heaviness). Removing the large rough seeds and serving a bit of black pepper, ginger, or lime with cucumber can help.*

SOME *TRIDOSHIC* SALAD COMBINATIONS

Lettuce and steamed asparagus

Lettuce and marinated artichoke hearts

Watercress and sliced summer squash

Lettuce, fresh peas and beets

Lettuce, sprouts, carrots, and beets

Lettuce, sprouts, carrots, and spinach

Lettuce, sprouts, summer squash, and beets

Lettuce, artichoke hearts, cucumber, and spinach

Cucumber, sprouts, carrots, and radish

ABOUT OILS

Ghee *is the highly preferred fat in Ayurveda, being light,
easy to digest and potentiating to many of the foods with which
it is served. It is, however, not much of an option on most salads. Sunflower
oil is a reasonable and less expensive alternative. It offers fewer medicinal
benefits, but is a rich source of essential fatty acids and has no cholesterol.
Like ghee, it is agreeable to all* doshas.

*Sesame oil is specifically recommended when a warming effect is
needed. It grounds* Vata, *tonifies the female reproductive system and is used
for a wide variety of other conditions. Toasted sesame oil has greater flavor.
Sesame being hot and heavy is not recommended for* Pitta *or* Kapha.

*Walnut oil makes a good option for salad dressings, and can be used
much as olive oil is. A drawback is its short keeping time. Therapeutically,
it is useful in strengthening the liver and gallbladder. It can also be taken
internally as a mild laxative to expel tapeworms. Topically, it is applied to
the eyes to strengthen dim vision.*

*Olive oil, while warm and heavy, also stimulates clearing of the liver and
gallbladder. It is therapeutic in imbalances in both of these organs, and best
for* Vata.

*While safflower oil has been very popular in this country due to its poly-
unsaturated fat content, it is not particularly well- regarded in Ayurveda. It
is recommended for occasional, rather than regular use, as it can be inhibiting to longevity in the long run. Curiously, a study at the Linus Pauling Institute in this last decade indicated the same thing: rats fed safflower oil daily
had shorter life spans than those fed other oils.*

The vast majority of oils are warming and heavy in quality, including ses-ame, almond, apricot, corn, olive, peanut, safflower, soy, lard, castor, and salted butter. Unsalted butter, coconut, avocado, and sunflower oils are cooling in action, sunflower and avocado being mildly so. The cooling oils, with the exception of sunflower, are not recommended for Kapha and can increase Kaphic conditions such as high cholesterol levels. Ghee is one of the only fats considered light on the digestive tract by Ayurvedic standards. It should still be kept to a minimum for Kapha, being a fat and a good source of cholesterol.

Mayonnaise is initially cooling, but ultimately hot and heavy in effect, due to the eggs and oil in its makeup. Margarine is cold and difficult to digest and not often recommended by Ayurvedic physicians.

CARROT RAISIN SALAD

Preparation time: 20 minutes
−Vata, + Pitta, 0 Kapha*
0 Vata, mildly +Pitta, −Kapha**

Serves: 4-5
✿ ✹

> **5-6 large carrots (4 cups grated)**
> **½ cup raisins**
> **½ cup boiling water**
> **2 tablespoons rice vinegar**
> **1 tablespoon dry dill weed**
> **¼ teaspoon sea salt**
> **1 tablespoon apple concentrate**
> **¼ cup sunflower oil**
> **2 tablespoons mayonnaise (for Vata only, do not add if preparing for Pitta or Kapha)**

Pour the boiling water over the raisins in a small heatproof bowl. Let soak for 10 min-utes. Go on to wash, peel and grate the carrots. (You do not have to peel the carrots, but the dish will be sweeter and less bitter if you do.) Mix up the dressing in a small bowl, stirring the dill, salt and apple concentrate into the vinegar before adding the oil. Drain the raisins, discarding the water. Stir them into the salad. Add the mayon-naise if you are serving an all Vata group. Otherwise, serve the mayonnaise on the side as a garnish for Vata.

*With mayonnaise
**Without mayonnaise

FRESH COLE SLAW

Preparation time: 15 minutes   Serves: 4-6
+*Vata,* −*Pitta,* −*Kapha*   ✿   ✳

> ½ **large fresh cabbage (4 cups grated)**
> ½ **medium carrot (for color)**
> **2 tablespoons rice vinegar or lime juice**
> **1 tablespoon dry dill weed**
> ¼ **teaspoon sea salt**
> **Black pepper to taste**
> ¼ **cup sunflower oil**
> **1 tablespoon apple concentrate**

Garnish: 1 tablespoon fresh coriander leaves, chopped (optional)

Wash and finely grate the cabbage and carrot. In a small mixing bowl, whip together the vinegar, dill and salt with a fork. Add the black pepper. Stir in the oil and apple concentrate. Pour the whole dressing over the grated vegetables.

LEEK-DAIKON-SUNFLOWER SALAD

Preparation time: 10 minutes   Serves: 2-4
−*Vata, 0 Pitta,* −*Kapha**   ✿ 🍃 ❄

> ½ **to 1 fresh leek (the lesser amount for** *Pitta***)**
> **5 to 6 inches mild daikon radish (1 cup grated)**
> **2 tablespoons raw sunflower seeds**
> **1 tablespoon sunflower oil**
> **1 cup sunflower sprouts**
> **1 teaspoon rice vinegar**
> **Black pepper to taste**

Wash all the vegetables well; slice the leek and grate the radish. Warm the oil in a medium-sized skillet and add the leek. Saute until tender. Add the daikon and sunflower seeds and saute for another 2 to 3 minutes, until the daikon is tender but not crisp. Put the sunflower sprouts in a cool salad bowl and pour the sauteed mixture over them. Add the rice vinegar and pepper and stir.

Comments: This deceptively simple salad gets its unique flavor from its vegetables. Highly recommended.

**When the smaller amount of leek and mild daikon are used. A very pungent daikon could increase Pitta.*

SNOW PEA AND SPROUT SALAD

Preparation time: 10 minutes   Serves: 2-3
*+Vata, −Pitta, −Kapha**   ✿ ❋ ❄
*−Vata, 0 Pitta, 0 Kapha***

    2 cups fresh snow peas
    4 cups bean sprouts (mung)

Wash and de-stem the peas; steam them for 3 to 5 minutes. Rinse the sprouts and put them on top of the peas in the steamer, cover and steam another 2 minutes. Toss with PEANUT GINGER DRESSING (p. 214).

Without dressing.
**With dressing.*

ARTICHOKE HEART SALAD

Preparation time: 10 minutes   Serves: 2-3
*moderately + Vata, −Pitta, −Kapha**   ✿ ❋ ❄

    1 jar (6 ounces) marinated artichoke hearts
    1 cup fresh peas (or frozen, if you must)

Wash the peas. Steam them over hot water in a steamer until tender, about 5 minutes. Mix with the artichoke hearts and serve. Or, if you have unmarinated artichoke hearts, use SIMPLE OIL AND VINEGAR DRESSING (p. 213) for the dressing.

Moderately +Vata, especially if the peas are frozen

ASPARAGUS SALAD

Preparation time: 15 minutes   Serves: 4
−*Vata*, −*Pitta*, −*Kapha*   ✿ ✳ ⚘ ❄

1 pound fresh asparagus

Follow the instructions for SIMPLE STEAMED ASPARAGUS (p. 148). While the asparagus is steaming, prepare SIMPLE OIL AND VINEGAR DRESSING (p. 213). When the asparagus is tender, remove from heat, drain, and serve with the dressing.

Comment: This goes well with almost anything.

MARINATED BROCCOLI WITH WATER CHESTNUTS

Preparation time: 15 minutes, plus 1 hour marinade   Serves: 4
0 *Vata*, 0 *Pitta*, −*Kapha*   ✿ ✳ ⚘ ❄

½ pound fresh broccoli (2 cups, sliced)
8-10 water chestnuts (about ½ of an 8 ounce can)
3 tablespoons rice vinegar
1 tablespoon tamari
¼ teaspoon dry ginger
1 tablespoon honey
2 tablespoons sunflower oil

Wash the broccoli and slice the stalk and head thinly. Put 1 to 2 inches of water in a large saucepan, put in a steamer and bring the water to a boil. Place broccoli in steamer and cover. Steam 3 to 5 minutes or until bright green, tender and crispy (NOT olive drab and limp). Take off heat. Drain water chestnuts and slice in half.

In a small bowl, whisk the tamari and ginger into the rice vinegar. Stir in the honey, then the oil. Put the steamed broccoli and water chestnuts in a small deep bowl and pour the marinade over them. Cover and let sit for an hour (or more) at room temperature to bring out the flavors.

Comments: While this is billed as a marinade, you can serve this dish immediately if you need a quick and delicious salad pronto, without waiting for the one hour soak. If you are working with an all-*Pitta* crew, you can substitute an equal amount of brown rice syrup or maple syrup for the honey. However, this small amount of honey is unlikely to disturb *Pitta* seriously. Steaming a clove or two of garlic in with the broccoli makes a nice addition for *Vata* or *Kapha*.

GINGER MUNG SPROUTS

Preparation time: 10 minutes   Serves: 4-5
– Vata, mildly + Pitta, – Kapha   ✿   ✳   🍃   ❄

> **4 cups mung bean sprouts (½ cup dry, if you are sprouting them yourself)**
> **2 tablespoons sunflower or sesame oil**
> **½ teaspoon toasted sesame oil**
> **1 tablespoon fresh ginger root, minced**
> **2 tablespoons tamari (soy sauce)**
> **¼ cup raw almonds (optional)**
> **1 teaspoon honey (optional)**

Heat oil; add minced ginger and mung sprouts. Stir well on medium-high heat for 2 minutes. Add tamari, then almonds. Stir another 1 minute. Take off heat and stir in honey, if desired (is excellent both with or without).

Comments: This goes well as a hot salad with rice and MISO TOFU (p. 102) or TOFU AND MUSHROOMS (p. 104).

If *Pitta* is making this for her/himself, use all sunflower oil and skip the honey, then 0 *Pitta* effect.

MUNG BEAN SPROUTS, INDIAN-STYLE #1

Preparation time: 30 minutes   Serves: 4-5
– Vata, – Pitta, – Kapha   ✿   ✳

> **4 cups mung bean sprouts (½ cup dry, if you are sprouting them yourself)**
> **2 tablespoons sunflower oil**
> **1 teaspoon sea salt**
> **½ teaspoon turmeric**
> **⅛ cup water**
> **2 teaspoons coriander powder**
> **¼ teaspoon curry powder**
> **2 teaspoons brown rice syrup**
> **⅛ hot green pepper, chopped (optional, omit for *Pitta*)**

Wash sprouts in cold water. Heat oil in a skillet and add sprouts. Add salt, water and turmeric. Cover and cook for 20 minutes over low heat. When beans are soft, add remaining ingredients and mix well. Cook for 10 minutes.

Comment: This goes well with BUTTERMILK CURRY (p. 78) and rice.

INDIAN STYLE SPROUTS #2

Preparation time: 5 minutes   Serves: 4-5
0 Vata, − Pitta, − Kapha   ✿   ✳

> 1 cup mixed sprouts: mung bean, lentil, chickpea or amaranth
> 1 tablespoon sunflower or olive oil
> ⅛ teaspoon *hing*
> ½ teaspoon turmeric
> ¼ teaspoon sea salt
> 1-2 tablespoons lemon juice, or to taste

Warm oil in skillet. Add spices, then sprouts. Saute 3 to 4 minutes. Add lemon juice. Serve warm.

HOT SICILIAN SALAD

Preparation time: 30 minutes (or less)   Serves: 4
0 Vata, − Pitta, − Kapha   ✿   ✳   🐾   ❄

> 1 large bunch of fresh kale
> 2 medium red potatoes
> 1 medium carrot
> 1 tablespoon rice vinegar
> 1½ teaspoons dry oregano
> 1 teaspoon dry basil
> ½ teaspoon thyme (optional)
> ¼ teaspoon dry rosemary
> ½ teaspoon sea salt
> Black pepper to taste
> ½ to 2 teaspoons apple concentrate (available in health food stores)
> 2 tablespoons olive oil

Wash vegetables. Pour about an inch of water into a medium-sized skillet; bring it to a boil over high heat. Cube the potatoes into to ½ inch pieces, leaving on the peel.

Put them in the boiling water, cover and reduce heat to medium. Cook for 5 minutes. While potatoes are cooking, cube carrots into ½ to 1 inch pieces and chop the greens in 1 inch wide sections. Add the carrot and greens to the potatoes and cook for another 7 minutes covered, on medium heat.

While the vegetables are cooking, you can make up the dressing. Or relax for a few minutes and survey your domain. This is an easy recipe. When you are ready, put the vinegar in a small bowl and whisk the herbs, salt, pepper, and apple concentrate, in that order, into it. Stir in the olive oil. When the vegetables are cooked, that is, tender but not mushy, drain them. Pour the dressing over the salad and toss. Chill or serve at room temperature as you please (your gut will be more pleased with room temperature, in general).

Comments: Quite good. And perhaps impossible to find in Sicily. I based this on a much beloved soup that an old friend of Sicilian-American extraction used to make for me years ago in Carmel. If you are not attempting to balance *Pitta*, you can add 2 cloves of garlic to the cooking vegetables for a nice flavor. But the salad is quite flavorful as it is.

HOT POTATO SALAD

Preparation time: 45 minutes   Serves: 3-4
− Vata, + Pitta, + Kapha   ❄

      6 new or red potatoes
      ¹/₂ cup rice vinegar
      1 tablespoon stone ground mustard
      1 tablespoon dry spearmint
      1 teaspoon dill weed
      ¹/₂ teaspoon sea salt
      ¹/₂ cup olive oil
      ¹/₂ cup mayonnaise

Garnish: black pepper, freshly ground

Boil the new potatoes until tender, 20 to 30 minutes. While they are boiling, mix up the dressing: whisk the mustard, herbs and salt into the vinegar, then add the oil (essential order for best flavor). Stir in the mayonnaise. Drain the potatoes, let them cool enough to slice them, then slice them or cube them as you like. Put in a greased covered dish and stir in the dressing. Cook for 20 minutes or until warm. Garnish with freshly ground black pepper.

Comments: Why, do you ask, do you offer such an enticing recipe with no hope of consummation for *Pitta* or *Kapha?* Well poor *Vatas* should be able to enjoy their potatoes *somehow*. Seriously, there is an alternative for *Pitta* and *Kapha*. Make up the dressing for HOT SICILIAN SALAD (p. 208) and proceed as directed here. Quite good and only mildly, very mildly, aggravating to *Vata* as well. Or *Pitta* can reduce the vinegar and mayonnaise in HOT POTATO SALAD (p. 209) by half, letting the dish be neutral in effect.

YAM SALAD

Preparation time: 30 minutes   Serves: 3-4
− − *Vata, mildly* + *Pitta,* + *Kapha*   🐌 ❄

> 3 to 4 medium yams (3 cups chopped)
> 2 tablespoons mayonnaise
> 2 teaspoons stoneground mustard
> 1 tablespoon *umeboshi* vinegar
> 1 tablespoon rice vinegar
> 2 tablespoons water
> ¼ teaspoon ground cumin
> ¼ teaspoon freshly ground black pepper

Garnish: fresh chopped parsley

Wash the yams, then peel and slice them in ½ inch rounds. Put them in a steamer over water and steam until tender, about 15 minutes. While they are steaming, mix together the rest of the ingredients. Cool the yams slightly, enough to cut them into ½ inch cubes. Toss with the dressing and serve. Garnish with parsley if desired.

Comment: If you want this to calm *Pitta,* omit the mustard entirely.

ABOUT JERUSALEM ARTICHOKES

The Jerusalem artichoke offers coolness, lightness, and moisture. An excess could throw off Vata, *but in moderation it is fine for this* dosha. *It balances* Pitta *well. Its pronounced lightness suits* Kapha; *as does its high content of inulin, a starch rich in fructose rather than glucose. Fructose, the same sugar found in honey and many fruits, tends to aggravate blood sugar and weight far less than glucose; it also is balancing to* Kapha. *This American native was eaten by North American Indians for centuries boiled, baked and raw. Sent over to Europe in the 1600s as the "Canadian potato," it came* back as the "Jerusalem artichoke," for reasons murky to history as it is not Middle Eastern in origin. Its sender thought it tasted something like an artichoke, while the Italians recognized its sunflower ancestry by calling it a "girasole" or sunflower. It is highly regarded by Dr. K. M. Nadkarni, author of the Indian Materia Medica, as an aphrodisiac and enhancer of semen production.

JERUSALEM ARTICHOKE SALAD

Preparation time: 20 minutes   Serves: 2-3
very mildly +*Vata*, −*Pitta*, −*Kapha*   ✿   ✴   ❄

> **8 Jerusalem artichokes (about 2 cups sliced)**
> **3 tablespoons olive oil**
> **¹/₄ teaspoon sea salt**
> **3 tablespoons fresh parsley, chopped**
> **1 teaspoon fresh savory, chopped or ¹/₂ teaspoon dry**
> **Black pepper to taste**

Wash the chokes well and place in boiling water until tender, about 15 minutes. This is a step which requires some attention, as the chokes can get tough again if they are allowed to cook too long. Drain and slice or cube. Place in mixing bowl with rest of ingredients and let marinate 15 minutes or more.

Serve hot or cool.

DEVILED EGG SALAD #1

Preparation time: 20 minutes, including boiling the eggs   Serves: 1-2
−*Vata*, +*Pitta*, +*Kapha*   🍵   ❄

> **2 eggs**
> **1 tablespoon mayonnaise**
> **1 teaspoon stone ground mustard**
> **Sea salt and black pepper to taste**

Garnish: paprika

Hard-boil the eggs. Cool them in cool water and peel. Mash them in a small bowl with a fork and add the rest of the ingredients. Sprinkle with paprika for color and as a digestive. Serve on bread, crackers or *chappatis*. Good quick lunch.

DEVILED EGG SALAD #2

Serves: 1

0 Vata, +Pitta, −Kapha ✿ 🍵 ❄

> **1 egg**
> **1½ teaspoon stone ground mustard**
> **1 tablespoon fresh parsley, chopped**
> **2 tablespoons fresh raw vegetables, finely chopped, such as spinach,**
> **Watercress or summer squash**
> **Black pepper to taste**

Follow the directions for DEVILED EGG SALAD #1 (p.211). Light and good.

CURRIED EGG SALAD

Preparation time: 20 minutes, including boiling the eggs   Serves: 1-3
0 Vata, −Pitta, −Kapha* ✿ ✳ 🍵 ❄
−Vata, +Pitta, −Kapha**

> **4 eggs**
> **2 tablespoons sunflower oil**
> **1 teaspoon rice vinegar**
> **½ teaspoon ground cumin**
> **½ teaspoon mild curry powder**
> **2 tablespoons fresh coriander leaves, chopped**
> **2 tablespoons fresh vegetables, chopped: cucumber or zucchini is good**

Hard-boil the eggs. Cool the eggs and peel them. If you are making this dish for
Pitta, remove the yolks and set them aside for another use (garnish for a *Vata* salad,
for example). For the other *doshas,* the yolks can be left in. Mash the egg whites or
whole eggs with the rest of the ingredients and serve.

Comments: A pinch of saffron can be added for extra cooling for *Pitta*; it is an
extravagant gesture, admittedly.

*Without yolks
**With yolks

AVOCADO SPREAD

Preparation time: 10 minutes or less — *Vata, 0 Pitta, +Kapha*

Serves: 2

> 1 ripe avocado
> 1 tablespoon lime or lemon juice (about ½ fresh lime)
> ⅛ teaspoon garlic powder (optional, omit for *Pitta*)
> ⅛ teaspoon fresh ground black pepper
> 1 tablespoon fresh coriander leaves, chopped

Mash all ingredients together in small bowl.

CREAMY AVOCADO SALAD DRESSING

Serves: 2-3

— *Vata, 0 Pitta, +Kapha*

Use the same ingredients as above, omitting the coriander if you like. Add an additional:

> 4 tablespoons lime juice
> 4 tablespoons water (or to taste)

Blend in well. Serve immediately.

SIMPLE OIL AND VINEGAR DRESSING

Preparation time: 10 minutes — *Vata, +Pitta, +Kapha*

Serves: 6-8

> ¼ cup rice vinegar
> ½ teaspoon sea salt
> ¼ teaspoon freshly ground black pepper
> 1 clove garlic (unpeeled if you are working with any *Pitta*, minced otherwise)
> ½ teaspoon dry basil
> 1 teaspoon brown rice syrup, honey or apple concentrate
> ½ cup oil—olive or walnut are flavorful, sunflower also works fine

Whisk all the ingredients except the oil together in a small bowl or jar. Add the oil and mix well. Use immediately or let sit until needed. Makes ¾ cup of salad dressing. Use brown rice syrup if you are cooking for *Vata* or *Pitta*, honey if you are cooking for *Kapha* or *Vata*, apple concentrate for *Pitta* or *Kapha*. Sunflower oil and honey can be used for a fairly *tridoshic* dressing.

Comment: Quite tasty.

PARSLEY-PUMPKIN SEED DRESSING

Preparation time: 10 minutes   Makes: 2 cups
  −*Vata*, −*Pitta*, −*Kapha*   ✿ ❋

    1 bunch fresh parsley (3 cups chopped)
    ¼ cup pumpkin seeds
    ½ cup water
    ½ teaspoon sea salt
    2½ tablespoons lemon juice
    1 clove of garlic (omit for *Pitta*)
    1 tablespoon sunflower oil (if cooking for *Vata* alone, add one more tablespoon)

Wash and chop the parsley. Put all ingredients in blender and blend until smooth. Good on tossed salad. Makes about 2 cups.

Comment: This light and nutritious salad dressing is an excellent one for those dealing with lung, bladder, or prostate challenges.

PEANUT GINGER DRESSING

Preparation time: 10 minutes   Serves: 3-4
  −*Vata*, +*Pitta*, +*Kapha**   ❋
  −*Vata*, 0 *Pitta*, 0 *Kapha***

    2 tablespoons peanuts
    1 teaspoon fresh ginger root, peeled and minced
    ¼ cup water
    2 teaspoons tamari
    1 teaspoon tahini

Blend all ingredients.

*Is the effect the dressing served alone
**Is the effect when this is served on SNOW PEA AND SPROUT SALAD. (p. 205).

CONDIMENTS

ABOUT CONDIMENTS

The use of condiments is fundamental in Indian cooking and hospitality. Fortunately, they are also a wise way to balance a meal Ayurvedically. Condiments are generally simple and easy to prepare, and yet add a definite appearance of polish to a meal. Serve them in small bowls arranged on your dining surface. A meal need not be Indian in flavor to avail oneself of the pleasures of condiments.

Peppers, sliced onions, radishes, beets, carrots, lime pickle, and fresh ground black pepper all heat up a meal and stimulate agni. Salt, tamari, miso, and pickled ginger will do the same.

Fresh chopped coriander leaves, unsweetened shredded coconut, cucumbers, mint, raisins, and raw lettuce or sprouts cool a meal, bringing Pitta into the normal zone.

Plain yogurt initially cools, then warms. It is good for calming the palate after or during a spicy dish. It then ignites agni. Raitas made with yogurt and fresh grated vegetables and spices will be either warming or cooling depending on their constituents.

Many of the recipes mention condiments appropriate for balance.

Nuts, ground sesame seeds, black olives, and green olives are often added as condiments. While hot, they are also heavy, and so will usually not stimulate agni the way most warming foods would. They take energy to digest. Pumpkin and sunflower seeds tend to be a bit lighter and easier to digest. They can also be used as condiments, but again will not aid digestion.

Sea vegetables are another possible garnish. While they are rarely seen in a typical Indian meal, they are used medicinally in Ayurveda, and so make a good addition to an eclectically healing meal. Red Irish moss or carrageenan is utilized to strengthen the bladder and kidneys and as a support in chest and bronchial conditions. Its cousin, dulse, can be used for the same purposes. Hijiki is a rich source of calcium and can be mixed with land vegetables like carrots to good effect. Fucus (bladderwrack), is a specific in the relief of obesity and thyroid and kidney imbalances. Kelp, rich in iodine and minerals, serves effectively in prepared herbal seasoning combinations. Alone, applied as a powder to foods, its taste resembles that of dead fish too closely for this author's tastes! Most sea vegetables, being salty, calm Vata. They are best used well-rinsed in small quantities for Pitta and Kapha.

Spirulina and other blue-green algae on the market today are fresh-water rather than salt-water inhabitants. Rich in beta-carotene as well as protein *and B-12, they warm and balance* Kapha. *In excess they can aggravate* Vata *or* Pitta. *They are more likely to be used as a nutritional supplement than as a condiment, due to their taste and texture. But some adventurous spirits may add them powdered to soups, grains, or blended into fruit smoothie drinks.*

LIST OF POSSIBLE CONDIMENTS

Any of the following can be served depending on your needs and the needs of your guests or family. Put them out in small bowls:

unsweetened shredded coconut	*−Vata, −Pitta, +Kapha*
raisins, soaked	*0 Vata, −Pitta, −Kapha*
toasted sunflower seeds	*−Vata, 0 Pitta, 0 Kapha*
ground toasted sesame seeds	*−Vata, +Pitta, +Kapha*
pumpkin seeds, raw or toasted	*−Vata, 0 Pitta, 0 Kapha*
sprouts	*+Vata, −Pitta, −Kapha*
chopped lettuce	*0 Vata, −Pitta, −Kapha*
whole or chopped hot peppers, red/green	*−Vata, +Pitta, −Kapha* *Excess will +Vata*
sliced raw onions	*+Vata, +Pitta, −Kapha*
sliced raw radish, regular or daikon	*−Vata, +Pitta, −Kapha*
lime pickle	*−Vata, +Pitta, +Kapha*
fresh ground pepper	*−Vata, 0 Pitta, −Kapha*
salt	*−Vata, +Pitta, +Kapha*
fresh chopped coriander (cilantro) leaves	*−Vata, −Pitta, −Kapha*
fresh chopped mint leaves	*−Vata, −Pitta, −Kapha (Excess will* *+Vata)*
sliced cucumbers	*−Vata, −Pitta, +Kapha*
plain yogurt, cottage cheese, or prepared	*−Vata, −Pitta, +Kapha*
raitas	*(depends on preparation)*
almonds, cashews, or other chopped nuts	*−Vata, +Pitta, +Kapha*
mango chutney	*usually −Vata, +Pitta, +Kapha*
Bernard Jensen's powdered broth or seasoning (vegetable bouillon)	*0 Vata, −Pitta, −Kapha*
honey or other sweetener	*(depends on sweetener, see information* *about individual sweeteners)*
hijiki	*−Vata, +Pitta, +Kapha;* *rinsed −Vata, 0 Pitta, 0 Kapha*
dulse	*−Vata, +Pitta, +Kapha;* *rinsed −Vata, 0 Pitta, 0 Kapha*

FRESH CORIANDER CHUTNEY

Preparation time: 5 minutes
—Vata, —Pitta, —Kapha

Makes: 1 cup

✿ ✳ ⚶ ❄

> 1 bunch (¼ pound) fresh coriander leaves and stems (also known as cilantro or Chinese parsley)
> ¼ cup fresh lemon juice
> ¼ cup water
> ¼ cup grated coconut
> 2 tablespoons fresh ginger root, chopped
> 1 teaspoon barley malt or honey
> 1 teaspoon sea salt
> ¼ teaspoon fresh ground black pepper

Blend lemon juice, water and fresh coriander until coriander is chopped. Add remaining ingredients and blend until it is like a paste. Can be stored in covered container in refrigerator up to one week.

Comments: Excellent with *dals*, grains, curries, bread. Use sparingly. Superb condiment for *Pitta,* best made with barley malt for *Pitta.* The amount of sweetener is so small per serving, however, that either honey or barley malt could be used for *Pitta* or *Kapha* without harm.

Dr. Robert Svoboda recommends, for a delectably silky sauce, to leave out all the stems and just use the leaves. I tend to go somewhere in between, chopping in the tender upper stems as I chop the leaves and leaving out the coarse and heavy lower stem. I tend to be a tad lazy but also love the smoothness.

MINT CHUTNEY

Preparation time: 10-15 minutes
—Vata, —Pitta, —Kapha

Makes: ¾ cup.

✿ ✳ ⚶ ❄

> 1 cup fresh mint leaves, loosely packed
> 2 tablespoons grated coconut
> 1 tablespoon sesame seeds (optional, can be omitted for *Pitta* if you choose)
> 1 tablespoon lemon juice
> ½ teaspoon sea salt
> 1 tablespoon fresh ginger root, grated

1 teaspoon barley malt or honey
¼ cup water

Wash mint leaves, drain and chop. Put all ingredients into blender and blend until smooth like a puree or paste. Put in covered container and store in refrigerator. Use sparingly. Keeps for 4 to 5 days.

Comment: Good for spiffing up a simple tasting meal, such as TOFU AND VEGE-TABLES (p. 105).

SWEET MANGO CHUTNEY WITH ORANGE PEEL

Preparation time: 20 minutes or more   Makes: 1 cup
—Vata, 0 Pitta, —Kapha   ✿ ✳ 🍵 ❄

1 cup dried mangos
1 cup hot water
¼ teaspoon cardamom
¼ teaspoon dry ginger
¼ teaspoon cloves
1 teaspoon coriander powder
2 teaspoons organic orange peel, grated

Soak the mangos in the hot water for 15 minutes (longer if you like), then puree them in the blender with the rest of the ingredients. *Vata* can add a dash of lemon or lime juice.

Comments: A good mango "jam" on toast, crackers, or *chappatis.* A good digestive chutney, stimulating *agni.*

This can be made with fresh mangos if you have them. Here in the Southwest, they can be quite hard to find, and so we use the dried ones. The fresh ripe fruits are preferable, being less aggravating to *Vata* and easier to digest. If you use fresh ripe mangos in this recipe, substitute 2 fresh mangos for the dried mango and omit the water. Bon appetite!

SPICY MANGO CHUTNEY

Preparation time: 15 minutes   Makes: 1 cup
– –Vata, +Pitta, mildly +Kapha   ✿   ☙   ❄

> 2 ripe mangos
> 1/2 teaspoon dry ginger powder
> 1/8 teaspoon sea salt
> 3 tablespoons lime or lemon juice
> 1/8 teaspoon turmeric (optional, aids digestion of proteins and adds bit-
> ter and astringent taste)
> 2 teaspoons brown rice syrup or Sucanat
> 1/4 teaspoon fresh ground black pepper
> 1/8 teaspoon *pippali* (or 1/16 teaspoon cayenne)

Wash and peel the mangos. Slice them and put them in the blender with the rest of the ingredients. Puree.

Comments: This is an excellent chutney for stimulating *agni,* digestion and elimina-tion. It is also mildly diuretic. It is *hot* in taste. If you can obtain *pippali,* it is preferred to cayenne here. While both peppers stimulate *agni, pippali* is also rejuvenative and cayenne is not.

CASHEW CHUTNEY

Preparation time: 10-15 minutes   Makes: 1/2 cup
–Vata, +Pitta, +Kapha   ☙   ❄

> 1/2 cup cashews, raw-whole or pieces
> 1/2 teaspoon sea salt
> 1/2 teaspoon coriander powder
> 1 tablespoon lemon or lime juice
> 1/2 teaspoon fresh ginger root, grated
> 1/4 hot green pepper, chopped (optional)

Chop cashews finely. Add rest of ingredients and mix well.

Comment: This goes well with salads, grains or curries.

SPEARMINT CHUTNEY

Preparation time:
— *Vata,* — *Pitta, moderately* + *Kapha*

Makes: about 1½ cups.
✳

3 tablespoons dry spearmint leaves, crumbled
6 dates, finely chopped
¼ teaspoon black pepper
½-1 teaspoon sea salt
4 tablespoons raisins
1 teaspoon ground cumin
3 tablespoons lime or lemon juice
½ cup shredded unsweetened coconut

Mix all ingredients together well. Serve as a garnish to fresh fruit salads. Keeps refrigerated for up to 2 weeks.

Comments: Intense but delightful! This was originally inspired by suggestions in Dr. Nadkarni's *Indian Materia Medica.*

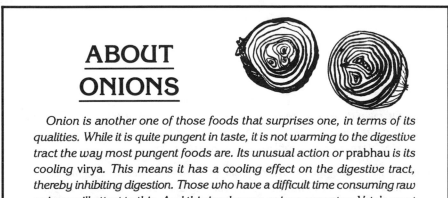

ABOUT
ONIONS

Onion is another one of those foods that surprises one, in terms of its qualities. While it is quite pungent in taste, it is not warming to the digestive tract the way most pungent foods are. Its unusual action or prabhau *is its cooling* virya. *This means it has a cooling effect on the digestive tract, thereby inhibiting digestion. Those who have a difficult time consuming raw onions will attest to this. And this is why raw onions are not on* Vata's *most recommended list. Cooking onions sweetens and lightens them, thereby making them balancing for both* Pitta *and* Vata *in gentle quantities. The pungency of onion in all forms makes it well-suited for* Kapha.

RAW ONIONS

Preparation time: 5 minutes   Makes: 1 cup
+*Vata*, +*Pitta*, −*Kapha*   ✿ ✳ ☙ ❄

> **1 large onion**
> **1 lemon**
> **1/2 teaspoon sea salt**
> **1/4 teaspoon freshly ground black pepper**

Slice the onion into a small bowl and squeeze the juice from the lemon over it. Stir in the salt and pepper. Pungent and antiseptic. Stimulates digestion in *Kapha*.

Comments: A standard side dish when *Kaphas* dine. To be used on whatever they like.

ROASTED ONIONS

Preparation time: 1 hour   Makes: 2 cups
−*Vata*, 0 *Pitta*, −*Kapha*   ✿ ✳ ☙ ❄

> **2 large onions**
> **1 teaspoon cumin seeds**
> **1 teaspoon Sucanat**
> **1 1/2 tablespoons *ghee***

Preheat the oven to 300 degrees. Grease a covered baking dish with *ghee*. Finely slice or chop the onions, as you please. Mix all ingredients in the covered dish, cover and bake for 50 minutes, or until the onion is tender.

Comments: This goes well with most *dals*, bean main dishes, and meals looking for a bit of extra spark. This demulcent and soothing dish is also an old Ayurvedic remedy for hemorrhoids. When eaten, they stimulate the circulation in the gut needed for healing.

ABOUT LEEKS AND GARLIC

The leek and shallot are relatives of the onion and behave in many of the same ways, but with a slightly milder action. They are good in soups, especially as a spring tonic.

Garlic, on the other hand, is hot and stays hot throughout its journeys in the gastrointestinal system. It is pungent, stimulating, antiparasitic, and dispels gas. It has all of the six tastes except sour. In cold weather, it is a useful Ayurvedic preventative for arthritis and nervous disorders. It calms Vata and Kapha and aggravates Pitta. It is excellent used both raw or cooked for bronchitis, pneumonia, asthma, and other flus and lung conditions. In the past, garlic oil has been used as an effective inhalant to relieve the acute symptoms of whooping cough in Indian children. Oil is the best medium for its activity, i.e., saute garlic before using it therapeutically.

Garlic, raw or sauteed, can be offered as a condiment in Ayurvedic meals.

BANANA *RAITA*

Preparation time: 10-15 minutes   Serves: 4-5
– – *Vata,* +*Pitta,* +*Kapha*

> 2 cups plain yogurt
> 1 teaspoon butter or *ghee*
> 1 teaspoon cumin seeds
> 1 teaspoon cardamom powder
> 1 teaspoon ground cumin powder
> 2 ripe bananas
> ¼ cup raisins (optional)

In medium pan melt butter or heat *ghee*. Add cumin seeds. When they turn brown, add yogurt and turn off heat. Add rest of spices. Cut bananas into ½ inch cubes or ¼ inch slices. Add to the yogurt mixture, stirring well.

Comments: This rich sauce goes well with soup, rice or cereal. Superb for *Vata*, fairly extravagant for everyone else.

BEET *RAITA*

Preparation time: 15 minutes   Serves: 5- 6
− *Vata, + Pitta, + Kapha.**

> **3 cups raw beets, grated**
> **1 bay leaf**
> **1 tablespoon sunflower oil**
> **¹/₂ teaspoon mustard seeds**
> **1 teaspoon sea salt**
> **1 tablespoon honey, maple syrup or rice malt**
> **2 cups yogurt**

Put 1 inch of water in a large saucepan, set in stainless steel steamer. Put grated beets in steamer, bring water to boil, cover and steam beets 2 to 3 minutes over medium heat.

Heat oil in small skillet; add mustard seeds and crumbled bay leaf. When mustard seeds pop, take skillet off heat. Put steamed beets, oil, spices and rest of ingredients in medium mixing bowl and mix well. Ready to serve. Can be chilled if desired.

Comment: Excellent garnish for bread, soup, rice or vegetables.

*If Kapha reduces yogurt to ½ cup, it is calming to Kapha.

CUCUMBER *RAITA*

Preparation time: 10 minutes   Serves: 4
− *Vata, mildly + Pitta, + Kapha**

> **1 cup fresh yogurt**
> **¹/₄ cup cucumber, peeled and finely diced**
> **1 tablespoon fresh scallions, finely chopped**
> **¹/₄ teaspoon dry ginger powder or 1 tablespoon fresh ginger root, peeled**
> **& finely grated**
> **¹/₈ teaspoon turmeric**
> **¹/₄ teaspoon ground black pepper**
> **¹/₈ teaspoon cinnamon (optional)**
> **¹/₄ cup fresh chopped coriander leaves**

Combine all ingredients in a medium mixing bowl. This goes well with most curries, *dals* and Indian dishes. Other vegetables, such as grated daikon radish or carrot, can also be used here.

*Fine for occasional use for Pitta & Kapha.

GINGER MARMALADE

Preparation time: 20-25 minutes
−Vata, +Pitta, −Kapha

Makes: 1 cup
❀ ❦ ❄

1 large fresh ginger root (1 cup grated)
1½ cups water
½ cup apple concentrate
1 tablespoon fresh organic lime or lemon peel, grated
½ teaspoon dry ginger powder

Peel and grate the ginger. Combine with water, apple concentrate, lime peel, and dry ginger and cook over medium-low heat until thick, 10-12 minutes. Keeps in refrigerator 3 to 4 days. Serve with tea and toast or *chappatis,* or as a garnish to your Indian curries.

Comments: Very good for stimulating *agni* and digestion in general.

Variation: Add 5 threads of saffron and ¼ teaspoon each of ground cloves, nutmeg and cardamom after cooking. Mix well. Good for colds, coughs and asthma. Based on suggestions from Dr. Nadkarni's *Indian Materia Medica.*

MATAJI'S *GARAM MASALA*

Preparation time: 40 minutes
−Vata, +Pitta, −Kapha

Makes: 1¾ cups
❀ ❦ ❄

5 cinnamon sticks, 3 inches long
⅛ cup whole cloves
½ cup cumin seeds
1 cup coriander seeds
⅛ cup whole black peppercorns

Pre-heat oven to 200 degrees. Mix all ingredients and put in roasting pan. Roast for 30 minutes on bottom shelf of oven. Stir occasionally. Cool. Blend in blender, sift, blend again until a powder. Store in a tightly covered jar.

Comments: This warming spice mix is used in soups and vegetables. Use sparingly! Very warming, stimulates digestion.

SNACKS

ABOUT SNACKS

Snacks are not a normal part of the ancient Ayurvedic program. One to two meals per day were considered ideal, and eating much between meals was regarded as an excellent way to ruin the digestive tone and create ama. Now, for some with blood sugar imbalances or erratic eating schedules, snacks even take the place of meals at times. These recipes are offered for the truly hungry belly. Most of the recipes under FRUITS (p. 174) also make excellent snacks.

ABOUT NUTS
AND SEEDS

Nuts and seeds are a tasty and simple snack. Ayurvedic medicine regards most nuts as restorative, nutritive and warm in their action. All of the nuts are also sweet, heavy and oily in quality, with the exception of dried coconut and apricot pits, which are still sweet and heavy, but drying.

The fattier the nut, the more aggravating it is to Kapha and Pitta. Brazil nuts, macadamias, peanuts, pecans, piñons, pistachios and walnuts are good examples. Most nuts, being heavy in attribute, are best eaten in small quantities by Vata. Unless a nut is cool and dry, such as coconut, it is best passed up by Pitta.

Like many other foods, nuts are valued for their medicinal activity. Filberts, hazelnuts and walnuts are considered aphrodisiac in action. Hazelnuts are also used as a general tonifier and strengthener to the stomach. Pistachio nuts are said to sedate and tonify the system, and are of benefit in debilitated conditions. Brazil nuts specifically are used as a laxative, for the relief of constipation and hemorrhoids; for this purpose they must be well-chewed and eaten no more than a couple of ounces at a time.

Peanuts are considered nutritious, laxative and emollient, being rich in B vitamins, vitamin E, iron, protein, and zinc. Beware if you are possessed of a sluggish liver or gallbladder, though, as the noble and fatty peanut is likely to only make these worse. It can also rather easily promote gas in Vata.

Almonds are most valuable, being used as a restorative, tonifier, nutritive, and nerve tonic. The therapeutic recipes using almonds here effectively stimulate a sluggish digestive tract as well.

Coconut is cooling, sweet, nutritive, demulcent, and laxative. Especially lovely for Pitta! Its fat can elevate cholesterol levels indirectly; it is best avoided by those with high cholesterol levels.

Pumpkin seeds serve all constitutions well, being rich in zinc, iron, and fiber. It is also used Ayurvedically as an eliminative for tapeworm.

Sesame seeds, like sesame oil, warm pronouncedly. They are good as a garnish or mixed with other seeds. They balance the ingestion of legumes for Vata to some extent.

Sunflower seeds are more nutritive than medicinal in action, being a generous source of potassium and zinc. They can be used by all constitutions with benefit.

Chia seeds promote endurance and strength; they are mildly warming and focussing in action.

Flax seeds are a rich source of essential fatty acids. While they are considered warming from an Ayurvedic perspective, they have an antiinflammatory action both internally and externally, most noticeably for Vata. They calm and relieve dry inflammations associated with the joints and skin. They also can be useful for relieving Kaphic bronchial congestion. Psyllium seeds are better suited to Pitta, being cooler, more moist and heavy. They also have an anti-inflammatory effect, primarily on the digestive tract. Both psyllium and flax seeds are used to stimulate elimination. Both need to be taken with adequate amounts of fluids and secondary digestive stimulants to be most effective in this role. Psyllium husks are actually more active than the whole seeds for this purpose. Simple digestive stimulants like cloves, cinnamon, cardamom, or black mustard seeds are in order if you are using these seeds on a regular basis, as they, especially psyllium, inhibit agni.

DRY ROASTED GARBANZOS

Preparation time: 40 minutes   Makes: 2 cups.
+Vata, +Pitta, – –Kapha   ✿   ❅

>   **2 cups cooked garbanzos**
>   **¹/₂ teaspoon garlic powder**
>   **¹/₂ teaspoon sea salt**

Preheat oven to 350 degrees. Mix all ingredients together and spread on a lightly greased cookie sheet. Slow cook them for 30 minutes or until the garbanzos are crisp on the outside, slightly tender on the inside.

Comments: This is an old Ayurvedic formula for restoring exhausted sexual energy, particularly in men (with the modern use of garlic powder—fresh garlic can also be used and roasted with the garbanzos). It is also used to relieve gas and stimulate urination. Dr. Nadkarni recommends that it be eaten at night, followed with a glass of warm milk, to relieve bronchitis.

Variation: The following modification is based on the spices in TASTY CHICKPEAS (p. 100). It provides an option for *Pittas* looking for a tasty and crunchy low-fat snack.

CURRIED ROASTED GARBANZOS

Makes: 2 cups

+*Vata,* −*Pitta,* −*Kapha* ✿ ❄

2 cups cooked garbanzos
1½ teaspoon coriander powder
1 teaspoon curry powder, mild
1 teaspoon sea salt
½ teaspoon turmeric

Combine all the ingredients and prepare as above for DRY ROASTED GARBANZOS (p.228).

TOASTED SUNFLOWER SEEDS

Preparation time: 20 minutes Makes: 2 cups
−*Vata,* 0 *Pitta,* 0 *Kapha* ✿ ✳ ☙ ❄

2 cups fresh raw sunflower seeds

Warm large heavy skillet (iron preferred) on low heat. After 2 minutes, add sunflower seeds. Toast for 15 to 20 minutes, stirring occasionally. Cool. Serve.

Comments: Good all-purpose munchie food; tasty garnish in salads, vegetables, main dishes. Rich in potassium and zinc.

SALTED CASHEWS

Preparation time: 5 minutes   Makes: 1 cup
− Vata, + Pitta, + Kapha   🐚 ❄

> **1 cup raw cashews, whole or pieces**
> **¹/₂-1 teaspoon sea salt**
> **1 teaspoon coriander powder**

Mix all ingredients together well and serve.

Comments: This is a flavorful substitute for commercially prepared fried nuts, and easier to digest. Good for parties. However, addictive!

DRY-ROASTED PUMPKIN SEEDS

Preparation time: 10 to 15 minutes   Makes: 1 cup
− Vata, 0 Pitta, 0 Kapha   ✿ ✴ 🐚 ❄

> **1 cup raw pumpkin seeds**
> **¹/₂ teaspoon ground cumin**
> **1 teaspoon coriander powder**
> **¹/₄ teaspoon turmeric**
> **¹/₂ teaspoon rock or sea salt**

Mix all ingredients in a large unoiled skillet and cook them over low heat until the pumpkin seeds begin to pop, about ten minutes. Stir, cooking another 1 to 2 minutes more. Cool.

Comments: The spices are added to enhance digestion of the seeds. The pumpkin seeds turn a lovely bright green in the roasting.

SUNFLOWER-PUMPKIN SEED MIX

Preparation time: 20 minutes   Makes: 2½ cups
− Vata, 0 Pitta, 0 Kapha   ✿ ✴ 🐚 ❄

Prepare dry-roasted pumpkin seeds as above and toast 1½ cups of raw shelled sunflower seeds at the same time in a separate skillet (see p. 229). When both seeds are done, mix them together.

SUN BALLS

Preparation time: 20 minutes — Vata, — Pitta, 0 Kapha*

Makes: about 2 dozen

½ cup plus 2 tablespoons toasted sunflower seeds (see TOASTED SUNFLOWER SEEDS (p. 229)
½ cup shredded, unsweetened coconut (omit for *Kapha*)
2 to 3 tablespoons raisins (omit for *Vata*)
¼ cup sunflower butter
1 tablespoon maple syrup
1 teaspoon almond extract
½ teaspoon coriander powder

Grind the sunflower seeds in a blender to a coarse meal. Mix all the ingredients together in a mixing bowl and press into 1 inch balls.

Comment: This is a good afternoon snack. See SUNBALL SWEETIES (p. 237).

*If a little extra dry ginger is added to Kapha's

SOAKED ALMONDS

Preparation time: Overnight — Vata, + Pitta, + Kapha

Makes: 2 cups.

½ pound raw almonds, organic if you can get them
2 cups water

Put almonds in small bowl. Pour water over almonds. Let sit overnight. Drain water and peel almond skins off. This makes a nice plump, yet raw, nut.

Comment: A few can be eaten by *Pitta* without harm.

Variation: If you are in a hurry, you can blanch the almonds. Bring the water to a boil and pour it over the almonds in a small heatproof bowl. Let them sit 5 minutes, then peel off the skins. They will come off quite easily. However, the high heat alters the oil in the almonds so they are not as calming to *Vata* nor quite as easy to digest.

SPICED UP YOGURT

Preparation time: 5 minutes

– –Vata, +Pitta, +Kapha

Serves: 1

❀ ✳ ᘓ ❄

> 1 cup plain yogurt
> 1-2 teaspoons blackstrap molasses
> ¼ teaspoon vanilla extract

Stir all ingredients together; serve.

Comments: The warm, oily, moist qualities of molasses make this especially good for calming *Vata*. At the same time it offers a mineral and vitamin rich mixture calming to the nerves (being rich in calcium, iron, sulfur, and B vitamins). Good alone as a snack or with BANANA MUFFINS (p. 144) for a fast lunch.

CHEVADO

Preparation time: 10 minutes

– Vata, – Pitta, moderately +Kapha*

Makes: 5 cups

❀ ✳ ᘓ ❄

> 1 cup ready-to-eat dry cereal flakes (wheat flakes, oat flakes, amaranth flakes, rice flakes)
> 2 cups ready-to-eat dry cereal with texture (Oatios, shredded wheats, Chex, etc.)
> 2 tablespoons sunflower oil (*Vatas* can increase this to as much as 6 tablespoons)
> 2 tablespoons coriander seeds
> 5 tablespoons shredded unsweetened coconut (omit for *Kapha*)
> 4 tablespoons sesame seeds (for *Vata* only)
> ½ cup raisins
> ½ cup pumpkin or sunflower seeds, or 1 tablespoon cashews
> ½ teaspoon turmeric
> ⅙ teaspoon *hing*
> ½ teaspoon sea or rock salt
> ½ teaspoon curry powder
> ½ teaspoon cinnamon
> 2 teaspoons Sucanat (omit for *Kapha*)

Heat oil in large saucepan over low heat. Add coriander seeds. Heat 30 seconds over medium heat, then add coconut, sesame seeds, raisins, cashews, and turmeric. Mix well. Add cereals and remaining ingredients. Heat over low heat for 3 to 5 minutes. Mix well, then cool. Chevado will stay fresh for about two weeks when stored in a tight container to protect from moisture.

Comments: This goes well with a hot beverage or as an afternoon snack. This is a delicious snack for *Pitta* and *Vata.* Adjusted as described below, it can also be a good snack for *Kapha.* The light dry qualities of it can imbalance *Vata,* which is why more oil is recommended for this *dosha.* A tasty *tridoshic* snack is to use rice cereals, 2 tablespoons sunflower oil, coriander, sunflower and pumpkin seeds, raisins, turmeric, *hing*, salt, curry powder, and cinnamon. *Vata* and *Pitta* can sweeten it up with Sucanat or raw sugar individually as they like, and *Vatas* can also add sesame seeds if they like.

When all ingredients are included. Using amaranth, oat, corn, or rye flakes, and no coconut, sesame seeds, cashews or Sucanat, moderately +Vata, 0 Pitta, −Kapha.

OAT CHEVADO

Preparation time: 15 minutes   Makes: 1½ cups.
+Vata, +Pitta, −Kapha   ✿ ✳ ﻌ ❄

    1 cup dry rolled oats
    1 tablespoon sunflower oil
    ½ teaspoon turmeric
    1 tablespoon raw sunflower seeds
    ¼ teaspoon sea salt
    ½ teaspoon curry powder
    ½ cup raisins
    ⅛ teaspoon cayenne or *pippali* (optional, good)

Heat the oil in a large skillet. Add turmeric, oats and sunflower seeds and cook over low heat for 10 to 15 minutes stirring occasionally so as to prevent sticking. Add remaining ingredients and mix well.

Comment: An odd but nourishing dry snack.

DESSERTS

ABOUT DESSERTS
AND SWEETENERS

In India, sweets are used to praise the Divine. Prasad, *Indian sweetmeats, are given to devotees at the close of a Hindu ceremony of worship much as wine and bread are received in a Christian communion ritual. Sweets are something special, an offering of love. They are also a way to pamper a guest and acknowledge the specialness of an occasion. Paradoxically, Ayurveda goes practical on us when it comes to desserts. While there are numerous recipes within the ancient tracts for sweet little goodies with therapeutic uses, when it comes to desserts, Charak is unequivocal: "After having taken food, one should never take such heavy articles as pastries, sweetened rice, (etc) . . . .Even when hungry, one should take these articles only in proper quantity." The reason, of course, is that Ayurveda is concerned with physical well-being, and a heavy sweet wonderfulness after a meal inhibits digestion, can create* ama, *and add weight. The sages were imminently masters of common sense. Whether you are as well, is of course, up to you.*

Our approach here is to wend a middle way. We have tried to offer as many light, easy to digest sweets as possible, with a few outrageous fatties for those special celebrations. People with any kind of yeast or fungal infection are best off avoiding sweets, as it can aggravate their condition. If you are working with a serious illness such as cancer, heart disease, or diabetes, you are advised to skip this section entirely. If you are not, well, trust your common sense. All of the recipes here offer alternatives to sugar, and many of them are wheat-free, if you need to avoid wheat.

Most sweeteners are cool, heavy and moist in attribute, making them calming to Vata *and* Pitta *and most imbalancing to* Kapha. *Honey is an exception, in that it warms, drys and provides astringency. It is a helpful sweet for* Kapha, *used in moderation and without cooking. Apple concentrate is another alternative for* Kapha, *being a tad lighter and dryer than most sweeteners. It is cool in nature, making it suitable for* Pitta *as well.*

A few other sweeteners are heating, among them jaggery and molasses. Sucanat, the organic granulated sugar cane juice developed in Switzerland, tastes mildly heating to us, but we may have to work with it a few more years before we can say for sure. Brown rice syrup, barley malt syrup, maple syrup, and plain old white table sugar are all cooling in nature. We have inclined toward the natural sweeteners as opposed to sugar in our recipes from personal experience. They have modest amounts of trace minerals and a bit of B vitamins and seem to provoke fewer shocking reactions on blood sugar mechanisms than the concentrated white favorite, sugar. Again, if you have blood sugar imbalances, even these natural sweeteners can be too much. In these cases, capitalizing on the sweetness of whole grains, sauteed carrots, sweet potatoes, and onions is more in order.

More information is provided about the sweeteners as they are used here. Bon appetit!

DATE DREAM BALLS

Preparation time: 45 minutes
−Vata, −Pitta, +Kapha

Makes 24-30 balls.

❀ ✴ ☙ ❄

    1 cup whole dried pitted dates (about ½ pound)
    2 tablespoons water
    2 tablespoons brown rice syrup
    1 teaspoon vanilla
    1 tablespoon organic tangerine peel (orange can be substituted)
    ¼ cup blanched almonds, chopped
    ¼ cup date sugar (or less)

Chop the dates finely. Mix the dates, water, rice syrup, vanilla, and tangerine peel in a small heavy skillet and cook over low heat for 10 to 15 minutes or until all the water has evaporated off and the dates are a thick mass. The thicker it is, the easier it is to work. Stir in the almonds and let cool. When cool, form into 1 inch balls (you can grease your hands with a bit of *ghee*, but basically you're going to get sticky with these). Roll the balls in date sugar (to get them dry enough to serve).

Comments: A very good and sumptuous rejuvenative. In ancient India, these would have been considered an aphrodisiac of sorts. They are delicious.

In general, dates calm *Vata* and *Pitta* and imbalance *Kapha*. Fresh dates are considered mildly heating in quality, and so are best for *Vata*. Dried dates are not as warming as fresh ones, and date sugar is cooler than either of these; both can be used by *Pitta* with good benefit. In Ayurveda, dates are used to strengthen the liver and are indicated for those dealing with alcoholism. They are also valued as an all-round tonifier and are used therapeutically to calm lung and bladder inflammations or chills and fevers.

ABOUT HONEY

Honey was highly esteemed by the ancients for its healing properties. Both the Indians and the Egyptians utilized it for a wide variety of conditions. One use was as a poultice applied directly to wounds to promote healing. Being a volatile sweet in the presence of heat, it can break down when used externally. For this reason, it is best to use honey cool or at room temperature. Left in hot places it will ferment, and used in baking it can create ama. If you are adding honey to a hot dish or beverage, it can be added at the end of preparation immediately before serving.

In India it is said that the effects of honey change over time, and that young honey—less than six months old—is healing for Pitta. *If you keep your own bees or have access to very fresh honey, this is a lovely thing to know. Otherwise, honey is best consumed by* Kapha. Vatas *benefit from occasional use of this sweet, as it is warm. Its dryness can aggravate* Vata *if over-used. In this recipe, the warmth and oiliness of the sesame more than counters this quality.*

SESAME SWEETIES

Preparation time: 20-30 minutes   Makes: 14 to 21 1-inch delicious balls.
− −Vata, +Pitta, +Kapha

  ½ **cup sesame seeds**
  ⅓ **cup honey**
  2 tablespoons raw sunflower seeds
  2 tablespoons tahini or sesame butter
  ½ **cup toasted wheat germ**
  ⅛ **teaspoon sea salt**
  ½ **cup unsweetened shredded coconut plus additional for garnish**
  1 teaspoon vanilla extract

Grind the raw sunflower seeds into a rough powder in the blender. Combine all ingredients into a stiff and slightly crumbly dough. Press into balls and roll in coconut.

Variation: Wheat-free version: Substitute ½ cup rough ground sunflower seeds for the wheat germ.

SUN BALL SWEETIES

Preparation time: 20 minutes   Makes: about 2 dozen
−Vata, −Pitta, +Kapha*
See SUN BALLS (p. 231) for ingredients list.

*Increase the maple syrup to ⅓ cup on SUN BALLS, (p. 231) and use additional coconut as a garnish, to roll the balls in. Makes a good simple dessert.

CAROB DELIGHTS

Preparation time: 45 minutes
−*Vata*, −*Pitta*, +*Kapha**

Makes: 3 dozen 2-inch cookies.

✿ ✳ 🐢 ❄

> **2 egg whites**
> **⅛ teaspoon cream of tartar**
> **¾ cup brown rice syrup**
> **1 teaspoon vanilla extract**
> **1 teaspoon cinnamon**
> **¼ teaspoon nutmeg**
> **2 tablespoons organic orange peel, grated**
> **¼ cup raisins (optional)**
> **2 tablespoons boiling water**
> **1 cup carob powder**
> **1½ cups shredded unsweetened coconut (plus ¼ cup more for garnish)**

Preheat oven to 300 degrees. Whip the egg whites with the cream of tartar until they are stiff enough to hold a peak; set aside.

In a separate bowl mix the brown rice syrup, vanilla, spices, orange peel, raisins, and water. Stir well. Stir in the carob, mix well. Fold in the egg whites and stir well. Fold in the coconut. Drop by the teaspoonful onto a greased cookie sheet. Garnish tops with shredded coconut. Bake for 15 minutes or until done.

Comments: Carob powder is sweet, light, dry, and astringent in nature. It is an extraordinarily rich source of potassium, containing 950 mg. per cup. It is most appropriate for *Pitta* and *Kapha,* and can be used by *Vata* when it is well-moistened, as it is here, or in a hot carob drink. It nourishes the lungs.

*A few of these would not be the end of Kapha; they are pretty light.

BUTTERSCOTCH BROWNIES

Preparation time: 30-40 minutes

−*Vata,* −*Pitta,* + +*Kapha**
−*Vata, mildly* +*Pitta,* + +*Kapha***

Makes: 2 dozen 1" x 1" x 3" bars
or 16 2-inch squares.

🐢 ❄

6 tablespoons *ghee*
1 cup Sucanat
¹/₂ cup rice or whole wheat flour
¹/₂ cup pecans or walnuts or coconut, chopped
¹/₄ cup sunflower seeds, raw (optional)
1 egg
1¹/₄ teaspoon vanilla extract
1 teaspoon baking powder
¹/₄ teaspoon sea salt

Preheat oven to 350 degrees. Warm the *ghee* in a medium-sized saucepan over low heat. Stir in the Sucanat. It will get moist like brown sugar, but will not dissolve the way brown sugar would. Measure the flour and nuts into a mixing bowl and immediately stir in the Sucanat-*ghee* mixture. Beat the egg in a separate small bowl and add in the vanilla to the egg. Add the baking powder and salt to the flour-Sucanat mixture, then combine the egg into the flour as well. Beat well. Spoon into an oiled 8 inch x 8 inch baking pan—if you want thicker brownies, you may not fill up the whole pan. Bake for 20 to 30 minutes or until a knife inserted into the middle of the brownies comes out cleanly. Cool and cut.

Comments: NOT for anyone looking to decrease *ama* or *Kapha*. Addictive and difficult to resist. You can use barley flour in this recipe; cut the *ghee* to 5 tablespoons and leave the flour at ¹/₂ cup. When doubling this rule, use two 8-inch square pans rather than one large pan, for best results.

*With whole wheat flour
**With rice flour

ABOUT CHOCOLATE

Chocolate was esteemed by the Incas, Mayans, and Aztecs for its energizing properties. It is warm, heavy and moist. The French novelist/philosopher Voltaire was said to sup on nothing but hot chocolate with coffee from rising until supper! Its high fat content and attributes make it most appropriate for Vata *and least helpful for* Kapha *and* Pitta. *Its caffeine is also aggravating to* Pitta.

ABOUT SUGAR

Sucanat is perhaps the healthiest, certainly the easiest, substitute for white sugar we know. Chemical-free and organic it offers a real alternative for those just beginning to wean themselves from the white stuff. It tastes much like brown sugar and has roughly the same texture and dryness, though more nutrients. As we have said, it tastes mildly warming to us, certainly not as hot as Indian jaggery or American molasses.

White sugar is cold, light, and dry. It can turn a Vata into a space cadet faster than just about any other substance we know. Its concentrated sweetness makes it inappropriate for Kapha. While it is often used in Ayurveda to calm Pitta, so many Pittas of my acquaintance also have Vata imbalances, that I would rather use more nutritive and weightier sweeteners, like the syrups.

True raw sugar cane, the unrefined sticks, are quite different from white sugar. Because they are still whole plants, they have moisture, coolness and minerals. Sugar cane is far more balancing than its refined counterparts. Calming to Vata, calming to Pitta, it moderately aggravates Kapha. Most "raw" packaged sugar does not fall in this category. If it has gotten to the state of being dried out and in packets, you can usually figure that it shares more with white sugar than with sugar cane. Curiously, high rates of dental cavities are reported with white sugar but not with sugar cane. It may be that the traces of nutrients and fluid in raw cane protect the teeth. In any case, the body seems to handle the whole food more effectively than the refined product. Sugar cane is diuretic in action.

Fructose is another sugar substitute that can be used freely by both Pitta and Vata. It is cool, sweet, light, and moderately dry. However, its concentrated sweetness imbalances Kapha—less than white or brown sugar, but quite a bit more than honey. In truth, fruits and honey are the best choices for Kapha when contemplating sweet.

COCONUT MACAROONS

Preparation time: 50 minutes
Makes: 2 dozen 2½" cookies
−Vata, − −Pitta, +Kapha
✻ ☙ ❄

1/4 cup raw almonds
4 egg whites
1/4 teaspoon cream of tartar
1/2 cup maple syrup
1/2 cup brown rice syrup
1/2 teaspoon baking powder
3 drops rose water (optional, lovely flavor if you have it)
3½ cups shredded unsweetened coconut (2/3 pound)

Preheat oven to 300 degrees.

Blanch almonds or soak them overnight (see SOAKED ALMONDS p. 231). Grind them in the blender or a nut grinder, set aside.

Beat egg whites and cream of tartar in a stainless steel, glass or enamel mixing bowl. Beat until stiff enough to peak. Whip in baking powder. In a separate bowl, combine the sweeteners, coconut, almonds, and rose water. Fold in the egg whites. Drop by the tablespoonful onto a lightly greased cookie sheet, mounding slightly into balls as you do. Bake for 30 minutes or until cookies are just turning golden around the edges and bottom. Remove from cookie sheet while warm, let cool on a plate.

ABOUT MAPLE SYRUP

Maple syrup, a native of North America, is cool, fresh, light, and moist like the Northern forests from which it is harvested. It is often recommended for calming Pitta. *It has a sprinkling of minerals and traces of B vitamins. It can be heated and used in baking, yet it is wise to take into account its distinctive flavor before randomly adding it to any dish. It is a good sweet to try on hot breakfast cereals in the morning. It is calming to* Vata *as well as to* Pitta. *It imbalances* Kapha, *being cool and moist. Its price may discourage overindulgence in this tasty item.*

CLASSIC OATMEAL COOKIES

Preparation time: 1 hour

Makes: 2 to 3 dozen 3 inch cookies.

−Vata, −Pitta, moderately +Kapha

🐌 ❄

> 1 cup date sugar or brown rice syrup, or any combination thereof
> ½ cup *ghee* or unsalted butter
> ⅛ teaspoon dry ginger
> ⅛ teaspoon ground cloves
> 1 teaspoon cinnamon
> 1 egg, beaten
> 1 cup oat flour or whole wheat flour
> ½ teaspoon sea salt
> 1 teaspoon baking powder
> 1½ cups rolled oats
> ½ cup raisins
> ¼ cup walnuts or raw sunflower seeds
> ¼ cup dates, chopped (optional)

Preheat oven to 375 degrees. Cream *ghee* (or butter) with sweetener in medium mixing bowl until smooth. Then stir in ginger, cloves and cinnamon. Next mix in beaten egg and vanilla.

In separate bowl, mix flour, oats and remaining ingredients. Then stir this dry mixture into the creamy *ghee* and egg. Spoon onto greased cookie sheet and bake for 15 minutes or until done (golden brown around the edges). Cool and remove from cookie sheet.

Comments: The *Kapha* in search of a decent *Kapha*-calming oatmeal cookie might start by cutting out all the extravagant sweetener and substituting ¼ cup apple concentrate. Then cut the *ghee* by ½, skip the dates, and use raisins or raisins and figs instead. You could increase the ginger and cloves to ¼ teaspoon each or more, depending on your tastes. The oat flour and rolled oats are fine as is, being warming. All and all, though, the ingredients add up to something heavy—good for an occasional nibble, but not an all-out glut.

This recipe is based on many I grew up with, with inspiration from *The Joy of Cooking.*

GINGER SNAPS

Preparation time: 1 hour   Makes: 3 dozen 3 inch cookies.
– – *Vata*, + *Pitta*, + *Kapha*   ✿ 🌰 ❄

     ½ cup *ghee* or unsalted butter
     ½ cup light (unsulfured) molasses
     ½ cup brown rice syrup
     1 egg, beaten
     2 teaspoons dry ginger powder
     1 ½ teaspoons cinnamon
     ¼ teaspoon ground cloves
     1 cup rice flour
     1½ cups oat flour (or 2½ cups whole wheat flour)
     2 teaspoons baking powder
     ½ teaspoon sea salt

Preheat oven to 375 degrees.

Cream the *ghee*, brown rice syrup and molasses together well. Beat in the egg. Add the spices to the liquid mix. In a separate bowl, mix the flours, baking powder and salt. Stir the dry mixture into the wet one. Spoon onto a lightly greased cookie sheet by the half-tablespoonful, leaving plenty of room around each cookie for it to spread (they do spread). Cook for 12 minutes or until golden brown around edges. Cool on the sheet, then remove.

Variation: GINGER SNAP FACES: Decorate each cookie with 2 raisins for eyes and a bit of orange peel for a grin, before putting them in the oven to bake. A fun one for kids.

ABOUT MOLASSES

   Molasses is hot, heavy and oily, perfect for Vata. *It disturbs* Pitta *and* Kapha *proportionally, however, one or two ginger snaps would not be the end of Pitta. Black-strap molasses is most heating in quality and is excellent added to hot water or milk as a Vata-calming beverage (see IRON-RICH BREAKFAST DRINK, p. 257 and HOT GINGER TEA, p. 265). Black-strap molasses tends to take over a dish the way a loquacious dinner guest can dominate a conversation. Light, unsulfured molasses has a milder flavor and fewer minerals, especially iron and calcium, but adapts more easily in recipes.*

ABOUT PRUNES

Prunes are warm, sweet, heavy, and laxative. Their laxative qualities make them relieving to Pitta and Kapha, in that they promote elimination and the release of the accumulated doshas. They are also a generous source of iron. They are too heavy and mobile for Vata to handle in any large quantity.

DELECTABLE PRUNE BARS

Preparation time: 1 hour
+ *Vata,* − *Pitta,* − *Kapha*

Makes: 2 dozen 1½ inch bars.

❀ ❋

2½ cups pitted prunes, finely chopped (about ⅔ pound)
1 cup apple juice
⅓ cup water
½ teaspoon cinnamon
¼ teaspoon allspice
½ teaspoon almond extract (optional)
1 cup barley flour
½ teaspoon baking powder
¼ teaspoon sea salt
1 tablespoon *ghee*
¾ cup water

Garnish: Cinnamon and organic lime or lemon peel

Preheat oven to 350 degrees. Simmer uncovered in a medium skillet the prunes, juice, water, and spices. Simmer them over low heat until they are thick, 20 to 30 minutes. Add the almond extract at the end of the simmering time. While prune mixture is cooking, stir together the rest of the ingredients (flour, baking powder, salt, *ghee*, and water) in a medium-sized mixing bowl. The mixture will be crumbly and not hold together. Do not let this slow you down. Lightly oil an 8 inch x 8 inch baking pan and pour/guide/dump the barley crust in. Press into place with your fingers— now it will hold together! Dust with cinnamon. Bake for 12 to 20 minutes or until slightly crusty.

When the crust is done, take it out and spread the prune mixture over it. Garnish with lime peel. (Or, if you can't find organic limes or lemons, cut a few thin slices of lime without the peel. This makes a striking garnish.) Put back in the oven and cook another 15 minutes. Cool and serve.

Comments: I wish I could say this was calming to *Vata*, as it is a great laxative. However, 100% of test cases so far have reported definite aggravation of *Vata!* To be eaten in moderation, i.e., 1 to 2 bars at a time.

SWEET POTATO HALVA

Preparation time: 1 hour (most of it unattended) Serves: 2-3
–Vata, –Pitta, +Kapha ✿ ✴ 🍃 ❄

2 ½ cups sweet potato, grated (about 2 large sweet potatoes)
2 cups whole milk or soy milk
½ cup raisins
½ cup blanched almonds or almonds and pecans
4 tablespoons *ghee*
1 teaspoon ground cardamom
15 to 20 threads of saffron

Preheat the oven to 400 degrees.

Grind the nuts in a blender into a fine powder. Wash and grate the sweet potato. Saute the sweet potato in 2 tablespoons of *ghee,* just enough to coat it. Stir in the milk and raisins.

Lightly grease an 8 by 8 inch baking pan or iron skillet and transfer the mixture to it. Cover and bake for 40 to 55 minutes or until all the milk is absorbed. If you need to, uncover the halva in the last 10 minutes of baking to allow the milk to dry. When all the milk is absorbed, stir in the rest of the *ghee*, nutmeal, cardamom, and saffron. Press back into a flattened shape. Add sweetener (such as brown rice syrup) if desired. Cut in small pieces and serve.

Comment: This delectable Indian dessert can also be made with butternut or buttercup squash or pumpkin in place of sweet potato. Rich in vitamins and entirely delicious.

INDIAN RICE PUDDING

Preparation time: 1 hour 15 minutes Serves: 4
–Vata, –Pitta, +Kapha ✿ ✴ 🍃

¾ cup basmati rice, uncooked
3 cups cow's milk
⅛ teaspoon saffron
15 cardamom seeds
3-5 tablespoons brown rice syrup, honey or maple syrup (depending how sweet you like it)

Garnish: 2 teaspoons organic lemon peel, grated and 2 tablespoons toasted unsweetened shredded coconut

Wash the rice until the water is clear. Combine the rice, milk, saffron, and cardamom seeds in the top of a double boiler. Cover and cook (with water in the bottom of your double boiler) over low heat for 1 hour. While it is simmering, you can toast the coconut in a dry skillet if you like, unless you have happened upon a source of pre-toasted unsweetened coconut. It just takes a few minutes, stirring occasionally so it does not get too brown. Let it cool. When the rice is done, stir in the sweetener and top with the lemon and coconut. Serve hot or cold.

Comments: A lovely, light, elegant dish, worthy of honored company. It is based on the saffron milk popular in India. I have never tried making it with goat's milk and honey, but it seems a perfectly tasty way to balance *Kapha*, perhaps with a pinch of dry ginger to cut the sweet. Use any of the sweeteners except honey if you want to calm *Pitta*.

Barley malt, rice bran syrup, sorghum, and maple syrup are all cool, heavy and moist: good for *Vata* and *Pitta*, to be avoided by *Kapha*. Brown rice syrup is a good choice if you are looking for a sweetener without much extra flavor of its own; it distracts least from the taste of a dish compared to the other syrups.

BAKED APPLES

Preparation time: 1 hour
0 Vata, − Pitta, − Kapha

Serves: 4

> 4 organic apples
> 2 cups apple juice
> 1 tablespoon cinnamon
> 1/4 teaspoon nutmeg or cardamom
> 1/4 teaspoon organic lemon peel or 1 teaspoon lemon juice
> 1/2 cup raisins
> 1/4 cup sunflower seeds
> *Ghee* or unsalted butter

Preheat the oven to 350 degrees. Wash and core apples. Place in 8 inch x 8 inch baking dish.

Mix the raisins, spices and seeds. Stuff this mixture firmly into the cored apples. Pour the apple juice into the pan, and dot the center of each apple with a dot of *ghee* or butter (optional). Cover and bake for 45 minutes or until tender.

Comments: A very satisfying dessert which also happens to reduce *ama* and promote elimination in a gentle sort of way.

Fruit juices and juice concentrates like apple or bottled cherry concentrate make good choices for sweeteners for *Kapha*. Raisin syrup (raisins and water ground in the blender as they do at Kripalu Yoga Center), dried figs and other ground dried fruits in moderation are other healing sweet options for *Kapha*. If you are a *Kapha* or working with a *Kaphic* imbalance, try eliminating all but fruit and honey from your sweets program and see how much lighter and clearer you feel (after the withdrawal pangs subside).

Variation: BAKED PEARS: proceed as above, slicing pears in half and removing core.

SHIRO

Preparation time: 30 minutes or less   Serves: 6-8
−Vata, −Pitta, +Kapha   ✳ 🍂 ❄

> 1 cup cream of wheat or bear mush, uncooked
> 1 cup Sucanat
> 2 cups milk or water or a combination of both
> 4 to 8 tablespoons *ghee* (the lesser for lower fat, the greater amount for a richer flavor)
> ½ cup mixed raw nuts: walnuts, blanched almonds, pecans or pistachios, chopped
> 1 teaspoon ground cardamom
> 4 tablespoons rose water
> 1 banana, chopped (optional: not everyday fare for *Pitta*, but fine here for a special treat)

Roast the cream of wheat or bear mush in *ghee* in a large heavy skillet over low heat, stirring constantly until color turns slightly brown and the grain becomes aromatic, about 4 minutes. Add liquid and increase heat to medium. Continue to stir until mixture begins to thicken. Add Sucanat, nuts, cardamom, rose water, and banana and cook uncovered until all liquid is absorbed and the *ghee* begins to separate out in little beads on the *shiro*. Press into a serving dish and cut into diamond shapes or as desired.

Comments: This rich brown Indian dessert offers a fitting conclusion to almost any Indian meal. Wheat-sensitive *Vatas* or *Pittas* can substitute an equal amount of cream of rice or Rice 'N' Shine cereal for the cream of wheat or bear mush. (Bear mush is a whole grain wheat cereal sold in some health food stores, and offers a nice texture if you can obtain it.)

A Desai family favorite.

KAPHA SHIRO

Preparation time: 30 minutes or less   Serves: 6-8
0 Vata, O Pitta, −Kapha   ✿   ✳   🐌   ❄

> 1 cup cream of rye cereal, uncooked
> 3 tablespoons *ghee*
> 2 cups soy milk (Edensoy Original works well)
> ¾ cup figs and/or raisins
> 1 teaspoon ground cardamom
> ¼ teaspoon dry ginger powder
> 1 tablespoon rose water
> 1 tablespoon raw honey (optional)

Follow the directions given above for *SHIRO*, browning the cream of rye, then adding in the soy milk and letting it thicken. Then add all the rest of the ingredients except the honey. When the liquid is absorbed and the *ghee* begins to bead up, take the *shiro* off the heat to cool. Stir in the honey, if desired. Serve hot or cool.

Comments: Yes! *Kaphas* deserve desserts too! However, the sweet and fat in most goodies inclines them in an opposite direction from *Kapha* calmness. This dessert is extravagant enough to feel like a dessert, but not so disruptive to *Kapha* that they will regret it. With 3 tablespoons of *ghee*, it is not recommended for daily consumption.

KHIR WITH NOODLES

Preparation time: 15 minutes   Serves: 3- 4
−Vata, −Pitta, +Kapha   ✳   🐌   ❄

> 2 ounces uncooked whole wheat noodles, finely crushed (about 1 cup crushed)
> 1 cup whole milk
> 5 almonds, blanched and slivered
> 1 teaspoon *ghee*
> ⅛ teaspoon ground cardamom
> 4 to 5 threads of saffron
> 1½ tablespoons brown rice syrup

Saute the crushed dry noodles in *ghee* until their color turns slightly brown. Add milk and bring to a boil over high heat for 4 minutes or until noodles are soft. Stir constantly to avoid lumping. When cool, add the rest of the ingredients.

Comment: As Mataji says . . . very good! A classic Indian treat.

TRIDOSHIC PAL PAYASAM

Preparation time: 20 minutes, plus chilling   Serves: 4-6

0 Vata, – Pitta, – Kapha*
– Vata, – Pitta, + Kapha**

     ☀ ☕ ❄

        1 quart soy milk or goat milk
        4 tablespoons *basmati* or brown rice, uncooked
        2 tablespoons honey
        ¹/₂ cup raisins
        3 cardamom pods
        ¹/₂ cup toasted sunflower seeds
        ¹/₄ cup shredded unsweetened coconut (optional)

Garnish: sunflower seeds and coconut

Grind rice in blender or grinder until it is a fine powdery meal. Mix the rice meal with ½ cup cold soy milk or goat milk.

Heat the remaining 3½ cups of soy milk in a medium saucepan. Stir in cold rice mixture and keep stirring until it comes to a boil. Remove seeds from cardamom pods. Add raisins and cardamom seeds to hot milk mixture.

Reduce heat to low and simmer for 5 to 10 minutes. The dessert will thicken a little, but basically it is a liquid-like dessert. Take off heat and stir in honey. Chill.

Comments: With thanks to *Laurel's Kitchen* for the original inspiration on this—it can be made with regular milk and cashews, as they suggest, for a *Vata*-calming treat. This recipe used with cow's milk and without the nuts can relieve diarrhea.

Goat and soy milk can be tricky things. Some *Vatas* find soy milk distinctly aggravating, while others get flatulent with the milk of goats. Cow's milk is usually most friendly to *Vatas*, as long as they are not sensitive to it.

*Without coconut.
**With coconut

MAPLE TAPIOCA

Preparation time: 30 minutes   Serves: 4

– –Vata, – Pitta, + Kapha*
0 Vata, – Pitta, – Kapha**

     ☀ ☕ ❄

6 to 8 dried apricots, peaches, figs, or prunes (optional, see Comments below)
5 tablespoons granulated (quick) tapioca
2 ½ cups milk, cow or goat
¼ teaspoon sea salt
2 eggs
⅓ cup maple syrup
½ teaspoon vanilla extract
⅛ teaspoon cinnamon
⅛ teaspoon ground cardamom

Optional topping: toasted blanched almonds, slivered, and toasted unsweetened shredded coconut, about 2 tablespoons of each.

Chop the dried fruit into ½ inch pieces. Place fruit, tapioca, milk and salt in the top of a double boiler and cook over boiling water for ten minutes, stirring only if the mixture begins to stick. Add maple syrup. Reduce heat and simmer 2 minutes on very low heat. Add maple syrup. In a separate small bowl, beat the eggs. Mix ½ cup of the hot tapioca mixture into the eggs to avoid curdling, then gradually add the egg mixture to the rest of the tapioca, cooking for 3 to 4 minutes more, stirring constantly. Add vanilla and spices, stir well. (Thanks to Angela for spicing.) Remove from heat and cool. Garnish with toasted almonds and coconut as desired. Serve warm or cold.

Comments: A soothing dish particularly in autumn and winter. Chilled, it makes an excellent summer dessert for *Pitta*. Whether or not you add the fruit is a matter of personal choice. From a strict Ayurvedic view, fruit and milk mixed together are *Viruddhashana*, a forbidden food combination. Cooked together, they are often fine. If working with an invalid or person with delicate digestion, I would omit the fruit. Tapioca is an especially good food for those recovering from illness, and will not create *ama*.

*With cow's milk
**With goat's milk

EGGLESS TAPIOCA

Preparation time: 5 minutes, 8 hour soak, 5 minutes more   Serves: 4

✱   ❮❯   ❄

Use the same ingredients and amounts as in MAPLE TAPIOCA (p. 249), but omit the eggs. Place the chopped fruit, tapioca and milk in a covered bowl and let them soak for 6 to 8 hours. Transfer these ingredients to a double boiler and bring to a boil over medium heat, stirring constantly. Simmer 2 minutes on very low heat. Stir in the maple syrup, salt, vanilla, and spices. Remove from heat and cool. Serve warm or cold. This makes a thicker dessert than MAPLE TAPIOCA.

KAPHA FRUIT CRUMBLE

Preparation time: 30 minutes   Serves: 4
0 Vata, − Pitta, −Kapha   ✿ 🌿 ❄

> 4 cups fruit: apples, apricots, blueberries, raspberries, cherries,
> peaches, pears or mangos
> 2 cups apple juice
> ¼ cup raisins
> 1 teaspoon cinnamon
> ¾ teaspoon coriander powder
> ⅛-¼ teaspoon dry ginger powder
> 1 tablespoon lemon juice
> 2-4 tablespoons honey (optional) or apple concentrate

Topping: 1 cup CRISPY GRANOLA (p. 284), fruit juice sweetened or otherwise
health-oriented brand and 1 tablespoon shredded unsweetened coconut

Wash fruit. Berries can be used whole; other fruit chop into 1 inch pieces; measure.
Pour apple juice into medium-sized saucepan; heat on medium. Put chopped fruit,
raisins and cinnamon in juice in saucepan, cook over medium heat for 20 minutes.
Remove from heat. Add coriander, ginger, lemon juice, and honey; stir. Spoon into
individual serving bowls and top with granola and coconut. Serve hot or cooled.

Comments: *Vata and Pitta* can eat this with warm fruit juice; *Kapha* as it is served
here. I work with many people of *Kapha* constitution who love sweets but who find
that most sweets imbalance them. This recipe is an exception to the rule, in that it
calms *Kapha* as it calms the sweet tooth as well. Use the higher amount of ginger
powder if you are cooking for *Kapha* or *Vata*, the smaller amount for *Pitta*, as it is
quite warming.

HEARTY RICE PUDDING

Preparation time: 2 hours, much of it unattended

Serves: 8

0 Vata, −Pitta, +Kapha

> ½ cup brown rice, uncooked
> ½ cup pearl barley, uncooked
> 3½ cup water
> ⅛ teaspoon sea salt
> 1¾ cups goat or cow milk
> 1 egg, beaten
> 1 tablespoon barley flour
> 1½ teaspoon cinnamon
> ¼ teaspoon nutmeg
> 1 tablespoon organic orange peel, finely chopped or grated
> 1 teaspoon *ghee*
> 2 teaspoons vanilla
> ¼ cup raisins
> 4 tablespoons apple concentrate

Preheat oven to 350 degrees.

Put the rice, barley, water, and salt in a saucepan to boil. Once they are boiling, cover, reduce heat to low and do what you'd like for 50 minutes. When the time is up, come back and mix them with the rest of the ingredients. Put the mixture in a lightly oiled casserole dish and bake for 45 to 50 minutes uncovered. Cool and cover.

Comments: Technically, this hearty dish should calm *Kapha*, if you only look at the list of ingredients, assuming you will use goat's milk rather than cow's milk. In reality, it is such a substantial character, it could only increase *Kapha*, unless consumed in very graciously small portions (a thimbleful, perhaps?) As delicious as its Indian cousin, but quite different.

BEVERAGES

ABOUT BEVERAGES

Beverages are considered an integral part of an Ayurvedic meal. It is not advised to pointedly separate beverages and solid foods, but to sip in moderation. This will enhance agni and moisten the food along with the salivation which takes place. Some liquids will definitely enhance agni, while others can suppress it. This depends on the makeup of the beverage and the amount drunk. A plain glass of room-temperature water or some warm tea are fine beverages to drink with a meal; a slice of lime or lemon in them will only enhance their ability to support agni. It is washing foods down with excessive amounts of icy drinks that is discouraged by Ayurveda. And rightfully so. In both Eastern and Western research, this has been shown to suppress gastric acid secretion and subsequent digestion.

Beverages can also be enjoyed as meals in themselves. Many of the drinks offered here make good snacks or easy meals.

Vegetable and fruit juices are valued for their medicinal properties and are often used to stimulate particular kinds of healing. Lettuce juice is recommended to calm nervousness and heart palpitations, while red cabbage juice is included in vegetable mixtures to heal chronic coughs, bronchitis, and asthma. Spinach juice has been used as a gargle for sore throats. Pomegranate juice is a specific for hemorrhoids. Onion juice was considered aphrodisiac, and was also used as a smelling salt after a fainting spell. Radish juice was valued for its ability to enkindle agni and appetite. Garlic juice is a specific for calming obstinate coughs and encouraging expectoration; it is used in asthma, bronchitis, pneumonia, and the flu. Beet juice was sniffed up the nose to relieve headache and toothache! Other uses are described in the recipes that follow.

ABOUT COTTAGE CHEESE

Cottage cheese is a lovely cooler for Pitta, and its moist heaviness makes it balancing for Vata as well. It can often be substituted for part or all of the sour cream or yogurt in a recipe, sometimes with the addition of a little lemon juice. This makes the recipe accessible for Pitta (see PITTA LASSI,) It is too heavy for Kapha to utilize regularly, although cottage cheese is less imbalancing to Kapha than hard cheeses by a long shot, being lighter than hard cheeses by a considerable measure. Cottage cheese is good served with fresh ground black pepper. This aids digestibility for all doshas and cuts Kapha.

LASSI

VATA LASSI

Preparation time: 5 minutes   Serves: 1
– Vata, mildly + Pitta, + Kapha

> ½ cup cottage cheese
> ½ cup yogurt
> ¾ cup water
> 1 teaspoon ground cumin powder
> 1 tablespoon honey or 3 large dates, pitted
> ½ teaspoon lemon juice

Blend cottage cheese, yogurt and water in blender. Add rest of ingredients and blend again. Drink at room temperature.

PITTA LASSI

Preparation time: 5 minutes   Serves: 1
– Vata, – Pitta, + Kapha

> ½ cup cottage cheese
> ½ cup yogurt
> ¾ cup water
> 2 teaspoons coriander powder
> 1 tablespoon maple syrup or 3 large dried dates, pitted

Blend cottage cheese, yogurt and water in blender. Add rest of ingredients and blend again. Drink at room temperature.

KAPHA LASSI

Preparation time: 5 minutes
−Vata, +Pitta, −Kapha

Serves: 1-2

✹ 🦢 ❄

>   ½ cup yogurt
>   1 cup water
>   2 teaspoons honey
>   ⅛ teaspoon each of: cinnamon
>   dry ginger powder
>   black pepper
>   ground cumin
>   3 cardamom seeds (about 1 pod)
>   1 tablespoon lecithin (optional)

Blend all ingredients well in blender. Drink at room temperature.

Comment: This drink has a bit of a kick—watch out!

ABOUT ALMONDS

Almonds are highly valued as a rejuvenative in Ayurveda. Ayurvedic practice recommends that almonds always be blanched, as they are in this recipe, as their skins are difficult to digest.

REJUVENATIVE ALMOND MILK

Preparation time: overnight soak, then 5-10 minutes
−Vata, −Pitta, +Kapha

Serves: 1

✿ ✹ 🦢 ❄

>   5 almonds soaked overnight in about cup water
>   1 cup milk
>   ½ teaspoon ground cardamom

In the morning, drain almonds and peel them. (The skin comes off easily when rubbed with your fingers.) In a small saucepan bring milk to boil. Pour hot milk, almonds and cardamom in blender. Blend well.

Comment: This very restorative drink is especially useful in fall and winter, or after a period of major exertion.

CANTALOUPE SMOOTHIE

Preparation time: 5 minutes

— *Vata*, — — *Pitta*, + *Kapha*

Serves: 2

✳

½ **fresh ripe cantaloupe**
½ **cup water**
¼ **teaspoon coriander powder**

Blend all ingredients together well in a blender.

IRON-RICH BREAKFAST DRINK

Preparation time: overnight soak, plus 5 minutes in morning

— *Vata*, — *Pitta*, — *Kapha*

Serves: 1

❀ ✳ 🍵 ❄

¼ **cup raisins**
¼ **cup unsulfured dried apricots or peaches**
1 **cup water**
⅛ **teaspoon dry ginger (*Kapha* only)**

Soak raisins and dried fruit overnight in water. A pint Mason jar works well. Next morning blend soaked fruit and water in blender. *Kaphas* need to garnish with a pinch of ginger to balance the drink for them.

Comment: *Vata* can add up to 1 tablespoon of molasses to this, blending with rest of ingredients in blender, for extra iron.

IRON-RICH YOGURT DRINK

Serves: 1-2

— *Vata*, — *Pitta*, moderately + *Kapha*

❀ ✳ 🍵 ❄

¼ **cup raisins**
¼ **cup unsulfured dried apricots, peaches or figs**
1 **cup water**
½ **cup yogurt, plain**

Follow directions as above, soaking fruit in water overnight. Then blend all ingredients in blender, mixing well.

Comments: This drink is an excellent digestive aid and toner. It is also mildly laxative in action.

MINT TULIP

Preparation time: 10 minutes   Serves: 4
— Vata, -Pitta, +Kapha   ✴ 🐌

> 10 fresh mint leaves, or 1 tablespoon dried mint
> 10 dates (about 1½ cup chopped)
> 1 tablespoon - ½ cup coconut
> Juice of ½ lemon (2 tablespoons)
> 1 tablespoon raisins
> 1 tablespoon frozen orange juice concentrate
> 1 cup fresh or frozen pineapple juice
> 3 cups fresh water

Blend all ingredients thoroughly in blender. Serve cool.

Comments: The only problem with this gloriously fresh and refreshing drink is its color, a pale caramel hue. If you're serving this for an elegant meal or summer afternoon, you might want to splash it up in some mint-colored goblets, perfectly matched to its flavor.

Cool and soothing.

DATE SHAKE

Preparation time: 5 minutes   Serves: 2
— — Vata, — — Pitta, +Kapha   ✴ 🐌

> 6 dates, pitted
> 1½ cups cow, soy, or goat milk
> ½ teaspoon vanilla extract
> ½ cup shredded unsweetened coconut

Place all ingredients in blender and blend. Serve immediately (or the coconut will begin to settle out).

Comments: Sweet, grounding and cool. Vata can add a pinch of cardamom or ground cloves for extra digestibility.

FIG SHAKE

Preparation time: 5 minutes Serves: 2
+Vata, −Pitta, −Kapha*

> **3 dried figs**
> **1½ cup apple juice**
> **¼ teaspoon ground cloves (optional, *Pitta* will do well to omit)**
> **½ teaspoon almond extract**

Blend all ingredients in blender.

*If served with cloves for Kapha; not Pitta.

HOT APPLE CIDER

Preparation time: 20 minutes, longer if you desire Serves: 4
0 Vata, −Pitta, −Kapha

> **1 quart apple juice, preferably chemical free organic**
> **1 small orange or tangerine (organic)**
> **1 cinnamon stick**
> **2 cloves**

Pour the juice into a saucepan to warm. Wash the orange or tangerine well and slice thinly, adding it to the juice. (NOTE: if you cannot get organic citrus, do not use the peel at all. Peel the fruit and then thinly slice it.) Add the cinnamon stick and cloves and simmer for 20 minutes or as long as you like.

Comments: If you have an all *Pitta* crew, you can eliminate the cloves, as they are quite heating. A variation on this recipe is to add 2 cups water during the heating. This harms no one, and much benefits *Kapha*, by cutting the sweetness of the fruit juice.

ABOUT MILK

Dairy is a builder, not a cleanser. Dairy is used as a prelude to some Ayurvedic cleansing therapies, to accumulate energy in one area prior to cleansing. It give grounding, mass, sweetness, and usually coolness to meals. For these reasons, it is excellent for children, teenagers, pregnant and nursing mothers, those seeking calm and grounding, and convalescents. It is superb for Vata, *miserable for* Kapha *(with a few key exceptions) and at times quite beneficial for* Pitta. *It offers calories, calcium, protein, and some vitamins. It builds bones and teeth, and in* Vata *strengthens the heart and nervous system. In* Kapha *it can do the opposite for the heart, adding congestion where it is not needed. Its cool sweetness is good for tonifying* Pitta, *if the appropriate dairy products are used.*

As Robert Svoboda points out in his excellent book Prakruti, Your Ayurvedic Constitution, *dairy has gotten a bad name in health circles more through its methods of preparation and mode of consumption than through its innate qualities. In the West, it is usually served cold, unspiced, homogenized, with other foods, and in excess. Its high-fat content, heaviness and coldness does not lend it to these uses. Served in this way, it can increase one's risk of heart disease, cancer or obesity. Dairy needs to be used skillfully and not in excess.*

Cow's milk was highly regarded by the Ayurvedic sages, being lighter and easier to digest than most dairy. It invigorates, and works well for both Vata *and* Pitta, *so long as they are not allergic to it. Unfortunately, cow's milk was introduced extremely early to Western babies of the post-war period, in the form of concentrated infant formulas. This may be part of the reason for widespread sensitivities to it as a food now. If it agrees with you (i.e., does not cause diarrhea, gas, congestion, or other discomforts) it is an excellent and balancing food, when properly prepared.*

Preparation is a key. There has been a lot of controversy over raw versus pasteurized homogenized milk in the last few decades. In Ayurveda, raw milk is recommended whenever possible, and milk is always boiled before serving. This high heat effectively kills bacteria in raw milk. It may also denature the proteins of pasteurized milk further, causing their breakdown into shorter amino acid chains which are then easier to digest. In general, boiling milk makes it safer and easier to digest; this is especially true of raw milk. The boiling process also warms a usually cold product as will the addition of warming spices such as cinnamon, cardamom, ginger, and black pepper. A bit of honey added after heating will also balance the qualities of the milk, warming and drying it.

Pasteurization has made the consumption of mass-produced milk safer in terms of eliminating the chance of bacterial infections for large groups of people. But its lower heating point (15 seconds at 161 degrees Fahrenheit or 30 minutes at 145 degrees Fahrenheit) does not make the milk more digestible nor does it eliminate the risk of potential viral contamination. The incomplete heating of pasteurization seems to cause the partial breakdown of milk proteins into tangled coils. These disorganized tangles are difficult for digestive enzymes to hold on to and break down. For some people, this may be why pasteurized milk causes them to be constipated, while boiled raw milk does not. The homogenization process is another controversial one. It apparently splits milk fats down into small enough globules that some pass into the blood stream whole, initiating a complex process which may lead to a greater tendency to create arteriosclerotic clots. Whether such a tendency actually exists is still being hotly debated in medical and health circles. In any case, the cow's milk extolled by the ancients is not the same as cow's milk sold in most markets today.

Goat's milk is more astringent and less mucus-forming than cow's milk; it is often well-absorbed by individuals with sensitivities to cow's milk. Its high buffering capacity makes it useful for calming and healing stomach ulcers. Pitta will usually tolerate goat milk well, and it can be used profitably in small amounts by Kapha. Its effect on Vata is variable. In ancient times goat's milk was used in India to stimulate milk production in nursing mothers. It was also considered a specific medicinal for excessive bleeding (due to its astringency).

Sheep's milk is a rare item which is calming to Kapha and Pitta. But if you cannot get it, be consoled by the fact that it is not nearly as highly regarded as cow's milk by most Ayurvedic physicians. Buffalo milk was another food recommended in the Ayurvedic sutras for its excellent ability to induce sleep. As an insomniac in New York City, you may be hard-pressed to come up with a buffalo, but will be well-served by safe tryptophan-rich cow's milk.

HOT SPICED MILKS

Preparation time: 10 minutes

HOT MILK #1

Serves: 1

— —Pitta, — —Vata, moderately +Kapha   ✳ 🫖 ❄

> 1 cup raw milk
> 2 teaspoons *ghee*
> 1 teaspoon or more coriander powder

Warm the milk and the *ghee* in a small pot, uncovered. When they are not, stir in the coriander and drink.

Comments: Really fine way to bring down *Pitta.*

HOT MILK #2

Serves: 2

—Vata, —Pitta, 0 Kapha*   ✳ 🫖 ❄

> 1 cup milk (goat milk for *Kapha*)
> 1 cup water
> ¼ teaspoon cardamom
> ¼ teaspoon dry ginger
> ¼ teaspoon cloves
> ¼ teaspoon caraway

Simmer all the ingredients in a small pot for 15 minutes or more. Strain and drink.

Comments: A good stomachic useful in atonic dyspepsia, from Dr. Nadkarni. Can be drunk after meals.

* —Kapha with goat milk

HOT MILK WITH NUTMEG

Preparation time: 10 minutes   Serves: 1
—Vata, 0 Pitta, 0 Kapha   ✿ ✳ 🫖 ❄

> 1 cup raw milk (goat milk for *Kapha*)
> ½ teaspoon ground nutmeg

Bring the milk to a boil, reduce heat and stir in the nutmeg. Simmer for 5 minutes, strain.

Comments: A good drink for calming the nerves or relieving insomnia. It is also used to relieve diarrhea in the summertime. Alright for occasional use by *Kapha.*

HOT MILK WITH CAFFIX

Preparation time: 10 minutes   Serves: 2
− *Vata*, − *Pitta*, − *Kapha* *   ✿   ✳   ꙮ   ❄

    1 cup milk (cow, goat or soy)
    1 cup water
    2 teaspoons Caffix, Roma, or other grain beverage (available in health-
    food stores, some supermarkets)
    2 teaspoons honey or maple syrup
    ¼ teaspoon dry ginger (for *Kapha* only)

Bring the milk and water to a boil in a small saucepan. Put one teaspoon of Caffix in
each of two mugs. Pour in the hot milk and water, add sweetener and spice and stir.

Comments: A nice after-dinner drink. Cinnamon, cardamom, nutmeg, or cloves
can be added, depending on your tastes and constitution. All of these spices would
be fine for *Vata*, *Pitta* or *Kapha*. *Pitta* would do best to stick with the cinnamon
and/or cardamom.

**For Vata, use cow's milk and either sweetener; for Pitta, use any of the milks and
maple syrup, and for Kapha, use goat or soy milk, honey, and ginger.*

HOT GINGERED MILK

Preparation time: 10 minutes   Serves: 2
− − *Vata*, 0 *Pitta*, 0 *Kapha*   ✿   ꙮ   ❄

    1 cup cow or goat milk (cow for *Vata*, goat for *Kapha*)
    1 cup water
    1 teaspoon freshly grated ginger root
    3-4 cardamom seeds
    ½-1 teaspoon *ghee*

Put milk, water, ginger, and cardamom into a small saucepan. Heat over medium-
high heat until boiling. Reduce heat immediately to low and simmer for 5 minutes.
Pour into individual cups and stir in *ghee*.

Comments: This hot drink is very calming to *Vata* and makes a good *anupanna*
(medium) for Ayurvedic medications which need to be taken before bed. (Check
with your practitioner if in fact this is helpful for you.) If you substitute ¼ teaspoon
dry ginger for the fresh ginger and use goat milk rather than cow, this is also calming
to *Kapha*. *Pitta* can skip the ginger altogether and enjoy a balanced beverage
thereby.

ABOUT SOY MILK

Liquid soy milk can be a good alternative to cow's milk, if you are sensitive to the latter. It is also less Kaphagenic *(imbalancing to* Kapha*) than cow's milk, when properly prepared. Lighter than cow's milk in its effect on the body, it cooks up easily in recipes. Like most high protein foods it promotes building, not cleansing. It is best used in restorative and maintenance programs. It can be warmed with cinnamon, cardamom, nutmeg or ginger and black pepper. Some* Vatas *do not tolerate it well. Dried soy milk powder and soy protein powder are much more difficult to digest than the whole liquid soy milks. Only the most stalwart* Pitta *is likely to be able to consume them without gas, as they are cold, heavy and dry. Whole soybeans and tempeh are often gas-producing as well. For adequate digestion they require much cooking and spicing, good* agni, *and a* Pitta *constitution.*

HOT SOY MILK

Preparation time: 5 minutes
0 Vata, − Pitta, 0 Kapha*

Serves: 1

✿ ✹ ぬ ❄

> **1 cup Edensoy Original soy milk**
> **Dash of cinnamon**
> **¹/₂ teaspoon barley malt, brown rice syrup or maple syrup (optional)**

Bring soy milk to boil. Immediately remove from heat and pour in a mug to serve. Stir in sweetener or drink plain, garnished with cinnamon on top.

Comments: Good before bedtime or when you are hungry and need a little extra protein.

*If Kapha drinks without sweetener and a pinch of dry ginger.

DIGESTIVE TEA

Preparation time: 5 minutes
−Vata, − −Pitta, −Kapha

Serves: 2

✿ ✹ ぬ ❄

> **2 cups water**
> **1 teaspoon coriander seeds (available in herb section of natural grocery or any Indian grocery)**
> **1 teaspoon fennel seeds**
> **1 teaspoon cumin seeds**

Bring water to boil. Put all the seeds in a blender. Pour in boiling water. Grind the seeds with the water; strain. Drink after any meal. Very good digestive aid.

MATAJI'S SOOTHING *CHAI*

Preparation time: 50 minutes   Serves: 6
− −*Vata, 0 Pitta, 0 Kapha*   ✿ 🍃 ❅

> 2 cups water
> 1 tablespoon fresh peppermint, 2 tablespoons dried, or 3 peppermint
> tea bags
> 1 quart cow or soy milk
> 1 cinnamon stick
> ¹/₄ teaspoon ground cloves
> 1 teaspoon dry ginger
> ³/₄ teaspoon ground cardamom
> 1 teaspoon black peppercorns
> 2 tablespoons to ¹/₂ cup sweetener (brown rice syrup, Sucanat or honey)

Bring water to a boil in a large saucepan and add peppermint in a tea ball. Remove
from heat and steep 20 minutes. Remove tea ball or tea bags. Add milk, spices, and
sweetener (unless you are using honey, in which case wait until the *chai* is finished to
stir it in). Heat and steep on low heat for an additional 30 minutes.

Comments: *Kapha* is best off using soy milk and the minimum of sweetener, preferably honey. This drink goes well with almost anything.

HOT GINGER TEA #1

Preparation time: 15-50 minutes   Makes 4 cups.
−*Vata,* +*Pitta,* −*Kapha*   ✿ 🍃 ❅

> 1 quart water
> 2 inches fresh ginger root
> Honey (as desired)
> Lemon (as desired)

Bring water to boil in saucepan or tea pot. Peel fresh ginger and slice it. When water
boils, add the ginger to the pot. Reduce heat to simmer and cook for 10-45 minutes,
depending on how pungent you want the tea to be. Strain and add honey (for *Vata*
and *Kapha*) and lemon juice (for *Vata*) if desired.

Comments: This tea is excellent for enkindling *agni.* Also good for sipping on a cold
wet day. Useful for colds, sore throats, bronchitis, and impaired circulation and
digestion.

HOT GINGER TEA #2

Preparation time: 5 minutes   Serves: 1
moderately +Vata, +Pitta, − −Kapha   ✿ ❄

> **1 cup water**
> **⅛ teaspoon dry ginger powder (a pinch)**
> **Honey (if desired)**

Bring water to boil, pour in cup, add ginger, stir. Add honey as desired.

Comments: Very good tea for *Kapha*, being warming and drying. To calm *Vata*, use molasses rather than honey for a healing brew. For "0" or *−Pitta*, use maple syrup and 1 teaspoon coriander powder.

BANSHA TEA

Preparation time: 5 to 10 minutes   Serves: 1
0 Vata, −Pitta, −Kapha   ✿ ✳ 🫖 ❄

> **1 teaspoon kukicha or bansha twigs, not green leaves**
> **1 cup boiling water or milk**

Pour water or milk over bansha in a tea ball or strainer in a tea cup. Steep 5 minutes or to taste. Serve milk and honey for *Vata*, sweetener for *Pitta* (milk is optional for *Pitta*), and water with or without a touch of honey and a pinch of dry ginger for *Kapha*.

Comments: Very good. Served straight without milk or sweetener, this beverage increases *Vata*.

MEDICINAL TEAS

Preparation time: 30 minutes or less   Serves: 1
0 Vata, −Pitta, −Kapha   ✿ ✳ 🫖 ❄
+Vata in Excess

CHAMOMILE: Bring 1 cup of water to a boil in a small saucepan. Add 1 tablespoon dried chamomile, turn off heat, cover and let sit ½ hour. Strain and serve. Good for soothing the nerves and as a before-bedtime brew. Calming to the digestion in the short run, but it should not be used daily or it may subtly inhibit gastrointestinal tract activity. (*+Vata, −Pitta, −Kapha in excess*).

CHRYSANTHEMUM: Bring 1 cup of water to a boil in a small saucepan, as with CHAMOMILE. Add 2 to 3 teaspoons chrysanthemum flowers (regular chrysanthemums grown organically in the garden are fine). Turn off heat, cover and let sit 15 minutes or more. Strain and serve. Lovely for calming *Pitta*. Soothing to eyes, liver, and psyche. *(+Vata, −Pitta, −Kapha in excess).*   Serves: 1   ✳

LEMONGRASS AND NETTLES: Bring 1½ cups of water to a boil in a small pot. Add 1 tablespoon lemongrass and 1 teaspoon nettles, turn the heat to very low and simmer for 5 minutes, covered. Turn the heat off and let sit another 20 minutes. Strain and serve hot or cold. Good summertime tea with a bit of sweetener. Tonifying to the kidneys and membranes, good for calming *Kapha* and *Pitta (0 Vata, −Pitta, −Kapha).*   Serves: 2   ❀ ✳ ?

PEPPERMINT: Bring 1 cup of water to a boil in a small spot. Add 1 teaspoon fresh peppermint or 2 teaspoons dried, turn off the heat, cover and steep 15 minutes or more. Strain and serve. Good for the nerves, weak digestion and heart palpitations due to nerve imbalances *(0 Vata, − −Pitta, −Kapha unless used in excess).*
          Serves: 1   ❀ ✳ ? ❆

SPEARMINT: Follow same directions as above for PEPPERMINT. Spearmint works primarily as a digestive stimulant. Good for dispelling gas, it can be mildly diuretic *(0 Vata, − −Pitta, −Kapha unless used in excess).*   Serves: 1   ❀ ✳ ? ❆

BORAGE-RASPBERRY-NETTLES-MINT: Bring 1 quart of water to a boil. Add 1 tablespoon borage, 3 tablespoons raspberry leaves (again, plain old organic garden variety are fine), 1½ tablespoons nettles and 1 tablespoon spearmint. Remove from heat, cover and steep 30 minutes or more. Strain and serve, hot or cool. Can be sweetened. Excellent post-partum brew. For a pregnancy tea, omit the borage. *(0 Vata with sweetener, −Pitta, −Kapha).*   Serves: 4   ❀ ✳ ? ❆
+Vata in excess

OSHA TEA
Preparation time: 30 minutes or more   Serves: 3-4
−Vata, +Pitta, −Kapha   ❀ ? ❆

    3 inches dried *osha* root
    1 eucalyptus leaf
    4 cups water

Bring the water to a boil; add the herbs and cover. Simmer on low heat for 30 minutes or more.

Comments: One of the queen of teas for winter. Excellent for preventing bronchial infections or "heading them off at the pass." *Osha* stimulates cilia, the small hair-like cells of the lungs and digestive tract. Through this action, it stimulates cleansing of the lungs and peristalsis in the digestive tract. Can be served with honey or other sweetener.

BARLEY TEA

Preparation time: overnight in crockpot, or 1 to 1½ hours   Makes: 4 cups
mildly +Vata, −Pitta, −Kapha*   ✿ ✳ 🍵 ❄

> ¼ **cup organic pearl barley (again, organic is important so as not to give
> yourself a dose of chemicals)**
> 8 **cups water**

Wash the barley well and put it and the water in a crockpot or large pot. Bring to a
boil, then simmer on low until the liquid is reduced to 4 cups. Strain and drink.

Comments: Excellent for soothing an inflamed bladder, throat, or gut. Also good for
mucous colitis. To calm fever, you can add 1 tablespoon Sucanat or jaggery and a
tablespoon of lime or lemon juice.

*Fine for occasional but not regular use for Vata

LAXATIVE BARLEY BREW

Preparation time: overnight in crockpot   Makes: 1 to 2 cups
0 Vata, −Pitta, −Kapha   ✿ ✳ 🍵 ❄

> ¼ **cup organic pearl barley (make this only if you can get organic barley,
> otherwise the process could concentrate toxins rather than relieve
> them)**
> 10 **cups water**
> ¼ **cup figs, chopped (without preservatives)**
> ¼ **cup raisins (without preservatives)**
> 2 **tablespoons licorice root**

Wash the barley well. Chop the figs, and grind the licorice dry in the blender for a
minute. Put all ingredients in the slow cooker and cook overnight, until the liquid is
reduced by half or more. Strain, drink the liquid.

Comments: One-half cup can be drunk at a time. This is one of those oddly arcane
recipes in the Ayurvedic tradition, inspired by directions in Nadkarni's *Indian Materia
Medica.* It is excellent for relieving *Pitta* and *Kapha* without aggravating *Vata*. A little
lavish on costly ingredients, though.

ZINGY HIBISCUS COOLER

Preparation time: 15 minutes Makes: 4 cups.
−Vata, −Pitta, −Kapha ✿ ✳ ❄

> **4 cups water**
> **2 cinnamon sticks**
> **¹/₂ teaspoon - 1 tablespoon fresh ginger root, grated**
> **¹/₄ cup dried hibiscus**
> **Honey or frozen orange juice concentrate to taste**

Bring water to boil in a medium saucepan. Add cinnamon sticks, ginger and hibiscus. Cover pot and reduce heat to low. Let simmer 10 minutes. Strain and serve unsweetened (tart) or add ½-1 teaspoon honey per cup (for *Vata* or *Kapha*) or 1-3 teaspoons orange juice concentrate (for *Pitta* or *Vata*). Refrigerate to cool for summer, or serve over enough ice to cool it. Good served hot in winter.

Comments: This bright, rose-colored tea makes a good alternative to Kool-Aid and other concentrated drinks for kids and adults. Using the smaller amount of ginger, it makes an excellent cooler for *Pitta* in summer. In winter, the vitamin C-rich hibiscus combination is a good flu reliever and preventive (use the greater amount of ginger for this). If you have hibiscus plants at home, you can use the flowers after they've bloomed for this brew, so long as you've utilized no chemicals in their growth. Or dried hibiscus flowers are readily found at most natural food and herb stores.

Some very fiery *Pittas* have trouble with even orange juice. Maple syrup is best used in these cases.

COOL MINT TEA

Preparation time: 30 minutes Serves: 4-6
−Vata, −Pitta, −Kapha* ✳

> **1 cup fresh peppermint leaves or ¹/₄ cup dried peppermint**
> **1 quart boiling water**
> **1 quart cold or room-temperature water**
> **2 tablespoons honey or rice syrup (optional, *Pitta* needs to drink this with rice syrup only and *Kapha* with honey only)**

Pour quart of boiling water over mint in teapot or other heatproof container. Cover; let steep for 20 minutes. Strain tea into pitcher or Mason jar; stir in sweetener. Add cool water, stir. Chill in refrigerator at least one hour, or serve immediately with a few ice cubes.

Comments: This is a great drink for aiding digestion and calming the nerves on a hot day. Spearmint or catnip can also be used. Good for people looking for flavorful non-caffeinated alternatives to juice or soda, also for those hooked on their iced tea in summer. 1-2 *bansha* tea bags (or cup *bansha* twigs) can be added for those looking for more of a caffeiney flavor.

*Unless drunk in excess, (i.e., one quart at a time) in which case it can +Vata (due to its light airy quality) and +Kapha (due to its chill).

FENUGREEK TEA

Preparation time: overnight soak, plus 5 minutes   Serves: 1
−Vata, +Pitta, −Kapha

> 1 teaspoon fenugreek seeds (*methi*)
> 1 cup water
> ½-1½ teaspoons honey (optional)

Mix fenugreek seeds and water in small container; a pint Mason jar works well. Soak overnight. In the morning boil the seeds and water. Strain the seeds and add honey if you like.

Comments: This tonifying and strengthening tea is good for the nerves and digestion. It strengthens the respiratory and reproductive systems. Not to be used in pregnancy, but a good builder before conception, and an excellent restorative in the 6 weeks after birth. Increases milk production. Good for weight loss due to excess water retention.

GOKSHURA TEA

Preparation time: 30-45 minutes   Serves: 1
0 Vata, −Pitta, −Kapha

> 1 tablespoon *gokshura* (plain old green goatheads, the weed)
> 2 cups water

Put water in a small heavy saucepan and bring to a boil. Add goatheads (*gokshura*), reduce to low heat and simmer uncovered for 30 to 45 minutes or until the liquid is reduced by half.

Comments: The irony of this quite healing brew is that *gokshura*, revered in India, is despised here as goathead—and with good reason. It is one of the most obnoxious weeds to step on, delivering a rapid and painful puncture wound via its barbed fruits. These same barbed fruits are the active ingredient in this tea. Perhaps, like me, you will derive a deep satisfaction from gathering up a handful of the blessed critters, popping them in water and having them benefit your health rather than wound it. Goathead/*gokshura* is calming and soothing in bladder infections and specifically rejuvenative for the kidneys—an excellent herb to prevent kidney infection, if you have a history of proceeding from bladder to kidney struggles. Traditionally, it is used with good results to encourage fertility, both female and male. It is a reviving tea for women postpartum. It tonifies and builds the kidney energy, often lacking these days through stress and unhelpful lifestyle practices.

Dr. Nadkarni, in his *India Materia Medica,* recommends a milk decoction specific for healing the male reproductive tract. A variation of it follows: Simmer 1 tablespoon of *gokshura* in 1 cup goat milk and 4 cups water over low heat until all of the water has evaporated. Stir in 1 tablespoon sesame seeds and 1 teaspoon raw honey; drink.

AJWAN TEA

Preparation time: 5-20 minutes — Serves: 1
−Vata, +Pitta, −Kapha   ✿ ✳ ☙ ❊

> ½ teaspoon *ajwan* seeds
> 1 cup boiling water

Pour the boiling water over the seeds in a cup. Let sit 5 minutes. Sweeten with ½ teaspoon raw honey if desired.

For a stronger brew, use the same amount of seeds in 2 cups water and simmer up to 20 minutes.

Comments: This is a very good brew for relieving lung or GI congestion. Prepared in the first (milder) way, children are usually willing to take it.

CARROT AND GINGER JUICE

Preparation time: 15-20 minutes — Serves: 2
−Vata, +Pitta, −Kapha   ✿ ✳ ☙

For this recipe, you need a vegetable juicer.

> 8 large carrots
> 1-2 inches fresh ginger root

Peel the ginger, wash the carrots.

Put the carrots and ginger through the juicer. Drink immediately if possible.

Comments: A beautiful tonic for the liver, especially if it is sluggish or has been abused. Best drunk on an empty stomach.

MIXED VEGETABLE JUICE

Preparation time: 15-20 minutes
−Vata, −Pitta, −Kapha

Serves: 2

❋ ✻ ૩๑

For this recipe you need a vegetable juicer.

> **1 large carrot**
> **3 stalks celery**
> **1 head lettuce**
> **1 bunch parsley**
> **2 small zucchinis (optional)**

Wash all vegetables well and put them through the juicer. Drink immediately.

Comments: Excellent nervine and diuretic.

VEGETABLE JUICES

		Especially rich in these nutrients
Carrot	−K & V, +P	Vitamin A, potassium, selenium, biotin
Watercress	−K & P, +V	Vitamin C, niacin, calcium, iron, copper
Beet	−K & V, +P	Folic acid, manganese
Parsley	−K & P, +V	Vitamins A & C, potassium, calcium, iron
Cabbage	−K & P, +V	Folic acid, pantothenic acid, Vitamin C, selenium
Celery	−K & P, +V	Sodium
Potato	−P & K, +V	Folic acid, niacin, phosphorus, potassium
Spinach	−K, +V & P	Protein (3.6 gm/oz), Vitamin A, biotin, folic acid, Vitamin E, sodium, potassium, iron, magnesium, manganese, zinc
Cucumber	−P & V, +K	Vitamin C, iron, copper

BREAKFASTS

ABOUT
BREAKFASTS

Whether or not you enjoy breakfast
is a personal matter. Vatas and those with blood sugar disorders often find
a solid breakfast a must. Kaphas frequently have little urge to eat before 10
a.m., and may only do so to be companionable. Pittas vary, but usually
need to eat something by mid-morning to waylay ferociousness. Many of
the dishes here emphasize whole cooked grains, as they are most grounding
and often are neglected in our culture.

TRADITIONAL *DOSAS*

Preparation time: overnight plus 30 minutes   Serves: 4
– – Vata, moderately + Pitta, moderately + Kapha*   ✿ ❋ 🍃 ❄

>   1 cup *urud dal* flour (available at Indian groceries)
>   1 cup rice flour (finely ground, also available at Indian groceries)
>   ½ teaspoon rock or sea salt
>   2 to 2½ cups water

These are remarkably simple if you follow the directions. If you don't, you could have
a sodden lump on your hands. So much for threats. Measure out the flours and salt
into a mixing bowl that can be covered; Tupperware works well. Add the water until
you have a batter the consistency of a thinnish pancake batter. Cover it and let it sit
overnight at room temperature. In the morning, get out a non-stick frying pan—very
important—and put a dab of oil, less than a teaspoon, in it. Heat the pan until hot.
Pour in ⅓ cup of batter and with a rounded spoon like a soup spoon, gently spread
the batter out from the center in a spiral motion. This is necessary because, unlike
American pancake batters, this batter will not spread on its own. It needs you to dis-
tribute it. You will end up with a *dosa* about 6 inches in diameter if this all goes
smoothly. As you get good at the technique, you can begin to make flashy *dosas* the
size of the kind you find in India. Start with something small enough to easily flip.
The *dosa* will bubble on top and get brown underneath. You can flip it just the way
you would any pancake. Let the other side brown, and serve. Or keep it warm in the
oven until all the *dosas* are done.

Comment: This goes very well with *MASALA* POTATOES (p. 275) or *dal*.

*Fine for occasional use for Pitta and Kapha.

DOSAS #2

Preparation time: overnight plus 45 minutes

Makes: 12

0 Vata, 0 Pitta, 0 Kapha*

mildly +Vata, 0 Pitta, −Kapha**

0 Vata, 0 Pitta, and mildly +Kapha; ***

     ✿　☙　❄

> 1 cup cornmeal
> 1 cup rice flour (the finely ground Indian variety—if you don't have this, use 1 cup barley flour or whole wheat flour)
> 1/2 teaspoon sea or rock salt
> 2 1/2 to 3 1/2 cups boiling water

Measure the dry ingredients into a Tupperware mixing bowl. Boil the water and pour over the flours, stirring well. Cover and let sit overnight. Add more water in the morning if you need to get the batter to a thinnish consistency. Follow the instructions for making *dosas* given above. The only difference with this batter is that it cooks more slowly. Be sure and let each *dosa* cook on medium heat until it is done and not sticky inside, about 2 to 4 minutes.

This also goes well with MASALA POTATOES or *dal*. Or, it can be tasty served with fruit, sweetened jam, or fruit fillings.

*With cornmeal and rice flour.

**With cornmeal and barley flour. Vata can offset this effect with ghee and a warming or sweet filling.

***With cornmeal and whole wheat flour. Vata can offset this with ghee and appropriate filling. Kapha is better off using a different flour.

MASALA POTATOES

Preparation time: 30 to 40 minutes

Serves: 3-4

0 Vata, 0 Pitta, 0 Kapha

     ✿　❋　☙　❄

> 2 red potatoes
> 1 medium parsnip
> 1/2 bunch leafy greens
> 1/4 onion, finely chopped
> 2 tablespoons sunflower oil or *ghee*
> 1/4 teaspoon black mustard seeds
> 1/8 teaspoon *hing*
> 1/2 teaspoon turmeric
> 1 inch fresh ginger root, peeled and chopped
> 1/2 to 2/3 cup water
> 1/2 teaspoon sea or rock salt
> 1/2 teaspoon coriander powder

Wash the vegetables and cube the potatoes and parsnips into ½ inch pieces. Chop the greens into 1 inch slices and finely chop the onion. Peel and finely chop the ginger root.

Warm the oil or *ghee* in a large skillet over low heat. Add the mustard seeds and *hing*, and warm until the mustard seeds pop. Stir in the turmeric and fresh chopped ginger root, then the vegetables. Add the water and cover and cook over medium heat until the potatoes and parsnips are tender and done, about 15 minutes. Stir in the salt and coriander and serve.

Comment: This goes deliciously with *DOSAS* (p. 274-75), or makes a good Indian-style substitute for hashbrowns.

COTTAGE CAKES

Preparation time: 45 minutes   Makes: 16 4" pancakes
 – *Vata, 0 Pitta, +Kapha*   🍵 ❄

> 1¼ cups oat flour
> ¼ cup barley flour or 1½ cups whole wheat flour
> ½ teaspoon sea salt
> 1 teaspoon baking soda (¾ teaspoon at high altitude)
> ½ teaspoon baking powder
> Dash of nutmeg
> 1-2 eggs
> 1½ tablespoons sunflower oil
> 1 cup cottage cheese
> ½ cup plain yogurt
> 1 cup + 2 tablespoons water
> 2 tablespoons brown rice syrup or maple syrup
> ½ cup fresh sweet blueberries (optional)

Mix all the dry ingredients, including the nutmeg, in a bowl. Beat the eggs well in the blender, then add the rest of the wet ingredients to the eggs in the blender and mix them well. Pour the liquid mixture into the dry one, stirring lightly and rapidly. Fold in the blueberries. Spoon the batter onto a hot and well-greased skillet or griddle. Cook on medium-high heat until the cakes bubble around their edges. Flip and cook until golden brown.

Comments: For years our family has been hooked on the cottage cakes served at O.J. Sarah's Restaurant here in Santa Fe. So we decided to create our own at-home version. These will work with one egg, but the cakes are lighter and more delicious with two.

One advantage of this recipe is that it offers a wheat-free alternative. Some people find oat flour more allergenic for them than even wheat flour. Others find it a welcome relief. Try for yourself. Varying the flours you use will achieve different effects. *Vatas* do best with the warming oat flour or grounding whole wheat, while *Pittas* benefit most from the cooling quality of the barley or wheat flours. If you are serving these to *Kapha*, a predominantly (light) barley with warming oat mix balances best. The less oil you can use in the cooking, the better for *Pitta* and *Kapha* A non-stick pan works well for this, and uses virtually no oil.

BUCKWHEAT PANCAKES

Preparation time: 45 minutes   Make: 1 dozen 6" pancakes
−*Vata,* +*Pitta,* −*Kapha**

    1 cup buckwheat flour
    1 cup oat bran
    3/4 teaspoon baking powder (1/2 teaspoon at high altitude)
    1 teaspoon baking soda
    1/2 teaspoon sea salt
    3 cups buttermilk (fresh)
    1 egg
    2 tablespoons sunflower oil

Mix all dry ingredients well in a bowl. In another bowl, beat egg and beat in buttermilk and oil. Add liquid mixture to dry mixture, stirring only enough to mix together. A few lumps are fine. Pour onto hot, oiled, evenly heated griddle or skillet. Turn over when bubbles appear on edges and underside is light brown.

Comments: Serve hot with honey, maple syrup, blueberry sauce or applesauce. Light and very good.

*The heat of the flours plus the sourness of the buttermilk make it unacceptable for Pitta. Substituting soy milk or cow's milk cools it down quite a bit for Pitta, but does not offer the same light taste.)

CORN CAKES

Preparation time: 15 minutes   Makes: 1 dozen 4" pancakes
+ *Vata*, + *Pitta*, − *Kapha**

Make up recipe for QUICK WHEAT-FREE BREAD, (p. 146). Put just enough sun-flower oil or *ghee* in a large skillet to keep the pancakes from sticking or use a non-stick pan without oil. Heat pan on medium-high; spoon in batter. Flip when the cakes begin to bubble along the edges and are golden brown underneath.

Comment: This goes well with stewed fruit or honey.

**O Vata with ghee and sweetener*

ABOUT CORN

One of the most revered grains among North American Indians, corn is a light, dry, warm grain with sweet and astringent tastes. Its attributes make it ideal for Kapha in all forms. It is only mildly imbalancing to Pitta or Vata when cooked or baked with liquids to moisten it, as in corn bread or atole. Toasted or dry roasted it is moderately imbalancing to them both. Sweet corn such as corn on the cob has much more moisture and a bit more cool-ness than does dried cornmeal, so it can be handled more easily by Vata and Pitta. Popcorn or corn chips present a greater challenge to the Vata digestive tract. They exacerbate the light dry qualities of the grain, making it most dif-ficult for Vata to break down and absorb. Corn has been used to calm an irritable bladder and as an adjunct in the treatment of kidney stones.

GORDO'S CREPES

Preparation time: 30 minutes   Makes: 8 8" crepes
O *Vata*, + *Pitta*, − *Kapha**
− *Vata*, + *Pitta*, + *Kapha***

     5 large eggs
     1/2 cup barley flour
     1/2 cup milk, (goat, cow, or soy)
     1/4 teaspoon sea salt

Beat all the ingredients together thoroughly with an egg beater, or in the blender. Pour ¼ cup of the batter into a hot, very lightly oiled skillet (or non-stick pan); spread by tilting the pan. Cook over medium-high heat until underside is brown; turn.

Serve with mango chutney, sweet or hot, ginger marmalade or blueberry sauce, or your favorite jam.

Comments: Not for the egg tee-totaller, these are scrumptious and easy. They can be made with whole wheat flour, if you desire. They were developed by a notorious *Pitta* for his sister and brother *Vatas* and *Kaphas.*

*With goat or soy milk and non-stick pan
**With cow milk and oiled pan

Variation: *PITTA CREPES: This is wild, but works:*

0 Vata, −Pitta, −Kapha

> **8 egg whites**
> **½ cup barley flour**
> **½ cup milk (goat, cow, or soy)**
> **¼ teaspoon sea salt**

Prepare as directed above. If you use a non-stick pan, this is an excellent low-cholesterol dish.

ABOUT EGGS

Master chef Julia Child has described the egg as "perfect, pristine, primal" food, and Western food scientists have tended to agree, regarding it as perhaps the best-balanced source of protein a human can eat. In India, eggs are not eaten nearly so widely as in the United States, in part because one takes a life when consuming an egg. The egg has also fallen into some disrepute with the public in the West, becoming almost synonymous with the forbidden word "cholesterol." From an Ayurvedic perspective, eggs are hot, heavy and oily in quality, making them somewhat challenging to digest. This heating effect is constant, regardless if they are served cold. In other words, a hard-boiled egg will heat up a body, and add mass. This effect is due almost entirely to the yolk of the egg; egg whites are actually quite different in quality, being cool, light and dry in attribute. This makes egg whites a useful source of protein for Pittas, and Kaphas as well. For a while there was a hullabaloo about raw egg whites creating a biotin deficiency. The protein in raw egg white, avidin, can in fact bind with the B vitamin, biotin, making it

unavailable. However, one would have to eat 2 dozen egg whites or more per day to create such an effect. While egg white is best not fed to infants under 12 months old (it can set off a food sensitivity to egg protein), it is a light and cholesterol-free food for people over one year of age.

Eggs calm Vata *well when fixed appropriately. This includes eggs in custards, puddings, souffles and baked goods. Most* Vatas *do fine with scrambled eggs or soft-boiled eggs. Fewer do well with plain hard-boiled eggs or fried eggs, the two most challenging ways to prepare an egg. Spicing these, as in DEVILED EGG SALAD (p. 211-12) makes them more manageable for* Vatas. Kaphas *are best off having an occasional egg in foods, such as muffins or souffles, at a rate of about one to three eggs per week, shunning the fried and raw varieties. Egg white alone is recommended for* Pitta. *At first this might seem quite limiting, which in fact it is. However, two egg whites can be substituted for each whole egg in most recipes. A variety of ways of approaching the white of the egg are offered here—in French toast and egg salad, among others. Another option for* Pitta *is to scramble one egg with a generous amount of SCRAMBLED TOFU (see p. 281).*

In recent years nutritionists have questioned whether or not eggs raise cholesterol. As in most things, it seems to be more related to the state of the individual body, rather than the food alone. Some people seem well able to eat an egg or two a day with nary a ripple in their cholesterol levels, while for others, this practice causes blood fats to soar. It may have a fair amount to do with the state of the individual's liver and trace mineral balance. A sluggish liver with a chromium deficiency elevates blood cholesterol relatively easily. A healthy hepatic response with adequate minerals and B vitamins generally keeps cholesterol levels at a happy state.

FRENCH TOAST

For *Vata*: Proceed as you would in any French toast recipe, whisking up a couple of whole eggs and adding a tablespoon of milk or two. Soak the bread and prepare as usual.

For *Pitta*: Separate egg whites, saving the yolk for other constitutions or animal friends of the family. Use one egg white per piece of toast, mix lightly with a fork, adding a pinch of salt if you like. We like to use a flavorful healthy bread like cinnamon-raison or orange date-nut; any which agrees with *Pitta* is fine. Soak the bread well in the egg whites and cook as usual on a lightly oiled skillet. Also calms *Vata*.

For *Kapha*: If you can find an all-rye or millet bread, you are in luck. You can soak the slices in either whole beaten egg or whisked egg white (as above for *Pitta*, low in fat.) Cook without oil on a non-stick pan. Delicious with a bit of honey and applesauce.

EGGS CHUPADERO

Preparation time: 1 hour　　　　　　　　　　　　　　　　Serves: 6
−*Vata*, +*Pitta*, −*Kapha*

6 eggs

Plus recipe for CURRIED POTATO PATTIES WITH CARROTS (p. 99)

Make up the recipe for CURRIED POTATO PATTIES WITH CARROTS. As they are browning, poach the eggs. Put one egg over each patty (there will be patties left over for another meal).

Comments: This goes well with MATAJI'S SOOTHING CHAI (p. 265) and makes a great Sunday brunch or company dish.

SCRAMBLED TOFU

Preparation time: 5-10 minutes　　　　　　　　　　　　　Serves: 2
−*Vata*, −*Pitta*, −*Kapha**

　　　½ pound (½ package) tofu
　　　1 tablespoon *ghee* or butter
　　　¼ teaspoon mustard seeds
　　　¼ teaspoon turmeric
　　　⅛ teaspoon *hing*
　　　¼ teaspoon sea salt
　　　¼ teaspoon black pepper
　　　⅛ teaspoon ground cumin

Warm *ghee* or melt butter in heavy skillet. Add mustard seeds and heat until they begin to pop. Add tofu, putting whole cube into skillet and then mashing it into small pieces with a fork in the skillet. Add rest of ingredients, stirring well. Cook on medium heat for 3 to 5 minutes.

Comments: A favorite of both authors, this goes well with toast, tortillas, or *chappa-tis.* This fast breakfast can include sauteed onions and pepper if you have an extra 5 minutes of preparation time. This modification is agreeable for balancing *Vata* and *Kapha,* but not *Pitta.*

*So long as Vata is not sensitive to tofu.

SPICY OATMEAL

Preparation time: 15 minutes or less   Serves: 2
— Vata, — Pitta, moderately + Kapha   ✿ 🦐 ❄

> ²/₃ **cup dry oats, regular or instant**
> **2 cups water**
> ¹/₄ **teaspoon salt**
> ¹/₄ **cup raisins**
> **1 cardamom pod (about 3-4 seeds)**
> ¹/₄ **teaspoon cinnamon**
> ¹/₈ **teaspoon ginger**

Put oats, raisins, salt, and water in small saucepan and bring to boil. Reduce heat to low and add rest of ingredients, breaking open cardamom pod to put whole seeds in the cooking cereal. Cover and cook on low until done, 2 to 10 minutes, depending on the type of oats used.

Comments: Can be served with *ghee,* maple syrup, and/or coconut. Good warming meal on a cold winter morning.

ABOUT OATS

Oats are sweet, warm, heavy, and moist, with a touch of astringency. Cooked in water, they balance Vata *and* Pitta. *Oats need to be lightened in order to be appropriate for* Kapha; *toasting does this. What is helpful for* Kapha *is not helpful for* Vata *in this case. The lightness of granola, a toasted oat dish, very commonly causes gas or bloating in* Vata, *unless it is very well-soaked with milk. It is excellent for* Kapha. *See CRISPY GRANOLA (p. 284).*

BREAKFAST RICE

Preparation time: 8 minutes

−Vata, −Pitta, 0 Kapha*

Serves: 2

❀   ☕   ❄

> 1 cup *basmati* rice, cooked
> 1 cup milk (cow, goat or soy)
> ¹/₄ cup raisins
> ¹/₄-¹/₂ teaspoon cinnamon (the lesser for *Pitta*, the greater for *Vata* and *Kapha*)

Put all ingredients in small saucepan; mix well. Cook on medium heat until hot, about 5 minutes.

Comments: Good with *ghee* and honey or maple syrup. TOASTED SUNFLOWER SEEDS (p. 229) or coconut make an agreeable garnish.

Variation: Use ¹/₈ teaspoon cinnamon and 1¹/₂ teaspoons coriander powder. Very cooling. *−Vata, − −Pitta, 0 Kapha.*

*Kapha should use goat or soy milk in order for this dish to be balancing.

HOT AMARANTH

Preparation time: 30 minutes

−Vata, mildly +Pitta, −Kapha*

Serves: 2

❀   ☕   ❄

> 1 cup dry amaranth
> 2¹/₂ cup water
> ¹/₈- ¹/₄ cup raisins

Garnish: shredded coconut

Bring water to boil in small heavy pot; stir in amaranth and raisins. Reduce heat to low and cover. Cook until cereal is soft and thick, about 25 minutes, stirring occasionally. Serve.

Comments: Sweet, protein-rich amaranth warms and energizes. Great start for a cool morning. Stores well in refrigerator; can be reheated for use the next day.

*Coconut garnish balances this dish to a neutral effect for Pitta

ABOUT AMARANTH AND QUINOA

Amaranth and quinoa are grains that are just beginning to be seen in Western markets. Their high-protein content makes them warming in nature. Amaranth is also rough and yet almost gelatinous in nature. It purifies the blood, helps heal hemorrhoids and can be a mild diuretic. It is widely utilized by the hill-tribes of India and mountain peoples of South America. Quinoa combines well with other grains and provides a warming drying influence.

CRISPY GRANOLA

Preparation time: 45 minutes
+Vata, +Pitta, −Kapha*

Makes: 7 to 8 cups.

❀ ✳

> **4 cups rolled oats**
> **1 cup oat bran**
> **1 cup raw sunflower seeds (grind half of them if you like, for ease of assimilation)**
> **¹/₂ cup pumpkin seeds (optional)**
> **1-1¹/₂ cups raisins**
> **¹/₂ cup dried apple or apricot, chopped (optional, tasty)**
> **3 tablespoons sunflower oil**
> **¹/₄ cup apple concentrate (available in health food stores)**
> **2 tablespoons cinnamon**
> **¹/₂-1 teaspoon dry ginger**
> **¹/₄ teaspoon ground cloves**

Preheat oven to 325 degrees.

Mix the dry ingredients together; I do it in an 8-cup measuring container to save time and washing. Combine the apple concentrate and the oil in a separate large bowl, whisk together. Mix in the spices, then add the dry ingredients. Mix well until the oats are coated. Spoon the mixture into one or two large shallow ungreased baking dishes. Bake until golden brown, about 30 minutes. Cool until crisp.

Comments: The extra dried fruit is tasty, if your digestive fire is good. Otherwise, its addition could be problematic. This granola is specifically designed to calm *Kapha*. It is likely to seem a bit mundane compared to the glamorous commercial granolas laden with sweet and fat. However, it calms *Kapha* far better than they do.

0 Pitta if you soak the granola in hot milk and add extra sweetener before serving.

Pitta Variation: Follow the recipe for *Kapha* above, and substitute wheat or barley flakes for the rolled oats. They are available at many health food stores. Oats, being warming, get more so after they are toasted. Wheat and barley are more cooling in action, and so are more appropriate for *Pitta*. The one cup of oat bran is fine to leave in, or wheat bran can be substituted. Omit the dry ginger and cloves and make the recipe as it stands. The sweetener can be increased if you like. Barley flakes can also be used for *Kapha*.

MORNING AFTER CEREAL

Preparation time: 10-15 minutes   Serves: 2
+*Vata*, +*Pitta*, − −*Kapha**   ✿ ✳ ☙ ❄

> ²/₃ **cup dry cornmeal**
> ⅛ **teaspoon** *hing*
> ¹/₂ **teaspoon whole cumin seeds**
> ¹/₄ **teaspoon fresh ground black pepper**
> ¹/₄ **teaspoon dry ginger powder**
> 1 **teaspoon turmeric**
> ¹/₂ **teaspoon sea salt**
> 1 **teaspoon coriander powder**
> 2 **cups hot water**
> 2 **teaspoons sunflower oil**
> 2 **teaspoons** *ghee*
> 2 **teaspoons honey**

Heat large heavy skillet on low heat for 1 to 2 minutes. Put in cornmeal and dry roast it for 5 minutes, stirring occasionally. As you roast it, add all the spices except the coriander. Add the oil and *ghee*, stirring well. Add the coriander, mixing well. Slowly add the hot water, stirring as you do to avoid creating lumps. Mix in honey immediately before serving.

Comments: This morning potion was originally described in *Charak* as a way of reducing the wages of sin, specifically for overeating and overdrinking, and to prevent diseases resulting from the same, such as diabetes, heart disease, parasites, and hemorrhoids.

It is also an excellent way to enhance *agni* and stimulate memory and intellect. It tastes much better than we imagined when we first read about it! If you've braved this combination successfully and wish to be true to the original, cut the water to ²/₃ of a cup and add a pinch each of *trikatu*, *triphala*, and horseradish.

*With extra ghee, 0 Vata

ABOUT MEAT, WINE, AND SMOKING

Alcohol, tobacco, red meat, and other items were not considered evil or inherently unhealthy by the ancient sages. They were considered Tamasic. Ayurveda has been a predominantly vegetarian form of healing for centuries due to the religious practices and perspectives of the vast majority of its Hindu practitioners. Yet originally it was not designed strictly for vegetarians. Fresh meat of young animals, fowl, and fishes was considered nourishing, when the animals were found in their natural surroundings and killed by non-poisonous means, such as arrows. And yet it is highly unlikely that the sages would recommend most meat, fish and fowl as it is produced today, under artificial conditions with no concern for the animal or the violence used in its death. Non-violent methods of living in the world were considered the foremost factor in promoting longevity and abundant ojas, more important than any food or herb. A return to this ancient wisdom is critical at this point for the longevity of all beings on the planet.

If you are not a vegetarian, using turkey, chicken or fish in these recipes tends to warm them. It also makes them a little heavier; you can adjust your condiments accordingly to enhance digestive fire.

Wine was used in ancient practice to dispel fatigue and enhance digestion. There are detailed descriptions of alcoholic preparations for healing included in the classic texts. Draksha is perhaps the best known example of an herbal wine for digestive stimulation. A variety of recipes for herbal wines are given in Frawley's excellent Ayurvedic Healing. Smoking was also used medicinally, with precise discussion of how, when, and what to smoke. Moderation and appropriateness was considered in each of these. Alcohol was acknowledged to badly aggravate Pitta when used to excess, especially in the summer. Smoking marijuana was known to imbalance Pitta and the digestive system and to cause melancholy and impotence. Tobacco could imbalance Vata, and often did.

Like other substances, it is recommended that if you use these items, that they be utilized with respect and awareness.

Appendix I
MOST FREQUENTLY ASKED QUESTIONS AND ANSWERS

Q. What about eating out?

A: It's unusual *not* to these days! You need to consider both what is being served and how it is prepared. A chef preparing food with openness, clarity, cleanliness, and awareness can mitigate a lot of the less positive qualities of the food itself. Along the same lines, *Vatas* eating at a fast-food place would probably not be terribly affected by the excess salt and fat such businesses offer. But she or he could be disturbed energetically by the rush, crush, bustle, and lack of awareness that most such places present.

You stick with the same basic principles. *Vata* looks for grounding, *Pitta* for cooling, *Kapha* looks for lightness. If you can get that in a restaurant, great. But to expect a restaurant to offer the same tailor-made eating you can get at home is probably unrealistic. The ancient texts recognized this, and actually advised against eating out. It is a personal choice. (For more specifics, see the chapter on Constitution, p. 8).

Q. What about leftovers?

A. Ideally, all food is prepared from fresh ingredients and eaten the same day. This has a maximally healing effect for the body. Again, realistically, often these days there may not be time to prepare a fresh meal from scratch. In my view, a healthy leftover from last night's dinner is preferable to skipping a meal (for *Pitta,* say) or eating a fast-food meal out (for any of the *doshas*).

Over the years, I have also begun to can more food at home when I need to preserve food. It seems to have a better effect than freezing, especially for *Vata* and *Kapha.*

Q. What about supplements?

A. Many people get nauseous if they take supplements on an empty stomach. Others with weak kidneys have a hard time with the concentrated load on these organs. You have to work with the individual situation, balancing nutritional needs with digestive ability. As a nutritionist, I still use them in my practice. I recommend supplements fairly often because I see a surprising number of trace mineral deficiencies with the depleted nature of American agriculture today. They are only useful if you can digest them. First you need to strengthen digestion and clear out *ama*, then you consider building. A clear system with strong digestive power is not the beginning state of many people seeking help for health problems. In general you will need fewer supplements in a clean strong system. Sometimes I see individuals so depleted they need to take some supplements immediately to give them the confidence to go on. But it is better to not put supplements on top of wastes; it only drives the wastes deeper.

You also consider what constitution you are working with when you buy yourself supplements. A *Vata* with poor digestion who is trying to protect her bones with piles of dry calcium pills is probably *not* going to be successful. Most *Vatas* are going to do better with liquid or oil-based preparations, not dry tablets. *Pittas* handle liquids, powders, tablets pretty well if their digestion is good. If it is not, then liquids and liquids in gelatin capsules work best. (You can prick the capsule with a pin and squeeze out the contents, if you do not want to consume the animal-based gelatin.) *Kaphas* often can handle powders and liquid forms of supplements. Something like oil-based vitamin E would be better for *Vata,* and *Kaphas* should try to find the dry forms of E, for example. *Kaphas* with strong digestion generally manage tablets and capsules alright. (There is more information in Appendix III on Nutritional Supplements for those who are interested.)

Speaking about bones, concern about osteoporosis is widespread. And yet a number of studies have indicated that the balance of calcium to phosphorus is as important or more important than simply getting enough calcium alone. As a meat-eating nation, our calcium to phosphorus ratio is 1:4. For healthy bones, you need a ratio closer to 1:1. One way to do this is to try to take lots of calcium supplements. But another way is to shift the ratio of foods you are eating. Seventh Day Adventists, vegetarians by practice, tend to have substantially lower rates of osteoporosis than the average American. They eat no phosphorus-rich meat. High phosphorus in meat, chicken and most fish can throw off our calcium balance. Dairy products, dark leafy greens and some fish (salmon and sardines especially) have a better balance of calcium to phosphorus. Magnesium and potassium are also important for holding calcium in the bones. These are especially prevalent in fruits, vegetables and grains. A healthy calcium-rich vegetarian diet is an important first step in prevention of osteoporosis. That and making sure that you do absorb your minerals, whether from food or supplements, through good digestion.

Q. What about fasting?

A. It depends on your constitution, the season, the climate, and your condition. A *Kapha* could probably do a 7 day juice fast in Florida in November. The same fast done by a *Vata* in upstate New York at the same time of year would likely be disastrous.

Fasts can be created using the same foods that naturally balance your constitution. But they are best done under the supervision of an experienced health professional, using Ayurvedic concepts of health care. There are secondary cleansing processes to be done, like sweating, or massage or breath, which are critical to the success of such a program.

Q. Could you say more about food combining from an Ayurvedic perspective?

A. Yes. *Viruddhashana* means forbidden food combinations. Basically, any diet or therapy which disrupts *Vata, Pitta,* or *Kapha* without releasing them from the body is considered unhealthy. What is appropriate can vary a lot from person to person.

Some basics to be avoided are:

1) taking in an excess of heavy foods at one meal, especially if *agni* is low, e.g., eating banana and avocado together.
2) Taking two foods together which are very contradictory in action. For example, milk is cooling, whereas fish is heating, even though both have a sweet taste. So their combination is to be avoided.
3) Combining sour foods with milk, like orange Juice and milk.
4) Eating cooling foods after *ghee*.
5) Eating heating foods after pork.
6) Eating *Vata* aggravating foods after exhaustion, exercise or making love.
7) Eating *Kapha*-aggravating foods after sleep or drowsiness.
8) Taking equal amounts of honey and *ghee* at the same time.

Q. What about *sattvic, rajasic* and *tamasic* foods?

A. *Sattvic* foods are those which purify the body and calm the mind. They are fresh foods. Pure milks, *ghee* and asparagus are some examples. *Rajasic* foods stimulate the body and mind to action. Coffee, garlic, onions, peppers, and hot spices would all fit into this category. *Tamasic* foods are those which dull the mind and incline the body toward inertia or disease. Spoiled food, chemicals, fried food, meat, cheeses, and heavy sweets are among these. Alcohol can be both *rajasic* and *tamasic* for some people, as it first stimulates them to activity or rage and then to sedation (or even stupor).

Q. Can you recommend a simple cleansing technique for the lay person?

A. Castor oil, a medicinal rather than cooking oil, has many therapeutic uses. It is an excellent way to clear *ama* out of the digestive tract (taking a modest ½ to 1 teaspoon) before bed when drunk with a medicinal tea like ginger.

Q. My family and friends think I'm crazy to think that food can make a difference in my health. I mean, low cholesterol and all that, fine, but not to eat a potato with them . . .

A. Trust yourself and keep working with awareness. Trying to convince anyone else about what you're doing only takes valuable energy you could put elsewhere. If the Ayurvedic program works for you, it will be obvious to them in the long run. Then you may have a receptive audience with interest rather than resistance. Pushing something on them is likely to be counterproductive.

Appendix II
Enlarged Food Guidelines for Basic Constitutional Types

NOTE: *Guidelines provided in this table are general. Specific adjustments for individual requirements may need to be made, e.g. food allergies, strength of agni, season of the year, and degree of dosha predominance or aggravation. The guidelines are based on Dr. Vasant Lad's, Ayurveda: The Science of Self-Healing (Lotus Press, 1984).*

▲ **Aggravates Dosha**
▼ **Balances Dosha**

	VATA		PITTA		KAPHA	
	NO ▲	**YES ▼**	**NO ▲**	**YES ▼**	**NO ▲**	**YES ▼**
FRUITS	Dried Fruits	Sweet Fruits	Sour Fruits	Sweet Fruits	Sweet & Sour Fruits	Apples
	Apples	Apricots	Apples (sour)	Apples (sweet)	Avocado	Apricots
	Cranberries	Avocado	Apricots (sour)	Apricots (sweet)	Bananas	Berries
	Pears	Bananas	Berries (sour)	Avocado	Coconut	Cherries
	Persimmon	All Berries	Bananas	Berries (sweet)	Dates	Cranberries
	Pomegranate	Cherries	Cherries (sour)	Coconut	Figs (fresh)	Figs (dry)
	Prunes	Coconut	Cranberries	Dates	Grapefruit	Mango
	Quince	Dates	Grapefruit	Figs	Grapes*	Peaches
	Watermelon	Figs (fresh)	Grapes (green)	Grapes (sweet)	Kiwi*	Pears
		Grapefruit	Kiwi †	Mango	Lemons	Persimmon
	NOTE: Fruits and	Grapes	Lemons	Melons	Limes	Pomegranate
	fruit juices are best	Kiwi	Limes (in excess)	Oranges (sweet)	Melons	Prunes
	consumed by	Lemons	Oranges (sour)	Pears	Oranges	Quince
	themselves for all	Limes	Papaya	Pineapples (sweet)	Papaya	Raisins
	doshas.	Mango	Peaches	Plums (sweet)	Pineapples	Strawberries*
		Melons (sweet)	Pineapples (sour)	Pomegranate	Plums	
		Oranges	Persimmon	Prunes	Rhubarb	
		Papaya	Plums (sour)	Quince (sweet)	Soursop	
		Peaches	Rhubarb	Raisins	Watermelon	
		Pineapples	Soursop	Watermelon		
		Plums	Strawberries			
		Raisins (soaked)				
		Rhubarb				
		Soursop				
		Strawberries				

VEGETABLES

Frozen, Dried or Raw Vegetables	Cooked Vegetables	Pungent Vegetables	Sweet & Bitter Vegetables	Sweet & Juicy Vegetables	Raw, Pungent & Bitter Vegetables
Beet Greens*	Acorn Squash	Beets	Acorn Squash	Acorn Squash	Asparagus
Broccoli†	Artichoke	Beet Greens	Artichoke	Artichoke*	Beets
Brussels Sprouts	Asparagus	Carrots†	Asparagus	Butternut Squash	Beet Greens
Burdock Root	Beets	Daikon Radish†	Bell Pepper	Cucumber	Bell Pepper
Cabbage	Butternut Squash	Eggplant†	Broccoli	Olives	Broccoli
Cauliflower	Carrots	Fenugreek Greens	Brussels Sprouts	(black or green)	Brussels Sprouts
Celery	Cucumber	Garlic	Burdock Root	Parsnip†	Burdock Root
Fresh Corn†	Daikon Radish	Horseradish	Butternut Squash	Potatoes (sweet)	Cabbage
Eggplant	Fenugreek Greens*	Green Olives	Cabbage	Pumpkin	Carrots
Jeru. Artichoke*	Green Beans	Kohlrabi†	Fresh Corn	Rutabagas	Cauliflower
Jicama*	(well-cooked)	Leeks (cooked) †	Cauliflower	Spaghetti Squash*	Celery
Kohlrabi	Horseradish †	Mustard Greens	Cucumber	Tomatoes	Fresh Corn
Leafy Greens*	Leeks (cooked)	Onions (raw)	Celery	Winter Squash	Daikon Radish
Lettuce*	Mustard Greens	Onions (cooked)*	Green Beans	Zucchini	Eggplant
Mushrooms	Okra (cooked)	Peppers (hot)	Jeru. Artichoke		Fenugreek Greens
Onions (raw)	Olives (black &	Pumpkin †	Jicama		Garlic
Parsley*	green)	Radish	Leafy Greens		Green Beans
Peas	Onion (cooked)	Spinach†	(Esp. Collards,		Horseradish
Peppers	Parsnip	Tomatoes	Dandelion,)		Jeru. Artichoke
Potatoes (white)	Potato (sweet)	Turnips	Lettuce		Jicama
Spaghetti Squash†	Pumpkin	Turnip Greens	Mushrooms		Kohlrabi
Spinach*	Radish		Okra		Leafy Greens
Sprouts*	Rutabaga		Olives (Black)*		Leeks
Tomatoes	Scallopini Squash		Parsley		Lettuce
Turnips	Summer Squash		Parsnip		Mushrooms
Turnip Greens*	Watercress		Peas		Okra
	Winter Squash		Peppers (green)		Onions
	Yel. Crkneck Squash		Potatoes (sweet)		Parsley
	Zucchini		Potatoes (white)		Peas
			Rutabaga		Peppers
			Scallopini Squash		Potatoes (white)
			Spaghetti Squash		Radish
			Sprouts		Scallopini Squash

*These foods are OK in moderation.
†These foods are OK occasionally.

Appendix II (cont.)

	VATA		PITTA		KAPHA	
	NO ▲	YES ▼	NO ▲	YES ▼	NO ▲	YES ▼
GRAINS	Cold, dry, puffed cereals Barley‡ Buckwheat Corn Millet Oats (dry): Granola Oat Bran Quinoa Rice Cakes‡ Rye Wheat Bran (in excess)‡	Amaranth* Oats (cooked) All Rice (including brown rice) Wheat Wild Rice	Amaranth‡ Buckwheat Corn Millet Oats (dry) Oat bran* Oat Granola Quinoa Rice (brown)‡ Rye	Barley Oats (cooked) Rice (basmati) Rice cakes Rice (white) Wheat Wheat Bran Wheat Granola	Oats (cooked) Rice (brown) Rice (white) Wheat	Amaranth* Barley Buckwheat Corn Granola (low-fat) Millet Oats (dry) Oat bran Quinoa Rice (basmati, small amount with clove or peppercorn) Rice Cakes‡ Rye Wheat Bran‡
ANIMAL FOODS	Lamb Pork Rabbit Venison	Beef‡ Chicken or Turkey (white meat) Duck & Duck Eggs Eggs	Beef Egg Yolk Duck Lamb Pork	Chicken or Turkey (white meat) Egg white Freshwater Fish* Rabbit	Beef Duck Freshwater Fish‡ Lamb Pork	Chicken or Turkey (dark meat) Eggs (not fried or scrambled with fat) Rabbit

LEGUMES	Black Beans Black-Eyed Peas Chana Dal Garbanzos Kala Chana* Kidney Beans Common Lentils Lima Beans Navy Beans Pinto Beans Soy Beans Soy Flour Soy Powder Split Peas Tempeh White Beans	Freshwater Fish Seafood Shrimp In Moderation: Aduki Beans Black Lentils Mung Beans Red Lentils Soy Cheese Soy Milk (liquid) Tepery Beans Tofu Tur Dal	Seafood Venison Black Lentils Red Lentils Tur Dal	Shrimp* Aduki Beans Black Beans Black-Eyed Peas Chana Dal Garbanzos Kala Chana Kidney Beans Common Lentils Lima Beans Mung Beans Navy Beans Pinto Beans Soy Beans Soy Products: Soy Cheese Soy Flour* Soy Milk (liquid) Soy Powder* Split Peas Tempeh Tepery Beans Tofu White Beans	Seafood Shrimp Venison † Black Lentils Mung Beans* Kidney Beans Common Lentils Soy Beans Cold Soy Milk Soy Cheese Soy Flour Soy Powder Tempeh Cold Tofu	Aduki Beans Black Beans Black-Eyed Peas Chana Dal Garbanzos Lima Beans Kala Chana Navy Beans Pinto Beans Red Lentils Hot Soy Milk* Split Peas Tepery Beans Hot Tofu* Tur Dal White Beans
NUTS		In moderation: Almonds Black Walnuts Brazil Nuts Cashews	Almonds Black Walnuts Brazil Nuts Cashews English Walnuts	Coconut	Almonds Black Walnuts Brazil Nuts Cashew Coconut	

*These foods are OK in moderation.
†These foods are OK occasionally.

Appendix II

	VATA NO ▲	VATA YES ▼	PITTA NO ▲	PITTA YES ▼	KAPHA NO ▲	KAPHA YES ▼
		Coconut English Walnuts Filberts or Hazelnuts Macadamia Nuts Peanuts‡ Pecans Pine Nuts Pistachios	Filberts Macadamia Nuts Peanuts Pecans Pine Nuts Pistachios		English Walnut Filberts Macadamia Nuts Peanuts Pecans Pine Nuts Pistachios	
SEEDS	Psyllium‡	Chia Flax Sesame Pumpkin Sunflower	Chia Flax Sesame	Psyllium Pumpkin* Sunflower	Psyllium Sesame	Chia Flax* Pumpkin* Sunflower*
SWEETENERS	White Sugar	Barley Malt Syrup Brown Rice Syrup Fructose Juice Concentrates Most fruit Honey Jaggery Maple Syrup Molasses Sucanat Sugar Cane Juice	Honey* Jaggery Molasses	Barley Malt Syrup Brown Rice Syrup Maple Syrup Fruit Juice Concentrate Fructose Sucanat* Sugar Cane Juice White Sugar*	Barley Malt Syrup Brown Rice Syrup Fructose Jaggery Maple Syrup (in excess) Molasses Sucanat Sugar Cane Juice White Sugar	Raw Honey Fruit Juice Concentrates, esp. Apple and Pear

CONDIMENTS

Chili Pepper*	Black Pepper*	Black Sesame Seeds	Black Pepper*	Black Sesame Seeds	Black Pepper
Ginger (dry)*	Black Sesame Seeds	Chili Peppers	Coconut	Coconut	Chili Pepper
Ketchup	Coconut	Daikon Radish*	Coriander Leaves	Cottage Cheese*	Coriander Leaves
Onion (raw)*	Coriander Leaves*	Garlic	Cottage Cheese	Dulse (In mod. if	Daikon Radish
Sprouts*	Cottage Cheese	Ginger	Dulse (well-rinsed)	well-rinsed)	Garlic
	Grated Cheese	Gomasio	Ghee	Hijiki*	Ghee*
	Daikon Radish	Grated Cheese	Hijiki (well-rinsed)	Grated Cheese	Ginger (dry esp.)
	Dulse	Horseradish	Kombu	Kelp	Horseradish
	Garlic	Kelp	Lettuce	Ketchup	Lettuce
	Ghee	Ketchup	Mango Chutney	Kombu*	Mint Leaves
	Ginger (fresh)	Mustard	Mint Leaves	Lemon, Lime	Mustard
	Gomasio	Lemon	Sprouts	Lime Pickle	Onions
	Hijiki	Lime		Mango Chutney	Radish
	Horseradish	Lime Pickle		Mango Pickles	Sprouts
	Kelp	Mango Pickle		Mayonnaise	
	Kombu	Mayonnaise		Papaya Chutney	
	Lemon	Onions (esp. raw)		Pickles	
	Lettuce*	Papaya Chutney		Salt	
	Lime	Pickles		Seaweeds,*	
	Lime Pickle	Radish		well-rinsed	
	Mango Chutney	Salt (in excess)		Sesame Seeds	
	Mango Pickle	Seaweed, unrinsed		Soy Sauce	
	Mayonnaise	(in excess)		Tamari	
	Mint Leaves*	Sesame Seeds		Yogurt	
	Mustard	Soy Sauce			
	Onion (cooked)	Tamari*			
	Papaya Chutney	Yogurt (undiluted)			
	Pickles				
	Radish				
	Salt				

*These foods are OK in moderation.
†These foods are OK occasionally.

Appendix II (cont.)

	VATA NO ▲	VATA YES ▼	PITTA NO ▲	PITTA YES ▼	KAPHA NO ▲	KAPHA YES ▼
		Seaweeds				
		Sesame Seeds				
		Soy Sauce				
		Tamari				
		Yogurt				
SPICES	Neem Leaves*	Ajwan	Ajwan	Fresh Basil Leaves*	Almond Extract*	Ajwan
		Allspice	Allspice	Black Pepper*	Amchoor	Allspice
		Almond Extract	Almond Extract*	Cardamom*	Tamarind	Anise
		Amchoor	Amchoor	Cinnamon*		Asafoetida
		Anise	Anise	Coriander		Basil
		Asafoetida	Asafoetida	Cumin		Bay Leaf
		Basil	Basil	Dill		Black Pepper
		Bay Leaf	Bay Leaf	Fennel		Caraway
		Black Pepper	Caraway*	Mint		Cardamom
		Caraway	Cayenne	Neem Leaves		Cayenne
		Cardamom	Cloves	Orange Peel*		Cinnamon
		Cayenne*	Fenugreek	Parsley*		Cloves
		Cinnamon	Garlic (esp. raw)	Peppermint		Coriander
		Cloves	Ginger	Rose Water		Cumin
		Coriander	Horseradish	Saffron		Dill
		Cumin	Mace	Spearmint		Fennel*
		Dill	Marjoram	Turmeric		Fenugreek
		Fennel	Mustard Seeds	Vanilla*		Garlic
		Fenugreek*	Nutmeg	Wintergreen		Ginger (dry esp.)
		Garlic	Onion (esp. raw)			Horseradish
		Ginger	Oregano			Mace
		Horseradish*	Paprika			Marjoram
		Mace	Pippali			Mint
		Marjoram	Poppy Seeds*			Mustard Seeds

Mint
Mustard Seeds
Nutmeg
Onion (cooked)
Orange Peel
Oregano
Paprika
Parsley
Peppermint
Pippali
Poppy Seeds
Rosemary
Rose Water
Saffron
Sage
Savory
Spearmint
Star Anise
Tamarind
Tarragon
Thyme
Turmeric
Vanilla
Wintergreen

Rosemary
Sage
Savory
Star Anise
Tamarind
Tarragon*
Thyme

Neem Leaves
Nutmeg
Onion
Orange Peel
Oregano
Paprika
Parsley
Peppermint
Pippali
Poppy Seeds
Rosemary
Rose Water
Saffron
Sage
Savory
Spearmint
Star Anise
Tarragon
Thyme
Turmeric
Vanilla*
Wintergreen

DAIRY

Goat Milk
(powdered)

All Dairy OK
in moderation:
Buttermilk
Cows Milk
Hard Cheese
Soft Cheese
Goat Milk (liquid)*
Goat Cheese

Salted Butter
Buttermilk
(commercial)
Hard Cheeses
Feta Cheese
Sour Cream
Yogurt

Unsalted Butter
Cottage Cheese
Most Mild Soft
Cheeses—like
farmer's cheese
Ghee
Cows Milk
Goats Milk

Butter
Cheeses of all kinds
Buttermilk
(commercial)
Cows Milk
Ice Cream
Sour Cream
Yogurt

Ghee
Goats Milk
Diluted Yogurt
(1: 4 pts or more
with water)

*These foods are OK in moderation.
‡These foods are OK occasionally.

Appendix II (cont.)

	VATA		PITTA		KAPHA	
	NO ▲	YES ▼	NO ▲	YES ▼	NO ▲	YES ▼
OILS		Ice Cream* Sour Cream* Yogurt All oils are fine, especially sesame	Almond Apricot Corn Safflower Sesame	Ice Cream Dilute Yogurt (1: 2-3 pts water) In Moderation: Avocado Coconut Olive Sunflower Sesame Soy Walnut	(undiluted) Avocado Apricot Coconut Olive Safflower Sesame Soy Walnut	Almond Corn Sunflower (all in very small amounts)
BEVERAGES	Apple Juice Caffeine Carob ‡ Carbonated Drinks Cold Dairy Drinks Cranberry Juice Fig Shake Bernard Jensen's Mineral Broth & Seasoning ‡ Icy Cold Drinks Pear Juice Pomegranate Juice Pungent Teas ‡ Prune Juice ‡ V-8 Juice ‡	Alcohol* Almond Rejuvenative Drink Aloe Vera Juice Apricot Juice Banana Shake or smoothie Berry Juice Carrot Juice and Carrot-Veg. Combinations Carrot-Ginger Juice Cherry Juice Chocolate Coconut Milk and Smoothies Coffee	Alcohol Banana Shake or Smoothie Berry Juice (sour) Carbonated Drinks Cherry Juice (sour) Coffee Sour Juices and Teas Pungent Teas Caffeine Carrot Juice (in excess) Carrot-Ginger Juice Carrot-Veg- Combination ‡ Chocolate Cranberry Juice	Almond Rejuv. Drink Aloe Vera Juice Apple Juice Apricot Juice Berry Juice (sweet) Mixed Veg. Juice (fresh, see recipes) Carob Cherry Juice (sweet) Coconut Milk Coconut Smoothies Cool, Dairy Drinks Date Shake Fig Shake Goat Milk Grain Teas: Cafix, Roma, Pero	Almond Rejuv. Drink Banana Shake or Smoothie Carbonated Drinks Cold Dairy Drinks Icy Cold Drinks Sour Juices & Teas Alcohol (in excess) Coconut Milk Chocolate Date Shake & Smoothie Grapefruit Juice Highly Salted Drinks, such as canned or commercial bouillons)	Aloe Vera Juice Apple Juice Apricot Juice Berry Juice Caffeine* Carob Carrot Juice Carrot-Ginger Juice Other Carrot Juice Combinations Cherry Juice (unless sour) Cranberry Juice Coffee* Fig Shake Hot Spiced Goat Milk Grain Teas: Cafix

Herb Teas:
Alfalfa ‡
Barley ‡
Blackberry
Borage*
Burdock
Chrysanthemum*
Cornsilk
Dandelion
Hibiscus*
Hops ‡
Jasmine ‡
Mormon Tea
Nettle ‡
Passion Flower ‡
Red Clover‡
Strawberry*
Violet ‡
Wintergreen*
Yarrow
Yerba Mate ‡

Hot Dairy Drinks
Date Shake
Grain Teas:
Cafix, Roma, Pero
Grape Juice
Grapefruit Juice
Lemonade
Mango Juice
Miso Broth
Mixed Veg. Juice
Hot Spiced Milk
Orange Juice
Papaya Juice
Peach Nectar
Pineapple Juice
Salted Drinks
Sour Juices & Teas
Soy Milk, well-spiced & hot*
Herb Teas:
Ajwan
Bansha
(with Milk*
Sweetener)
Basil
Catnip
Chamomile
Cinnamon
Cloves
Comfrey
Elder Flowers
Eucalyptus
Fennel

Grapefruit
Highly Salted Drinks
Ice Cold Drinks
Lemonade
Orange Juice*
Miso Broth
(in excess)
Papaya Juice
Tomato Juice
V-8 Juice
Herb Teas:
Ajwan
Basil‡
Cinnamon‡
Cloves
Eucalyptus
Fenugreek
Ginger (fresh)
Ginseng
Hawthorne
Hyssop
Juniper Berries
Mormon Tea
Osha‡
Pennyroyal
Red Zinger
Rosehips‡
Sage
Sassafras
Wild Ginger
Yerba Mate

Grape Juice
Mango Juice
Peach Nectar
Pear Juice
Pomegranate Juice
Prune Juice
Soy Milk
Vegetable Bouillon
(e.g. Bernard
Jensen's
Mineral Broth and
Seasoning)
Herb Teas:
Alfalfa
Bansha
Blackberry
Barley
Borage
Burdock
Catnip
Chamomile
Chicory
Chrysanthemum
Comfrey
Cornsilk
Dandelion
Elder Flower
Fennel
Hibiscus
Hops
Jasmine
Lavender

Lemonade
Licorice Tea
Miso Broth
(in excess)
Orange Juice
Papaya Juice
Soy Milk (cold)
Tomato Juice
V-8 Juice
Herb Teas:
Comfrey*
Licorice
Lotus‡
Marshmallow
Oat Straw*
Red Zinger
Rosehips‡

Grape Juice‡
Mango Juice
Mixed Vegetable
Juice
Peach Nectar
Pear Juice
Pomegranate Juice
Pungent Teas
Prune Juice
Soy Milk, Well-
Spiced & Warm
Low-salt vegetable
bouillons like
Bernard Jensen's
Mineral
Broth and Seasoning

Herb Teas:
Ajwan
Alfalfa
Barley
Basil
Bansha
Blackberry
Borage
Burdock
Catnip
Chamomile
Chicory
Chrysanthemum
Cinnamon
Cloves
Corn Silk

*These foods are OK in moderation.
‡These foods are OK occasionally.

Appendix II (cont.)

VATA		PITTA		KAPHA	
NO▲	YES▼	NO▲	YES▼	NO▲	YES▼
	Fenugreek		Lemon Balm		Dandelion
	Ginger (fresh)		Lemon Grass		Elder Flowers
	Ginseng*		Licorice		Eucalyptus
	Hawthorne		Lotus		Fennel*
	Hyssop		Marshmallow		Fenugreek
	Juniper Berries		Nettle		Ginger (dry, esp.)
	Lavendar		Oat Straw		Ginseng*
	Lemon Balm		Orange Peel*		Hawthorne
	Lemon Grass		Passion Flower		Hibiscus
	Licorice		Peppermint		Hops
	Lotus		Raspberry		Hyssop
	Marshmallow		Red Clover		Jasmine
	Oat Straw		Rose Flowers		Juniper Berries
	Orange Peel		Saffron		Lavendar
	Osha		Sarsaparilla		Lemon Balm
	Pennyroyal		Spearmint		Lemon Grass
	Peppermint		Strawberry		Mormon Tea
	Raspberry*		Violet		Nettle
	Red Zinger		Wintergreen		Orange Peel
	Roseflowers		Yarrow		Osha
	Rose Hips				Passionflower
	Saffron				Pennyroyal
	Sage				Peppermint
	Sarsaparilla				Raspberry
	Sassafras				Red Clover
	Spearmint				Rose Flowers
	Wild Ginger				Saffron
					Sage
					Sarsaparilla*

NOTE: Dilute Fruit Juices 1:1 with water for Kapha and drink in moderation

Sassafras
Spearmint
Strawberry Leaves
Violet
Wild Ginger
Wintergreen
Yarrow
Yerba Mate
Spirulina and other
blue-green algae

OTHER

Spirulina and other
blue-green algae*

Spirulina and other
blue-green algae‡

*These beverages are OK in moderation.
†These beverages are OK occasionally.

APPENDIX III
SOME BASIC INFORMATION ABOUT NUTRIENTS

Nutrient	Function	Deficiency	Excess	Affect on Dosha, Other Information
Vitamin A	Strengthens mucous membranes, immune, adrenals, eyes	Infections, night blindness	Frontal headache, drowsiness, liver pain	*Pitta* seems to have the greatest need for this nutrient.
Vitamin D	Essential for calcium, magnesium & zinc absorption	Calcium not absorbed, bone & teeth problems	Similar to A	Sunlight is the best source. D is especially important when the calcium intake is low, as often happens on a *Kapha* diet.
Vitamin E	Antioxidant, detoxifier, membrane lubricator, protects hormones	Dry skin, muscle weakness, adrenal exhaustion, nerve problems	Gastrointestinal-like flu which disappears when E is stopped; blood clots slower	Dry form of E best for *Kapha & Pitta*, oily form best for *Vata*.
Vitamin K	Essential for blood clotting	Excessive bleeding	Unusual	Usually not available in over-the-counter formulas. It is made by bacteria in our guts; antibiotics increase our need for this nutrient.
Vitamin C	Antioxidant, detoxer, (especially for heavy metals) maintains collagen, energy, adrenals	Bleeding gums, heavy metal buildup possible, adrenal fatigue	Diarrhea, possible kidney stones	C is hot & sour & so is most appropriate for *Vata & so is least for Pitta*. If *Pitta* must take C, no more than 1500 mg of BUFFERED C is recommended.
B Vitamins: Thiamine (B₁)	Heart, circulation, nerves	Edema, heart failure, irritability, ear problems, fatigue, memory loss	At very high doses: nervousness, sweating, tachycardia, low blood pressure	Good sources: rice bran, soy flour, wheat germ, (pork).

Nutrient	Function	Deficiency	Toxicity	Comments
Riboflavin (B₂)	Detoxifier of chemicals in liver, eyes	Light sensitive, eyes red, sensitive, liver pulse affected	Nontoxic—high doses could cause itching	B-2 is bright yellow in color; this is what turns urine yellow-ish green after taking a multiple or stress vitamin.
Niacin	Energy, vasodilation, digestion, skin, mind	Diarrhea, indigestion, dermatitis, irritability, insomnia, memory loss, higher cholesterol	Liver damage, itching, burring	Small doses useful for *Vata*, high doses most aggravating to *Pitta* with *Vata* a close second.
Pyridoxine (B₆)	Protein metabolism	PMS, irritability, bloating, anemia, skin lesions	Permanent numbing of extremities may result	Keep B-6 under 200 mg/day. Acts as a diuretic & can act as a mood elevator; enhances the absorption of many minerals. Especially useful for *Kapha*.
Cobalamin (B₁₂)	Nerves, blood, energy	Anemia, glossitis, damage to Central Nervous System	Unusual	Found only in animal products, bacteria (fermented food) and some algae, like Spirulina.
Pantothenic Acid	Sinuses, smooth muscle of gut, adrenals	Infections, weakness, digestive problems, hayfever, heart and nerve disorders	Unusual—diarrhea	Seems relatively neutral to all *doshas*. In very large doses (1,000 mg or more) could aggravate *Vata*.
Folic Acid	Hair, skin, mood	Anemia, Gastrointestinal problems, hair loss, glossitis	Promotes estrogen and growth	Frequently low in post-natal women, also children. Seems relatively neutral for all *doshas*. An excess (over 800 mcg/day) can imbalance *Kapha*.
Biotin	Energy, maintenance of skin, hair, sweat glands, nerves, marrow, sex glands	Skin peeling, testosterone & adrenals may get low	Unknown—could be imbalancing to other Bs	More biotin is needed with Candida infection.

APPENDIX III
SOME BASIC INFORMATION ABOUT NUTRIENTS

Nutrient	Function	Deficiency	Excess	Affect on *Dosha*, Other Information
Choline & Inositol	Nerves, cholesterol	Fatty liver, edgy	Liver could get sluggish	Best to use in a system clear of *ama*.
Calcium	Muscle contraction & relaxation, nerve conduction, vision, teeth, bones	Leg cramps (esp. at night), bone breakage, malformation, irritability	Unusual, unless with concurrent Vit. D excess—then calcification of soft tissues	*Agni* needs to be strong to assimilate Ca—is especially difficult for *Vata* to absorb as a supplement. May be needed in non-dairy (*Kapha*) diet.
Magnesium	Muscle relaxation, nerve conduction, holds Calcium in bone, digestion, heart muscle, skin, liver detoxification	Insomnia, irritability, tired-wired feeling, constipation, skin problems	Laxative	Excess disturbing to *Vata*. Insufficiency frequent in stressed conditions for all *doshas*.
Phosphorus	Nerve nutrient, works with Calcium & Magnesium in bone & teeth, energy	Bone loss, muscle weakness, fatigue	Bone reabsorption, hypocalcemia, overstimulation of Parathyroid Hormone	Homeopathic useful for nerves. Rarely needed as a regular (not homeopathic) supplement. Abundant in food, especially lecithin.
Sodium	Acid-base balance, adrenal support, osmotic balance, nerves, blood pressure	Nausea, anorexia, muscle weakness	Excess H$_2$O intake, diarrhea, *Pitta & Kapha* blood pressure rise, edema, anemia, lipemia	Calms *Vata*, aggravates *Pitta* and *Kapha*.
Potassium	Same as Sodium above, plus maintains heart depression	Fatigue, physiologic depression, heart arrhythmia	Vomiting, weakness, mental confusion, diarrhea, heart & Central Nervous System	Similar to Magnesium above. Deficiency more common than one might guess, especially under stress. Rich food sources include fresh carrot juice, sunflower seeds, avocado.

	Function	Deficiency	Excess/Toxicity	Notes
Iron	Blood, immune energy, catecholamine synthesis, digestion, O$_2$ to brain	Anemia, low energy, shortness of breath, frequent infections	Liver toxicity, shock, acidosis, prolonged blood clotting time, increase in respiratory & pulse rates (acute)	Liquid tonics preferable to solid pills for absorption in all *doshas*.
Zinc	Immune, reproductive, endocrine, works with A	White spots on nails, decreased sense of taste & smell, night blindness, frequent colds and/or infections	Diarrhea, can compete with Calcium, Magnesium, Iron for absorption	*Pitta* often seems to need more Zn. If taken as a supplement, must be after meals—on an empty stomach this mineral can be nauseating.
Manganese	Ligaments, blood sugar, thyroid, brain metabolism, works with essential fatty acid metabolism	Aching or "creaky" knees, diabetes, other blood sugar imbalance, "tired" brain	Muscle fatigue, impotency, nerve condition similar to Parkinson's	*Vata* often seems to need more. Alfalfa is a rich source.
Chromium	Blood sugar metabolism, heart	Craving for sweets or alcohol, increased risk of heart attack	Vomiting, diarrhea, excess not toxic but can weaken liver, kidneys	Especially important for *Kapha*. Brewer's yeast & whole grains are good sources.
Iodine	Thyroid metabolism, which affects brain, basal metabolic rate	Goitre, lower body temperature	Brassy taste, Gastrointestinal irritation, edema	Especially important for *Kapha*. An excess can imbalance *Vata* and aggravate *Pitta*.

Other: Copper, blood; Silica, hair and nails; Selenium, immune strength, heart strength and liver detoxification.

APPENDIX IV
GLOSSARY
OF ENGLISH AND SANSKRIT TERMS

Absorption: the active receiving of nutrients into the cells and tissues of the body.

Aduki beans: small red kidney-shaped beans which are popular in many Asian cuisines. Strengthening to the kidneys. Also known as azukis. Available in health-food, Chinese and Indian groceries.

Agni: the sacred Hindu god of fire, representative of the cosmic force of transformation. Also, digestive fire.

Ahamkara: ego; sense of separate self; body intelligence.

Alterative: restorative and cleanser.

Ajwan: wild celery seed, Indian spice, warming in action, decongestant. Available through Indian groceries.

Ama: internal toxins, usually resulting from incomplete digestion or elimination or improper metabolic functioning.

Amalaki: also known as *amla, Emblica officinalis.* It is an Indian medicinal herb for digestion, the part of *Triphala* calming to *Pitta.* Its fruit is unusually rich in vitamin C.

Amchoor: dried mango slices or powder, sour in taste, made from unripe mangos. Used in dals and other dishes to stimulate digestion. Available in Indian grocery stores.

Amla: sour in taste. See also *Amalaki.*

Anabolic: building phase of metabolism.

Analgesic: relieves pain.

Anthelmintic: helps eliminate parasites, including worms, bacteria and fungus.

Antispasmodic: calms spasms.

Anupana: substance that provides a medium in which medicinal herbs can be taken, like hot milk or *ghee.*

Ap: water, the element.

Aperient: mildly laxative in action.

Aphrodisiac: healing and tonifying to the reproductive organs, thereby invigorating to the sexual energy and the body as a whole.

Apple concentrate: concentrated apple juice, available in bottles in health-food stores. Bernard Jensen Products makes a good one. A good sweetener for *Kapha* and *Pitta,* and not overly aggravating to *Vata.* Frozen apple juice concentrate from the supermarket can also be used, although it is more watery and may contain more pesticides.

Aromatic: foods or herbs rich in essential oils, usually with a strong scent, which stimulate or calm digestion. Examples: coriander, peppermint.

Artav: female reproductive tissue and/or function

Asafoetida: see *hing.*

Assimilation: the process of absorption.

Asthi: bone tissue

Astringent: contractive cooling taste, therapeutic in small amounts.

Atharva Veda: one of the four ancient Sanskrit texts known as the *Vedas,* contains information about the practice of Ayurveda.

Aura: the body's energy field, which is produced and sustained by *ojas.*

Avila: cloudy.

Barley: pearl barley, available in supermarkets and health food stores. Cooling and diuretic in action.

Basmati: a richly scented rice, valued in India for its ease of digestion, and served on special occasions. Here in the United States, the selection of *basmati* is more limited and less fragrant, yet still useful in its gentle effect on the digestive system.

Basti: medicated enema.

Bhasma: an ash form of Ayurvedic medicines and/or gems.

Bhuta: material element.

Bibhitaki: Terminalia bellerica, the herb which is calming to *Kapha* in the Ayurvedic preparation *Triphala.*

Bitter: a cold taste which assists digestion and cleansing when used in small amounts.

Black cumin seeds: an herb available in Indian groceries, also known as *siya zira* or *shah zira.*

Brown basmati: an American version of Indian basmati, which is closer in action and effect to brown rice. Cooks much slower than Indian basmati or Texmati.

Brown rice: nourishing whole grain which is most appropriate for *Vata.* Heavy, slightly warming in action.

Brown rice flour: nutritive dry rough heavy flour made from brown rice, found in some health-food stores. Good for adding texture to some dishes, and quite different from finely ground Indian rice flour.

Brown rice syrup: a malted sweetener made from brown rice and barley. Calming to *Vata* and *Pitta,* it is found in health-food stores.

Buddhi: individualized cosmic intelligence, understanding.

Cardamom: a sweet and warming spice which is sold in three forms: in the pod, in individual seeds, and as ground seed. It provides the characteristic flavor of many Indian sweets. Calming to all *doshas.* Found in the herb and spice section of most groceries.

Carminative: relieves intestinal gas and bloating.

Catabolic: the phase of metabolism in which elements are broken down. Digestion is a catabolic process.

Cathartic: powerful laxative for rapid cleansing; not to be over-used.

"Cellophane" noodles: pasta made from mung bean flour, used in Asian cooking and sold in Asian groceries and the import section of some supermarkets. Slippery, slimy, and tasty!

Chakra: vital energy center of the body.

Chala: mobile.

Chana Dal: the split version of *Khala Chana,* Indian chickpeas. *Chana dal* looks like wrinkled yellow split peas; they calm *Pitta* and *Kapha.* They can be found in Indian stores.

Chappati: tasty Indian flat bread, usually made of wheat flour. May also be called *rotis or rotalis.*

Chappati flour: finely ground whole-wheat low-gluten flour found in Indian groceries. also called *ata.* Eases the making of *chappatis* and other Indian breads.

Charak: author of *Charak Samhita,* one of the classic Ayurvedic textbooks still available today.

Chitta: collective or conditioned unconscious.

Cholagogue: stimulates liver and gallbladder function.

Chyvanprash: Indian rejuvenative jam, highly regarded. Quite sweet.

Colitis: inflammation of the colon, with excessive secretion of mucous. Often connected with food sensitivities.

Coriander: a cooling herb which is a valuable digestive aid. It is sold as the whole seed, ground seed, or in leaf form. The leaf is often called "cilantro" or "Chinese parsley." Found in most herb sections, produce sections, and in Chinese, Mexican, and Indian groceries. It is a hardy herb which is relatively easy to grow.

Cumin: a popular spice in both Indian and Mexican cooking, it is calming to all *doshas.* Available in most herb sections and in Indian and Mexican groceries.

Curry leaves: see *neem*.

Demulcent: gentle and soothing in action, especially to the skin and membranes.

Dal: nourishing Indian soups made from a variety of legumes. Can also refer to the individual beans or peas, such as *urud dal* (split black lentil) or *chana dal* (split chickpea) or *mung dal* (split mung bean).

Dhatu: one of the seven basic tissues of the body.

Diaphoretic: increases perspiration, thereby enhancing cleansing through the skin.

Digestive: an herb which stimulates digestion.

Distension: abdominal bloating, usually from excess gas. Often related to an imbalance in *Vata*.

Diuretic: increases urination.

Dosha: one of the three basic types of biological energy, which determine individual constitution: *Vata, Pitta,* and *Kapha.* It can also mean the excess of one of these in nature.

Drava: liquid.

Dyspnea: difficult breathing.

Edema: water retention, results in swelling.

Electrolyte: vital minerals, especially sodium, potassium, calcium, and magnesium.

Emetic: induces vomiting.

Emmenagogue: stimulates the onset of menstruation.

Emollient: softening, soothing, and tonifying in action, especially used externally on the skin.

Enteritis: inflammation of the small intestine. Often associated with bacterial or other infection.

Expectorant: stimulates discharge of phlegm from the lungs and throat.

Febrifuge: relieves fever.

Fennel seeds: an easy to find spice which is sweet and cooling and aids digestion. Look in the herb and spice section of most groceries.

Fenugreek seeds: odd looking spice which is yellow, with flat surfaces and an almost square shape. It is bitter, pungent, sweet and warm. It can be found in most herb stores or Indian groceries. Indian cooking also uses the sprout and greens of these seeds, known as *methi*.

Garam masala: literally "warming spices," a mixture to enhance digestion.

Gastritis: inflammation of the stomach. Often related to *Pitta*.

Gastrointestinal tract: the organs from the mouth to the anus which are involved with ingestion, digestion, absorption, and elimination of food.

Ghee: clarified butter, highly valued in Ayurveda. Enhances absorption.

Ginger: a spice available in both fresh and dried forms. It is warming and pungent and easily found in the produce and spice sections of most stores.

Goat milk: available in fresh, powdered and evaporated forms. Generally available in health-food stores, increasingly available in supermarkets. Calms *Kapha* and *Pitta,* neutral or sometimes aggravating effect on *Vata.*

Gool: see *jaggery.*

Gout: metabolic condition involving pain and inflammation, often of the lower joints.

Guna: quality, attribute.

Guru: heavy.

Haritaki: Teminalia chebula, the herb most calming to *Vata* in the Ayurvedic prepara-tion *Triphala.*

Hemorrhoids: enlarged veins in the lower rectum or anus due to congestion in circu-lation or digestive tracts.

Hing: strong-smelling Indian herb, also sold as asafoetida. it is useful for reducing gas and excess *Vata.* It can be found in Indian groceries and sometimes in the import section of health-food stores or groceries.

Jaggery: Indian lump sugar, golden brown in color and somewhat like molasses in flavor. Also known as *gool* or *goodh.* Sold in Indian groceries.

Jala: water, the attribute.

Jinenjo noodles: also known as wild yam soba noodles, made of Japanese wild yam and wheat, tasty and easy to fix. Found in Asian and some health-food stores.

Kapha: earth-water constitution.

Karma: effect.

Karmendriya: organ of action, e.g., tongue, vocal cords, mouth, hands, feet, geni-tals, anus.

Kashaya: astringent.

Katu: pungent.

Kathina: hard

Khala chana: dark brown Indian chickpeas, smaller than American garbanzos, and often easier to digest. Available in Indian groceries.

Khara: rough

Khir: a cool Indian dessert made with sweetened milk and rice or noodles.

Kichadi: A healing stew of mung beans, basmati rice, vegetables and spices

Kombu: a dark green dried seaweed, useful in dispelling gas and adding minerals to beans or soups.

Lablab: butter beans, used in south Indian cooking.

Laxative: promotes elimination through bowel movements.

Lobhia: black-eyed peas.

Laghu: light.

Lavana: salty.

Madhu: pre-digested sweet taste, such as honey.

Madhura: sweet taste which needs to be digested.

Mahat: cosmic intelligence.

Majja: nerve and marrow tissue.

Malabsorption: the inability to effectively absorb nutrients from the gastrointestinal tract.

Malas: bodily waste products; urine, feces, perspiration.

Mamsa: muscle tissue

Manas: conditioned mind.

Masala dosa: traditional dish of Indian crepe-like cakes with a potato stuffing, popular as a breakfast dish. *Dosa* can also be served with *dal.*

Masur dal: red lentils. Found in health-food, Indian and Middle Eastern stores.

Marma: energy pressure point.

Math dal: tepary beans, small brown legume with a slightly peanut-like flavor, found in Indian groceries. Reputed to calm all *doshas.*

Medas: fat tissue.

Methi: fenugreek greens, with a fragrant bitter taste. Easily grown. Available in the summer in Indian food stores.

Microflora: the bacteria and other microbial organisms growing in the body, most predominantly in the large intestine.

Millet: tiny yellow round grains, available in health- food and Korean groceries. Calming to *Kapha.*

Miso: fermented soybean paste, salty in flavor. Used to season broths, soups and tofu. Sold in Asian and health-food stores.

Mrudu: soft.

Mung beans: the whole beans are small and green in color, calming to *Pitta,* mildly imbalancing to *Kapha,* and variable in effect for *Vata* (some *Vatas* digest them well whole, others do not). Sold in Oriental, Indian and health-food stores. The bean from which bean sprouts are grown.

Mung dal: the split version of mung beans. Hulled they are yellow and look like chipped yellow split peas. Available in all Indian stores and some health-food stores. Calming to *Vata* and *Pitta,* mildly imbalancing to *Kapha.*

Mustard, black: whole seeds, a very frequently used spice in Indian cooking. Warming, stimulates digestion. Available in Indian groceries and herb stores.

Nasya: nasal application of herbs and oils.

Neem leaves: also known as curry leaves, *Azadirachta indica,* a bitter herb useful for *Pitta* and *Kapha.* Can sometimes be found fresh in the refrigerator section of Indian groceries, which is much preferable to its dried form, which often has little potency left.

Nirama: conditions free of *ama.*

Nephritis: kidney inflammation.

Nervine: strengthens and tonifies the nerves; can sedate or stimulate.

Nutritive: gives nourishment to the body.

Ojas: essential energy of the body, our energy "cushion."

Okasatmya: diets or lifestyles which have become non-harmful to the body through regular and habitual use.

Pancha Karma: the five purifying practices of Ayurveda: *vamana, virechana, basti, nasya,* and *rakta moksha.*

Papadum: a paper-thin Indian wafer made of *urud dal* flour. In the north of India it is called *papar.*

Peristalsis: the rhythmic and essential movement of food through the digestive tract.

Pippali: Indian long pepper, highly valued for its abilities to stimulate digestion and rejuvenation. Found in most, but not all, Indian groceries.

Pitta: fire-water constitution.

Prabhau: the specific action or special potency of an herb or food, beyond any general rules which might apply to it.

Prana: the vital life force in the universe.

Pranayama: breathing processes, potent in balancing energy and health.

Prakruti: primal nature; also our biological constitution at birth.

Prasad: blessed food.

Prayatna: effort.

Prithvi: earth.

Puja: devotional worship.

Pulao: a seasoned rice dish with vegetables or meat.

Purgation: the use of moderate to strong laxatives to expel excess *Pitta* or *Kapha* from the system, also known as *virechana.*

Rajas: quality of energy and action.

Rajma: red kidney beans, calming to *Pitta.* Available in most supermarkets and health-food stores.

Rakta: blood.

Rakta Moksha: ancient practice of blood letting.

Rasa: taste; also plasma; also feeling.

Rasayana: rejuvenative.

Rejuvenative: revitalizer.

Rice flour: a finely ground white flour available in Indian and Chinese groceries. Also known as "rice powder." Finer than brown rice flour, which is sold in health-food stores, rice flour calms *Pitta* as well as *Vata.* Small amounts of Indian rice flour can also be useful for *Kapha.* Substitute ⅞ cup rice flour for every cup of whole wheat flour in recipes.

Rice vinegar: a fine light mild vinegar, sold in Asian groceries and the import section of some supermarkets and health-food stores.

Rig Veda: most ancient scripture of India.

Rishis: ancient Indian sages.

Rock salt: more stimulating to digestion than sea salt. Found in Indian groceries, sometimes sold as "black salt." Kosher salt sold in supermarkets is a good substitute.

Rotalis: see *chappati.*

Ruksha: dry.

Sama: has *ama.*

Samskara: collection of sensations and experiences.

Sandra: solid, dense.

Sara: mobile.

Samkya: school of philosophy which is underlying much Ayurvedic practice.

Sattva: quality of clarity, harmony and balance.

Sedative: calms.

Saffron: fragrant yellow spice calming to all *doshas.* Expensive and sometimes hard to find. Available in good herb stores and some Indian groceries.

Sea salt: available in most health food stores.

Sesame oil: regular or toasted (tasty), found in Asian and health-food stores. Warming and heavy.

Shamana: palliation therapy, neutralizing toxins by enkindling *agni* or stimulating digestion through fasting.

Shiitake mushrooms: fresh or dried black Chinese mushrooms, found in Asian and health-food stores. Immune stimulant and tonifier. They are most inexpensively used in their dried form, although their fresh form is more likely a richer source of immune substances.

Shukra: reproductive tissue.

Sita: cool, cold.

Slakshna: slimy.

Snigda: oily.

Srota: channel for the movement of energy through the body.

Sthira: static.

Sthula: gross.

Stimulant: enlivens.

Stomachic: strengthens and tonifies stomach function.

Sucanat: evaporated organic sugar cane juice, with a taste and texture similar to brown sugar. Sold in health-food stores, it is an easy first step away from white sugar toward more whole foods. Most calming to *Vata,* it is moderately calming to *Pitta* and aggravates *Kapha.*

Sukshma: subtle, minute, fine.

Sunflower butter: a thick butter made from sunflower seeds. Rich in zinc and B vitamins.

Sunflower oil: neutral in flavor and rich in polyunsaturated fatty acids. Neutral in its effect on all *doshas.* Generally sold in health-food stores, sometimes in supermarkets.

Sushrut: author of *Sushrut Samhita,* one of the three great Ayurvedic classics still available today.

Svedana: steam therapy to stimulate cleansing through perspiration.

Tahini: ground sesame paste. Warming and heavy like the sesame seeds from which it is made. Found in jars or cans in health food stores and Middle Eastern groceries.

Tamas: quality of inertia, resistance and grounding.

Tamari: a soy sauce made without wheat.

Tamatra: sense organ, e.g., ears, skin, eyes, tongue, nose.

Tamarind: a sour pulp used frequently in Indian cooking to enhance digestion, also known as *imli.* Sold in Indian groceries in one pound cakes or as a paste. The pulp has more flavor.

Tejas: the essence of cosmic fire underlying mental activity, transmitted through *ojas* to the digestive tract.

Texmati: an American grown rice which is a cross between Indian *basmati* and Carolina long-grain white rices. Available in health-food stores. Cooks up rapidly, similar in effect to *basmati* (but probably less potent).

Tikshna: sharp.

Tikta: bitter

Tofu: white soybean curd. Available in the produce section of supermarkets, also in Asian or health-food stores. Calming to *Pitta,* mildly increasing to *Kapha,* it is a bland-flavored item that perks up with seasoning. Cool in action. Some *Vatas* tolerate it well, others do not.

Tridosha: the three constitutions, *Vata, Pitta,* and *Kapha.*

Tridoshic: foods or herbs suited to all three constitutions, such as asparagus, *ghee* and *basmati* rice.

Triphala: powerful Ayurvedic herbal combination for elimination and rejuvenation.

Toovar dal: also known as *tor dal* or *arhar dal,* this yellow split pea-like legume is fiery in action. Available in Indian groceries, often oiled.

Tulsi: holy basil, much respected in India. The seeds can be purchased from some nurseries in the U.S.

Turmeric: bright yellow powdered spice which enhances the digestion of protein. Widely available in the spice section of most food stores.

Umeboshi plums: sour, rose-colored pickled plums, enhancing to digestion. Used as a condiment, available in Asian and health-food stores.

Umeboshi vinegar: a sour light Japanese vinegar made from umeboshi plums, found in the same outlets.

Urud dal: whole, this bean looks small and black. It is also known as black lentil or black gram. Split and hulled, it looks quite different, being ivory in color. The split form is what is usually used in these recipes. Warm and heavy, it is restorative to *Vata* in small quantities. Available through Indian groceries.

Urud dal flour: the ground version of black lentil. Used in making *masala dosas and papadums.* Also found in Indian groceries.

Ushna: hot.

Vagar: the combination of spices warmed in oil or ghee to initiate the cooking of an Indian dish, or to flavor it afterward.

Vagbhata: the elder and the younger authors of the third great classical text in Ayurveda, the *Ashtanga Hridaya and Ashtanga Samgraha.*

Vaidya: Ayurvedic physician.

Vamana: therapeutic vomiting.

Vata: air-ether constitution.

Vasodilator: opens the blood vessels by relaxing them.

Vayu: air.

Vedas: the four ancient scriptures of India.

Vikruti: current imbalance or disease state.

Vipaka: post- digestive effect of a food or herb.

Virechana: purgation therapy.

Viruddhashana: forbidden food combination.

Virya: the energy of a food or herb and its effect on the body's digestive power, heating or cooling in action.

Vishada: clear.

Appendix V

Food name equivalents in Latin, Sanskrit & Hindi.

Latin	English	Sanskrit	Hindi
Abelmoschus esculentus	okra	tindisha	bhindi
Actinidia arguta	kiwi		
Alaria esculenta	kelp		
Aleurites moluccana	filberts	askhota	akhrot
Allium ascalonicum	shallot		ek-kanda-lasun
Allium cepa	onion	palandu	piyaz
Allium porrum	leek		
Allium sativum	garlic	lasuna	lasan
Allium schoenoprasum	chive		
Aloe vera	aloe vera	ghrita-kumari	ghi kanwar
Amaranthus sp.	amaranth		chua-marsa?
Anacardium occidentale	cashew	shoephahara	kaju
Ananas comosus	pineapple		ananas
Anethum graveolens	dill		
Annona muricata	soursop		
Annona squamosa	custard apple	shubba	sharifah
Anthriscus cerefolium	chervil		
Apium graveolens	celery	ajmoda	ajmoda
Arachis hypogaea	peanut	buchanaka	bhuising
Armoracia lapathifolia	horseradish		
Artemisia dracunculus	tarragon		
Asparagus officinalis	asparagus		marchuba
Avena sativa	oats		
Bertholletia excelsa	brazil nut		
Beta vulgaris	beet		chukander
Beta vulgaris var. cicla	chard		
Bixa orellana	annato		senduria
Brassica alba	white mustard	svetasarisha	sufedrai
Brassica caulorarpa	kohlrabi		
Brassica juncea	brown mustard	rajika	rai
Brassica napobrassica	rutabaga		
Brassica nigra	black mustard	sarshapah	kalorai
Brassica oleracea var. acephala	collards		
Brassica oleracea var. botrytis	cauliflower		
Brassica oleracea var. capitata	cabbage		kobi
Brassica oleracea var. italica	broccoli		
Brassica oleracea var. gemmifera	brussels sprouts		

Appendix V (cont.)

Latin	English	Sanskrit	Hindi
Brassica rapa	turnip	raktasarshapa	shulgam
Cajanus indicus or *cajan*	tur dahl	adhaki	tor
Camellia theifera	black tea		chai
Capsicum annuum	cayenne or red pepper	marichiphalam	lal
Capsicum frutescens	chili pepper		jhal
Capsicum frutescens var. grossum	bell pepper		
Capsicum frutescens sp.	paprika		
Carica papaya	papaya		popaiyah
Carthamus tinctorius	safflower	kamalottara	kusumbar
Carum carvi	caraway		shiajira?
Carya illinoensis	pecan		
Caryota orens	jaggery	benkhajur	ramguoah
Castanea sativa	sweet chestnut		
Ceratonia siliqua	carob		
Chenopodium album	lambs' quarters	vastuk	chandan betu
Chondrus crispus	carrageen, Irish moss		
Cicer arietinum	whole: chickpea, garbanzo (U.S., Spain)		safaid or kabulichana
	whole: small Indian black chickpea	chanaka	kala or desi chana
	split: chana dal		chana dal
Cichorium endivia	endive		
Cichorium intybus	chicory		hinduba
Cinnamomum zeylonicum	cinnamon	gudatvak	dalchini
Citrullus vulgaris	watermelon	chaya-pula	tarbuz
Citrus aurantifolia	lime		
Citrus aurantium	bitter orange	swadu-naringa	narengi
Citrus bergamia	Indian sour lime	jambha	nimbu
Citrus limonum	lemon	limpaka	jambira
Citrus medica	citron	karuna	maphal
Citrusparadisi	grapefruit		
Citrus reticulata	tangerine		
Citrus sinensis	orange		
Cocos nucifera	coconut	tranaraj	nariyal
Coffea arabica	coffee	mlechca-phala	kafi
Cola acuminata	kola nut		
Coriandrum sativum	coriander	kustumbari	kottmir
Corylus avellana	hazel nut		findak

Appendix V (cont.)

Latin	English	Sanskrit	Hindi
Crocus sativus	saffron	bhavarakta	zaffran
Cubeba officinalis	cubeb	sungadha-muricha	sitalachini
Cucumis melo var. cantalupensis	cantaloupe	kalinga	khurbuj
Cucumis melo varieties	honey dew, other melons		
Cucumis sativus	cucumber	sakusa	kankri
Curcurbita pepo	pumpkin	kurlaru	safed kaddu
Cucurbita pepo var. melopepo	zucchini		
Cuminum cyminum	cumin	ajaii	safed jeera
Curcuma longa	turmeric	rajani	haldi
Cydonia oblonga	quince		
Cymbopogon citratus	lemon grass	bhustrina	ghandatrana
Cynara scolymus	artichoke		hatichuk
Daucus carota	carrot	shikha-mulam	gajar
Dioscorea sp.	yam	raktalu	lal-gurania
Diospyros sp.	persimmon	tinduka	taindu
Dolichos biflorus	horsegram	kulatha	kulthi
Dolichos lablabtypica	butter bean	simbi	sim
Elettaria cardamomum	cardamom	ela	chhoti elachi
Eruca vesicaria subsp. sativa	arugula, rocket		
Eugenia aromatica	clove		
Fagopyrum esculentum	buckwheat		kaspat
Ferula assafoetida	hing, asafoetida	bhutnasan	hingra
Ficus carica	fig	anjira	anjir
Foeniculum vulgare	fennel	madhurika	badi
Fragaria sp.	strawberry		
Fucus vesiculosus	bladderwrack		
Gelidium cartilagineum	agar-agar		chinai-ghas
Gentiana sp.	gentian	kiratatikta	karu
Glycine max or soja	whole: soybean		bhat
	split: soy dal		bhat ya patrijokra
Glycyrrhiza glabra	licorice	yashti-madhu	mithilakdi
Helianthus annuus	sunflower	arkakantha	hurduja
Helianthus tuberosus	Jerusalem artichoke	hastipijoo	
Hordeum vulgare	barley	yava	jave
Humulus lupulus	hops		
Ipomoea batatas	sweet potato		ratalu
Jasminum officinale	jasminemakki	mallika	motiya

Appendix V (cont.)

Latin	English	Sanskrit	Hindi
Jatropha manihot	cassava, tapioca		
Juglans nigra	black walnut		
Juglans regia	English walnut	akshota	akhroot
Lactuca sativa	lettuce		kahu
Laminaria saccarhina	kelp sp.		galpar-ka-patta
Laurus nobilis	bay		
Lens esculenta or culinaris	commonbrown lentils also red, pink, black in color	masurika	masur
Lepidium sativum	watercress	chandrasura	chansaur
Linum usitatissimum	linseed, flaxseed	uma	tisi
Lycopersicum esculentum	tomato		bilatee baigun
Mangifera indica	mango	amva	am
Matricaria chamomilla	chamomile		babunphul
Medicago sativa	alfalfa		lasunghas
Melia azadirachta	neem	ravipriya	nim
Mentha sp.	mint		
Mentha piperita	peppermint		paparaminta
Mentha spicata	spearmint		pahadi pudina
Morus rubra	mulberry		
Musa paradisiaca var. sapietum	banana	vana laxmi	kela
Myristica fragans	nutmeg and mace	jati-phalam	jayphal
Myrtus caryophyllus (see also Eugenia aromatica)	clove	lavangaha	laung
Nasturtium officinale (see also Lepidium sativum)	watercress		
Nephelium litchi	lichee		lichi
Nigella sativa	black cumin	Krishna-jiraka	kala-jira
Ocimum basilicum	sweet basil	bisva tulasi	babui, tulsi
Olea europaea	olive		
Opuntia dillen or ficus-indica	prickly pear	vidara-vishvasaraka	phani manasa
Origanum majorana	marjoram		sathra
Oryza sativa	rice	vrihi	dhan
Panicum miliaceum	millet	china	china
Papaver sp.	poppy		
Pastinaca sativa	parsnip		

Appendix V (cont.)

Latin	English	Sanskrit	Hindi
Persea americana	avocado		
Petroselinum sativum	parsley		
Peucedanum graveolens	dill	misroya	sowa
Phaseolus acomitifolius	tepery beans		math
Phaseolus aureus or	whole: mung bean	mada?	sabat mung
radiatus	split: mung dal		mung dal
Phaseolus limensus	lima bean		
Phaseolus mungo	black gram or		sabat urud (whole)
	black lentil		urud (split)
or			
Phaseolus roxburghii	black gram		uiud
Phaseolus vulgaris	kidney bean,		rajma
	string bean,		bakla
	navy bean		
Phoenix dactylifera	date	pinda-kharjura	pindakhejur
Pimenta officinalis	allspice		
Pimpenella anisum	anise	shatapushpa	saonf
Pinus gerardiana	pine nut		gunobar
Piper longum	Indian longpepper	pippali	pimpli
Piper nigrum	black pepper	maricham	gulmirch
Pistacia vera	pistachio		pista
Pisum sativum	whole: green pea	saheela	kerav, mattar
	split: American		
	split pea		
Plantago major	plantain		lahuriya
Plantago psyllium	psyllium seed		lahuriya?
Prunus amygdalus	almond	badama	badam
Prunus armeniaca	apricot		jardalu
Prunus avium	sweet cherry		
Prunus cerasus	sour cherry		alu-balu
Prunus domestica sp.	plum, prune		alu
Prunus persica	peach		aru
Prunus serotina	black cherry		
Punica granatum	pomegranate	dadima-phalam	anar
Pyrus communis	pear	amritphala	nashpati
Pyrus malus	apple	sebhaphala	seb-safargang
Pyrus sp.	crabapple		
Raphanus sativus	radish	moolaka	mula
Rheum rhaponticum	rhubarb		
Rhodymenia palmata	dulse		

Appendix V (cont.)

Latin	English	Sanskrit	Hindi
Ribes grossularia	gooseberry		
Ribes nigrum	black currants		
Ricinus communis	castor oil	eranda	endi
Rosmarinus officinalis	rosemary		rusmari
Rubus idaeus	garden raspberry		
Rubus strigosus	raspberry		
Rubus villosus	blackberry		
Saccharomyces cerevisiae	brewer's yeast		
Saccharum officinarum	sugar cane	ikshu	ganna
Salvia officinalis	sage		salbia-safakuss
Santalum album	sandalwood	srigandha	safed chandan
Sassafras albidum	sassafras		
Satureja hortensis	savory		
Satureja montana	winter savory		
Secale cereale	rye		
Sesamum indicum	sesame	tila	til
Smilax officinalis	sarsaparilla		
Solanum melongena var. esculentum	eggplant	vartaku	begun
Solanum tuberosum	potato		alu
Sorghum vulgare vars.	sorghum		
Spinacia oleracea	spinach		palak
Stellaria media	chickweed		
Symphytum officinale	comfrey		
Taraxacum officinale	dandelion		dudal
Thea sinensis	tea		
Theobroma cacao	cocoa		
Thymus citrodorus	lemon thyme		
Thymus vulgaris	thyme		ipar
Torula saccharomyces	torula yeast		
Trigonella foenum-graeceum	fenugreek	medhika	methi
Triticum sativum	wheat	yava, godhuma	gehun
Urtica dioica	nettle		bichu
Vaccinium sp.	blueberry		
Vaccinium oxycoccus	cranberry		
Vanilla planifolia	vanilla		
Vicia faba	broad bean		
Viguna sinensis	black-eyed peas (American)		
Viguna uniquiculata Subsp. catiang	cow pea black-eyed pea (Indian)		lobhia

Appendix V (cont.)

Latin	English	Sanskrit	Hindi
Vitis vinifera	grape	dakha	angur
Withania coagulans	vegetable rennet	asvagandha	akri
Zea mays	corn	yavanala	makka
Zingiber officinale	ginger	srangavera	sonth (dried) adrak (fresh)

BIBLIOGRAPHY

AYURVEDA

Caraka Samhita, translated by Dr. R. K Sharma and Vaidya Bhagwan Dash, volumes I and II, Chowkamba Sanskrit Series Office, Varanasi, India, 1976. Classic Ayurvedic medical texts.

Clifford, Terry, *Tibetan Buddhist Medicine and Psychiatry: The Diamond Healing.* Samuel Weiser, Inc., York Beach, Maine, 1984. Scintillating Western approach to this topic.

Donden, Dr. Yeshi, *Health Through Balance: An Introduction to Tibetan Medicine,* translated and edited by J. Hopkins, Snow Lion Publications, Ithaca, New York, 1986. Highly recommended.

Frawley, Dr. David, *Ayurvedic Healing: A Comprehensive Guide,* Passage Press, Salt Lake City, Utah, 1989. Excellent.

Frawley, Dr. David and Dr. Vasant Lad, *The Yoga of Herbs: An Ayurvedic Guide to Herbal Medicine,* Lotus Light, Wilmot, WI 1986. The resource on the Ayurvedic use of herbs.

Frawley, Dr. David, Editor, *Herbal Energetics Chart,* Lotus Light, Wilmot, WI, 1987. Quick reference quide from *Yoga of Herbs.*

Garde, Dr. R. K., *Ayurveda for Health and Long Life,* D. B. Taraporevala Sons and Co. Private Ltd., Bombay, 1975. Good history and perspectives.

Heyn, Birgit, *Ayurvedic Medicine,* translated by D. Louch, Thorsons Publishing Group, Rochester, Vermont, 1987. A German introduction.

Lad, Dr. Vasant, *Ayurveda: The Science of Self-Healing,* Lotus Light, Wilmot, WI, 1984. The best introduction in the West. Much excellent information.

Nadkarni, Dr. K.M., *Indian Materia Medica, volumes I and II,* Popular Prakashan Private Ltd., Bombay, 1976. Extensive material on Indian herbs.

Sushruta Samhita, volumes I, II and III, translated by K. L. Bhishagratna, Chowkhamba Sanskrit Series Office, Varanasi, 1981. Classical Ayurvedic surgical texts.

Svoboda, Dr. Robert E., *Prakruti: Your Ayurvedic Constitution,* Geocom, Albuquerque, New Mexico, 1988. Beautifully written, clear book on this topic.

Tierra, Michael, *Planetary Herbology,* Lotus Light, Wilmot, WI 1988. An integration of Chinese, Western and Ayurvedic herbs.

ABOUT COOKING, FOOD, HERBS, ET AL.

Ballentine, Martha, *Himalayan Mountain Cookery, The Himalayan International Institute,* Honesdale, Pennsylvania, 1981. Good introduction.

Ballentine, Dr. Rudolph, *Transition to Vegetarianism..* The Himalayan International Institute, Honesdale, PA. 1987. Highly recommended for those who are new to vegetarian eating. Provides a clear, safe, enjoyable path to meat-free, wholesome eating.

Ballentine, Dr. Rudolph, *Diet and Nutrition: A Holistic Approach,* The Himalayan International Institute, Honesdale, Pennsylvania, 1978. Well-written introduction to Western nutrition, with Ayurvedic overtones.

Colbin, Annemarie, *The Natural Gourmet,* Ballantine Book, New York, 1989.

Colbin, Annemarie, *Food and Healing,* Ballantine Books, New York, 1986. Very thorough understanding of how food affects body and energy.

Colbin, Annemarie, *The Book of Whole Meals,* Ballantine Books, New York, 1983. Tasty approach to macrobiotic cuisine.

Desai, Yogi Amrit: *Philosophy of Kripalu Yoga* and *Kripalu Yoga I and II, Kripalu Center,* Box 793, Lenox, MA 01240. More about the practice of Kripalu yoga, with yoga postures and breathing and dietary recommendations.

Ecology Action, "Organic Gardening with Bountiful Gardens," 1990 Catalog, Ecology Action, 5798 Ridgewood Road, Willits, California, 95490. Lots of great information from the folks who originated *How to Grow More Vegetables* by John Jeavons.

The Epic of Man (sic.), edited by Life, Time, Inc., New York, 1961. Many photos of finds from the Indus civilization.

Estella, Mary, *Natural Foods Cookbook, Vegetarian Dairy-Free Cuisine,* Japan Publications, Tokyo, New York, 1985. Macrobiotic—but not much philosophy—just good recipes.

Glenn, Camille, *The Heritage of Southern Cooking,* Workman Publishing, New York, 1986. This woman is a fabulous cook! In no way Ayurvedic or even low-fat, but inspiring in its culinary excellence.

Hoffman, David, *The Holistic Herbal,* The Findhorn Press, Findhorn, Moray, Scotland, 1983. A lovely herbal.

Jaffrey, Madhur, *An Invitation to Indian Cooking,* Vintage Books, New York, 1983.

Jaffrey, Madhur, *World of the East Vegetarian Cooking,* Alfred A. Knopf, New York, 1989. Two excellent resources with lots of information about Indian foods and cooking methods. I am especially partial to the latter.

Kroeger, Hanna, *Allergy Baking Recipes,* Johnson Publishing Company, Boulder, Colorado, 1976. This little booklet offers some good options for the individual on a wheat-free diet.

Lust, John, *The Herb Book,* Bantam Books, New York, 1974. Compact and thorough coverage of most Western herbs.

MacEachern, Diane, *Save Our Planet: 750 Everyday Ways You Can Help Clean Up the Earth,* Dell Trade Paperback, New York, 1990.

McGhee, Harold, *On Food and Cooking: The Science and Lore of the Kitchen,* Charles Scribner's Sons, New York, 1984.

Moore, Michael, *Medicinal Plants of the Mountain West,* Museum of New Mexico Press, Santa Fe, New Mexico, 1979.

Moore, Michael, *Medicinal Plants of the Desert and Canyon West,* Museum of New Mexico Press, Santa Fe, New Mexico, 1989. This man knows his stuff! And he is a good writer to boot.

Nichols Garden Nursery, "Herbs and Rare Seeds," 1990 Catalog, 1190 North Pacific Highway, Albany, Oregon, 97321. Good source for Tulsi seeds, saffron crocus bulbs, and other unusual Indian and Western herbs.

Robertson, Laurel, and Carol Flinders and Bronwen Godfrey, *Laurel's Kitchen,* Bantam Books with Nilgiri Press, Petaluma, California, 1976. Great, well-balanced vegetarian cookbook. One of my favorite sections is "The Keeper of the Keys," an extraordinarily sane look at how crazy we have gotten in terms of caring for and feeding ourselves.

Rombauer, Irma S., and Marion R. Becker, *The Joy of Cooking,* The Bobbs-Merrill Company, Inc., New York, 1952. The American classic.

Root, Waverly and Richard de Rochemont, *Eating in America: A History,* William Morrow and Company, Inc., New York, 1976. Where else would you find that Americans eat huge numbers of mustard seeds? (On our hotdogs, of course.)

Sahni, Julie, *Classic Indian Vegetarian and Grain Cooking,* William Morrow, and Company, Inc., 1985. An excellent source on Indian cooking, with little overlap with Madhur Jaffrey's books.

Seeds of Change Diversity Catalogue, 1990, 621 Old Santa Fe Trail, #10, Santa Fe, New Mexico 87501. Great selection of rare western and Indian seeds.

Weed, Susun, *Wise Woman Herbal for the Childbearing Year,* Ash Tree Publishing, Woodstock, New York, 1985. Lovely, practical information from a Western herbal perspective.

Index

ABOUT THE AUTHORS

Amadea Morningstar Amadea studied human biology and nutrition at Stanford University and the University of California at Berkeley, graduating with a B.S. in nutrition and food sciences from Berkeley in 1975. She did graduate work in nutrition at the University of Texas at Austin and has a Masters in counseling from Southwestern College in Santa Fe.

She has been a practicing nutritionist and teacher for fifteen years. She became interested in Ayurveda in 1983 through the work of Dr. Vasant Lad and Lenny Blank. Through study of the Ayurvedic classics and practical application, she began to incorporate Ayurvedic principles into her private practice and classes.

She has been on the faculty of The Ayurvedic Institute in Albuquerque, New Mexico since 1984 and acts as a nutritional consultant to other schools and practitioners. Her articles have appeared in The Ayurvedic Wellness Journal and other publications. She has also written *Breathe Free Naturally* with Daniel Gagnon, due out in the fall, 1990 (Lotus Press).

She began painting in 1979 inspired by artist Dolores Chiappone.

Amadea lives in the country north of Santa Fe, New Mexico with her husband Gordon Bruen and their daughter Iza.

Urmila Desai She began her life long interest in nutrition and food in the small Indian village of Halol, a western village of Gujarat Province. At the age of 19, Urmila married Yogi Amrit Desai. Since that time she has been closely involved with the development and practice of yoga, health, and cooking activities.

Her inspiration for Ayurvedic recipes has grown from her practice of a spiritual lifestyle.

In 1986, she was diagnosed as having early stages of colon cancer. She focused her attention on the healing properties of food and diet, and through deep relaxation and proper lifestyle, she completely healed herself of all signs of cancer in the body.

In 1989, Urmila met Amadea Morningstar, who came to the Kripalu Center for Yoga and Health, located in Lenox, Massachusetts. Founded by her husband, Kripalu Center is currently the largest residential health center in the United States, accommodating over 10,000 guests a year. Amadea had come to the Center to give cooking classes and to lecture on Ayurvedic cooking principles. They began a relationship at that time based on their many years of creative cooking and decided to co-author this cookbook.

Urmila is the mother of three children, who are grown.

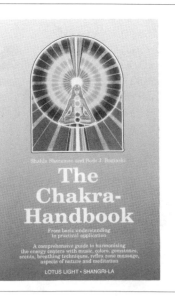

Two Classics in the field with combined sales of more than 70,000 copies.

Ayurveda: The Science of Self-Healing

$11.95 (postpaid); 176 pp.; 5½ x 8½;
paper; ISBN: 0-914955-00-4

The Yoga of Herbs

$13.95 (postpaid); 255 pp.; 5½ x 8½;
paper; ISBN: 0941-524248

Ayurveda: The Science of Self-Healing, by Dr. Vasant Lad, and *The Yoga of Herbs,* by Dr. David Frawley and Dr. Vasant Lad, together constitute the most complete and accessible guide for the western reader to the practice of the world's oldest healing system, Ayurveda.

Ayurveda: The Science of Self-Healing introduces the reader to the Indian philosophical principles of healing, with a detailed discussion of diagnostic techniques and treatments, listing western herbs and spices used for healing. More than 50 charts, diagrams and tables, many photographs and a full glossary and index complete this most practical guide.

The Yoga of Herbs is a complete and detailed guide to herbal therapies, against the background of Ayurvedic medical theory and practice. This handbook is a must for the beginning and/or practising herbalist. The text is enriched with handsome drawings, diagrams and charts.

Herbal Energetics Chart

$5.95 (postpaid); 10½ x 13½; laminated 2 sides;
ISBN: 0941524-29-9

THE HERBAL ENERGETICS CHART, edited by Dr. Frawley, references the qualities, preparation, indications and uses of commonly available western herbs, according to the therapeutic principles of Ayurveda—and does it at a glance! This attractive laminated guide contains a world of information for only $5.95.

LOTUS PRESS

PO Box 2AC
Wilmot, WI 53192

SOURCES
FOR
HERBS AND PRODUCTS

Herbs & Spices

Wholesale:
Lotus Light
PO Box 2AC
Wilmot, WI 53192
414/862-2395

Retail:
Lotus Fulfillment Services
33719 116th St., Box AC
Twin Lakes, WI 53181

Herbal Products
& Essential Oils

Wholesale:
(includes Ayurvedic
products):

Lotus Light
PO Box 2AC
Wilmot, WI 53192
414/862-2395

Retail:
(Ayurvedic products):

Lotus Fulfillment Services
33719 116th St., Box AC
Twin Lakes, WI 53181

These sources will be happy to provide
Ayurvedic products available for mail order.

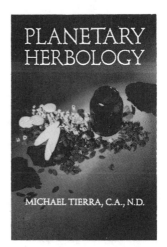

AROMATHERAPY
To Heal and Tend the Body
by Robert Tisserand ISBN: 0-941524-42-6
224 pp.; 5½ x 8½; paper; $9.95

The use of aromatic oils to soothe both physical and psychic disorders was recognized in early Egypt and has been rediscovered as a pleasant treatment for a wide range of ailments. The therapeutic properties of the essential oils, together with the relaxation induced by the massage, have been found particularly helpful for stress-related problems. Robert Tisserand's first book, *The Art of Aromatherapy* has become a classic text.

ENCHANTING SCENTS

by Monika Junemann

$9.95; 123 pp.; paper; ISBN: 941-524-36-1

The use of essential oils and fragant essences to stimulate, activate and inspire body, mind and spirit.